PIETAS

SELECTED STUDIES IN ROMAN RELIGION

BY

H. WAGENVOORT

LEIDEN / E. J. BRILL / 1980

PIETAS
SELECTED STUDIES IN ROMAN RELIGION

STUDIES IN GREEK AND ROMAN RELIGION

EDITED BY H. S. VERSNEL

IN CO-OPERATION WITH F. T. VAN STRATEN

VOLUME 1

LEIDEN / E. J. BRILL / 1980

PIETAS

SELECTED STUDIES IN ROMAN RELIGION

BY

H. WAGENVOORT

LEIDEN / E. J. BRILL / 1980

Published with financial support from the
Netherlands Organization for the Advancement of Pure Research
(Z.W.O.)

ISBN 90 04 06195 9

Copyright 1980 by E. J. Brill, Leiden, The Netherlands

All rights reserved. No part of this book may be reproduced or translated in any form, by print, photoprint, microfilm, microfiche or any other means without written permission from the publisher

PRINTED IN THE NETHERLANDS

CONTENTS

Foreword VII
In memoriam Hendrik Wagenvoort 1886-1976 by H. L. W. Nelson XI

I. Pietas 1
   (Rede uitgesproken ter aanvaarding van het ambt van hoogleeraar aan de rijksuniversiteit te Groningen den 24en Mei 1924)

II. Diva Angerona 21
   (*Mnemosyne* ser. III, 9, 1941, 215-217)

III. Profānus, profānāre 25
   (*Mnemosyne* ser. IV, 2, 1949, 319-332)

IV. Gravitas and Maiestas 39
   (*Mnemosyne* ser. IV, 5, 1952, 287-306)

V. Felicitas imperatoria 59
   (*Mnemosyne* ser. IV, 7, 1954, 300-322)

VI. Cupid and Psyche 84
   ('Apuleius Märchen von Amor und Psyche' in: R. Merkelbach - G. Binder, *Amor und Psyche*, Darmstadt 1968, 382-392)

VII. The Golden Bough 93
   ('De gouden tak', *Hermeneus* 31, 1959, 46-52; 72-79; 92-100)

VIII. The Goddess Ceres and her Roman Mysteries 114
   ('De dea Cerere deque eius mysteriis Romanis', *Mnemosyne* ser. IV, 13, 1960, 111-142)

IX. On the Magical Significance of the Tail 147
   ('Zur magischen Bedeutung des Schwanzes', *Serta Philologica Aenipontana*, 1961, 273-287)

X. The Origin of the Goddess Venus. 166
('De deae Veneris origine', *Mnemosyne* ser. IV, 17, 1964, 47-77)

XI. Orare, precari 197
(*Verbum. Essays dedicated to H. W. Obbink*, Utrecht 1964, 101-111)

XII. Augustus and Vesta 210
(*Mélanges Carcopino*, Paris 1966, 965-978)

XIII. Characteristic Traits of Ancient Roman Religion. . . 223
('Wesenzüge altrömischer Religion', in: *Aufstieg und Niedergang der römischen Welt* I, 2, 1972, 348-376)

Index of authors cited 257
Index of subjects. 262

FOREWORD

Hendrik Wagenvoort died in 1976, twenty years after his retirement as professor of Latin at the University of Utrecht. On that occasion, in 1956, his pupils presented him with an edition of his collected papers, the 'Studies in Roman Literature, Culture and Religion'.[1] Anyone acquainted with his erudition, *curiositas* and interest in Roman and other religions, will have endorsed the wish formulated by A. D. Nock in his review of this book:[2] 'We must hope that its author will enjoy many years of health and strength and produce the material for more than another volume of *opuscula*'. By this time, now that we can survey the results of another twenty years' scholarly work, that wish appears to have been granted: there is more valuable material than could possibly be collected in one volume. In their foreword to 'Studies' the editors wrote: 'All those articles that have appeared in *Mnemosyne* which are easily accessible, we have rigorously omitted as they would have taken up all our available space'. Since the year in which these words were written, however, no part of the world seems to have been sacred from an educational 'nouvelle vague', which has, in a different way, negatively affected the 'accessibility' of the *Mnemosyne* papers. For, as is generally known, Wagenvoort used to write his contributions in an elegant, smooth and witty, but by no means easy, Latin.

In these circumstances, and considering the importance and influence of Wagenvoort's work, a team of editors, for the greater part not pupils of Wagenvoort in the strict sense of the word, has taken the initiative of publishing another collection of Wagenvoort's papers in an English translation. We realize that no translation can ever reflect the charm and pointedness of the original, but considered this a sacrifice to be made to intelligibility. For the rest, alterations have been restricted to an unavoidable minimum. We have not censured ideas which may appear antiquated nowadays: one of our aims was to provide a piece of a history of

[1] Leiden, E. J. Brill, 1956.
[2] *Class. Philol.* 53 (1958), 141.

scholarship. We have refrained from adding recent literature in text or foot-notes. Neither did we see a reason for 'correcting' the slightly rhetorical tone noticeable from time to time: it often betrays the origin of an essay as a lecture, a favorite activity of the author. The sometimes rather whimsical way of citing, so characteristic of many scholars of Wagenvoort's generation, has been mended only if the references were obscure or misleading.

Naturally the majority of contributions have been selected from the work that has appeared since 1956, but some of the most important publications of the previous period have also been included such as the inaugural address at Groningen in 1924. Beginning with this lecture, down to the latest extensive essay, the one on 'Characteristic Traits of Ancient Roman Religion' of nearly fifty years later, this collection illustrates Wagenvoort's unflagging, pious devotion to the study of the (early) Roman religious experience and expression.[3] But there are also samples of his explorations in less familiar fields, such as his reflections on the 'Golden Bough' and the origins of 'the Märchen of Cupid and Psyche', which show many points of coherence and both have a Roman starting-point.

It has not escaped us that a number of the *Mnemosyne* articles bear a critical, sometimes even slightly polemical nature. 'Gravitas and Maiestas', 'Felicitas imperatoria', 'The Goddess Ceres', 'The Origin of the Goddess Venus', all had their origin in discussions with scholarly opponents, for the most part as book reviews. We have included them with pleasure and conviction.[4] Wagenvoort's critical work has often met with emphatic approval and praise. In his commemorative address J. H. Waszink [5] devoted an extensive passage to this quality and lauded the deceased in Horatian terms

---

[3] For a fairly complete bibliography of the publications down to 1956 see 'Studies', 299-304. The titles of the recent publications may be found in the annual survey of work by Dutch scholars in *Mnemosyne*.

[4] The pleasure was nourished by the conviction that publication of this critical work was also a matter of justice. The other part of the discussion has been published many times in various forms. See e.g. G. Dumézil, *La religion romaine archaïque* (Paris 1966), 33ff.; second edition 1974, 36ff.; idem, *Idées romaines* (Paris 1969), 125-152.

[5] J. H. Waszink, *Hendrik Wagenvoort* (23 augustus 1886 - 15 januari 1976), *Jaarboek van de Koninklijke Nederlandse Akademie van Wetenschappen* (1976), 1-7.

as a *censor honestus* and a *candidus iudex*. A. D. Nock, in the review mentioned above, expresses his regret that in the 'Studies' this aspect could not be paid more attention to. However, there is another, equally important, consideration. It was precisely these reviews and discussions which provided Wagenvoort with the opportunity to reconsider and test former theories. Sometimes this induced a modification, it always provoked new, sharper formulation, and very often the result was a new and original interpretation of the problem under discussion.

The collection has been organized in a strictly chronological order. A thematical arrangement would, so we found, result in an unacceptable chronological arbitrariness. Moreover, Wagenvoort liked to elucidate one theme from various view-points in a short period of time. An instance of this will be found in his treatment of the terms 'Orare, precari' and his 'Augustus and Vesta'. Another is the juxtaposition of 'The Märchen of Cupid and Psyche' and 'The Golden Bough', where the chronological principle has been abandoned only in appearance: the former is a German revision of a lecture given in 1954.

Five editors have contributed to the publication of this book. The original instigation we owe to Prof. M. J. Vermaseren, whose great familiarity with Wagenvoort's work, based on his close friendship with the author, was a continuous stimulus and expressed itself in numerous suggestions. We are indebted to Prof. H. L. W. Nelson, Wagenvoort's successor in the chair of Latin at Utrecht, for his permission to publish an 'In memoriam' by his hand. Thanks to his good offices the Netherlands Organization for the Advancement of Pure Research was found willing to grant a subsidy which made the publication possible. The editors wish to express their sincere gratitude to this Organization. J. N. Bremmer and F. T. van Straten have been concerned in the selection of the material from the beginning. They have also undertaken the time-consuming and hard task to read and check large parts of the translation and shared proportionately in proof-reading and compiling of the indices. Besides his share in these activities, the undersigned, coordinator and general editor, has performed the duties belonging to his job, among them the initial compilation of the material, and suggested the selection which was to be the basis of this volume.

Pietas was the title of Wagenvoort's inaugural address at Groningen. 'There is no doubt', the editors of 'Studies' wrote, 'that you gave us unwittingly more than mere professional learning: you gave us a glimpse in your daily life of that *pietas* that you made the subject of your first inaugural address'. And Nelson concludes his 'In memoriam' by the words: 'It seems to me that even today, now that his obituary must be written, this term is the most suitable one with which to conclude the survey of his life'. For once it was unnecessary to invent a title: it presented itself. *Pietas* is not only the characteristic of the life and work of Wagenvoort, it is also the expression of the high esteem his pupils, both the direct and the indirect, feel for the humane scholar that was Wagenvoort, an esteem which never leads to slavish imitation but lives on in the inspiration his works continue to give. The editors of the 'Studies in Greek and Roman Religion' consider themselves fortunate to have the opportunity of starting this new series with the present volume.

H. S. VERSNEL

IN MEMORIAM HENDRIK WAGENVOORT 1886-1976

Hendrik Wagenvoort's final illness which preceded his death was relatively short: it lasted about five weeks. Until 6 December 1975 he had been tirelessly active both in scholarly and in other domains; on that date, however, he was taken to the Nursing Home of Utrecht after suffering a stroke. He died on 15 January 1976, just over 89 years old.

Wagenvoort was born in Minnertsga in Friesland (municipality of Barradeel in the vicinity of Franeker) on 23 August 1886. His father came from the very rural village of Harfsen in the 'Gelderse Achterhoek' (the former county of Zutphen forming the eastern part of the present-day province of Gelderland), in Minnertsga he was headmaster of a primary school. But since his father moved from Minnertsga to Utrecht in 1888 in order to act as headmaster of another school, Utrecht was the city where Hendrik Wagenvoort grew up, the city which occupied a central place in the memories of his youth. Not only did he spend his school-years there, but he also completed his university studies there in 1911. In 1930 he was to return to the cathedral city for good, this time as professor of Latin language and literature.

Wagenvoort studied classics from 1904 to 1911. In the year in which he graduated (1910) he competed for a prize organized by the Municipal University of Amsterdam. The competitors had to write a paper on Horace's 'Roman Odes' and the language in which it was to be written was Latin. Two of the entries were awarded prizes: one of them was Wagenvoort's.[1] This success

---

[1] Wagenvoort's rival for the prize was Aloysius Slijpen, later professor at the Catholic University of Nijmegen. The latter also used his entry as the basis of a dissertation; he graduated on 20 January 1920 at the Municipal University of Amsterdam (the title of his thesis: *Disputatio critica de carminibus Horatii sex quae dicuntur Odae Romanae*). The jury which had to judge the two papers rated Slijpen's entry higher than Wagenvoort's and gave the former the first prize (a gold medal). In a commemorative speech delivered in 1976 before the Koninklijke Nederlandse Akademie (the Royal Dutch Academy) J. H. Waszink made the following remarks about the verdict (see *Jaarboek van de Kon. Nederl. Akad. van Wetenschappen*, 1976): 'Slijpen was strictly philological in his work—the term "close reading"

led to his decision to elaborate his paper on Horace into a dissertation. He took his doctor's degree shortly after, on 18 March 1911, in Utrecht. The title of his thesis, supervised by P. H. Damsté, was *De Horatii quae dicuntur Odis Romanis*.

The distinction conferred on his paper earned the young doctor a grant which enabled him to study abroad for a year (1911-12): he spent the first six months in Göttingen and the rest of his time in Rome.[2] In the Roman capital he enjoyed the hospitality of the German Archeological Institute, but since, in those days, there was no chair of archeology at Utrecht, Wagenvoort's teacher Damsté, who had arranged for the grant, thought it best that Wagenvoort should go first to Göttingen. This would enable him to obtain some knowledge of the subject before taking up residence with the archeologists in Rome.

After his return from Italy Wagenvoort, like most classical scholars in the Netherlands in those days, started his career as a teacher at a classical grammar school. From 1912 to 1919 he taught at Arnhem, and from 1919 to 1924 in The Hague, in both places at a Protestant 'gymnasium'. If we consult the list of his publications—a list which became extremely long in the course of the years—we find various titles dating from the time when he worked as a school-teacher—contributions to both national and foreign reviews, no less than four of which deal with the philosopher Seneca. At the same time Wagenvoort made the author Seneca accessible to schoolboys: in 1917 there appeared an anthology of Seneca's epistles to Lucilius, *Seneca's brieven aan Lucilius*, accompanied by a highly instructive commentary, which obtained considerable fame in grammar-school circles within a relatively short time and continued to be reprinted until after the Second World War. In addition to this Wagenvoort had another 'best seller' written as a school-textbook to his name: *Varia Vita* (first

comes to mind when we read his paper—while Wagenvoort constantly kept the historical and religious background in view; we could say that he gave the poems their place in space and time. That, in a period in which classical studies were devoted almost exclusively to philology, the gold medal should have gone to Slijpen, will surprise nobody in retrospect'.

[2] When Wagenvoort reminisced amongst his friends he enjoyed talking about his stay in Göttingen. As far as his teachers there were concerned, he had a particular veneration for Friedrich Leo.

published in 1927), a sketch of the philosophical and religious currents in Rome at the beginning of our era. These successes were no accident, for both books showed clearly that Wagenvoort had other ambitions besides purely scholarly ones: he was aware of the potential power of the popularization of his subject, and he therefore willingly addressed himself, on occasion, to a 'wider audience'.

In 1924 Wagenvoort was appointed professor of Latin language and literature at the State University of Groningen. His inaugural lecture, entitled *Pietas*, can be said to have heralded a theme which was to be central to his later research: the religions of the Roman people and, shortly afterwards in a broader sense, of the other peoples who had inhabited the Roman Empire. In his Groningen period his attention was primarily devoted to the religions and religious currents which flourished in the last decades of the Republic and the days of Augustus. His particular preference was for the question of what influence religion had had on the public life and literature of that time (for example the poet Virgil),[3] but he also displayed a strong interest in the emperor Augustus himself, the great restorer of the ancient Roman cult of the State.

In the meantime, owing to the retirement of P. H. Damsté in 1930, the chair of Latin at Utrecht became vacant. Wagenvoort accepted the invitation to succeed his master and settled in Utrecht, this time for good. The topic of his inaugural lecture came as no surprise to those acquainted with his scholarly interests: *Pax Augusta*. In the course of the thirties, however, a shift gradually took place in the orientation of his research. The cult of the State of the days of the emperor Augustus had contained a number of primeval elements which had such a primitive character that the Augustan authors and poets who wrote about them no longer understood them. Wagenvoort now turned his attention to these primitive 'survivals' and set himself a new objective: the reconstruction of the religious thought of Rome's earliest inhabitants. In order to make up for the scarcity of material which might serve for

---

[3] The best known publication from this period is: 'Vergils vierte Ekloge und das Sidus Iulium', *Mededelingen Kon. Ned. Akademie v. Wetenschappen*, afd. Letteren 67A n⁰ 1, 1929, included in English translation in 1956 in the volume *Studies in Roman Literature, Culture and Religion* (p. 1ff.).

an interpretation and which originated from the ancient world itself, he made widespread use of the results of ethnological research.[4] Various 'dynamistic' concepts, to which ethnologists who had studied Melanesian religions had drawn attention (e.g. 'mana', 'taboo', etc.), played a particularly important part in his attempts to explain ancient Roman religious terms (cf., for example, his book published in 1941, *Imperium, studiën over het 'mana'-begrip in zede en taal der Romeinen*; in 1947 an English version of this work appeared with the title *Roman Dynamism, Studies in Ancient Roman Thought, Language and Custom*.[5]

Wagenvoort was well aware of the fact that his means of approaching ancient Roman religion entailed, in his own words, a 'difficult experiment, not without dangers'. But what he did achieve was that the all too classical halo with which the Romans had been surrounded for centuries was somewhat weakened: it emerged that primitive, even 'dynamistic', Romans *had* existed, and it was worth a piece of daring to break through to this aspect of Roman life too. When certain of his arguments were criticized Wagenvoort used to quote, not without irony, a Latin proverb which he had derived from his own name: *aude ac perge*, 'waag en voort!', 'dare and proceed!'. This was the motto which he wished to see placed both over his personal aspirations and over his scholarly work.[6]

---

[4] The first study in which this new approach is clearly visible is 'Caerimonia', *Glotta* 26 (1937) p. 115ff.; an English translation is to be found in *Studies in Roman Literature, Culture and Religion*, p. 84ff. The linguistic-historical and religious-historical conclusions of this study were also included by Wagenvoort in the article '*Caerimonia*' which he later contributed to the *Realenzyklopädie für Antike und Christentum* (II (1954), 820ff.). *Caerimonia* is etymologically connected with *caerulus, caeruleus;* it is consequently derived, like the two adjectives, from **caerus*, 'dark'. On this basis Wagenvoort postulates that the original meaning of *caerimonia* was 'darkness', 'mystery' etc.—i.e. that area especially reserved for the caste of priests.

[5] H. J. Rose contributed to the English translation.

[6] Wagenvoort, moreover, received numerous tokens of approval and recognition of his scholarly work. It would be going too far afield to investigate all of these in this obituary. I shall only recall that Wagenvoort was a member both of the Koninklijke Nederlandse Akademie and the Koninklijke Vlaamse Akademie van Wetenschappen (the Royal Dutch Academy and the Royal Flemish Academy of Sciences). He was also chairman of the Nederlands Genootschap van Godsdiensthistorici (the Dutch Society

So much for Wagenvoort's research. Now a word about his teaching. From the fact that the chair of Latin passed from Damsté to Wagenvoort in 1930, in other words from master to pupil, we are by no means entitled to conclude that the didactic approach to the teaching of Latin at the university of Utrecht remained unaltered. If anything, the contrary is true. P. H. Damsté was a classical scholar in the old Dutch tradition; in his case, as in that of most other classical philologists of his generation, classical Latin—the language—was at the centre of his interests. The practice of textual criticism was not only the basis of scholarly research but also of university teaching; textual interpretation only followed in the second place.[7] Owing to Wagenvoort's arrival, however, the position was reversed. The study of texts, from then on, was largely subordinated to a cultural-historical objective: the reconstruction of the life of the Romans—above all their religious life—in Antiquity. This new approach met with a great response amongst the students, as is evident, for example, from the large number of doctoral theses that were completed under Wagenvoort's supervision between 1930 and 1956: 36. If we add the two theses from the Groningen period we reach a total of 38—a very high number, at least in the sector of classical languages.[8]

So far I have virtually limited myself to discussing Wagenvoort's university activities. If I were to leave it at that this sketch of his personality and his life would be incomplete. One of Wagenvoort's characteristic qualities was that he also felt the need to be active outside the —somewhat closed—circle of the university. These activities are too numerous for me to give a detailed summary of them here, however. They covered a very varied field; they were

of Religious Historians). The State University of Ghent accorded him an honorary doctorate.

Membership of the Nederlandse Akademie entailed a rather curious subsidiary function: as chairman of the 'Iudices' of the 'certamen poeticum Hoeufftianum' he had to act every year as adjudicator of a whole series of Neo-Latin verse entries.

[7] Damsté had also always aspired to tread in the footsteps of his revered master from Leiden C. G. Cobet.

[8] On p. 305-306 of *Studies in Roman Literature, Culture and Religion* there is a survey of the dissertations completed under Wagenvoort's supervision.

partly social and partly devoted to popular scholarship, and they also comprised ecclesiastical functions. Wagenvoort wrote a great many articles and other contributions intended for circles of readers who could not be regarded as fellow-specialists. If we draw up a list of Wagenvoort's publications which includes those outside the specialized sphere of the author, we find an amazing quantity of non-classical reviews, yearbooks, literary anthologies, and introductions to literary and religious history. The fact that he had much to do with the 'Nederlands Klassiek Verbond' (the Dutch Classical Association), the 'Genootschap van Leraren aan Gymnasia' (the Society of Grammar-School Teachers) and other societies meant that he had to make numerous speeches. On top of this there were his administrative duties. Just to give a few examples: he was president of the 'Provinciaal Utrechts Genootschap' (the Provincial Society of Utrecht) and of the 'Utrechtse Volksuniversiteit' (the Extra-mural University of Utrecht), and he was on the committee of the 'Utrechtse Openbare Leeszaal' (the Public Library of Utrecht) and of the 'Volksuniversiteitsbibliotheek' (the Library of the Extra-mural University), etc. As far as his ecclesiastical and social functions are concerned I must also confine myself to a few instances: he was a deacon in the Reformed Church, a member of the Commission for the unemployed (during the economic crisis in the thirties), and on the governing board of the 'Utrechtse Diaconessenhuis' (the Nursing Home of Utrecht) and the Sanatorium 'Zonnegloren' (at Soest, in the province of Utrecht).[9]

Two rules of life made such activities possible: a continual readiness to divide up rigorously all his available time and an unflagging interest in what he himself referred to with a quotation from St Augustine: *varia, multimoda vita et inmensa vehementer*, 'a life varied, full of changes and exceedingly immense'.[10] Sometimes one had the impression that he even put his hours of leisure to observing 'a life full of changes'. Whoever accompanied him on one of his walks in peaceful surroundings, far from the bustle of

---

[9] It goes without saying that Wagenvoort presided over countless university councils, commissions and other gatherings. We need only recall that in 1948/9 he acted as Rector Magnificus of the University of Utrecht.

[10] Cf. Augustine, *Confessiones* 10, 17, 26.

everyday life, soon discovered that he had a habit of taking in everything that went on around him; he was, to use a slightly archaic Dutch term, *'gewarig'*, ('aware'); he even noticed the sounds and the movements of birds and knew how to identify them. This interest in all that lived was, as one might well imagine, partly the result of an innate character structure. To this, however, we must add the conviction that only he who takes an interest in living man and his surroundings is in a condition to give a true consistency to what, since the Renaissance, we have called *humaniora*.

In 1956 Wagenvoort reached the age of 70 and went into retirement. Since he was to continue to perform all the duties which he had performed in the past contemporaneously with his work at the university, however, the year 1956 constituted no more than a slight break with what had gone before. He continued until 1960, for example, to act as president of the 'Nederlandse Organisatie voor Zuiver Wetenschappelijk Onderzoek (ZWO)' (Dutch Organization for Pure Scientific Research), a post which had been conferred on him in 1951. He went on fulfilling other functions, such as the chairmanship of the 'Commissie voor Geesteswetenschappen' (the Commission for the Humanities) still longer. Nor did he even give up teaching. Throughout the 1950s the influx of students who, because of their inadequate preliminary training, had to have a Latin interview became ever greater, and Wagenvoort consequently organized elementary Latin university courses immediately after his retirement. He performed his new task for five years, now acting as associate professor of the University of Utrecht. Since he was dealing with students who were considerably older than the average grammar-schoolboy, and who wished to attain their objective in a far shorter time, he even prepared an entirely new course for them.

As anyone who knew Wagenvoort might have expected, he continued his scholarly research steadily and tenaciously. On the list of his publications we therefore also find a long series of writings mainly devoted to religious history which date after 1956, the most recent being of 1974. But this does not mean that he then stopped writing for good. On the contrary: the papers he left included a manuscript containing extensive material for a new book: it was on *Phanes*, the immortal god of light and the primitive deity worshipped by the Orphics. A subtitle—of the utmost significance if we take the author's great age into account—indicated the contents and the angle of the work: *Studies about the Golden Light and the Dark Shadows*.[11] The editors of the present volume initially cherished the hope that they might be able to publish one of the sections of the manuscript posthumously. On closer inspection, however, it transpired that the fragmentary nature of these sections made such an undertaking impossible.

Despite the activities which Wagenvoort performed in the period of almost twenty years which followed his retirement, the last two decades of his life were not entirely bereft of difficulties or displeasures. He too felt the effect of the years on his body. The attack which was to prove fatal to him in December and early January 1975/76 had had a precursor in January 1966. Fortunately the paralysis then appeared to be more or less limited. Nevertheless much of his willpower and determination was required in order to adapt his way of life to the new circumstances. Before the year 1966 was out he was once more afflicted by misfortune: in the summer his wife Catharina Maria Knook died; he had been married to her since 1912.

I have already mentioned various facts and events which throw some light on Wagenvoort's personality and behaviour. He was a man whom his pupils were eager to have supervise their theses; he was also a man who was frequently approached by commissions, councils, organizations, unions and societies of the most varied nature: he was requested to act as a member, preferably as a member of the board or as chairman. His friends, of course, wondered what the secret of Wagenvoort's 'popularity' was. They agreed that if one were to describe his behaviour and his attitude to others such qualifications as jovial and affable could hardly be applied. It was often apparent, furthermore, that outsiders, who had no more than a superficial acquaintance with Wagenvoort, found him

[11] There were also other occasions which showed how, as Wagenvoort advanced into his eighties, he took an ever greater interest in the concepts which ancient man had about the souls of the dead. Particularly relevant are two extensive articles written by him on this period: 'The Journey of the Souls of the Dead to the Isles of the Blessed', *Mnemosyne* 1971 p. 113ff. and 'Nehallennia and the Souls of the Dead', *ibid.* p. 273ff.

reserved, not to say slightly surly. And he did indeed have a tendency to adopt a reserved attitude towards the arguments of those who met him for the first time. Only when he saw that his interlocutor seriously wanted to expose his ideas to him did there follow a genuine reaction on his part: a reaction, moreover, which soon led him to the very essence of his interlocutor's ideas—a sober reaction, but sometimes of a typically humorous sobriety. Because he sincerely tried to understand other people's point of view there soon developed between himself and those who had anything to do with him a sense of trust.[12] It was probably mainly because of his readiness to listen and his capacity again and again to master a new subject that he was so much in demand as a chairman.

His relationship with his pupils was similar. He was not the sort of man who allowed his own point of view to obtrude, let alone who forced it on others. Wagenvoort did not found, and did not wish to found, a 'school' of his own—a school, for example, with a special method of religious-historical research. The subjects of the dissertations which he suggested were always adapted as far as possible to the personal preference and disposition of the graduates. What he expected from these graduates was that they should show him their work regularly. Whoever did not do this soon received a card with the brief and laconic invitation to 'drop in'.

The circle of friends which assembled around Wagenvoort in the course of the years—or better still, the decades—was always large, not only in the years of his professorship but also in those of his retirement. The greater his age, the more the visits he received on his birthday assumed the character of a festive meeting of

---

[12] Wagenvoort was very ready to investigate and enquire into the point of view of others not only in oral discussions, but also in discussions which cropped up in the course of his research and in his reviews. His reviews deserve a special mention: they excel in subtle judgements, and the points for and against are carefully assessed. This does not mean to say, however, that Wagenvoort never made malicious remarks about the publications of others. Especially when he believed that an author had advanced an unproven view with excessive facility he was capable of reacting with terse irony. His verdict on the French religious historian G. Dumézil which appeared in his article 'Felicitas imperatoria' (*Mnemosyne* IV, 7, 1955, p. 301, n⁰ 3), won the greatest renown: 'Iterum Dumézil Dumezilia tractat'. (see below p. 60 n. 8).

former colleagues, former pupils and other old faithfuls. His last—eighty ninth—birthday on 23 August 1975, was no exception to this rule.

Over twenty years ago, in 1956, an anniversary volume [13] was presented to Wagenvoort by his pupils and former pupils. A term was then sought which might express Wagenvoort's attitude and his other activities as briefly and concisely as possible, and the editors chose the Latin word which he had used as the title of his first inaugural lecture: *Pietas*. It seems to me that even today, now that his obituary must be written, this term is the most suitable one with which to conclude the survey of his life.

Utrecht, February 1979.   H. L. W. NELSON

[13] The title of this volume (published by E. J. Brill, Leiden) has been quoted above in notes 3 and 4. The term *pietas* is to be found in the foreword (p. V see *supra* p. X).

I

PIETAS

Certain words are typical of their time. After a long process of spiritual conflict the solution, the liberating idea, is crystallized in these words and comes as a marvel so clear and so pure that they are passed from hand to hand in amazement; they are recognized as a precious property of lasting value, not only for the individual who coined them, but for the community at large. Sooner or later, however, a new period sets in, with new problems which supersede the old; a new catchword is issued and the older one is forgotten until a later time, when it is discovered once more and reinstated with a new value, for, now that the men who coined the word are no longer there, to the eyes of the later spectator it is the word which makes its mark on men. It is such a word that I wish to discuss in this paper. These, however, are not the lines which I imagine my teaching to be following in the future: I hardly consider myself qualified for what I might call a 'synthetic' practice of philology—although I would be delighted if my treatment of my subject were to be regarded as an attempt at it.

If an archeologist is so fortunate as to find a terrain for his excavations where a series of different towns have emerged and disappeared, where different civilizations have flourished and faded or have been destroyed by force, he can make his research bear fruit in two ways: by a vertical section and by a horizontal section of the terrain. A vertical section might make it possible, for example, to analyse the development of ceramics in the area in question by way of the fragments of pottery found in the successive strata. A horizontal section, on the other hand, brings to light the remains of a given culture in a certain period and makes it possible, by considering the various phenomena in their context, to form an idea of the life of a human community, with all its variegations, in the distant past. Well, the same can be said of scholarly research into antiquity, but with one important difference: while it may be possible for the archeologist to combine both methods of research, the student of classical antiquity is faced by such an extensive task that he must necessarily limit himself to one of the two methods. He will therefore either choose the vertical section, and will devote his life to the history of language or literature, art or religion, law or political institutions, social-economic conditions or philosophy, script or texts—or he will choose the horizontal section and will devote himself to the study of a single period, but in the multiple unity which life, in all its manifestations, entails. In the first case his research has no time limit, but is narrowly confined in space. In the second case there is no limitation of space, but research is restricted to a brief period of time. I am fully aware that this distinction can seldom be applied absolutely in practice, and we are only really entitled to speak of emphasis. But in so far as the distinction *can* be made I am more attracted by the synthetic character of the horizontal method, and it is this method which I wish to apply to the Augustan period.

In the present study of the word *pietas* I propose to investigate exclusively the meaning of this word in the period of transition from the Republic to the Monarchy. For we are here dealing with a perfectly transparent crystal which was formed during a remarkable process of spiritual conflict: the interaction between an outlook based on Greek philosophy and a Roman sense of reality and statemanship, a process which led—more than was once thought—to the creation of Augustus' principate.

Gaston Boissier described the development of Hellenism in Rome in a paper entitled 'A propos d'un mot latin'.[1] The Latin word was *humanitas* and he, like others before and after him (I am thinking of Schneidewin [2] and Reitzenstein [3] in particular), demonstrated that the term "humanity" was a creation of the Roman mind intended to express the revelation made to the Romans by the Hellenistic currents of their time, cosmopolitanism and individualism. Here too, then, we have a similar catchword, and I shall pause by it because I wish to show that it is no coincidence if, after the days of Varro and Cicero, it lost its lustre and its force

---

[1] *Revue des deux Mondes*, 36 (1906), 762ff.; 37 (1907), 83ff.
[2] *Die Antike Humanität*, Berlin 1897; cf. Th. Zielinski in *N. Jhrbb.* I (1898), 1ff.
[3] *Werden und Wesen der Humanität im Altertum*, Strassburg 1907.

as a slogan, while the age of Augustus chose as its catchword the *pietas* which formed the theme, as it were, of Virgil's epic and provided the standpoint from which Livy wrote his works of history—to mention only two authors.

Alexander the Great had amazed the Greek world by placing the vanquished nations of the empire which he conquered on an equal footing with his subjects of Greek extraction, and he thus became the first man to put cosmopolitanism into practice. Thereafter it was above all the philosophers of the Stoa who elaborated this new principle on a theoretical level and elevated to a doctrine the idea that it was not the chance of being born in a certain geographical area which determined the value of the individual, but that the mere fact of being human ennobled man, and consequently that world citizenship comprised the brotherhood of mankind. It was primarily the representatives of the Middle Stoa, Panaetius and Posidonius, who, in a period running roughly from 150 to 50 B.C., transferred the seeds of the Hellenistic world-view to Rome. They did so directly by way of their widely-read works, and indirectly through their personal contact with influential Romans. We know of the intimate friendship of Panaetius, as well as of his compatriot the historian Polybius, with the younger Scipio and his circle in Rome, a friendship which dates from about 144 B.C.[4]

In this circle the concept of *humanitas* was expressed in a single word; indeed, the word was newly coined for the purpose and does not seem to have appeared before the end of the second Punic war.[5] It is not identical to cosmopolitanism in so far as the Roman preference for action rather than thought immediately focussed the vague and generalized Greek theory on practice. This had two results. In the first place it became a concept which incidentally admitted an unlimited number of nuances since it could be regarded as a norm in almost every sphere of life and could be applied everywhere in a particular way. Thus *humanitas*, so much richer in meaning than the English 'humanity', could also imply beneficence, magnanimity, disinterestedness, kindness, courtesy, gratitude, tact, love for wife and child, for parents and relatives, as well as

---
[4] Cf. A. Schmekel, *Die Philosophie der mittleren Stoa*, Berlin 1892, 6.
[5] Boissier, *op. cit.*, 763.

elegance, joyfulness, wit, literary taste and education in general, every property, in short, which can derive from the desire for dignity of the human being as such. And in the second place *humanitas* would not have been a Roman concept if, like Hellenistic cosmopolitanism, it had excluded love of one's country, or had allowed for an apathetic attitude towards the fatherland. The Greeks, even the Greek philosophical sects, attached little importance to patriotism after the great period of the Persian wars. Indeed, even in their philosophical speculations on the ideal form of government, they were only really acquainted with the narrow confines of the city state. But a man like the younger Scipio, who once thought it his duty to set Carthage on fire, and those who, together with him, enthusiastically experienced the Hellenic renaissance, would certainly never have accepted a doctrine which did not take the rights of their country into account. The satirical poet Lucilius, who belonged to the circle of Scipio and must have known of Panaetius' teachings (although this does not necessarily mean he was a Stoic), says, in one of his surviving fragments,[6] that virtue consists, among other things, in:

> Commoda praeterea patriae sibi prima putare
> deinde parentum, tertia iam postremaque nostra.

The interests of our country come first, then those of our parents and, in the third and last place, our own. Here too the principle of humanity had its importance. The feeling that the interests of the State, the common welfare, should be the dominant principle in the life of the individual, had run in the Romans' blood for centuries, and the Roman Hellenists did not deny their origin. But even Cicero, who, assures us in his *De Republica*[7] that the state has absolute power over the individual and that we can only dispose freely of ourselves in so far as our country does not need us, gives, in his *De Officiis*, instructions about international relations based on principles of humanity which could have been prescribed for our own time. We thus read:[8] 'There are, however,

---

[6] Marx 1337f.
[7] *De Rep.* I 4, 8.
[8] *De Off.* I 11, 33-35; cf. II 8, 26ff.; *de Rep.* III 23, 35; *p. Balbo* 5, 13; Sall. *Cat.* 9, 3ff.; Livy XXX 42, 17; Virgil *Aen.* VI 851ff. (cf. Norden's commentary on these lines); Prop. III 22, 19ff.; *Mon. Anc.* 26.

certain duties which we owe even to those who have treated us unjustly. For even retribution and punishment have limits, and I am inclined to think that it is sufficient for the aggressor to repent of his wrong-doing both so that he will refrain from it in future and so that others may hesitate to turn to crime. In a commonwealth, moreover, the rights of war must be strictly observed. For there are two means of adjudging a dispute: one is by negotiating, the second by force, and since the former is typical of man and the second of beasts, we should only resort to force when it is not possible to negotiate. We can indeed go to war if our object is to live in peace unharmed, but once we are victorious we should spare those who were neither cruel nor inhuman in warfare'.

Here, moreover, we can speak of an interaction of Greek speculation and Roman conviction. On the one hand the Romans displayed a tendency to limit the rights of the state over the individual. On the other hand, however, a Greek like Panaetius who, for the sake of propaganda in Rome, also smoothed over some of the sharper edges of the inflexible doctrine of the Early Stoa, seems to have made concessions to Roman patriotism and, in his book on duty from which Cicero borrowed a large part in his *De Officiis*, put duty to one's country in the first place.[9] We thus see how Cicero, who had come into contact with the last representatives of Scipio's circle and who, though no philosopher himself, acquired considerable merits both in his own day and in ours by adapting Greek philosophical writings, gave an important place to humanity in his outlook upon life. So important was this place that when, in later centuries, the Greek-Hellenistic cultural ideal was again revived, and the idea of humanity again came to the fore, Cicero was a primary source of inspiration and the new culture thus also contained a Roman element.

But we now come to the question—and to my true topic—of why it was that, after the days of Cicero and his like-minded supporter Varro, humanity quite suddenly turned into a concept of secondary importance. Why, in the literature of the succeeding period, is it hardly ever mentioned, and then only as the name of one virtue among many others? This phenomenon has often been

---

[9] Cic. *de Off.* II 17, 58; cf. Schmekel, op. cit., 32, 445.

remarked upon, and attempts have been made to explain it. Reitzenstein has rightly pointed out that the doctrine of *humanitas* was first adopted in Rome by aristocratic circles, and he adds: 'es ist eine gewaltige Leistung dieser Aristokratie, deren Verkommenheit der Historiker so gern hervorhebt, dass sie diesen Begriff prägen und zu derartig allgemeiner Anerkennung bringen konnte, wie unser Lexikon das zeigt. Sie schuf damit zugleich die Werte, welche die Fortdauer der römischen Nationalität sicherten'.[10] But when he also maintains that humanity turned into the moral of a certain class which necessarily disappeared with the collapse of the aristocracy after the horrors of the civil war and the rise of a new empire which could not deny its democratic origin in spite of everything, it seems to me that he is failing to take certain factors into account. In the first place humanity was not an exclusively moral concept of which a particular class could claim a monopoly—and indeed, why should that monopoly also be acknowledged by others? It entailed, rather, certain consequences, especially in the domain of practical statecraft, which even the democratically-minded citizens of Rome could appreciate. That they did so seems to me to be evident from what follows: in his *De Officiis* Cicero attributes all the evils which had afflicted the Roman empire in recent years to the fact that man had lost sight of the requirements of humanity. 'For', he writes,[11] 'since men behaved so cruelly to their fellow citizens, nobody saw anything wrong in the ill-treatment of allies'. Earlier, according to him, the Roman empire had reposed more on benefaction than on injustice, but it was above all the triumph of Sulla which marked a turning-point in history and brought the commonwealth to its knees. 'And these evils came about', he adds, 'because we preferred to be the object of fear rather than of love and affection'. Now, Cicero was no aristocrat: he stood midway between aristocracy and democracy. Yet it is evident that he was opposing Sulla, who belonged to the aristocracy, in the name of humanity. Still more indicative is the fact that the democrat Sallust, who was anything but well-disposed towards Cicero, fully agrees with him on this point in his *Bellum Catalinae*.[12]

[10] *Op. cit.*, 16ff.
[11] *De Off.* II 8, 27.
[12] *c.* 9-11.

There is also a second factor. If we look closely we see that it was not after Cicero's death that humanity began to lose a sizeable amount of its significance: it had already done so during his lifetime, and particularly in his own convictions. In the last years of his life Cicero himself started to doubt the strength of the principle which found its expression in *humanitas*, and at last consciously dethroned humanity as an ethical monarch and replaced it by piety.

Of the meaning of the word *pius* and *pietas* [13] Wissowa [14] says that the Romans meant the conduct of the man who performed all his duties towards the deity and his fellow human beings fully and in every respect. As *pietas adversus deos* (piety towards the gods), he goes on to say, the concept comes very close to *religio*, which gradually replaced it to such an extent that *pietas* came to denote, in a more restricted sense, the fulfilment of duty and virtuous behaviour of men to one another, and particularly between blood relatives and relations by marriage. Now, it is most remarkable that in the works of Cicero we should find the very opposite development to the one described here, and, in view of the fact that this phenomenon is of particular importance for the continuation of my argument, I propose to clarify it and to support it with certain quotations. In the rhetorical tract *De Inventione*, written, according to Cicero himself,[15] in his youth, he distinguishes between *religio* and *pietas*, and defines the latter as the virtue 'which admonishes us to do our duty to our country or our parents or other blood relations'.[16] He gives more or less the same definition later in the same work, but with this difference: he reverses the order and puts blood relations before the fatherland.[17] In his oration against Verres of the year 70 B.C. he regards it as inconceivable that a man like Heius could sin to such a degree against

---

[13] On the etymology cf. amongst others Jordan, Königsb. ind. lect. hib. 1882/83, p. 13.

[14] Roscher Lex. s.v.

[15] *De Or.* I 2, 5.

[16] *De Inv.* II 22, 66. *religionem eam, quae in metu et caerimonia deorum sit, appellant; pietatem, quae erga patriam aut parentes aut alios sanguine coniunctos officium conservare moneat.*

[17] *ibid.* II 53, 161: *pietas, per quam sanguine coniunctis patriaeque benevolum officium et diligens tribuitur cultus.*

his *humanitas*, his *pietas* and his *religio* as to sell the images of the home-gods of his ancestors for a paltry sum of money.[18] In this trio of virtues *humanitas* obviously means a sense of self-respect as a human being, *pietas* is mainly piety towards one's ancestors, and *religio* veneration for the gods. In his oration for Plancius of 54 B.C. he asks: 'what is *pietas* if not a feeling of gratitude towards one's parents',[19] and, in a tract on rhetorical divisions [20] which probably dates from the same year, he distinguishes between righteousness towards the gods, which he calls *religio*, and righteousness towards one's parents, which he calls *pietas*. In his *De Republica*, which he also began in 54, he prescribes: 'observe righteousness and piety, which is not only strictly due to parents and relations, but also to one's country.[21] Even in the Brutus of 46 B.C., written three years before his death, we read: 'Had he but behaved with as much piety towards his country as he did towards his brother!' [22]

As we see clearly from these quotations, which are so essential to my argument, up to the year 46 Cicero uses *pietas* at one moment in connection with blood relations and at another with the fatherland, and, frequently, with both.[23] But after that year this suddenly

[18] *Verr.* IV 6, 12: *videamus, quanta ista pecunia fuerit, quae potuerit Heium, hominem maxime locupletem, minime avarum, ab humanitate, a pietate, a religione deducere.*

[19] *p. Plancio* 33, 80: *quid est pietas, nisi voluntas grata in parentes?* Cf. ibid. 12, 29.

[20] *Partit. Orat.* 22, 78: *in communione autem quae posita pars est, iustitia dicitur, eaque erga deos religio, erga parentes pietas, . . .*

[21] *De Rep.* VI 16: *iustitiam cole et pietatem, quae cum magna in parentibus et propinquis, tum in patria maxima est.*

[22] *Brutus* 33, 126: *utinam non tam fratri pietatem quam patriae praestare voluisset.*

[23] There are two important passages on *pietas* in the works of Cicero which I have not included in this survey. They appear in two orations, belonging to the *orationes IV post reditum habitae—de Domo* 41, 107 and *de Harusp. Resp.* 9, 19, two speeches probably delivered in 57 and 56 B.C. respectively. Here an emphasis is laid on the *pietas erga deos* long before 45 B.C. In itself this is in no way surprising. It is perfectly possible that a man like Cicero, who was many-sided but was not tied to any single principle, could have come across the idea of *pietas* in the course of his reading before becoming fully aware of its significance. But we must be cautious: doubts have often arisen about the authenticity of these four orations (see for example M. H. Leopold, *De orationibus IV quae iniuria Cic. vindicantur*, Leiden 1890), and even if they are authentic the question still remains of whether they

changes. In May and June of 45 he wrote his *De Finibus*, in which he says, amongst other things: 'without an explanation of nature we cannot understand *pietas adversum deos* (piety towards the gods) and what great gratitude we owe to them.[24] The following year he put the last touches to his *De natura deorum*. At the beginning we find this important passage: 'It seems probable to me that, if piety towards the gods disappears, also loyalty and the *societas generis humani* (the community of the human race, in other words humanity!) and that particularly excellent virtue, righteousness, will disappear.[25] And he later writes resolutely: *est enim pietas iustitia adversus deos*, for piety is righteousness towards the gods,[26] while in the *Topica*, also of 44, *pietas* is described as 'equity to the gods in heaven'.[27] I shall be quoting two other passages which fully confirm my conclusion presently. What is this conclusion? We can see clearly that, since the year 45, *pietas* has changed its content for Cicero, or at least that the emphasis has shifted, and that instead of being applied to one's country, parents and relatives, it is applied, in the first place, to the gods.[28]

were rewritten and published later—this, as Schaum has shown, was the case with *de Domo* (*De consecratione domus Ciceronianae*, Mainz 1889, only known to me from Schanz). The text runs as follows, *de Domo* 41, 107: *nec est ulla erga deos pietas, si honesta (deest) de numine eorum ac mente opinio; de Harusp. Resp.* 9, 19: *quam volumus licet, patres conscripti, ipsi nos amemus, tamen nec numero Hispanos nec robore Gallos nec calliditate Poenos nec artibus Graecos nec denique hoc ipso huius gentis ac terrae domestico nativoque sensu Italos ipsos ac Latinos, sed pietate ac religione atque hac una sapientia, quod deorum numine omnia regi gubernarique perspeximus, omnis gentis nationesque superavimus*. The last utterance is anyhow of the greatest interest and expresses so accurately the concept which we otherwise only encounter in the last years of Cicero's life that it is quite conceivable that we have here some evidence concerning the history of this oration.

[24] *De Fin.* III 22, 73; *nec vero pietas adversum deos, nec quanta iis gratia debeatur, sine explanatione naturae intellegi potest.* Cf. moreover *de Fin.* V 23, 65 and *Deor. nat.* II 61, 153.

[25] *Deor. nat.* I 2, 3: *in specie autem fictae simulationis, sicut reliquae virtutes, item pietas inesse non potest, cum qua simul sanctitatem et religionem tolli necesse est, quibus sublatis perturbatio vitae sequitur et magna confusio;* (4) *atque haud scio an pietate adversus deos sublata fides etiam et societas generis humani et una excellentissima virtus, iustitia, tollatur.*

[26] *Ibid.* I 41, 116: *est enim pietas iustitia adversus deos.*

[27] *Top.* 90: *atque etiam aequitas tripertita dicitur esse, una ad superos deos, altera ad manes, tertia ad homines pertinere; prima pietas, secunda sanctitas, tertia iustitia aut aequitas nominatur.*

[28] Of course piety in the previously accepted sense also appears, e.g. XIII *Phil.* 20, 46ff.

Two questions immediately arise: what is the cause, and what the significance, of this phenomenon? I shall try and provide an answer to both. We know that during the second civil war which raged between Pompey and Caesar from 49 to 46 Cicero, after much deliberation, openly committed himself in favour of Pompey's party. After Pompey had been defeated decisively Cicero was pardoned by Caesar and even treated with honour. But his active energy had been completely crushed. Domestic troubles, above all the death of his beloved daughter Tullia, had contributed to this. Henceforth he withdrew from public life and spent most of his time far from Rome, on his country estates. He sought consolation in his books, and, after initially returning to his earlier rhetorical studies, he started in 45 to dedicate himself in earnest to the study of philosophy, which naturally meant that he immediately set about publishing adaptations of Greek philosophical writings. In so doing he did not limit himself to a single sect but, eclectic as he was, sought consolation and wisdom in many thinkers and many systems. This, however, does not prevent us from being so fortunate as to be able to identify the source which directly influenced Cicero's attitude to *pietas*. In the first place we possess a tract by Sextus Empiricus. As Schmekel has shown,[29] this tract, like a large portion of the first book of Cicero's *De Natura Deorum*, takes its analysis of the theology of the Stoa from the philosopher Posidonius. There we find quoted the passage:[30] ἔστιν ἡ ὁσιότης δικαιοσύνη τις πρὸς θεούς. This is literally the same as what we found in Cicero's work: *est enim pietas iustitia adversus deos,*—'for piety is righteousness towards the gods'. We can therefore assume that we are confronted with a quotation from Posidonius both in Sextus Empiricus and in Cicero. We can say more. We know that when Cicero composed his *De Officiis*, which consists of three books, he used Panaetius as his chief source in the first two books and Posidonius in the third. In the third book we also read as follows: 'It is absurd of some people to say that they do not wish to harm their father or their brother for their own interest, but that the rest of their fellow-citizens are a different matter. These people maintain that they are not legally bound to, and have no common

[29] *op. cit.*, 85-104.
[30] *Adv. phys.* I 124.

interests with, their fellow-citizens, a concept which destroys all social relations. Those, however, who say that we must respect our fellow-citizens but need not respect people of foreign nationality thereby destroy the universal community of mankind, and when this vanishes kindness and generosity, goodness and righteousness will totally perish. Those who effect this destruction must be regarded as lacking all piety towards the immortal gods, for it is the gods who have established the community of mankind which these men wish to uproot'.[31] Here again, in a concept very probably borrowed from Posidonius, we encounter the same attitude towards *pietas*, but it is also strikingly obvious where the difference between the humanity taught by Panaetius and the piety, the ὁσιότης of Posidonius, resides. They are not concepts which exclude one another entirely and which stand in opposition to each other; they even share, up to a point, the same content. Or better still: piety includes humanity as a whole, but approaches it from a different angle. Panaetius regarded man as a rule to himself. According to him true religion consisted in the knowledge of truth which can only be attained through philosophy. Posidonius introduces the deity: it is not by living our lives as we please that we get to know truth and happiness, but by listening to the calling, a calling from the deity to man. Only this piety, this faith in his calling, will make it possible for man truly to practise humanity. Whoever excludes the deity, on the other hand, ends up by acting out of self-interest. This was the discovery which Cicero had obviously just made when, in the passage I have already cited, right at the beginning of his *De Natura Deorum*, he admitted: 'It seems probable to me that if piety towards the gods disappears, also loyalty and the community of the human race—humanity—and that particularly excellent virtue, righteousness, will disappear'.[32]

[31] *De Off.* III 6, 28: *Nam illud quidem absurdum est, quod quidam dicunt, parenti se aut fratri nihil detracturos sui commodi causa, aliam rationem esse civium reliquorum. Hi sibi nihil iuris, nullam societatem communis utilitatis causa statuunt esse cum civibus, quae sententia omnem societatem distrahit civitatis. Qui autem civium rationem dicunt habendam, externorum negant, ii dirimunt communem humani generis societatem, qua sublata beneficentia liberalitas, bonitas iustitia funditus tollitur. Quae qui tollunt, etiam adversus deos immortales impii iudicandi sunt. Ab iis enim constitutam inter homines societatem evertunt.*

[32] *Deor. nat.* I 2, 4.

It is not of course enough simply to bring to light this alteration in Cicero's convictions about the meaning of piety. If this were the case we would only be learning something which is already known to us from elsewhere: the mystical-religious element in Posidonius' philosophy and Cicero's tendency, in his last, sombre days, to seek consolation in a doctrine which did not just turn man's attention to himself, but allowed for the possibility of divine intervention in human affairs. But the principle of piety which we have now encountered acquired an immense political significance: I shall try to show that it was an attempt to provide a moral justification for the Roman policy of conquest and, at the same time, the philosophical background, the philosophical sanction, of Augustus' principate.

Whenever alarming circumstances arise in some state or other, whenever people start to fear for the safety of the state, they usually soon express the desire that all powers should be concentrated in the hands of a single strong personality. Such a tendency also appeared in the Roman Republic at the time of the civil wars. In Cicero's *De Republica* it is expressed over and over again, and he attributes the almost prophetic declaration to Scipio: 'in matters of government there are curious cycles and, as it were, periods of change and vicissitudes. To know these changes is the task of the philosopher, but to see them in the distance while steering the ship of state, when the course can still be regulated and controlled—that is unquestionably the work of a great citizen and a man almost divine'.[33] That, then, is the ideal statesman destined to have a major role in the ideal government; it is the citizen who, as we also see elsewhere,[34] compels everybody, with the force of his authority and with legal punishments, to do what the philosophers could only persuade a few individuals to do—and that with great difficulty—with their philosophical arguments. It is the man who deserves to be called *princeps rei publicae*, 'the first citizen'.[35] But this tract, which must have been published in 51, was not yet familiar with the new concept of *pietas*, and the author was consequently confronted by certain difficulties.

[33] *De Rep.* I 29, 45.
[34] *Ibid.* 2, 3.
[35] *Ibid.*, 21, 34.

I shall turn to the nature of these difficulties after a preliminary observation.

The subjugation of Greece by Rome gave rise to extensive speculation. Indeed, the Greeks could hardly help wondering why their country, which wielded the sceptre in the domain of the mind, should be subordinated to Rome, whose cultural level was so much lower. This led to all sorts of accusations from the Greek side, and it is easy to guess the main point of debate, even if this conjecture were not supported by facts. The Romans were told that they did indeed pride themselves on their sense of justice, and, later particularly, on their humanity, but that their world conquest could hardly be based on their humanity and that they were far from practising what they preached. To play this trump against the conquerors became such a common practice that as early as 155 B.C., when the Athenians sent an embassy of three philosophers to Rome, one of them, Carneades, delivered an oration to the Romans in which he argued that it was not law which regulated the dealings between men and states, but self-interest: the Romans had always acted according to this principle, they who had conquered the entire world by coveting and robbing the property of others. Had they not been exclusively devoted to their own interests and had they been prepared to behave with righteousness, they would have surrendered all their conquests and returned to their lowly hovels of primitive times.[36] How deep an impression this argument made appears from the fact that the old and revered Cato, who was firmly devoted to tradition, ordered the philosophers to leave the city as quickly as possible.[37] He felt that the attack was directed against the fundaments not only of Roman law, as Schmekel pointed out in his *Philosophie der mittleren Stoa*,[38] but also of the Roman state. Had it only been the law which was affected Schmekel would have been right in saying that no police-measure could arrest the influence of Greek attitudes such as these on the young Romans, but that one idea had to be set against another, and that this counterbalance was provided by the Stoa of Panaetius. But it was also a question of the state, and although

---

[36] *Ibid.*, III 6, 9; 12, 20ff.
[37] Plut. *Cato* 22ff.
[38] *op. cit.*, 455.

Rome could rightly claim that she had, on the whole, carried out her conquests in a moderate and conciliatory spirit, and had infringed humanity, the fruit of Panaetius' doctrine, as little as possible, it could hardly be claimed that the wars had been conducted according to the principle of humanity and were justified by that principle. If not by that principle, however, by which principle? A satisfactory solution to this problem was vital to the Roman state: relations with Greece were particularly difficult since Rome actually felt inferior to the conquered country, but did not wish to be inferior.[39] The Romans' only hope of justification was to place theory and practice, thought and action, on the same level: this is the profound meaning which lurks in Cicero's words when he puts the statesman next to, or rather, above, the philosopher. But then at least one condition had to be fulfilled: the action had to be morally justified. And we need only read the third book of Cicero's *De Republica*, which was wholly dictated by Panaetius' doctrine (fragments alone survive, but these tell us enough), to see how difficult it was to justify Roman expansionist policy in a world which was thinking more and more along Greek lines. It is no coincidence that Carneades' oration should be quoted in this same third book, and St Augustine has preserved the arguments advanced against it. 'The reply on the side of justice', he says, 'was that conquest was just because servitude is in the interests of such men, and is established for their benefit when it is rightly established, that is, when the wicked are deprived of the licence to do evil, and when those conquered will be better off than they were before being conquered'.[40] We see how weak the support provided by Panaetius' rationalism was on this point. But in the last years of his life Cicero made a surprising discovery which seemed to provide him with a perfectly satisfactory solution. What if every state had its destiny! What if the deity had called Rome to found a world empire! What if the Roman conquests had not come about from a ruthless urge to further the Romans' own interests, but from faith in the divine calling, from that sense of duty which silences every human voice before the voice of the

---

[39] Cf. my article 'Het cultureel program van Keizer Augustus', in *Tijdschrift voor Geschiedenis* 1924, 161-188.

[40] Augustine *de Civit. Dei* XIX 21, 2 = Cic. *de Rep.* III 24, 36.

deity, in brief—from *pietas*! This had been the discovery of the great Posidonius, and how thankful the Romans, especially those of a later generation, were to him for it, will appear to us in due course.

It would be wrong to assume that Posidonius violently distorted his own convictions in order to curry favour with the Romans, even though his entire work, in so far as it is known to us, is dominated by a conciliatory tendency. For the dogma of piety in Roman statecraft is entirely in accordance with his doctrine as we know it from elsewhere; he sees every terrestrial event as determined by the divine law and, whatever he does, man must appreciate his dependence. I believe that we do Greek philosophy in general, and the Stoa in particular, an injustice if we assume, as, for example, Norden does,[41] that its reflections were simply determined by the attempt to establish in theory what the Romans had long been doing in practice, for the theory goes far beyond practice in that, in a vision of genius, it provides practice with a new, hitherto unknown, worth.

After the days of Cicero humanity no longer played a part of any significance, but *pietas* became the device of the new Roman state, piety in the sense in which we have encountered it. And there is a striking phenomenon which, I believe, proves clearly to what an extent the new concept, the new dogma, had become the common property of all educated Romans. Both in literature and in the plastic arts writers and artists soon started to personify the virtue of piety according to the old concept of love for parents and relatives, and to venerate her as a goddess.[42] As early as 181 B.C. her first temple was dedicated in Rome, later to be followed by a second, and countless coins were struck with her name and image. This continued until 41 B.C., when the triumvir M. Antonius had *denarii* struck with the image and name of Pietas through the intermediary of his brother. But then this process suddenly came to a halt, and it was not until the time of the emperor Tiberius that we again find her image on coins and her name on altars, an expression of reverence which recurs very frequently in the later imperial period. We can observe the very same process in literature:

[41] Comment. *Aen.* VI 851-53.
[42] Cf. for the following Wissowa in Roscher Lex. s.v.

in Plautus' comedies the goddess is mentioned often; she appears nowhere in the Augustan period, but is named repeatedly thereafter in Seneca, Statius and Claudian. Needless to say, there can be no question of chance in this phenomenon. In the same period, which was infused with piety in any case, a violent and conscious reaction has apparently developed against the personification of the virtue and its being honoured as a goddess, a reaction which lasted as long as 'piety' remained the political catchword, i.e. until Augustus' death. The explanation seems simple enough to me: one cannot make a goddess of a concept which primarily implies the right attitude of man to the deity. *Religio*, for example, was never made into a deity! The fact that this idea was accepted generally and without exception can be considered a proof of the existence and popularity of the dogma I have discussed.

The way in which Augustus himself affected this development with his reform of the cult of the state is too well-known for me to have to analyse it extensively here. When the senate decreed that a golden shield with an inscription should be placed in the Curia Julia in his honour, that happened, as he himself reports in the Monumentum Ancyranum, *virtutis clementiae iustitiae pietatis causa*: for the sake of his observance of virtue, tolerance, righteousness and piety. But there is no better source for getting to know the aspirations of the *princeps* than the literature which he inspired. And of course we first think of Virgil, who made the *pius* Aeneas the hero of his epic at the pressing request of Augustus himself.[43] If the poet puts the piety of his hero so much in the fore as to have him say of himself: *sum pius Aeneas*, 'I am the pious Aeneas,'[44] a detailed analysis shows with complete certainty how, from start to finish, he had the same ideal before his eyes as the one cherished by Cicero in the last years of his life. Right from the beginning, for nowhere—or so it seems to me—is his object clearer than in the fourth book, one of the first which he wrote, where Aeneas' stay at Dido's court in Carthage is described. A great many serious studies have been devoted to the delineation of the characters

---

[43] Serv. *Praef.* I p. 2, 10 Th. I have discussed the question of why Aeneas was chosen, and not Augustus himself, as the poet had originally planned, in the above-mentioned article.

[44] *Aen.* I 378.

in this book; scholars have wondered what we should make of a character like Aeneas who, after having yielded to his love for Dido and after having basked at length in the luxury the queen offered him, suddenly changed when the goddess warned him to remember his calling and, without letting himself be moved by Dido's touching laments and pleas, rapidly made ready to leave. I shall not go into the emphasis which the poet repeatedly gives to the amount of effort and self-control which this attitude cost Aeneas precisely because he felt that one moment of weakness would make him waver in the decision he had taken.[45] The main point, however, is that, in this tragic conflict, we see depicted a clash between self-interest and the divine calling. Aeneas is the hero because he sacrifices his own desires, his own love, for the formidable task of seeking a new land for the fugitives from Troy for whom a glorious future lay in wait. I wish to make two points in this connection. When the unhappy queen, beside herself with grief, sees Aeneas sailing away, she calls out: 'Behold, that is the honour and faith of him of whom they say that he carries with him the home-gods of his fathers and that he took his old and decrepit father on his shoulders.[46] She therefore bases her lament on Aeneas' piety, which she cannot understand in a more elevated sense. And after that, as she flings her curses after him in her powerless rage, she cries prophetically that an avenger of Carthaginian blood will arise to complete the deserved punishment in a bitter war against Aeneas' descendants.[47] What does this mean? It means that the war with Hannibal and the Punic wars in general were a result of Aeneas' piety, or, in other words, deprived of poetic symbolism, that they were a necessary consequence of Rome's obedience to the divine calling.[48]

Rome's greatness and world conquest as a fruit of piety—this is also illustrated in the theme of Livy's ambitious work of history. Livy, too, was a friend of Augustus'; he, too, started his work

[45] *Aen.* IV 331ff.; 395; 448ff.
[46] IV 597ff.
[47] IV 625ff.
[48] Cf. also R. Heinze, *Vergils epische Technik*, Leipzig-Berlin 1915, 301ff. N.B. the remarkable, and at first sight curious, combination of encomia with which Virgil glorifies the young Marcellus: *Heu pietas! heu prisca fides invictaque bello dextera!* etc. VI 878ff.

shortly after the transition from the Republic to the Monarchy. This young man, too, had evidently fallen under the charm of the new dogma which both explained the past and assured the future, and while Augustus forged the future into a world empire of peace, Livy set about reviving the past. He no longer had to hesitate about reviewing the endless series of wars, for the calling of the state made them inevitable. Apart from civil war, which he abhorred, he frequently mentions a *bellum pium*, a war waged on the basis of pious considerations.[49] The arguments he advances for this usually appear particularly weak to us and often consist exclusively in the affirmation that war was never begun before an indemnity had been requested through the intermediary of the priestly college of the *fetiales*, and that it was then declared with the usual ceremonies. It may be worth noting in this connection that Augustus inaugurated his religious reforms before the battle of Actium by reviving this custom after an interval of over a hundred years, and by declaring war on Cleopatra in person, as a *fetialis*, according to the ancient rite.

I no longer feel bound to show how this same concept is frequently (albeit, as a rule, incidentally) put into words by other writers and poets—I have particularly Ovid and Propertius in mind—but I would still like to mention a poet who ran into curious difficulties owing to the new concept of *pietas*, coined for the state and hallowed by the emperor—Horace. Although he never lost his heart exclusively to one philosophical sect and was also an eclectic, Horace's sharply critical mind, with a subtle sense of humour on the surface and a tempered pessimism deeper down, was far more inclined towards the doctrine of Aristippus, Epicurus and Lucretius than towards the Stoa which he often mentions with sympathy, but to which he was not really prepared to accord more than a smile. He too knew of another piety, besides a firm love for relatives and friends, but it was not that of the Stoic-Roman dogma, nor was it that of his master Lucretius, although it stood nearer to the latter. J. Woltjer has explained to us [50] what Lucretius under-

[49] E.g. *bellum pium* Livy I 32, 12; *arma pia* IX 1, 10; XXX 31, 4; *bellum iustum piumque* XXXIX 36, 12; *bellum pie indicere* I 22, 4 etc.

[50] 'Religio en Pietas bij Lucretius', *Versl. en Meded. Kon. Ak. v.W. afd. Lett.* XI (1912) p. 239ff; see p. 246. The remarks about *pietas* in Cicero on p. 245 are, as I hope to have shown, wrong.

stood by *pietas*: it is the peace of mind which stems from the correct, Epicurean concept of the gods and which preserves man from the fear of death. In Horace we only have to think of the observance of religious duties which he, too, followed, not because he attributed a deeper significance to it, but because he shared the current view that a distinction should be made between three sorts of religion: that of the philosophers, that of the statesmen and that of the poets. Only the first is the true religion, but it is unsuited for the people. For the sake of the people it was essential to display a formal reverence for the gods invented by politicians and poets, and Horace was therefore in full agreement with the revival of the cult of the state by Augustus. But he poked as much fun at the piety of his friend Virgil as he did at the glorification of Aeneas, the forefather of the Julian line. 'When we have descended to where father Aeneas, the rich Tullus and Ancus are, we are dust and shadow', he says in one of his Odes,[51] and he herewith denies the divinity and immortality of Aeneas. With equal impassivity he disregards the official concept of *pietas*: I am only aware of his having alluded to it specifically once, but then with tremendous irony. This is in the so-called 'Roman Odes', at the beginning of the third book where, whatever we may think of the context, he is certainly referring to Augustus' rule and his determination to glorify his reign even in the domain of religion. In Juno's well-known speech the goddess warns the Romans that excessive piety (*nimium pii*) should not put it into their heads to want to rebuild Troy once more.[52] You never can tell, he means, where pious fanaticism will drive the leaders of our people. One wonders at this point how anyone could ever have regarded Horace as a subservient court poet who wrote what he was told to write.

But I have now come to the end of my observations. I hope that the development of this concept of *pietas* has shown that, in the transition from Republic to Monarchy, the interaction of Greek-Hellenistic philosophy and Roman statecraft was a factor of some significance, and that this interaction did not originally develop by either of the two surrendering its autonomy to the

---
[51] *Od.* IV 7, 15ff.
[52] *Od.* III 3, 57ff.

other, but as a parallel emotion, as the result of the great spiritual currents of the time.

Finally: the concept of humanity seemed to be a plant from a Greek seed cultivated in Roman soil, and if we wish to characterize it with some names, we must mention Panaetius and Scipio. The same was true of the idea of *pietas*, taken from Greece but brought to flower in Rome: it is inseparable from the names of Posidonius and Cicero. Consequently Greek wisdom and Roman energy collaborated harmoniously and aspired together towards the ideal commonalty of mankind for over two hundred years. After Augustus' death this came to an end. Under Tiberius Pietas again came to the fore as a goddess, but nobody could find a new standard for the practice of community life—unless, that is, we search outside the sphere of Hellenism. For, under the same Tiberius, the ethics of Christianity were summarized in a couple of words: love of God and our neighbour—this was piety and humanity combined. Now, however, they were no longer directed towards self-preservation but towards self-surrender. I cannot help feeling that this development contains an element visible to anyone willing to see it: the fullness of time.

II

DIVA ANGERONA

Everyone knows how often both in ancient and more recent times scholars have attempted to interpret the nature and name of the goddess Angerona. And yet to me we seem to have made hardly any progress in this attempt. Aust [1] and Wissowa [2] have collected the relevant passages from ancient authors and other documents which I think it unnecessary to copy out. Neither the disease of *angitia* nor 'worries to be dispelled,' as urged on us by the ancients, are of any help towards an interpretation. Mommsen [3] thought Angerona was a goddess in charge of the New Year. He sought to derive the name from *angerendum*, ἀπὸ τοῦ ἀναφέρεσθαι τὸν ἥλιον. The explanation was accepted by Wissowa but rightly rejected by others (Walde-Hofmann s.v. '*ganz unwahrscheinlich*'). Recently Eva Fiesel [4] and Altheim [5] have sought an Etruscan origin for the name and connected it with the gentilitial name *anχarie, ancarie, anχaru, ancaru*. The suggestion is rejected by Vetter,[6] and I cannot agree with it either. To the arguments offered by Vetter I can add the following. First, the derivatives in Latin of Etruscan names ending in -*u* usually end in -*ōnius* not -*ōnus*.[7] Secondly, the name *Angĕrōna* seems to fit very well into a large series of such names belonging to truly Roman (or Sabine) goddesses.

First of all we have *Abeonam, Adeonam, Intercidonam*, all

[1] *RE* I, 2189ff.
[2] *Rosch. Lex.* I, 348ff; *Rel. u. Kult.*² 241.
[3] *CIL* I p. 409.
[4] *Language* 11 (1935) 122ff.
[5] *Hist. of Rom. Rel.* (1938) 114f. *Latona* is not comparable, being undoubtedly formed differently (cf. also Walde-Hofmann s.v.).
[6] *Glotta* 28 (1940) 197: 'The conjectures are ingenious but not well grounded. Phonetically there is the difficulty that the family name, which was certainly borrowed by the Etruscan from the Italic, when reproduced in Latin always has the *tenuis* (c, ch) whereas in the name of the goddess it is always the *media*. The supposition of an Etruscan goddess *ancaru* is unproven'.
[7] Cf. e.g. Nehring, *Glotta* 13 (1924) 14; also Stolte *ibid.* 14 (1925) 289ff. A late attestation of the form *Angeroniae* (*Gloss. Labb.* p. 12) is not relevant.

named after an action and that, if I am not mistaken, in popular speech on the analogy of those that follow. For, secondly, several similar names of goddesses have come down to us derived from substantives, the best known of which are *Bellona* (or *Duellona*) and *Pomona*. To these we must at once add *Populona*, later combined with Juno as *Iuno Populona*. The word here is substantival, not adjectival in form, and after a while the Romans did not hesitate to corrupt it into '*Populonia*'.[8] Then *Mellona* [9] and *Bubona* [10] can be added to the list. It may perhaps be rash to designate *Annona* as a member of this company,[11] since I have the same doubt whether a goddess of that name is ancient as I do in the case of *Orbona* [12] and *Fessona*.[13] Even if these were really goddesses believed to care for the bereaved and infirm, I for one should rather suppose that the names were formed at a later period on the analogy of the others. Against that, I have no hesitation in adding *Vallon(i)a*,[14] a goddess who reigned over valleys according to Augustine, *C.D.* 4, 8. The fact that this name is written with -i- in one single case seems to me no good reason to regard it as having been formed in any other way. In *Populona* we noted the same variation, and later we have it also in *Fessona* (thus in Augustine, *C.D.*, 4, 21; the inferior codices have *Fessonia*) and in *Mellona* (thus in Augustine, *C.D.* 4, 34, but *Mellonia* appears in Arnob. 4, 7ff.).

Thus if she who presides over *bellum*, war, is called *Bellona*; over *populus*, the people, *Populona*; over *mel*, honey, *Mellona*; over *boves* (*bubos*? cf. *bubīle* or *ovīle*), cattle, *Bubona*; over *valles*, valleys, *Vallona*, it is natural to enquire whether Angerona too can be referred to a substantive indicating the thing over which the goddess presides.

With this in view it certainly seems worth considering the adjective *angustus*, from which we easily derive a substantive

[8] Cf. W. Otto, *Philol.* 64 (1905) 172.
[9] Cf. Peter, *Rosch. Lex.* 2, 1, 203.
[10] Cf. Wissowa, *R. u. K.*² 199, 10; on the etymology of the word see Walde-Hofmann s.v. *būbulus*.
[11] Cf. Oehler, *RE* 1, 2320; Wissowa, *R. u. K.*² 302.
[12] Cf. Wissowa, *R. u. K.*² 244.
[13] Cf. Peter, *Rosch. Lex.* 2, 1, 298.
[14] Cf. Peter, *Rosch. Lex.* 2, 1, 228.

angus(-ĕris): cf. *onustus(onus)*, *augustus* (**augus*), *vetustus* (**vetus*). Nor do I know what else that obsolete noun could have meant but '*angustias*', 'narrows'. Thus we are led immediately to the further question, in what sense a Roman goddess Angerona could be thought of as a goddess of **angerum* or 'narrows'.

We know from ancient sources that in the small sanctuary of Volupia there stood a statue of Angerona *ore obligato obsignatoque*.[15] It is a great subject of controversy what this posture can have meant. Not to make too long a story of it, I myself do not doubt that W. F. Otto [16] and Altheim [17] have the right answer in connecting Angerona with the *Dea Tacita*,[18] or Silent Goddess, and interpreting her as goddess of the 'silences' or the *manium tacitorum*, i.e. the 'silent' or infernal shades. It is further worth mentioning that there was a connection between Angerona, in whose honour the *Divalia* were held on 21 December, and Larenta, to whom special honours were paid every year on 23 December. She is compared by Wissowa (*op. cit.* p. 235) with the *Dea Tacita*, whom he calls 'eine Indigitation der Larenta'. Moreover a point not to be overlooked is that Larenta herself seems to have been a goddess of the underworld at whose 'tomb' we know that the *flamen Quirinalis* offered a sacrifice for the dead on her feast day.[19] This tomb was called by Wissowa a *mundus*, 'that is a grave usually closed and opened only on the feast day as a suitable place of sacrifice in the Roman view for the underworld gods, since it constituted in a sense a passage between the world above and the world below'. Altheim [20] supports this view. Whether such a place is rightly called a *mundus* is a question of small consequence for my own suggestion. Whatever view we take, the passage from Angerona to certain *fauces Orci*[21] is not a long one. Such 'narrows', through which it was believed that the infernal beings could be reached,

---

[15] *Masur. Sab. ap. Macr.* 1, 10, 8; cf. Plin. *N.H.* 3, 65; Solin. 1, 6.
[16] *Rosch. Lex.* 4, 823.
[17] *Op. cit.* 115
[18] Cf. E. Tabeling, *RE* 4 A 1997.
[19] Wissowa, *R u K*.² 233ff.
[20] *R. R. G.* 1, 14ff.
[21] Though I still think the word *mundus* less appropriate, in this respect I must correct what I wrote in the discussion quoted in the next note p. 56.

were once frequent in Italy. There is no need for me here to repeat what I have recently published at greater length.[22]

Therefore I ask, what is to prevent us believing that Angerona presided over those *angera, or angustiae, or 'narrows', 'through which death is reached' (Sen. *H.O.* 1773)? In my opinion it all agrees very well together.

[22] 'Orcus , *SMSR* 14 (1938) 33ff.

III

PROFĀNUS, PROFĀNĀRE

Anyone who scours the dictionaries in the desire to learn the real meaning of the verb *profanare* can hardly avoid finding himself befogged. Ernout and Meillet seek to distinguish two homonymous verbs, one derived from the adjective *profanus* and meaning the same as English 'desecrate', the other derived from *pro fānō* and meaning 'sacrifice', 'consecrate' (*sacrificare, consecrare*). Against them Walde-Hofmann is convinced that there is only one verb, the original meaning of which was 'to sacrifice', but refers us to Danielsson's theory (*Eranos* 3 (1898)58) that the verb did mean ' 'to sacrifice' but had originally been confined to 'abstracting the human share of the victim" as opposed to '*pollūcēre*', 'to offer the θεομορία' or divine share. Thus in his opinion it did not at *first* have the sense of sacrificing so much as of abstracting part of the offering for human use. Walde-Hofmann also adds that the verb was used by Ovid in the sense of 'lifting the consecration'. Other dictionaries either simply group the directly contrary senses of consecrating and lifting the consecration under one and the same lemma or like Ernout and Meillet assert that there were two homonyms. The commentators too, especially those on Cato and Varro, appear to flounder in dreadful confusion. Several of them, like Gesner and Schneider, assume that the verb *profanare* was at first used in the sense of consecrating and later switched back into the completely opposite sense.

Hardly anyone with experience of this matter will be satisfied by these views. It is perhaps not unexampled that one and the same verb should have two contrary senses, but the language used in Roman religious services must necessarily have resisted such an ambiguity, which according to normal feeling would of course have jeopardized the successful outcome of the rites. Perhaps it may be objected that the sense of the adjective *sacer is* equivocal. The word did contain an idea which was already as strange to Roman minds in historical times as to our own today, and we cannot in fact render it exactly except with the help of the Indonesian word *tabu*, which of course holds the same ambiguity. But it is impossible that such a sense could have been latent in the verb *profanare*. Otherwise it could never have signified the sharing of the sacrificial feast with the people. There is the further point that if the matter were otherwise the same sense would necessarily have been found in the adjective *profānus*, where there is in fact not the least trace of it. Finally the conjecture that the verb is formed from two homonyms is of no help at all, since it leaves us completely in the dark as to how, in a divine service, people could use the same word in two totally opposed senses, without injuring the ceremony.

In our study of this question it seems appropriate to start with the adjective *profanus*. For there is a considerable controversy how the meaning of this word is to be explained etymologically. Surely it contains *fānum*, that is, 'holy place, shrine, temple', but what the prefix *pro-* can signify is by no means immediately apparent. Yet there are those who have shown the way to a true explanation. Wackernagel for instance (*Sprachl. Unters. zu Homer* p. 240) after pointing out that in several verbal compounds *pro-* means the same as Dutch or German '*weg*'—English 'away'— *prohibēre* is one of them—correctly adds that in some languages this prefix has the same force in nominal compounds. He compares the Sanskrit *pra-parṇa*, 'whose leaves have fallen' i.e. 'are not to be seen',[1] the Latin *pro-fundus*, 'whose bottom is not to be seen', and others, with the additional note: 'Should *profanus, profestus* therefore be added to the list, as opposites of *sacer, festus* in the sense that *pro-* indicates the absence of the following concept— *profesti dies* the days on which there is no longer a festival, *profana* the places from which a *fanum* is absent (literally, has been lost)?' Not even the ancient grammarians were unaware of this function. Festus for instance (p. 256 L.) thus deals with the adjective *profundus*: '*profundum dicitur id quod altum est ac fundum longe habet*', whence it would follow that in his opinion *pro-* meant nothing but 'a long way off'. Nevertheless I am convinced that more careful consideration can throw new light on the question.

[1] My colleague J. Gonda adds the ἅπαξ εἰρημένον *pra-nīḍa* which is said of a bird leaving the nest.

It is a well-known fact that the early Romans had remarkable difficulty in rendering abstract notions. But there is hardly any notion so abstract as that of expressing—especially with one clear part of speech like *weg* or 'away'—something which a short while previously was present and is now no longer to be seen but is vanished from view. The Latin language lacks even a particular word for this notion, which is of course why it has often recourse to the combination *non comparere*.

There are peculiarities even about the Dutch or German particle *weg*. Experts assure me that in ancient times it was pronounced *ǝweg*, cfr. the English 'away', and meant 'on the way', '*en route*'. Consequently, even though the thing that does not appear is inanimate human skills are attributed to it and it is said to have departed. The same thing is found in the Italian *via*, Danish *bort(e)*, Swedish *bort(a)* (ancient *braut*, to which also a conjunction was prefixed—*ibraut, ibrott*, properly 'on the way', the same therefore as *weg*, 'away'). And in fact early Latin did have a similar term. *Pro* was used to express 'far', or rather 'so far as to be no longer discernible'. This little word survived in Classical Latin as an interjection. Many dictionaries translate this 'oh! ah! alas!' By contrast Lindsay (*The Latin Language* p. 618) is both brief and accurate, '*prō* seems to be merely the preposition (adverb) *prō*, "forth", lit. "away with (it)!"' Here there is an excellent parallel in the Greek φροῦδος (< προ-οδος). Anyone who has properly understood this usage will see how it could come about that the interjection sometimes took the accusative, sometimes the vocative. There is no doubt that originally it governed the accusative, e.g. *pro scelus* (i.e. strictly 'away with the crime', Mart. 2, 46, 8); *pro nefas* (Sen. *Ag.* 35); *pro facinus ingens* (*Oct. praet.* 147). And how did it later come to take a vocative? This becomes clear the moment we look closely at Ter. *Ad.* 447:

Pro di immortales, facinus indignum!

The commentators on this passage generally say that *pro* here takes a vocative, and I for one have no doubt that that is what Terence intended. It is equally clear in my opinion that the writer who first used these words in this order punctuated them differently:

Pro, di immortales, facinus indignum!

That is, 'Away with the shameful deed, immortal gods!' Thus here too *prō* in early times governed the accusative. Let us compare Ter. *Phorm.* 1008 '*Pro di immortales, facinus miserandum et malum!*' [2] I am almost certain that the vocative in an exclamation of indignation after *pro* was modelled on a text from some religious service and had in this way become so well-worn and commonplace that step by step the particle *pro* came to be used almost with an artificial meaning. Accordingly we can in broad outlines agree with Wackernagel's theory that the prefix *prō* means the absence of the thing to which it is prefixed, but he did not sufficiently realize how it acquired this sense. For it cannot be right that *profāna*, as he alleges, were 'locations lacking a *fānum*'—'where a *fānum* had been lost'!—principally for the reason that in Old Latin the adjective *profānus* [3] was used primarily not of places but of things. Ernout and Meillet seem to me right in having thought that this adjective originated in the expression *prō fānō*, in the same way as *proprius* from *prō prīvo*.[4] The *prō fānō* did not mean the place in front of the temple, however, but *fānō* was a true ablative of separation and *prō fānō* meant the same as 'away from the temple' and was properly used of things which had previously been in the temple, and consecrated. This opinion is not in conflict with those already proposed by ancient commentators. For instance Servius Danielis (*Aen.* 12, 779; cf. Macr. *Sat.* 3, 3, 4) writes, '*profanum* properly means a thing converted from religious to human use'. Thus, if I am right, the sense of the adjective properly speaking is not 'unconsecrated' but 'no longer sacral', and the verb *profanare* derived from it is to be understood as meaning 'lift the consecration'. And this is the point on which I insist, in early times *profanare* meant nothing else but 'lift the consecration from man or thing'.

[2] The same rule must have given rise to such locutions as Ter. *Eun.* 943 '*Pro deum fidem, facinus indignum*', where *deum fidem* (*imploro* understood) has been substituted for the vocative *di immortales*. Later, when this was no longer understood it occasioned such combinations as *pro deum fidem* (Ter. *Andr.* 237), *pro divum fidem* (Enn. *Sat.*18), *pro fidem* (Plaut. *Amph.* 376).

[3] Regarding the short -ŏ- in prŏfanus cf. M. Leumann, Stolz-Schmalz [5] p. 91 and 102.

[4] It is also probable that the adjective *profundus* is to be explained in this way, the surface or 'top' of the water being regarded as 'a long way from the bottom'. *Profestus* however may have been formed on the analogy of *profanus*.

We find it still used in this sense in two passages of Cato, now rather far distant from one another, that is chapter 50 and 132, but in the opinion of qualified scholars [5] intended by Cato himself to be read in the same sense. The first passage (*de agr.* 50, 2) is:

'*Ubi daps* profanata *comestaque erit, verno arare incipito*'.

Gesner annotates '*profanare* here means *consecrare*' and refers to passages of Varro and others which I shall deal with later. But it seems to me that the explanation '*cum daps (deo) consecrata et (a populo) comesta erit*'—'when a sacrificial feast is consecrated (to the deity) and eaten (by the people)'—can at once be rejected. Nobody at any time was ever allowed except on certain definite conditions (and that rarely—I shall discuss them later) to consume consecrated food except as a holy sacrament after the performance of certain rites, a case which is unthinkable here. The religions of the whole world abound with such rules. A reference to the prohibition among the Jews on eating the bread in the temple at Jerusalem will be enough. Hörle (*Catos Hausbücher*, 1929) refers to Gesner's opinion in connection with the words (c. 131) *dapem.... facito* and says that in this passage Cato has substituted *dapem facere* for the obsolete phrase *dapem profanare*. Therefore if we follow him *profanare* will here mean '*sacrificare*', and many others including Hooper and Ash in their English version (Loeb, 1934) have agreed with him. But I am convinced they are wrong. When the *daps* (sacrificial feast) is ritually offered to the deity there must perforce be a sacral act. But a sacral act means some form of consecration, which is customarily performed by a contact, as I have lately explained at some length (*Roman Dynamism*, 1947 ch. 1). A priest may lay his hands on it or the offering be placed on the altar. But if the food is nevertheless given to the human worshippers to eat, this can only be done after it has previously been *profanatum*—'deconsecrated'—: the consecration must be lifted by some ritual. The strict sense in which in those early times sacrifices offered to the gods were forbidden for popular and profane use has been more than sufficiently demonstrated by Pfister (*Religion d. Griechen u. Römer, Bursians Jahresber.* Suppl. Bd. 229,

[5] Schneider *ad* ch. 132; Jos. Hörle, *Catos Hausbücher* (*Stud. z. Gesch. u. Kult. d. Altert.* Vol. 15 H. 3/4) p. 87.

pp. 115f.) with a great deal of evidence from Latin and other languages. There are rules from different cults on how, if at all, human beings may share in the sacrificial meals and victims. Either this was altogether prohibited,[6] which needs no explanation because of course it was based on an interpretation handed down from time immemorial, or secondly, it was permissible to consume part of them provided it was not taken outside the temple precinct,[7] and this occurred mainly in chthonian cults (cf. Puttkammer p. 62f.). The point of the restriction seems to have been correctly understood by Robertson Smith (*The Religion of the Semites*, 221). 'The unmistakable sense of this rule' he writes 'is that the meat is not ordinary but sacred meat and its consumption is part of the cult action and must be completed before the people leave the sanctuary.' The third and last possibility was that everybody should take away some portion to eat at home. This, however, is never found at Rome except in foreign cults (cf. Wissowa, *RuK*[2] p. 420). The second kind of rule, where food offered to the gods and then freed for human use was forbidden to be taken outside the temple, is first mentioned among the Romans in the worship of Silvanus, on the authority of Cato (*de agr.* 83) and *C.I.L.* VI 1, 576 (= Dessau II 4915) (cf. F. Boll, *ARW* 13 (1910) p. 575, 2.). There has been a good deal of disagreement about the true nature of Silvanus. The very name of course has been taken to indicate a god of the woods, by the ancient Romans no less than by more recent writers. Against that Deecke and others have associated him with an Etruscan god named Selvans. Whatever the case, if the name *Silvanus* is derived from *silva* it must necessarily be considered an adjective which in early times was attached to a different god. Wissowa's conjecture (pp. 213ff.) that this was Faunus seems probable. If correct, it is noteworthy that according to the most recent investigations (see E. C. H. Smits, *Faunus, Diss. Utrecht.* 1946 *passim*) Faunus was also an underworld deity. It may be so.

[6] Cf. F. Puttkammer, *Quo modo Graeci victimarum carnes distribuerint*, diss. Regimontana (1912) p. 6of.
[7] *CIL* VI 1, 576 (= Dessau II 4915) '*Extra hoc limen aliquid de sacro Silvani efferre fas non est*'—'It is not lawful to take anything from the sanctuary of Silvanus outside this threshold'; Cato *agr.* 83 '*Ubi res facta erit, statim ibidem consumito*'—'Where the thing has been done, there at once consume it'. Cf. Ada Thomsen, *ARW* 12 (1909) 468.

Our subject here, however, is not Silvanus but Jupiter, not a temple but a household ceremony.

Another example of the same thing was current at the Tithe of Hercules at the *Ara Maxima*, which I shall deal with more fully below, and which we may certainly assume was in origin Greek rather than Roman. It follows therefore, that the private rite mentioned in passing by Cato certainly stands by itself and is not to be compared with the other ceremonies we have considered so far. Here a sacrificial feast offered to the gods was none the less consumed by human beings. I must at once ask, is it probable that in the opinion of the early Romans this could happen without the need of some ritual? It is, if you believe Wissowa (*RuK* ² p. 419): 'After the *exta* have been offered (*extis redditis*) the rest of the animal (the *viscera*,) is "profane' and eaten by those present'. But it would certainly be surprising. Anyone even moderately versed in Roman religion must know that such a proceeding would seem to them contrary to the order of nature. To take one example, when an enemy city had been captured its free inhabitants did not at once automatically become slaves, but it was necessary that they should be passed under the yoke so that they 'lost their heads' as it was called (*Roman Dynamism* pp. 155ff.). In the same way it was the custom for every inauguration to be lifted by an 'exauguration', every *confarreatio* (the most solemn form of marriage) by a *diffarreatio* (the corresponding divorce). Equally in my opinion even in early times a consecration of any kind could not be nullified except by some *profanatio*. The evidence that this was what Cato meant in his chapter 50 is provided, if I am not mistaken, by his chapter 132. The passage has been thus edited by Keil (I have changed the punctuation just before the end):

'*Dapem hoc modo fieri oportet. Iovi dapali culignam vini quantum vis polluceto. Eo die feriae bubus et bubulcis et qui dapem facient. Cum pollucere oportebit, sic facies: "Iupiter dapalis, quod tibi fieri oportet in domo familia mea culignam vini dapi, eius rei ergo macte hac illace dape pollucenda esto". Manus interluito, postea vinum sumito: "Iupiter dapalis, macte istace dape pollucenda esto, macte vino inferio esto." Vestae, si voles, dato. Daps Iovi assaria pecunia, urna vini Iovi caste.* Profanato *sua contagione. Postea dape facta serito milium, panicum, alium, lentim*'.

These words are by no means clear at first glance. The last sentences especially ('*Daps Iovi....contagione*') are decidedly unclear, and moreover there is a good deal of disagreement among scholars about the text. Our distinguished countryman Popma thought that '*pecunia*' should be amended to '*pecuina*', a reading accepted by Hooper and Ash, who thus translate: 'The feast to Jupiter consists of roasted meat and an urn of wine'. This at any rate is inaccurate, since according to Popma it was not a question of roast meat but of meat 'prepared and dressed for roasting'. You may suppose they were deceived by the first appearance of the words, not grasping the real meaning of the word *pecunia*, and considering that a sacrificial feast intended for Jupiter could hardly if at all consist only of wine, because even though we refrain from asking how the word *daps* could have such a meaning, in chapter 50 it is transparently clear that the *daps* in question here was customarily eaten. But what are we to make of *assaria pecunia*? The adjective *assarius*, as we see in the *Thesaurus L.L.*, occurs nowhere else, unless we allow Bücheler's emendation in Seneca *Apoloc.* 11 of *homines assarii* i.e. *viles*—'mean, worth (not) one (single) ass'. Yet a substantive *assarius* with the same sense as *as* on the testimony of Charisius [8] was in use in early Latin and is still found in Varro (*l.l.* 8, 71). But what *pecunia* in this passage really means Wissowa so far as I know is the only one to have realized (*RuK* [2], p. 410, 10), after Keil's capitulation, 'for me it is sufficient in these formulae, our knowledge of which is very uncertain, to have restored the reading of the archetype'. Wissowa observes, quite rightly, that the puzzle is solved by these words of Paulus (p. 287 L.) restored by Scaliger: 'A sacrifice is said to be *pecunia* when in aid of the fruit and field crops *mola pura*, grain and salt, is offered, because all those household things we now call *pecunia* consist of these.' I refrain from asking whether this special use of the word *pecunia* can be fully explained. At least we do seem to be able to infer from the words quoted that *mola salsa*, the simplest food of the early Romans, was called *pecunia* whenever it was offered to any deity. You may plausibly suspect that Cato thought of baked bread when he talked of *mola*. On the contrary,

[8] 1, 76, 3 '*Assarius ab antiquis dicebatur, nunc as dicitur non assis*'.— '*Assarius*', 'was used by the ancients, where we now say *as* rather than *assis*'.

in my opinion Wissowa was wrong to have punctuated the words as he did '*assaria, pecunia*' making it seem as if he thought the *assaria* stood for *caro assa*, roast meat. We have seen that it is never found anywhere else in this sense. And if I am not mistaken the epithet *assaria* means that one *as* (worth or weight) of *mola* would have been enough for the sacrificial feast. If we consider that in the year 250 B.C., without forgetting that it was a year of excellent harvests, a bushel of corn was sold for one *as* (Mommsen, *Röm. Staatsrecht* I⁶ p. 836), this interpretation seems not impossible.⁹

It is just as difficult to work out the end of this sentence. With the older Italian commentators I have put the stop after *caste*, because I am convinced that the dative *Iovi* cannot possibly belong to the verb *profanato*. If it has been correctly transmitted, the repetition of the name of Jupiter seems to be explained by the mention of the goddess Vesta in the immediately preceding words. For the whole section concerns a sacrifice offered to Jupiter. But if anybody wants to seize the opportunity, writes Cato, of including Vesta in the sacrifice, there is no religious objection provided that Jupiter gets his due, an *as* of *pecunia* and an *urna* of wine. Where *caste* belongs is not so easy to decide. But since it is *not* superfluous only if it goes with what follows, whereas it becomes superfluous if joined with the preceding sentence, I prefer the former. We may in particular compare Cato's immediately preceding words, '*manus interluito, postea vinum sumito*':¹⁰

The words which follow, '*profanato sua contagione*', in my opinion have been generally misunderstood. Because *contagio* is generally used in a bad sense, meaning a polluting or befouling touch, several scholars accepting the view that *profanare* in this passage has the sense of 'offering in sacrifice' or 'consecrating' and thinking the

---

⁹ In the time of Polybius (cf. Mommsen) in the richest parts of Italy board and lodging in an inn cost half an *as* per day. Cf. also Plin. *N.H.* 19, 54 'food too was to be had for an ass'. On *mola salsa* offered to the gods see Plin. *ibid*. 18, 7; Serv. *Ecl.* 8, 82.

¹⁰ Cf. Cic. *Leg.* 2, 24 '*Caste iubet lex adire ad deos*'—'The law is that the gods are to be approached in a state of purity'; C. Iulius Caesar Strabo, *Adrastus* (Ribbeck, *Trag. Rom. Fragm.*³ p. 263), '*Cum capita viridi lauro velare imperant / prophetae sancti, caste qui purant sacra*'—'when the holy prophets command heads to be veiled with green laurel, and purity in those who handle the offerings'.

text must therefore be corrupt, followed the example of the *editio princeps* in emending *sua contagione* to *sine contagione*, a conjecture which we still find defended by Marquardt-Wissowa (*Röm. Staatsverw.* 3 ² p. 150, 8). Hooper and Ash indeed do not follow in their footsteps but translate, 'Present it to Jupiter religiously, in the fitting form', and neglect what is in my opinion the most necessary part of the ceremony, the act of eating briefly mentioned in chapter 50 above. Without doubt here still as in early times *profanare* is equivalent to 'remove the religious prohibition from things previously consecrated', *contagio* quite properly means a 'polluting touch', *sua* however must concern some rite, and what Cato is really saying is, 'then convert that sacrifice to human use by lifting the consecration through the method of touch prescribed for that purpose.' What that method was has not come down to us.[11]

The verb *profanare* was often used in this sense later as well, as in Ov. *Her.* 7, 129, '*Pone deos et quae tangendo sacra profanas*', or *Am.* 3, 9, 19 '*Scilicet omne sacrum mors importuna profanat*'.[12] But in Varro (*l.l.* 6, 54), we encounter a quite different use of the word. He writes:

> '*Hinc fana nominata, quod pontifices in sacrando fati sint finem; hinc profanum, quod est ante fanum coniunctum fano; hinc profanatum quid in sacrificio † ad quae Herculi decuma appellata ab eo est quod sacrificio quodam fana[n]tur, id est ut fani lege sit. Id dicitur pollu⟨c⟩tum, quod a porriciendo est fictum: cum enim ex mercibus libamenta porrecta sunt Herculi in aram, tum pollu⟨c⟩tum est, ut cum profan⟨at⟩um*

---

[11] *Translator's Note.* In accordance with the preceding discussion Cato's Section 132 may now be rendered in English: 'The sacrificial feast is to be offered as follows. Offer a cup of wine, as much as you want, to festal Jupiter. Make the day a holiday for oxen and teamsters and those who perform the sacrifice. When you make the offering, say: "Festal Jupiter, since it is fitting that a cup of wine be offered for thy feast in my house among my people, to that end be thou exalted by the offering of this feast". Wash your hands, then take the wine: "Festal Jupiter, be exalted by the offering of this feast, be exalted by the sacrificial wine". Offer to Vesta, if you wish. To Jupiter the festal sacrifice is one as's worth of grain and salt, to Jupiter one urna of wine, to offer which you must be pure. Lift the consecration by the appropriate rite of touch. When the whole sacrifice has been performed sow millet, panic grass, garlic, lentils.'

[12] Cf. Ov. *Met.* 4, 390; Liv. 31, 44, 4.

dicitur, id est proinde ut sit fani factum: itaque ibi olim ⟨in⟩fano [13] *consumebatur omne quod profanum erat, ut etiam fit quod praetor urb⟨an⟩us quotannis facit, cum Herculi immolat publice iuvencam.'*

Varro thus begins by putting forward an etymological account of the word *fānum*, which I pass over. Then he proceeds to explain *profānus* in a way which I have already rejected; [14] finally he treats *profānātum* as a participle functioning as a substantive. It is most unfortunate that this text too has reached us in mutilated form but lower down the definition is repeated in much the same words. There it certainly appears that according to Varro *profānātum* is that 'which *fanatur* (as it were)' by some sacrifice, that is so as to be subject to the law of the *fanum* (temple)' or 'consequently made to belong to the *fanum*'. Thus in his opinion *profānāre* is 'to render *profānum*', but with the *pro-* meaning 'for', i.e. 'instead of', the *fānum*. But Lübbert (p. 3), Wissowa (*Röm. Staatsverw. l.c.*), Boehm (*RE* 8, 571), and others have observed that in this passage the notions of *profānāre* and *pollucēre* as so often are being confused. Boehm for instance writes, 'In the sacral terminology the part burned for the deity was called *polluctum*, the part handed over to the people was called *profānātum*.' And after quoting the passage from Varro he goes on, 'Marquardt convincingly demonstrates from the passages concerning the Tithe that the expressions *pollūcēre* and *profānāre* were often confused'. He is right there. *Pollūcēre*, an obsolete ritual term of uncertain etymology, is interpreted by Ernout and Meillet as '*placer des mets sur l'autel en vue d'un banquet de sacrifice, placer en offrande*'. If you believe Varro, *profānāre* means almost the same.

Finally Varro declares—at least if we are right to follow Vertranius in inserting the preposition *in* before *fano*—in the offering of the

---

[13] Lübbert, *Commentationes pontificales* p. 9 and Marquardt-Wissowa, *Röm. Staatsverw.* 3² p. 149 defend the omission of the preposition and understand by *fano* 'for the benefit of the temple'. Wrongly in my opinion.

[14] Nevertheless it is not all clear how this is to be reconciled with what follows. It is no help to maintain with Wissowa, *RuK* ² p. 468, 5 that *ante* is adverb, *fanum* however an adjective, so that '*profanum* is what was previously *fanum*, that is, belonging to the sanctuary' so that we have 'a mix-up of the notions *profanum* and *profanatum*'.

Tithe of Hercules at the *Ara Maxima* the rule mentioned above (p. 30) was in force that all meat destined for human use must be consumed in the temple itself, which agrees very well with the words of Servius Danielis (*Aen.* 8, 183), '... *ad Aram Maximam aliquid servari de tauro nefas est, nam et corium illius mandunt*'—'at the Ara Maxima no part of the bull may be kept, they chew up even its skin'.[15]

Nobody indeed will deny that Varro used the verb *profānāre* in the sense of consecrating or sacrificing. It seems noteworthy that so far as I know the word is never used in this sense except in connection with the Tithe of Hercules. Thus Festus (p. 270 L.) writes, '...*Hercules, cum ad aram, quae hodieque maxima appellatur, decimam bovum ... profanasset*'. Macrobius (3, 6, 11) quotes the words of Masurius Sabinus, a writer of the first century B.C., that a certain M. Octavius Herrenus '*instituit mercaturam, et bene re gesta decimam Herculi* profanavit'. It is worth remarking that Servius (*Aen.* 8, 363) though he did not name its author copied this passage almost word for word but at the end changed '*profanavit*' to '*dicavit*'—'dedicated'. In this he may have been influenced by his antiquarian studies, and thus hesitated to use the verb *profanare* in that sense. Nor can we say he was wrong!

The Tithe of Hercules was at first donated by private people, especially merchants, and used to be fairly modest (cf. Boehm, *RE* 8, 570f.). But since a share of the victims was allotted to the public—Tertullian indeed (Apol. 14, 1) makes mock of the fact that only a third was consumed by the altar fires—the Roman nobles soon began to use the custom as a means of gaining popular favour. Thus it came about that the Tithes turned into sumptuous banquets and, as Boehm remarks, in comedy especially the words *polluctum, polluctura*, and others from the same root came to comprehend all kinds of luxuries and delicacies. This is true, however, not only of *polluctum*! If we look more closely we soon find that it is even more the case with *profanatum*, because of course it signified that part of the offerings no longer consecrated but set aside for public use. How often then when people have said to one another, '*Hodie profanabitur ad Aram Maximam*',

---

[15] On the devouring of skin and bones in antiquity cf. Ada Thomsen, pp. 471ff.

though taught of old to think of the actual ceremony of (*profanatio*), they must have had in their mind's eye the luxurious banquets accompanying the sacrifice.

Whence it results that the two almost contrary senses of the verb *profanare* came about not because there originally existed two different verbs which later became more or less confused, but because the proper sense of the verb, which had not been lost even in more recent times, was 'to lift the consecration'. The very moment at which it began to mean 'sacrifice', or more precisely 'to donate a tithe and make a banquet for the people' the distance travelled by Roman popular morality in the century between Cato and Varro comes to the light.

Finally I observe that we may now be able, if I am not mistaken, to restore, with great probability, the deficiencies in that transmitted text of Festus (p. 242 L.). I shall subjoin the text as edited by Lindsay, who himself not only restored its quotation from Plautus but also adopted some words supplied by Scaliger. However, this text, as now entirely re-edited so far as possible by myself, differs from that previous version, first, in my having inserted in roman lower case material supplied in Marquard-Wissowa (*o.c.* p. 149) from some source or other and seeming to me correct, and secondly, additions of my own in italic capitals. I have the following further points to make. The final *t* of the words *licet* and *sicut* can still be made out in the codex. Against that, where I have proposed to read *populo*, the first and second letters have completely perished and for the third the previous editors put -*c*-. As for the final words, whether we read *consumi* or with Antonius Augustinus prefer *consumere* for what in the codex is read *consume*, we can hardly avoid restoring the correct meaning. We have seen above what this instruction really means, unless in the Tithe of Hercules it was no longer considered unlawful to consume the meat outside the sanctuary, so that the true reason for the instruction had faded from memory. Thus I think the text should be emended as follows:

'..... <*Plautus in P*>*seudolo (266): "atque in*
<*manibus exta teneam, ut porici*>*a*⟨*m*⟩ *interea loci*".
<*Porrigitur autem in mensis a*>*risque quod consecran-*

<dum est deo: quod profanatur con>tra it consumi-
<tur a vulgo profano. PROFANATA LICE>t ut Verrius eo-
<dem libro de significatu verbo>rum, sint dicta libe-
<RIORE SENSU PORRECTA, SICU>t arbitratur ob eam cau-
<SAM QUOD PARS DISTRIBUITUR POP>ulo, quia
profana ea
quoque, id est deo dic⟨a⟩ta, consumi est necesse.'

All that remains doubtful is the word *profana*. If it has been transmitted correctly, it must necessarily say the same as *profanata*, when explained on the authority of Festus by the word *dicata*. But we have already noted above that Servius changed the reading *profanavit* which he found in Masurius Sabinus to *dicavit*. For this reason I should have no further doubts but for the fact that in Varro's words already quoted exactly the same thing happens. There too (line 7) the reading transmitted is *profanum*, which Leonhardt Spengel changed to *profanatum*, followed by Kent, but not by Goetz and Schoell. However, it may be, if *profana* is the correct reading, it follows that it must mean the same as *profanata*.

IV

GRAVITAS AND MAIESTAS

Five years ago when I published the book *Roman Dynamism*, on the last page, as I had already done in the Dutch edition of 1941, I declared that I was quite aware of a rather venturesome element in my ideas which might quite easily earn the disapproval of certain experts. I added however, that I would welcome and indeed solicited any corrections, any judgments disagreeing with my own, provided they were offered with good will and in the sole desire of eliciting the truth. Hitherto my hopes, or rather my sure expectations, have not been disappointed. On the one hand there have been numerous testimonies of agreement which it is hardly for me to enumerate, nor is this the place. On the other objections perhaps have been equally numerous, including corrections and differing opinions on individual points. Though some of these, it goes without saying, I find difficult to accept, being not infrequently due to misunderstanding of my words, yet there are many cases in which I find that I was mistaken or careless. I have accordingly collected all of these and filed them, with the intention of publishing a retraction as soon as I get a chance.

Now, however, to use words attributed to the divine Augustus in Seneca's *Apocolocyntosis*, 'I can no longer hide or contain a grief which shame makes all the more severe'. Recently Georges Dumézil,[1] the eminent historian of Roman religion whom I have always highly esteemed, has thought proper to attack me as 'le plus actif des dynamistes contemporains', which he does not intend I fear as a title of honour. The picture he paints of my opinions is so wrong-headed and distorted as to drip *ira et studium* from every pore. If it is true that to understand everything is to forgive everything, we need not despair of patching things up between us. For it seems that all this displeasure emanates from one over-hasty judgment of my French colleague. I shall discuss it later. First I must demonstrate the arguments he has produced against my views.

[1] *Rev. de Philol.* 26 (1952) 7ff.

The first page of his article I reserve to the end. I begin with the second, where he begins his critical examination of my interpretation of the notions of *gravitas* and *maiestas*. I note at once that for unstated reasons he has inverted the order of treatment. First he deals with *maiestas*, then with *gravitas*. If we suppose that this is more or less by chance or of small importance, we are making a bad mistake. For this inversion serves my opponent's purpose of obscuring my real opinion as much as possible. Let us see how he renders my words. I had written on p. 120, at the very beginning of the short sub-section dealing with *maiestas*: 'Strictly speaking, this *maiestas* (*māg-ies-tāt-s*) or "being greater" does not belong to our present study, but it is difficult to leave it out of our consideration because it is important to observe how, in the long run, this notion either took the place of *gravitas* or for a long time occupied a place beside it as having a synonymous meaning'. And to avoid the possibility of misunderstanding, at the end, on p. 127, I again declared: 'It will be clear that, as I have observed at the outset, the word *maiestas* from its origin does not belong to the complex of *mana-* reminiscences. Yet through the emphasizing of various conditions of might and power it has gradually been amalgamated with it in many respects'.

This is how Dumézil renders this (on his p. 24): 'M. Wagenvoort n'a donc pas démontré sa thèse principale. D'autre part, *en posant que maiestas et gravitas sont synonymes*,[2] il a effacé des différences importantes'. Then again in his conclusion on p. 28 he writes: 'Ainsi, replacés dans l'ensemble de la vie et de la pensée romaines, *maiestas* et *gravitas*, *loin d'être deux désignations équivalentes*[2] d'une variété de force mystique ou de *mana*, apparaissent comme deux notions distinctes....'[3]

[2] My italics.
[3] It is true that in one of his numerous footnotes (p. 19, 9) he hides this rather than he brings it out into the open: 'Il est remarquable que, dans son utilisation de *maiestas*, M. Wagenvoort marque quelque réserve, pensant (pp. 119-128) qu'il s'agit d'un terme plus jeune que *gravitas* et qui même l'aurait supplanté dans certains emplois.....; admettant aussi, dans ses dernières lignes (p. 127), que ce mot, en tant que dérivé de *maior*, n'a pas appartenu dès le début "to the complex of *mana*-reminiscences"...' Dumézil is mistaken. I 'admitted' nothing nor was it necessary for me to 'admit' anything. Not only in my final lines but at the very beginning I stated that the two words did *not* mean the same, though occasionally—not everywhere but here and there—they came closer to one another in meaning and almost merged.

Dumézil is mistaken. I could hardly have said more clearly that the word *maiestas* in its proper sense has nothing in common with the notion of *gravitas*. Not only did I quite deliberately treat *gravitas* first, and *maiestas* after that, but it was quite necessary that I should do so. By inverting this order he corrupts the very sense of the whole discussion, he paints a distorted picture, and I doubt whether there is much consolation in his words (p. 27), 'La caricature fait souvent ressortir, dans sa déformation, un trait essentiel de l'original'.

As for the peculiar notion of *maiestas* itself, it is worth noticing how strikingly we agree with one another. I had written (p. 120) that the word in early times meant 'being greater'. '*Maiestas* then' I added (p. 123) 'was, from the beginning an attribute of the gods. As early as in Livius Andronicus' *Aegisthus* (fr. 8 R.) the godhead presents itself as "*maiestas mea*" '. Dumézil writes (p. 8), 'le rapport de *maiestas* à *maior, maius,* leur' (i.e. to the Romans) 'était évident', and adds (p. 10), 'Dans un de ses emplois le plus anciennement attestés, *maiestas* sert à situer les dieux par rapport aux hommes. Dans l'Égisthe de Livius Andronicus—le plus ancien témoignage— la divinité elle-même se qualifie déjà, au-dessus de l'action dramatique, par les mots "*maiestas mea*" '. Yet Dumézil refrains from mentioning this close agreement even in passing.

But, you may tell me, dear reader, though I may have started from the same notion, I very soon followed a different line and after the words just quoted immediately proceeded: 'Gradually, however, the distinction between the notions *gravitas* and *maiestas* became less marked'. Having previously declared, this reader may continue, (e.g. on p. 117) 'that originally *gravitas* was a heaviness caused by strong *mana*', you cannot deny that in course of time, according to you, the notion of *maiestas*, if not everywhere, yet 'in many respects', diverged into the sense which Dumézil disapproves and attacks. You are right, quite right—except for those last few words. Because Dumézil is very far from disapproving or attacking this sense. Instead, it is wonderful how much agreement there is between us. Let me recall my actual words: 'in the long run, this notion either took the place of *gravitas* or for a long time occupied a place beside it as having a synonymous meaning' (p. 120); 'through the emphasizing of various conditions of might and power it has gradually been amalgamated with it in many respects' (p. 127). Then what is Dumézil's verdict? I ask you to pay careful attention to his reasoning (p. 8): 'S'il était déjà chargé de prestige' (i.e. le mot *maiestas*)—'disons, pour suivre la mode: *s'il dégageait déjà du mana—ce n'était là*, en tout cas, *qu'un effet secondaire....*'.[2] Or (p. 18), 'dès lors, notion prestigieuse et notion confuse, *maiestas* rayonne du *"mana"*; mais nous ne nous lassons pas de répéter *que ce mana est secondaire, qu'il est le produit d'une évolution*'.

I applaud, though I could hardly believe my eyes on reading this, and I was all the more surprised on coming to the end of the article to read that the notions of *maiestas* and *gravitas* '*loin d'être deux désignations équivalentes d'une variété de force mystique ou de mana*, apparaissent comme deux notions distinctes...' etc. How these are to be reconciled I leave to Dumézil.

Of course I realize that, though Dumézil tries in vain to conceal by a number of evasions and self-contradictory arguments that he cannot help agreeing with me on the main issue, yet when the question arises in what passages the word *maiestas* has an almost 'dynamistic' force he often rejects my interpretations and arguments as in his opinion weak or even worthless. And please observe how he sets about refuting them.

When it was necessary to indicate my reason for dealing with *maiestas* immediately after *gravitas* (p. 123) I pointed out that in ancient writers the two notions were often associated, and continued, 'Beside the *maiestas* of the gods we find the *maiestas* of the Roman people', and gave examples. In order to reply to the question what *maiestas populi* really meant, I quoted definitions collected by Kübler, such as Cicero's '*maiestas est amplitudo ac dignitas civitatis*' (*de. or.* 2, 164). I found these definitions 'all vague and obscure'. And I do not think my Paris colleague will want to contradict me there, because he repeatedly states that the word properly speaking has a comparative force, almost a hierarchical one. He says, for instance, (p. 9) that the word signifies 'le rang supérieur qu'occupe une catégorie par rapport à une ou à plusieurs autres'. In the passage quoted, however, and others like it such a meaning is not at all evident. For that very reason I continued in the same strain: 'The very core of the question is all the more clearly defined by the jurist Proculus discussing a clause appearing in treaties of alliance such as are mentioned in Cic. *Balb.* 35'. (References to Cicero and Proculus here follow). 'We have here a fundamentally correct idea of the comparative notion implied in *maiestas*....., the *maiestas populi Romani*, the "being greater" or "superiority" of the Roman people, must always be measured according to its position compared with the surrounding world'. Here Dumézil attacks me. After himself quoting the words of Proculus and—in a note—Cicero he comments (p. 11), 'Si l'on tient à voir du *mana* dans le rapport naturel de positions qu'exprime ici *maiestas*, il faudra.....' And up to this point I had not in this context even muttered the word *mana*! On the contrary I had added, 'This', i.e. that *maiestas* is the attribute of a people exceeding others in power and strength, 'is shown by many passages', and quoted four of them. Here I choose one, Liv. 23, 43, 10, '*Hannibalis virtutem fortunamque extollit, populi Romani obterit senescentem cum viribus maiestatem*'—'he extolled the valour and good fortune of Hannibal and disparaged the aging majesty and declining strength of the Roman people'. I conclude the paragraph with these words, 'In the same sense Vergil, *Aen.* 12, 820ff. says....' (followed by six lines).

'*In the same senso*' i.e. the sense I was discussing a few lines above—'the "being greater" or "superiority" of the Roman people'. Though this must be clear as day to anyone else, Dumézil chooses to interpret my words differently. He seems to suppose they refer not to the preceding words but....to the following paragraph! After requoting the six lines, '*pro Latio obtestor, pro maiestate tuorum*', he proceeds, 'M. Wagenvoort suggère de comprendre ici *maiestas* comme "the *mana* of the ruling tribe" et cite le témoignage d'un ethnographe d'après lequel, pour exprimer qu'ils sont dominés par les Britanniques, les Maoris de la Nouvelle-Zélande disent qu'ils sont "sous le *mana* des Britanniques"' (p. 10). Then he informs us that the poet here means the Latins, the offspring of Saturn father of Jupiter Latiaris, a point which was already noted by Servius, and I do not know who could have been ignorant of it since you will find it explained in any commentary published for the use of schools.

Dumézil is mistaken. I never said what he attributes to me.

Consider. After having assembled many passages concerning *populi maiestas* I could not help asking myself whether they were all much alike or whether perhaps one or other among them exhibited a meaning which was somehow primitive in modern terms. A question as necessary as it is difficult. Necessary, because we have often seen it established that a word has this tendency. Difficult, however, because it is often a case of different shades of meaning, which not only may easily deter us but on the contrary risk leading us on too boldly in pursuit of variations which have no real substance. It is because I always have this danger in view that I hold myself completely ready to consider opposing opinions and acknowledge myself in the wrong—'Any *constructive* criticisms or suggestive remarks offered in a friendly spirit will also in future be thankfully received' (Preface p. XI).

But if I am asked this question about the phrase *maiestas populi* what shade of meaning I consider primitive, I have already given my reply in the following paragraph: '*Maiestas populi* in the primitive sense, is the "*mana* of the ruling tribe" (Lehmann above (p. 119)', whereupon I quoted from the same author, to illustrate this meaning, the example of the New Zealand Maoris. Do we encounter this meaning in the passages quoted? I grant that in the following section, under pressure of space, I wrote rather too briefly and succinctly. I wanted to say and should have said that this primitive meaning was apparent in at least one passage. 'The loss of this superiority-*mana*', I wrote, 'is referred to by Livy (*loc. cit.*) when he uses the graphic expression *senescens maiestas.*' This is the argument which Dumézil needed to refute. The points he made at such length from the Proculus and Vergil passages were mere shadow-boxing. It is true he did not altogether neglect the Livy reference, but he relegated it, as less handy to his purpose, and as usual, to a footnote. After arguing in his main text (p. 11), 'Aussi sa *maiestas*' (i.e. of Rome) 'n'a-t-elle pas été la conséquence fortuite, mais la justification presque juridique, presque rationnelle, de son accroissement et de son empire, pour lesquels sa force militaire n'a été qu'un moyen', he subjoins the footnote: 'C'est ce que ne comprend pas le Carthaginois Hannon quand, pour détacher les sénateurs de Nola de l'alliance de Rome, alors en grande difficulté, *Hannibalis virtutem fortunamque extollit, populi*

Romani obterit senescentem cum viribus maiestatem (Tite-Live, XXIII, 43, 10)'. This is altogether beside the point. First the words quoted are not Hanno's but Livy's, the subject speaks for itself, and Livy states unequivocally, 'Hanno... spoke *through an interpreter*' (§ 9). Secondly, every schoolboy knows what to think of those speeches inserted by ancient historians. *'C'est que, pour les anciens, elles constituent un ornement indispensable de l'histoire'* (Henri Bornecque, *Tite-Live* (1933), p. 155; cf. his whole chapter *'Les Discours'*). Thus *senescens maiestas* is a phrase attributed to Hanno but really Livy's. Whether the majesty of Rome at that moment of time had really 'aged' or not is of no concern to us here. One thing we do note—Livy was undoubtedly using words which would have been clear to every Roman reader. What does the verb *senescere* really mean? Men, animals, trees *senescunt*, 'grow old', 'an age' (*aetas*) too may 'grow old' (Cic. *Cat.* M. 38), so may a field (*ager*) (Ov. *a.a.* 3, 82), presumably in a figurative sense (i.e. to become exhausted, 'tired'). 'Strength' (*vires*) may 'grow old' (Sall. *or. Macr. ad. pleb.* 19). Livy himself combines the proper and the figurative sense, *'Hannibalem ipsum iam et fama senescere et viribus'*, (29.3.15). A state too of course could grow old (*senescere civitatem otio ratus*, 'considering that a state could be aged by ease'—1, 22, 2). Surely it must be clear to everyone that even in the passage I quoted the words *senescens maiestas* no longer have anything of the comparative meaning but flatly correspond here to the definition devised by Dumézil himself (p. 18): 'il' (i.e. the sense of the word *maiestas*) 'tend à devenir la notation non plus d'un *rapport*, mais d'une qualité, appartenant inconditionnellement à une personne divine ou humaine, c'est-à-dire déjà ce que nous appelons "majesté"; dès lors, notion prestigieuse et notion confuse, *maiestas* rayonne du *"mana"*'?

I should not wonder if there were misgivings to be overcome on two points at least, before you were ready to follow me here. First, you may ask, do I think Livy was a man of so little learning that he offers us examples of primitive and uneducated speech? God forbid! But I have already dealt with this question on the first page of the Introduction, which I can only ask you to look up and first of all study the words quoted from Nathan Söderblom, which are too long to repeat here. In any case it is of the greatest importance to understand that what we are usually concerned with here are 'expressions the original meaning of which not only does not strike them' (i.e. the Latin authors) 'but which, moreover, as possible recollections of primeval national belief, as links in a chain connecting their own time with bygone ages, altogether escape their attention'. But if you ask me secondly whether I really believe that the passage of Livy is the only one in Latin literature in which the indicated meaning occurs I shall reply cautiously that, if not, I know nowhere where the meaning is so plain. Since this applies not only to *maiestas* but also to *gravitas*, I think it useful here to insert a brief digression.

How often when his ears tingle does a man of our time say, 'Somebody is talking about me'. How is this to be understood? Are we to take it that our friend has been caught in the toils of vain superstition? Not at all, we are all convinced he is engaged in completely senseless word play. But when we see that M. Cornelius Fronto had already written in the second century (*Ep.* 2, 2 1.f.), 'But the matter gave rise to a long, long talk about you, much longer than that between you and the quaestor about me. I am sure your ears must have been tingling in the forum'; or read in Pliny (*N.H.* 28, 24) 'it is generally thought that absent persons know by the tingling of their ears that others are talking about them'; or if that charming poem comes to mind (*A.L.* 452), once falsely attributed to Seneca, '*De tinnitu auris*', are we not then conscious of a link between ourselves and people of that very remote age? But if Apuleius (*Apol.* 48) or some magical papyrus [4] informs us that according to the ancients this tingling was often caused by magical art, and moreover that the origin of the superstition was agreed by competent judges to be attributable to magical beliefs,[5] what I ask should we conclude? Nobody I imagine will maintain that we ourselves when using this expression believe in magic. They are words used casually but survivals all the same

---

[4] Griffith-Thompson, col. III p. 35 (18)ff., quoted by Abt, *Die Apologie des Apuleius von Madaura u. die ant. Zauberei*, 1908; cf. also H. E. Butler and A. S. Owen in their note (1914) on the passage.

[5] Cf. e.g. Gulick, 'Omens and Augury in Plautus', *Harvard Studies* 7 (1896) 245f.; Bachtold-Stäubli, *Wörterb. d. Dtsch. Abergl.* VI and sources there quoted; also Riess, R.E. 1, 87, 12ff.; X. Wolters, *Notes on Antique Folklore*, diss. Utrecht 1935, p. 47ff.

from a time when such words were by no means casual. What times were they? The Roman period perhaps? Not even that would be generally accepted. 'When the Roman people appears in history', I wrote (p. 3) 'it is well past the primitive stage', and Pliny for example speaks with too much caution to be rashly suspected by us of such folly. Yet he did stand much nearer to its origins than we do. Moreover the passage of Apuleius informs us that his case was far from being the same as that of all his contemporaries.

Let me give another example. Whenever one of us sneezes we have a habit of saying 'Bless you!' What do we really mean by that? We really mean nothing. The voice of past ages speaks through our mouths, ages when our distant ancestors were convinced that sneezes were caused by the action of spirits. This question too is raised by Pliny (*N.H.* 28, 23): 'When people sneeze why do we salute them, as even Tiberius Caesar, by general agreement the most serious of men, is said to have done in his carriage, while some even think it more proper to address them by name?' Anyone reading Pliny's whole treatment of this subject, where he raises the question whether 'words and spells can have magic force' (28, 10) will readily agree with me that though he does not answer the question himself but thus gives his own verdict, 'taken one by one the verdict of our wisest men would be against the idea', yet all the same he stands wondering and hesitant among all these obscure and inexplicable phenomena. There is no need to quote other passages to demonstrate the special meaning attributed by early men to sneezes (such as Hom. *Od.* 17, 541ff.; Xen. *Anab*, 3, 2, 9 etc. cf. Wolters, pp. 44ff.). I must again emphasize that neither our own countrymen today nor Pliny's contemporaries so far as they are educated and civilized are to be thought of as habitually terrified of ghosts. But neither is this manner of speech or other sayings of the same kind for that reason to be completely overlooked. On the contrary they do really advertise that there was once a time when things were different.

If these two examples do not suffice, consider a third. There is a very common saying here in Holland whenever in a family or in a meeting of friends the conversation dries up and there is a sudden silence. We say, 'a clergyman is passing', but in English they say 'an angel is passing'. Again it is Pliny the Elder who assures us (28, 27) that such remarks originate in very ancient roots of superstition. After giving a long list of superstitions he writes, 'Then it has been noticed that a sudden silence at a dinner party occurs only with an even number of diners'. Though the sudden silence is here associated with the even number of diners, it is quite clear from what immediately precedes it that the ancients feared the presence of some higher being. Such customs were adopted, he says, 'by those who believed that gods were present at all transactions and appointments and therefore sought to placate them even for their own lapses'. This is not the place to enquire whether Pliny was thinking of real deities or of spirits, as Wolters thinks (pp. 93ff.). Cicero at any rate in a similar context declared that the minds of the immortal gods must be conciliated (*de har. resp.* 23). But this is neither here nor there. All I have tried to do is demonstrate by example how easily it may happen that after many centuries our words, even unknown to us, may betray religious or magical notions long since buried in oblivion.

I only wanted to insist on this point, that we ourselves, no less than Roman writers twenty centuries ago, quite frequently use words or locutions the original meaning of which is completely hidden from us and none the less shines through for anyone who considers them carefully. When I argued therefore that Livy's words *senescens maiestas* betrayed something like a magical significance, I did not in the least maintain that Livy himself was conscious of it—any more than Dumézil himself necessarily had in view, when he wrote (p. 8) 's'il était déjà chargé de prestige' (i.e. the word '*maiestas*'), the magical origin of the word 'prestige' (Lat. *praestigiae*). But here you have something he cannot or will not understand. I wrote for instance on p. 107, 'Admiration and reverence for the magic power of speech, particularly of oratory, are often expressed in terms borrowed directly from worship', and added two examples, Tac. *Dial.* 4, 4 and Quint. *Inst. Or.* 12, 11, 30. Quintilian at the end of this work extols '*ipsam...orandi maiestatem, qua nihil dii immortales melius homini dederunt*'—'the very majesty of oratory, than which the immortal gods have given man nothing better'. But just listen to my Paris colleague! 'On se demande' he writes (p. 13) 'comment M. Wagenvoort a pu placer ce texte (le seul de ceux qu'il cite qui contienne *maiestas*) [6] parmi les témoignages d' "admiration or reverence for the magic power of speech" '. On these words he then comments in a footnote, 'où "magic power", le contexte le prouve, est à prendre au sens littéral'.

Dumézil is mistaken, and I have never seen anything more absurd. First, if I had thought Quintilian so vainly superstitious, it would not have been necessary for him to *borrow* words from religion. But further, if you look up the context, you will find that the matter under discussion there was the epithet *gravis* combined with certain nouns. The immediately preceding sentence was, 'There is, in addition, the *gravitas* of magic words, e.g. "*terroribus omnibus verba graviora*" (referring to a magician's conjurations, Quint. *decl.* 10, p. 206, 1 L.)'. Here of course I am speaking of magic in the literal sense. In my following words, which have just been quoted, I merely wished to indicate, as surely everyone must realize, that the remarks even of scholarly writers give evidence of the almost religious reverence accorded to great eloquence. This is all the more apparent from the fact that there is now no mention of *gravitas* nor any connection with the preceding words.

It is impossible for me to reply to all these points one by one. Having decided to return to the question one day at greater length and in terms of a more permanent record, I have for the present sufficiently demonstrated Dumézil's method of argument. One thing, however, I cannot pass over in silence before going on to the notion of *gravitas* which was my primary concern. Or rather both aims turn out to be the same. For I am talking of those passages where the notions of *maiestas* and *gravitas* turn out to be in some way linked. On p. 121 of my book I had compared two passages of Ovid (*Met.* 9, 268ff. and 4, 539ff.) and then written, 'On the strength of this comparison alone it may be asserted that the very poet who dared to employ the word *gravitas* still in its real sense must accordingly have equally felt the etymological sense of *maiestas*'. Since in these passages there was mention of apotheosis conferring superhuman stature I had quoted some other passages where the same conjunction was noted. Finally I had

---

[6] Please note that this passage in my book does not even deal with *maiestas* but with *gravitas!*

passed the reader on to S. Eitrem's essay 'The Size of the Heroes' (*Symb. Osl.* 8 (1929), 53ff.), where the matter was dealt with much more fully. So what does Dumézil comment? 'Mais, de ces petits faits littéraires' (*sic*) 'comment tirer la notion précise et constante, presque juridique, que nous avons dégagée?' (p. 19).

In Eitrem's essay, where neither the word *mana* nor anything like it occurs, on p. 55 we read, 'Superhuman dimensions are indeed *a primitive means of expression to characterize the religious quality* both of heroes and of gods,[2] and in portraiture just the same feature recurs'. Therefore, too, according to Eitrem, a man really expert in such questions, we do indeed here catch 'des survivances de mentalité primitive' which Dumézil (p. 19, 6) contends cannot be elicited from it without violation of sense ('forcément').

How then when we find the same thing happening elsewhere? It will be enough to recall some passages where a prophet is described as filled with a divine afflatus. We read for example in Ovid (*Fast.* 6, 537ff.):

Parva mora est: caelum vates ac numina sumit
fitque sui toto pectore plena dei.
Vix illam subito posses cognoscere: tanto
sanctior et tanto, quam modo, maior erat.[7]

Is it absurd to conclude on the poet's testimony that the prophet from that moment partook of a certain *maiestas* and that it would not be so 'inutile donc de supposer un rapport de cette *maiestas* bien concrète, bien physique, avec quelque forme de "sacredness"' (Dumézil p. 19, 7)? I let alone that it was not properly physical or subject to the senses. As Vergil saw very well. Of the Euboean Sibyl (*Aen.* 6, 48ff.) he writes:

pectus anhelum,
et rabie fera corda tument; maiorque videri
nec mortale sonans, adflata est numine quando
iam propiore dei.[8]

[7] 'It does not take long: the prophetess absorbs heaven and its holy spirit and her whole heart fills with the god. Suddenly you would hardly recognize her, she is so much more holy and so much *taller* than before.'

[8] '... .her breast heaves and her wild heart swells with frenzy; she looks taller and her voice sounds more than human, as she is breathed on by the close-felt *numen* of the god.'

The poet is well aware that he is expressing a psychic event in physical terms, as Servius too understood very well, in thus annotating the lines: '*Maiorque videri*—was seen in the manner in which the presence of *numen* was manifested in those prophesying; which deceived human appearances. Whence "*maiorque* videri" because it was not really so'. Dumézil himself rightly observes, 'ce signe' (i.e. *maiorem fieri*)' et quelques autres, par lesquels le poète veut rendre sensible un grand changement de condition, est certes intéressant à relever' (p. 19). He refrains from asking what caused the ancients to express their feelings with such an image. For there is no doubt that in the passages quoted the poets are trying to express the manner in which a certain *maiestas* is implanted in a prophet full of the deity. Or if anyone still hesitates to agree with me, let us examine Valerius Flaccus 4, 548ff. The prophet Phineus is brought on stage:

> ....*hic demum vittas laurumque capessit*
> *numina nota ciens. Stupet Aesonis inclita proles*
> *Phinea* ....
> ....: *tam largus honos, tam mira senectae*
> *maiestas infusa; vigor novus auxerat artus.*[9]

Well? Are these again 'des petits faits littéraires'? *Maiestas* is imparted to a prophet touched with the holy spirit, and this cannot possibly not be 'quelque forme de "sacredness"'[10] Nor is it in any way by chance that we have the coincidence of this *maiestas* and that *maiorem fieri* in the divine frenzy of prophecy which I noted in Ovid's lines quoted above, in the context of apotheosis. Not even Dumézil has dared to deny such an obvious fact. But he adds (p. 19, 8), 'Mais, de cette association, on n'est

---

[9] '....here at length he takes the fillet and the laurel, summoning the *numen* he knows so well. The illustrious son of Aeson wonders at Phineus, at his great grandeur, the marvellously infused majesty of age. A new vigour swells his limbs.'

[10] Cf. A. D. Nock's very just observation (*A. J. Ph.* 65 (1944) 103: 'Such phrases as *maiestas laesa, maiestas violata* have a distinct suggestion of sacrilege: cf. Ulpian, *apud Dig.*, XLVIII, 4, 1: *proximum sacrilegio crimen est, quod maiestatis dicitur* (and in Ulpian it is still an offence against the Roman people and not against the princeps). *Maiestas* is almost the secular counterpart of *numen*.'

pas en droit de conclure que la notion matérielle a été, historiquement, dans le développement de la langue et de la pensée latines, 'l'origine" de *maiestas*'. It seems to be very difficult for my colleague to quote the words of another accurately. Again and again I have declared in emphatic terms, 'the word *maiestas* from its origin does not belong to the complex of *mana*-reminiscences' (p. 127). But 'in the long run' (p. 120) the notions of *gravitas* and *maiestas* have not so much coalesced as approached one another in meaning, so that again and again they were easily combined or assimilated with one another. In my investigation of the reason for this phenomenon I think it was I who first formulated it as follows: (p. 120): 'As soon as the powers of *mana* are personified and definitely distinguished from its bearers—stone, tree, spring, etc.—i.e. as soon as man had learnt to look upon himself as an individual and to confront himself with mysterious powers as individualities, he came upon a criterion more striking as a means of comparison than heaviness, namely size'.

But whatever you may think of my manner of answering the question, you may at once ask another: Is it so? Are you convinced that the Romans of the Augustan age were still conscious of that primitive meaning—even assuming that you had worked it out correctly? On p. 121 you find my reply: 'Not much of it can have remained in the mind of the average Roman'. All the same, as I explained at the time, and as can be inferred also from the examples I have just quoted, so far as *maiestas* is concerned that consciousness had not altogether disappeared from the minds of men. I had previously shown and shall again briefly insist below that the same was true of *gravitas*. I beg and pray the reader to bear in mind two points, which I perforce repeat again and again. First, the two terms are in my opinion comparable, to the extent that what I consider the primitive meaning of *gravitas* is also its principal, native meaning, whereas the same meaning of *maiestas* is ancient but not principal. Secondly, even though I have rightly interpreted the passages of Ovid, Vergil, and Valerius Flaccus, I do not acknowledge that I have thereby accused them of magical superstitions. They spoke in the manner of their ancestors; if they had gone on to interpret their words they would have done so in their own manner.

Among the objections made by Dumézil to my account of the word *gravitas* is the following (p. 25), 'Ces liaisons mécaniques des emplois figurés de *gravis*—et c'est là ce qu'il y a peut-être de plus fatal à la thèse de M. Wagenvoort—sont tournées exactement à l'inverse de la notion de *mana*, force non matèrielle, mais mystique'.

Dumézil is mistaken, partly perhaps through my own fault, since it may be that I did not insist enough on this point either. Yet on p. 106 I had quoted Thurnwald's words,[11] 'this (*mana*) is represented in a manner *perceptible by the senses*', and myself added, 'The reader will do well to stamp on his memory the last words', and I had thought that what followed spoke for itself. But it will be better to linger a little longer over it. The point is this. It is true that initially investigators were convinced that the notion of *mana* was purely psychical and almost mystical—Codrington, for instance, who was the first to make use of the idea, said: 'There is a belief in a force altogether distinct from physical power, which acts in all kinds of ways for good and evil.....This *mana* is not fixed in anything [2]...' Hocart (*Man* 14 (1914), 100) considers the term 'out and out spiritualistic', Marett (*ARW* 12 (1909), 191) calls it 'quite immaterial'. But gradually we have come to understand how slippery these concepts are. 'The beliefs, customs, and usages connected with the Polynesian terms *mana* and *tapu* are so widely diverse that if we were to attempt to formulate definitions which would cover all of them, such formulations would be of such a general character that they might be attributed to any human culture'.[12] The chief thing we have learned, however, is that these peoples do not make the same distinction between the psyche and the *physis*, between soul and body as we do. Söderblom

---

[11] *ARW* 27 (1929) 101. Cf. p. 103: 'Es ist die Kraft der überragenden Persönlichkeit, deren *Analogiebild* auch in der Naturerscheinung erlebt und *auf dem Wege des sinnengebundenen Denkens in konkreter Weise symbolisiert* wird. Auch handelt es sich nicht bloss um ein "alter ego", ein Zweites Ich, sondern vielmehr um ein besonderes, in den Menschen befindliches "Fluidum", dem die *soziale Auszeichnung* einer Person zu danken ist. Die konkreten Formen, in denen das Mana vorgestellt wird, werden natürlich immer mit dem gesamten Gedanken und Anschauungssystem, dem Lebens- und Weltbild, dem Mythen- und Sagenbereich des betreffenden Volkes, kurz mit seiner Denkart und Geistesverfassung in Einklang gebracht.'

[12] R. W. Williamson, *Essays in Polynesian Ethnology*, ed. by R. Piddington (Cambridge 1939), pp. 264f.

(*Das Werden des Gottesglaubens* (1926), p. 67) had made a considerable advance when he wrote, 'Sometimes power is thought of as more personal, like a will or spirit or one of their attributes, sometimes more material like a medicine or electricity'. And Lehmann (*Mana* (1916), 41) had already prepared the transition when he reasoned, 'For the concept of *mana* is not attached only to spirits or people, or things but refers simply to the efficacy exerted by such existences, which in a primitive thought process is imagined as visible and *treated like an object*'.[2] And van der Leeuw (*Phänomenologie der Religion* (1933), p. 255) is not far wrong: 'Power and substance are in the primitive realm of thought not different concepts. It is therefore just as possible to speak of "soul power" as of "soul substance". In both cases what is meant is either some powerful substance or a power residing in a substance'.

I am sorry that I cannot find the passage where one investigator stated that *mana* as often as not was subject to the senses and could virtually be cut out of the body with a knife. However, descriptions of this kind have reached us from various regions. E. E. Evans-Pritchard [13] relates: 'A Zande told me: 'Azande think that witchcraft is inside a man. When they used to kill a man in the past they cut open his belly to search there for witchcraft-substance. . . . . .Azande think that witchcraft-substance is a round thing in the small intestine'; and later (p. 42): 'For the Zande mind is logical and enquiring within the framework of its culture and insists on the coherence of its own idiom. If witchcraft is an organic substance its presence can be ascertained by post-mortem search' (cf. also pp. 21ff.). Other testimonies could be produced,[14] but I think this should be enough, added to those already offered in the book. A fatal mistake has indeed been made, but not by me.

Dumézil says correctly that I relied on three arguments to support my theory: first, *gravis*, *gravitas* are used repeatedly as epithets of things and people, to which in remote times, as I attempted to prove in my opening chapters, the same occult force was attributed; secondly, in other languages related to Latin

[13] *Witchcraft, Oracles and Magic among the Azande*, (Oxford 1937), p. 40; cf. what follows. I am grateful for this reference to my colleague H. Th. Fischer, Professor of Anthropology.

[14] As S. Santandrea in *Africa*, 11 (1938), 467ff.; J. D. Viccars *ibid.* 19 (1949), 221.

but absolutely different from it, words meaning *gravitas* appear similarly in ancient times to have meant an occult force comparable with *mana*; thirdly, in classical literature still a certain special *gravitas* is attributed to gods and heroes which seems to have been derived from the same source.

But how does Dumézil argue against me? First, my opening chapters have not proved what they were supposed to prove. 'Ils ne peuvent donc rendre le service qu'il leur demande ici' (p. 20). Here there is a complete absence of argument. How do the French put it? 'La mort par phrase?' Moreover, and here there is no lack of argument, he convicts me besides of error in my interpretation of several passages. There is one to which I immediately agree. Where I attempted to explain the real meaning of *grave imperium*, I should not have quoted Liv. 39, 51, 6. Dumézil rightly points out that the words there have a different sense from that I suggested. As for the rest, I will here be brief. It is in fact the part of my book which in other quarters too has encountered much more opposition than the rest. While the greater number of these objections are of the same kind as those I have treated above, there are other arguments calling for honest and careful scrutiny, which, however, would require more space than I have at my disposal here.

Secondly, even though we establish that in other languages too the meaning of similar words from the same beginning has advanced to the same end, nothing, so Dumézil argues, has been proved by such an argument and we are no further on. If silence gives consent, I give it. What other response could there be? If anyone is anxious to know what absurdities such reasoning can lead to, let him read the objections with which I am confronted in the footnote on p. 22, 1. A further point—all the examples which my colleague J. Gonda had collected from more recent Sanskrit literature [15] are rejected wrongly, on the ground that Vedic (p. 22) is 'la seule forme du sanscrit qui puisse éclairer le vocabulaire latin'. I deny that my Utrecht colleague's argument can be rejected in this fashion. This is what he wrote (*Bull.*, p. 130): 'Parce que l'essence de la classe brahmanique, et par conséquent des brahmanes qui

---

[15] Which he not only allowed me to copy (*Rom. Dyn.*, pp. 108f.) but several of which also he later dealt with in the *Bull. of the School of Oriental & African Studies* 12, 1 (1947), 124ff.

font fonction de guide spirituel, fait un avec le fond ultime et premier de l'être, avec le "sacré" lui-même, l'hypothèse n'est pas inadmissible que le guru indien, dont la vénération donnait, à la longue, naissance à un vrai culte, doive son titre au fait qu'il était, au point de vue *"mana"*, plus "lourd" que les autres hommes'. 'M. Gonda's explanation is no more than a hypothesis' says Dumézil (p. 22, 3). As Gonda himself said. It is, however, a hypothesis which explains what has not been explained before. The fact that his examples are not taken from actual Vedic speech is not sufficient to refute it. First, if a Greek word is not found in Homer, we do not usually at once conclude that it is a recent introduction. Secondly, anyone who has to admit that in the more recent literature a particular superstition occurs but then still denies that it has existed in those regions from the beginning then has the onus of explaining how it crept in at a later period. Dumézil's final argument, printed in italics, is this: the fact that an almost similar transition of meaning occurred both in Hebrew and in Sanskrit is no proof that the same thing happened in Latin. Indeed it is not. It may not be *proof* of a conjecture but still very much in its favour if it offers the first explanation of a point hitherto not understood, as seems to occur expressly with the Hebrew *kābōd*.

Thirdly, it may be that in individual cases I pressed the argument too strongly. For instance, concerning the Vergil passage, *Aen.* 6, 412ff., others [16] as it now seems rightly have argued that the poet had undoubtedly translated these words from the Greek, that the Greek author had in his mind's eye some splendid specimen of an athlete. And Norden writes, 'But also the special theme of the boat filling with water when a massive living body gets into it from its very peculiarity gives us to suppose that Vergil did not invent it'. Although Norden—quite differently from Dumézil— thinks this image was very unusual and although I also wonder what can have induced Vergil to take it from a Greek source, nevertheless I concede that the passage was not well chosen for bolstering my argument. But I did quote many others and I am not at all moved by Dumézil's rhetorical question, 'Comment les flagorneries de Lucain au dieu Néron, de Stace au dieu Domitien, par exemple, nous renseigneraient-elles sur les authentiques

[16] F. Bömer, *Gnomon* 21(1949), 356; he too quoted Norden.

croyances religieuses des contemporains de Caton, et de leurs ancêtres?' I reply, that they are flatteries is nothing to the point. If, as we have seen above, even our words not infrequently still reflect primitive and altogether obsolete superstition, why should the same not be the case with the authors of the Roman imperial age? There is the further point that the six quotations I included from Ovid and in part fully discussed are not even mentioned by Dumézil. None the less he adds, 'M. Wagenvoort n'a donc pas démontré sa thèse principale'. Please note the 'donc'!

Why all the fuss? Why am I reluctantly drawn into argument against all my habits and inclinations? Why can we not use some moderation in examining each other's opinions and conjectures and offering our own for what they are worth?

At the end of his review of my book J. Bayet noted (*REL* 26 (1948), 448): 'M. H. Wagenvoort n'a pas connu les livres de M. G. Dumézil. C'est dommage. Il y aurait trouvé (par exemple) de quoi affirmer et clarifier son explication du *tigillum sororium*'. And yet I had known a good part of his work, with admiration too, though here and there—and even this author will not blame me for that—I put a question mark. But my book was not dealing with Roman religion, though it could hardly fail to touch on it quite frequently. I was not concerned with the gods of Rome, who had nothing in common with the *numina*. And yet on the very first page of his article Dumézil inveighs against a school of writers (leaving no doubt that I belong to it) who 'en sont arrivés à former une véritable doctrine qui séduit de jeunes esprits, et même quelques autres, moins jeunes. Suivant cette école, la religion romaine des temps historiques serait encore tout près de ses origines, d'origines très humbles; ce n'est que tardivement, presque sous nos yeux, et sans jamais atteindre un plein succès, que les Romains seraient parvenus à dégager quelques dieux du vaste et larvaire champ de "forces"—de *mana*, localisé plutôt que personnalisé—dans lequel ils pensaient vivre et qu'ils ressentaient intensément'.

Dumézil is mistaken. And this mistake is the source of all this misery. In attacking me he defends himself. Yet so far am I from not recognizing any really Roman gods that two years ago in a brief account of the ancient Roman religion [17] I wrote as follows:

---

[17] In the work *Het oudste Christendom en de antieke Cultuur*, ed. J. H. Waszink, W. C. van Unnik, Ch. de Beus, vol. I (1951), 124.

'In the first place it must be observed that in their earliest development both among individuals and the community magic and religion (including the belief in live, or as we should now say "personal", gods) tended to become merged with one another, and that men were not for that reason troubled with any feeling of inconsistency'. I then worked this out at length. I refuse to be numbered among those authors, if there are any, who make an 'abstraction des grands dieux hiérarchisés de la religion romaine la plus ancienne pour ne voir partout qu'un chaos de "centres de force" quasi automatiques' (Dumézil p. 16), although I reserve to myself absolute freedom of judgment in deciding which deities are to be credited with an original and authentic divinity and how far that may go.

Is it too much to hope that even in these questions the truth may gush forth from such a conflict of opinion? I do not see why, if only we ourselves do not set our faces against it. If I for one have said anything out of season, I am sorry.

V

FELICITAS IMPERATORIA

A discussion of Harry Erkell, *Augustus, Felicitas, Fortuna. Lateinische Wortstudien*. Göteborg, Elanders Boktryckeri Aktiebolag, 1952.

Recently in the journal *Museum* (59, 1954, 199-201) I published my notice of the above book. It is a useful work of great learning ranging over a great variety of sources. Nevertheless I briefly indicated at the time that I thought the author was here and there in error, primarily where he was discussing the notion of *felicitas*. Since that was not the proper place to deal with the question at greater length, it seemed preferable to avail myself of the hospitality kindly put at my disposal by the present journal for publication of my essay.

The question at issue is this. Everybody knows that in the literature both of the Republic and of the imperial age there was frequent reference to the *felicitas* of Roman *imperatores*. What was meant by that term? Or rather—because hardly anybody will deny that it had various meanings—is it possible for us to follow it in its birth, growth, and various modes of stabilization? So far as the adjective *felix* is concerned, whatever its final sense, it is well enough established that it means much the same as *fecundus, fertilis*. But how could men in the metaphorical sense be said to be *felices*?

Previously this question had been tackled by F. Taeger,[1] A. Passerini,[2] L. Berlinger,[3] M. A. Levi,[4] whose opinions Erkell carefully records. Though they may disagree on particular points,

---

[1] *PhWS* 53 (1933) 930ff. (in a review of R. M. Haywood, *Studies on Scipio Africanus*).

[2] 'Il Concetto antico di Fortuna', *Philol.* 90 (1935) 90ff.

[3] 'Beiträge zur inoffiziellen Titulatur der römischen Kaiser. Eine Untersuchung ihres ideengeschichtlichen Gehaltes und ihrer Entwicklung'. *Diss. Vratislav.* 1935.

[4] 'Auspicio imperio ductu felicitate', *Rendiconti R. Istit. Lomb.* 71 (1937/8) 113, 51.

they are all convinced of one thing, that *felicitas* is properly a certain force innate in human beings and belonging to the order of nature, '*forza immanente, concetto puramente italico*' (Passerini, 93) 'power as well as a quality' [5]—a notion derived from magical ideas. I myself had agreed with these, as Erkell noticed, when I wrote in my book *Roman Dynamism*,[6] 'this *felicitas* is not regarded as "fortune" subject to chance but as evidence of personal excellence: *"Ego enim sic existimo, in summo imperatore quattuor has res inesse oportere, scientiam rei militaris, virtutem, auctoritatem, felicitatem"* Cic. *imp. Cn. Pomp.* 28)'.[7] Erkell takes a contrary line, not frivolously but with numberless parallels collected with the help of the *Thesaurus*. After taking due account of the opinions of others he thus concludes (p. 50), 'The problem is evidently the same in regard to the German *Heil* and the Roman *felicitas*—independent magical force or divine blessing?' Before continuing I think we must pause a while. It is not that I want to join with Erkell in framing the question so sharply. Quite the contrary. If we do not proceed with the greatest caution there is a danger that some angry man, moved by the mere suspicion that we were about to accuse the Scipios of base magical frivolities, might mount a bellowing Pegasus and spurring madly upon us shake the campus with the continuous thunder of hooves—in some philological review [8]! Consider how often we have seen one of our contemporaries, after pronouncing that he had never been ill, 'touch wood', in an apotropaic gesture. Even though we may be convinced that his nervous

---

[5] H. Mattingly, *Coins of the Roman Empire in the British Museum* 4 (1940) L n. 1 (not as mistakenly given by Erkell, p. 125, 4, 1).

[6] P. 61. To a book which unfortunately has not yet appeared, *Thesaurismata*, dedicated to Ida Kapp, W. H. Friedrich has contributed an essay 'Caesar und sein Glück'. (To our knowledge, the book has never appeared. Editors.)

[7] 'For this is what I think. A commander-in-chief has need of four things, military science, valour, authority, the luck of a born winner'.

[8] Cf. G. Dumézil, '*Maiestas* et *Gravitas*', *R. Phil.* 26 (1952) 7ff. where he seeks to refute my observations in Chapter 4 of my book *Roman Dynamism* (1947). I replied in *Mnemos.* vol. V (1952) 287-306 ('Gravitas et Maiestas'); my opponent defended himself very briefly in 'Maiestas et Gravitas, II', *R. Phil.* 28 (1954) 19f. Without the slightest apprehension I leave the reader to decide between us. He will have no difficulty in proving himself a better judge than Dumézil seems to give him credit for. Once more *Dumézil dumezilia tractat*.

reaction betrays a superstition deeply rooted in the primitive past, do we then immediately accuse him of floundering blindly in a fog of religious prejudice? Or should we rather decide that these are survivals of very ancient notions with a content of which the man himself is scarcely or not at all conscious? But if such things can occur in our own century, what is to prevent our believing that in the age of Rome, which was so much nearer to rude and uncivilized times, there existed much more frequent survivals in words and rite of superstitions of the same kind?

It will at once be clear why the Erkell method of procedure causes me misgivings. For he begins by quoting a definition of *felicitas* from Augustine (*C.D.* 4, 18f.; cf. 4, 21.23.24; 5, 24) and to a large extent relies on these passages throughout the chapter. But what help is that? St. Augustine lived at a time as remote from the Ciceronian age as we are from the end of the Middle Ages. Even supposing it can be asserted that from the evidence of his words he knew nothing of any magic, what then? I do not see that we are any further in determining the original significance of the notion of *felicitas*, especially *felicitas imperatoria*. Erkell himself (p. 51) asks, 'Is St. Augustine reliable in this respect, or have we good reason to suspect here a theoretical construction for purposes of propaganda or for other reasons?' But in the first place, this has nothing to do with it. It would have been better to ask, 'Is St. Augustine reliable in this regard, or have we good reason to think it probable that if ever *felicitas* had anything to do with magic, any consciousness of it would in the course of so many centuries have faded beyond all recall and perhaps altogether vanished?' And who could answer No?

I am not overlooking that Erkell added to the Augustinian definition one by Cicero, from the *Epist. ad Corn. Nep.* frgm. 2,5 (= Amm. Marc. 21, 6, 13) '*Neque enim quicquam aliud est felicitas nisi honestarum rerum prosperitas vel, ut alio modo definiam, felicitas est fortuna adiutrix consiliorum bonorum, quibus qui non utitur felix esse nullo pacto potest. Ergo in perditis impiisque consiliis, quibus Caesar usus erat, nulla potuit esse felicitas, feliciorque meo iudicio Camillus exsulans quam temporibus isdem Manlius etiam si, id quod cupierat, regnare potuisset*'. Erkell holds that these definitions are somewhat different but none the less contends that both mean 'a sort of divine blessing'. Meanwhile Cicero's last words, from *feliciorque* to the end, are not quoted by him. Doubtless they do not agree nearly so well with his own interpretation, because it is not so easy to understand how Camillus could have owed more to the favour of the gods for his exile than Manlius for his kingdom if he had achieved it. But the whole passage does become clear once we realize that the ideas in question are not really ancient but of much more recent date and not altogether detached from Greek philosophy. We shall see later, however, how little Cicero himself was consistent in his use of the term *felicitas* and in interpreting the idea.

Not only at its very outset but throughout this short work there is scarcely any regard for chronological order. On p. 53 we read, 'The nature of the source material makes it impossible to give a strictly chronological account', but there seems to have been no endeavour whatever to achieve this laudable, if unattainable, aim. On the same page we find quoted in succession Seneca, Martial, Augustine, Macrobius, Rhetor ad Herennium, Quintilian! Yet there was a good deal to give Erkell pause for thought. I can immediately produce three considerations which deter me from accepting his interpretation.

A. If the Romans of republican times really thought, as Erkell maintains, that the *felicitas* was inherent in the favour of the gods, or indeed rather that the two were one and the same, it is difficult to see why it pertained almost solely to *imperatores* (generals in the field, commanders-in-chief) 'It is always someone' says Erkell 'who holds *imperium*' (p. 59). 'To sum it up we can ... say ... that it mainly indicates fortune and success in war, that the good fortune or success are mostly attached to an individual not a community, that it particularly often represents something complementary to *virtus* both in Roman and in non-Roman field commanders' (pp. 68f.; cf. also p. 128). A little further on (p. 69) he tries to remove this difficulty. 'These words' (*felix, infelix*, in Livy) 'are applied 4-5 times as often, it is true, to words of military or political significance as to others. They rarely say anything about the happiness or unhappiness of people in their private life. That can be explained, however, by the fact that Livy himself takes so little interest in people's private life.' This argument seems to me to betray a certain horror vacui, first because it was sufficiently demonstrated earlier (e.g. p. 59) that the word *felicitas* in Cicero too almost always indicated something peculiar to an *imperator* and he at least cannot be accused of not caring about people's private lives. There is the further point, as we shall find, that for as far back as we can see things were never different.

B. In like manner we learn to our surprise that this *felicitas* on the testimony of Latin writers was to be found not only among the Romans themselves but also among foreigners and even among the enemies of the Roman people. I have already quoted Erkell (under A, p. 68, cf. also p. 67: 'Just as Livy generally uses Roman expressions when he speaks of other peoples, he puts the words *felicitas virtusque* into the mouths of non-Romans'). He also quotes Livy 42, 12, 2; 22, 58, 3; 30, 12, 12; 30, 30, 23.[9] But this too is not peculiar to Livy. Similar things are found elsewhere:

> Nep. *Timol.* 2, 1 *Huc Timoleon missus incredibili felicitate Dionysium tota Sicilia depulit.*
> Cic. *inv.* 1, 94 .... *si qui hostium vim et copias et felicitatem augeat.*
> Cic. *Att.* 6, 6, 3 *Parthi...., qui posteaquam incredibili felicitate discesserunt.*

The Ciceronian passages are bound to strike us more than the rest, since there the *felicitas* is attributed actually to the enemy and we shall not easily be convinced that in writing these words the author envisaged some favour granted by the gods.

The same thing occurs already in the passage of Livy quoted by Erkell (42, 12, 2)—he is talking about Perseus—'*nec dicere pro certo posse, utrum* felicitate *id* quadam *eius accidat, an, quod ipse vereatur dicere, invidia adversus Romanos favorem illi conciliet*'. On the use of the pronoun *quadam* Erkell adds, 'The small reservation *quadam* may be based on the thought that from the Senate's point of view Perseus cannot really have possessed *felicitas*'. The explanation is not absurd but I fear it comes too pat. Cicero,

[9] This place perhaps has less force, because though it is Hannibal who is speaking, he is praising M. Atilius, a Roman.

who did not judge it necessary to add the pronoun in the passages above, none the less uses it elsewhere, when it is a question neither of foreigners nor of enemies: *off.* 1, 118 '*nonnulli tamen sive* felicitate quadam *sive bonitate naturae . . . rectam vitae secuti sunt viam*'—'yet many there are who by a sort of *felicitas* or by natural goodness . . . . have kept to a straight path of life' (cf. Sen. *dial.* 5, 17, 2; Quint. 6, 3, 56). Here though *felicitas* is not said in a military sense yet it seems to me that the frequent addition of the pronoun *quaedam* rather suggests a certain ambiguity, and obscurity almost, in the word.[10]

C. If we believe Erkell (p. 128), finally, the magical sense of the word reappears in Pliny (*N.H.* 26, 19), '*Cur Caesaris miles ad Pharsaliam famem sensit, si abundantia omnis contingere* unius herbae felicitate *poterat?*'—'Why did Caesar's men feel hunger at Pharsalia if abundance of food could have been given them by the *felicitas* of a single plant?' Perhaps, he adds, it may also be present in Tertullian (*anim.* 50, 4 = p. 381, 19), '*Quaenam et ubinam* felicitas aquarum, *quas nec Johannes baptizator praeministravit nec Christus ipse discipulis demonstravit?*'—'What and where is the *felicitas of the waters* which neither John the Baptist has administered nor Christ himself demonstrated to his disciples?' He seems not to have noticed what a marvellous thing this would have been. How could it possibly have happened that a word till then free of all magical significance could suddenly become imbued with that sense in the imperial age? You will search Erkell for an explanation in vain. There is the further point that such a meaning is also present in other literature. I think first of all of two places in Vergil (it is of no great importance that the adjective *felix*, not the substantive *felicitas* is used):

[10] Things are different in Cic. *Brut.* 4 '*Sed quoniam* perpetua quadam felicitate *usus ille* [*Q. Hortensius*] *cessit e vita . . . .*', where Kroll notes: ' "*quadam*", I should say, is little different from "almost" '. In reality this *quadam* belongs rather to *perpetua* than to *felicitate*. Cf. also Weissenborn on Liv. 29, 26, 5. Similarly Florus, 2, 20, 1 '*Victa ad occasum Hispania populus Romanus ad orientem pacem agebat, nec pacem modo, sed* inusitata et incognita quadam felicitate *. . . opes et . . . regna veniebant*'. (In English, where 'a sort of', 'a certain' are so often the natural translation of *quidam* and its declension, the question whether the qualification applies more to the adjective or the noun tends to disappear. *The Translator*).

Georg. 2, 126f. '*Media fert tristis sucos tardumque saporem* felicis *mali*'.

Ladewig-Jahn here rightly comments, '*felicis mali,* because blessed with healing power'. We may contrast Servius' note, where after first attempting to interpret the *felix malum* as the *malum* of an *arbor felix* he goes on, '*Aut certe "felicis" salubris; nulla enim efficacior* [11] *res est ad venena pellenda*' More to the point is the fragment of Oppius, the grammarian, from the end of the Republican age (Münzer, *RE* 18, 743, 25) in Macrobius (*Sat.* 3, 19, 4), where he speaks of the lemon, 'it is extremely fragrant, and put among clothing kills moth. It is also said to be an antidote to poisons. Pounded with wine and drunk it saves life by its powerful cleansing effect'. Macrobius adds his own comment, 'You see that here the lemon is actually named and all the indications are that Vergil (*Georg.* 2, 127) though he did not use the name was referring to it; .... for Oppius' reference to the putting of lemons among clothing ... we may quote the poet Naevius in his Punic War where he talks of a *citrosam vestem*—'lemony garment'. Similarly *felix oliva* cannot simply be taken as *fecunda oliva*. This is seen clearly enough if we compare these two Vergil quotations: *Aen.* 6, 229ff. '*Idem ter socios pura circumtulit unda spargens rore levi et ramo* felicis olivae *lustravitque viros*' and *Aen.* 7, 750ff. '*Quin et Marruvia venit de gente sacerdos fronde super galeam et* felici *comptus* oliva ... *vipereo generi et graviter spirantibus hydris spargere qui somnos cantuque manuque solebat* ...' For *arboribus felicibus* see below p. 78. The term has almost the same force in *Aen.* 9, 771ff., '*Inde ferarum vastatorem Amycum, quo non* felicior *alter ungere tela manu ferrumque armare veneno*'.

Ladewig-Jahn rightly comments, 'By *ung. tela* simply the poisoning is meant, by *armare* the use of the poisoned arrows in war'; cf. 10, 140. It is well known that less highly civilized peoples tend to regard poisoning as an art for magicians.[12] But look at the difficulties the good Servius is led into by this passage. His note reads: 'felicior *peritior; nam in ungendis telis non est felicitas, sed peritia*'. But how the word *felicitas* could mean the same as *peritia* he fails to explain.

[11] On the magical nature of the term *efficax* cf. *Roman Dynamism* p. 128.
[12] Cf. e.g. Hutton Webster, *Magic. A Sociological Study* (1948) 393.

I think I have made it plain enough why at first glance Erkell's treatment seems to me not very convincing. Therefore I have determined to look once more into this question myself, at greater length than previously. I shall refer to the earlier writers first, quoting post-Augustan writers only when necessary, not because there is nothing useful to be gleaned from them but because they are governed by a more and more alien climate—Greek above all— and have little by little almost entirely lost from view what *felicitas* really meant. To begin with we have three very ancient passages deserving our closest study. They are: a) The Senatorial decree of the year 201 B.C. about the triumph of Scipio Africanus in Cicero *fin.* 4, 22; b) Temple inscription of the year 179 B.C. dedicated to the *Lares Permarini* (guardian gods of sea voyagers) in Livy, 40, 52, 5; c) Fragment of a speech of Aemilius Paullus delivered in the year 167 B.C., quoted by Valerius Maximus, 5, 10, 2. Thus all are earlier than the middle of the second century. Erkell deals with the first and second (p. 58), the third and most important he does not even mention.

I Fragm. Sen. Cons. a. 201 a. C. n. ap Cic. *FIN.* 4, 22

> '*An senatus, cum triumphum Africano decerneret,* "quod eius virtute" *aut* "felicitate" *posset dicere, si neque virtus in ullo nisi in sapiente nec felicitas vere dici potest?*'

Which Africanus is meant seems hardly in doubt. It must have been Maior. Otherwise we should have expected an additional epithet like *Minor* or *Posterior*. Besides which cf. *imp. Cn. Pomp.* 47 and what Haywood there notes about the peculiar *felicitas* attributed to Africanus Major. Nor, so far as I can discover, is there any disagreement among scholars on the point. Cf. e.g. Baiter, in his Index Nomin. Cicer. s.v., Taeger in the review already quoted, Passerini (93). All this I mention because Erkell describes my second passage (Liv. 40, 52, 5) as 'the oldest example of *felicitas*', and this cannot be right unless he thinks the Ciceronian quotation above refers to the younger Africanus.

Erkell himself, however, is right in his verdict that 'Cicero is really confounding two different meanings of *felicitas*. His own discussion applies to the philosophical concept of *beatitudo* while the Scipio example refers to military success'. In other things, however, I find him mistaken. He objects to Taeger, for instance, who thinks that Cicero was quoting literally from the formula for a triumphal decree, 'We must however envisage the possibility that Cicero is perhaps not quoting the words literally but with slight changes. Thus *virtus* could stand for *fortiter*, *felicitas* for *feliciter*. I know of no other passage in which *virtute* and *felicitate* occurred in a decree of triumph.' To this I reply; 1. It is absolutely incredible that Cicero, wishing to define true *felicitas*, should have appealed to a passage where the word does not even occur. 2. It is equally incredible that he should have substituted for the actual words of a decree a manner of speech absolutely incongruous with such a decree—as would be the case if we believed Erkell. 3. I wish he had informed us how many decrees of triumph he knows which have been handed down word for word. It is true that he himself on p. 56 takes us back to Livy 38, 48, 14f. '...*in ea civitate, quae ... in sollemnibus verbis habet, cum supplicationem aut triumphum decernit:* quod bene ac feliciter rem publicam administrarit'. But the one thing does not exclude the other, as is clear enough from the words I quote below from Cicero. It is indeed most probable that the combination of the words *virtute felicitate* was not at all rare in decrees of that kind, when we find that it was used by the Senate in decreeing an equestrian statue: Cic. *Phil.* 5, 40f. '... *senatus consultum his verbis censeo perscribendum: cum a M. Lepido imperatore ... saepe numero res publica et bene et feliciter gesta sit ... senatum populumque Romanum pro maximis plurimisque in rem publicam M. Lepidi meritis magnam spem in eius* virtute, *auctoritate* felicitate *reponere ... eique statuam equestrem ... statui placere'*. Cicero again is witness that a similar formula was used in decreeing thanksgivings. In *Phil.* 14, 37 Cicero himself moves in the Senate: '... *ob eas res senatum existimare et iudicare eorum trium imperatorum* virtute, *imperio, consilio, gravitate, constantia, magnitudine animi,* felicitate, *populum Romanum foedissima crudelissimaque servitute liberatum, ... uti ob eas res bene, fortiter feliciterque gestas ... praetor urbanus supplicationes per dies quinquaginta ad omnia pulvinaria constituat'* (cf. also § 28). In consideration of all this I cannot imagine what prevents us supposing that a place was found for the same words also in decrees of triumphs.

There are two things to note above all. First, the *felicitas* of an *imperator* is almost always closely linked with his *virtus*. Secondly, there are often other qualities added, such as *auctoritas, auspicium, imperium, consilium, gravitas, constantia, magnitudo animi, ductus, fides*. Erkell, relying on passages from Cicero and especially Livy, thinks that *felicitas* is to be distinguished from all the rest by the fact that they are inherent in the man himself while it alone is given to man by the gods. And it really is the case that in several passages this was how the Romans felt. We may take *imp. Cn. Pomp.* 47 (cf. Erkell, p. 45), 'Reliquum est ut de felicitate, quam praestare de se ipso nemo potest . . . timide et pauca dicamus . . . Fuit enim profecto quibusdam summis viris quaedam [13] ad amplitudinem et ad gloriam et ad res magnas bene gerendas divinitus adiuncta fortuna'. But though I join with Erkell in thinking Passerini was wrong to scent magic here, none the less in my opinion both the phrase 'to say a few diffident words' and 'a sort of' are evidence that the speaker feels he has strayed into an area which he himself finds obscure. However that may be, are we any further? Exactly the same thing applies to *virtus* itself, which is quite often attributed to the favour of the gods. True, the contrary opinion is also found here and there, as in Cicero *n.d.* 3, 86 'virtutem autem nemo unquam acceptam deo rettulit'—but nobody has ever maintained that *virtus* was received from the gods'.[14] But compare

> Cic. *n.d.* 2, 79 'mens fides virtus concordia unde nisi ab superis defluere potuerunt?'
> Liv. 10, 24, 16 'Iovem optimum maximum deosque immortales se precari, *ut ita sortem aequam sibi cum collega dent,* si eandem virtutem felicitatemque *in bello administrando daturi sint*'.
> Liv. 38, 48, 7 '*Te, L. Scipio, appello, cuius ego mihi* . . . virtutem felicitatemque pariter *non frustra* ab diis immortalibus precatus sum'.

What do you think? Are we to suppose for the future, in reliance on these and similar quotations, that the Romans really conceived of *virtus* as a gift of the gods, not a quality innate in a human being?

---
[13] For this pronoun see p. 64 above.
[14] See J. B. Mayor's very full note on this place, where he begins: 'The statement is very far from the truth'.

All such questions are vain—if we do not at least make an effort to discover with what shade of meaning Cicero or Livy invested the word *felicitas,* and in such a way as to understand by what route a term which initially meant the same as *'fertilitas, fecunditas'* in the end came to mean 'happiness'. The question is all the more pressing because in early times the quality seems to have been regarded as peculiar to an *imperator* or commander-in-chief.

We must suppose that the actual decree we are considering had some wording as follows: *'Quod P. Cornelii Scipionis Africani* virtute felicitate *res publica bene et fortiter gesta est, et diis immortalibus honorem haberi iubemus et P. Cornelio Scipioni Africano triumphum decernimus'*. Madvig rightly remarks in his note on the passage: 'Cicero uses the disjunctive particle (*aut felicitate*), although in decrees the two were usually associated, to indicate that neither one nor the other could be said by anyone who chose to follow the Stoics'. We must in any case always start from this very close and ancient association of the two words *virtus* and *felicitas* and keep our ears closed to the usage of more recent authors who frequently oppose the two concepts to one another, as in these passages:

> Rhet. ad Her. 4, 27 *'Alii fortuna dedit* felicitatem, *huic industria* virtutem *comparavit'*.
> ibid. 4, 28 *'hominem laudem egentem* virtutis, *abundantem* felicitatis?'
> Cic. *inv.* 1, 94 (see above p. 63).
> Cic. *imp. Cn. Pomp.* 10 '... *ita res a L. Lucullo ... est administrata, ut initia illa rerum gestarum magna atque praeclara non* felicitati *eius sed* virtuti, *haec autem extrema, quae nuper acciderunt, non* culpae *sed* fortunae *tribuenda esse videantur'* (cf. etiam § 47).
> Cic. *Sull.* 83 *'ego sim tam demens, ego committam, ut ea quae pro salute omnium gessi, casu magis et* felicitate *a me quam* virtute *et consilio gesta esse videantur?'*
> Cic. *Mil.* 6 '... *nec postulaturi (sumus) ut, si mors P. Clodii salus vestra fuerit, idcirco eam* virtuti *Milonis potius quam populi Romani* felicitati *adsignetis'*.

Cic. *Marc.* 19 (to Caesar) '*Qua re gaude tuo isto tam excellenti bono, et fruere cum fortuna et gloria, tum etiam natura et moribus tuis, ex quo quidem maximus est fructus iucunditasque sapienti* (!). *Cetera cum tua recordabere, etsi persaepe* virtuti, *tamen plerumque* felicitati *tuae gratulabere . . . tantus est enim splendor in laude vera, tanta in magnitudine animi et consilii dignitas, ut haec a* virtute *donata, cetera a* fortuna *commodata esse videantur*' (cf. E. p. 52f.).
Nep. *Lys.* 1, 1 '*Lysander . . . magnam reliquit sui famam, magis* felicitate *quam* virtute *partam*'.
Nep. *reg.* 2, 3 '*Hic*' (Dionysius), '*cum* virtute *tyrannidem sibi peperisset, magna retinuit* felicitate'.
Liv. 6, 27, 1 '*Camillus, consilio et* virtute *in Volsco bello,* felicitate *in Tusculana expeditione . . . insignis*'.

I have purposely quoted many passages of this kind in order to give Erkell his due. It is clear that already in the first century B.C. *felicitas* and *fortuna* were regarded as more or less one concept (see especially *imp. Cn. Pomp.* 10 and *Marc.* 19). There is no doubt, however, that we here have traces of the influence on the Roman mind both of Greek philosophy (note *sapienti*, Cic. *Marc.* 19) and of the popular religion of the Greeks (note *fortuna* equated with *felicitas*, Cic. *imp. Cn. Pomp.* 10; *Marc.* 19, for 'the Greek Tyche appears in the Roman world under this name', Erkell p. 131). That is why I take pleasure in Erkell's own words (p. 75) (though in a different context), 'Still more dangerous than translation into another language is translation from one world of religious ideas into another'. This is the very thing the Romans were forced to do when they tried to interpret their set and solemn early words in the new light shed by the Greeks. More than once already we have had a glimpse of the laborious nature of this task and the vexations that it caused in Livy himself. As in the passage already quoted (38, 48, 7ff., where § 7 according to the ancient rule closely couples the words *virtus* and *felicitas* ('*Te, L. Scipio, appello, cuius ego mihi, succedens in vicem imperii tui,* virtutem felicitatemque *pariter non frustra ab diis immortalibus precatus sum*'). And yet by adding *pariter* ('both qualities in equal measure'— Weissenborn) he makes it plain enough that he in no way identifies the two qualities, in hendiadys as it were. There is the further point that in § 15, in no uncertain terms, he separates the two words: '*si grave ac superbum existimarem* virtute *gloriari, pro* felicitate *mea exercitusque mei ... postularem ...*'.

Cicero too uses almost this language:

> dom. 16 '... *quia videbam id, quod omnes, quod nos de Cn. Pompeio polliceremur, id illum fide, consilio,* virtute, *auctoritate,* felicitate denique sua *facillime perfecturum*'.

Truly, the addition here of the adverb *denique* clearly shows that though it fits in with the other standard qualities *felicitas* is regarded as of a different order from them.

> *prov.* 35 '*Quare sit in eius tutela Gallia, cuius fidei,* virtuti, felicitati *commendata est: qui si* Fortunae muneribus *amplissimis ornatus saepius eius deae periculum facere nollet ...*'.

Here too Cicero's ears first caught the stock vocabulary of solemn terms but then with a sudden transition to 'Fortune's gifts' with great clarity tells us what he meant by *felicitas*.

'But' someone may rightly ask 'do you not see that you are begging the question? By what right do you suppose that *virtus* was considered inherent in human nature, whereas *felicitas* by contrast was conferred on man from outside, presumably by the gods?' Before I reply, let us hear my second witness.

II. TEMPLI INSCRIPTIO A. 179 A. C. N. AP. LIV. 40, 52, 5f.

> '*Supra valvas templi tabula cum titulo hoc fixa est "duello magno dirimendo, regibus subigendis caput patrandae pacis ad pugnam exeunti L. Aemilio M. Aemilii filio auspicio, imperio,* felicitate *ductuque eius ... classis regis Antiochi ... fusa contusa fugataque est*'.

It is unfortunate that these words have not been transmitted in full and that a few of them have been lost (on which see Weissenborn). But the actual words are not of overwhelming importance for us. Two things at once stand out. First, *virtus* itself is missing from the list of titles of glory, secondly *felicitas* is not given the final place, being followed by *ductus*. On the first point we are left in doubt, because it may of course be that the word *virtute* is one of those which has dropped out. But we are under very little compulsion to supply it here because not only in the authors (Cic. *S. Rosc.* 136 '... *eaque omnia deorum voluntate, studio populi Romani,* consilio et imperio et felicitate *L. Sullae gesta esse intellego'*), but also in public inscriptions (CIL I ¹626 '*Ductu auspicio imperioque eius Achaia capta, Corinto deleto'*, where even *felicitas* is lacking) such omissions occur.

The second point I have noted, however, does deserve careful consideration. '*felicitas*' is placed between '*imperium*' and '*ductus*'. What *imperium* meant in early times I discussed at length in my book *Roman Dynamism*, Chapter 4, (cf. p. 66, '*imperium* originally meant "chief's *mana*", *imperare* "to transfer *mana*" and *imperator* "the chief who transfers *mana*" '). Erkell (pp. 111f.) is uncertain whether I was right or not but correctly observes (p. 112, 1), 'This theory is disputed by many'. He could have added that many others have agreed with it.[15] I myself have carefully considered all the opposing arguments and persist in my opinion, but neither can nor will go into it here at length. I simply refer my readers to what I have already written. Even those, however, for whom *imperium* is not nor ever has been anything but '*die oberste mit Commando und Jurisdiction ausgestattete Amtsgewalt*' (Mommsen, *R St.* I ³, 22) will readily concede that if *felicitas* as Erkell contends was from the very start due to the favour of the gods it is remarkable that it should here have been listed between *imperium* and *ductus*. For *ductus* is usually coupled as closely as possible with *virtus, imperium,* and *auspicium.* Compare

---

[15] Cf. e.g. G. van der Leeuw, *De Gids* (1942) 130; J. Bayet, *REL* 26 (1948): '*une lumineuse investigation sur* imperare'; A. Brelich, *SMSR* 21 (1947/8) 150, who though he was in no way ready to accept the main argument of the book (unjustifiably afraid that the foundations of the true Roman religion might be shaken by it) thus concludes his review: 'Independently of the fundamental theory, with which one may disagree, the volume contains some excellent solutions on questions of detail. Here too I must content myself with a single example, the chapter on *"imperium"*, which with good reason gave its title to the original edition of the work.' It was with some pleasure that I found individual chapters which had greatly angered and been abused by some singled out by others for praise.

Plaut. *Amph.* 196 '(*ut haec nuntiem uxori suae*) *ut gesserit rem publicam* ductu, imperio, auspicio *suo*' (compared with 191f. '*id vi et virtute militum victum atque expugnatum oppidum est imperio atque auspicio mei eri*'.
Cic. *har. resp.* 3 '*suo* ductu et imperio'.
Inscr. Augustea ap. Plin. *N.H.* 3, 136 '*Caesari divi filio Aug*. . . . *S.P.Q.R. quod eius* ductu auspiciisque *gentes Alpinae* . . . *sub imperium p. R. sunt redactae*'.

For this reason it seems that Erkell's reasoning (p. 59) must be rejected: '*Felicitas* can also mean good luck of an entirely profane kind, but to speak of such a thing in a formal inscription on a temple and combine it with *imperium* and *auspicium* would be not only a fault of style but even blasphemy. The only possible meaning here is indeed 'divine blessing', 'divine luck', and the like, and *felicitas* has just as sacral a sound as *imperium* and *auspicium*.' For *felicitas* would thus become the cuckoo in the nest. Just turn the inscription into your own language and you will feel how languidly, how unwillingly almost, *ductus* would follow it.

The question takes on an entirely different aspect the moment we realize that *felicitas*, as plainly accords with the nature and etymology of the term, means a force innate in men, having in its origins nothing to do with the gods. Just as an *arbor felix* grows good fruit, so a *homo felix* produces 'well conducted affairs', or good campaigns. To us highly cultured people perhaps such a comparison may appear strange and foreign, but anyone expert in such matters will at once recognize how readily it would occur to rather less cultured minds—just as they may often attribute the very fertility of the soil to their chief or king, as has been amply demonstrated by others and is also everywhere evident in my book. *Felicitas* belongs by definition to the *imperator*,—or rather did so. For among the Romans, especially among the more cultured ones whose writings we read, the notion became almost completely obsolete after the Greeks had taught them otherwise, and perhaps even before. None the less, in the minds of the people its traces remained and came to the surface as we shall see more clearly below. With this in view we must start with my third piece of evidence.

III. Aemilii Paulli Or. Frgm. a. 167 a.C.n. ap. Val. Max. 5, 10, 2

'*Cum* in maximo proventu felicitatis nostrae, *Quirites, timerem ne quid mali fortuna moliretur, Iovem ... Iunonemque ... et Minervam precatus sum ut, si quid adversi populo Romano immineret, totum in meam domum converteretur*'.

On the use of the verb *provenire* in Krebs-Schmalz (*Antibarb.* 2, 417) we read, 'This verb according to Ruhnken on Ov. *heroid.* 15, 14 is a term of agriculture, and standard in this sense. It is all the more remarkable that we do not find it in Cato or Varro. It is not found in Cicero, once in Caes. *Gall.* 5, 24, 1 *frumentum angustius provenerat*, but only in this one place. Otherwise *provenire* is not unusual in neo-classic and late-Latin (examples follow, many of which are in Columella). *Provenire* and *proventus* are used just as frequently in a metaphorical sense, nowhere in Cicero but in Caes. *Gall.* 7, 29, 3; 7, 80, 2' (later examples follow). 'Unusual however, and not to be imitated is the use, frequent only in Tacitus, of *provenire* = "succeed" ... even though *proventus* = "the fortunate outcome" is classical in Caes. *civ.* 2, 38, 2'.

The instructions here given for using the classical language are now of no concern to us. The collated material is of some interest, but corrections and additions must be made. In what are called classical times even Sallust uses the verb *provenire*, in a metaphorical sense but clearly indicating an agricultural mode of speech, *Catil.* 8, 3, '*Sed quia* provenere *ibi scriptorum magna ingenia* ...' a mode of speech therefore no longer technical which became very popular with later ages (cf. Plin. *Ep.* 1, 13, 1; Quint. 12, 10, 11; Iust. 13, 1, 12; Sen. *Dial.* 9, 5). Sometimes, where the original meaning of the word is scarcely any longer recognizable, yet the writers somehow seem to keep it still in view, as in Liv. 45, 41, 6 '*Aliarum deinde secundarum rerum velut proventus secutus*' where Weissenborn correctly notes: '*velut* is added because Livy still has in mind the original meaning of *proventus* ('sprouting' of new growth, emergence of fruit). Against that Caes. *B.G.* 7, 29 *secundos rerum proventus* cf. *B.C.* 2, 38'. And truly the sense became gradually weakened. 'Grow' or 'increase' became 'turn out well' or 'succeed' (thus in Caes. *B.C.* 2, 38, 2 '*Multum ad hanc rem probandam adiuvat adulescentia, magnitudo animi*, superioris temporis proventus [= successus], *fiducia rei bene gerendae*'. Moreover there was a *vox media: bene evenire* > *evenire*, as in Caes. *B.G.* 7, 29, the passage quoted by Weissenborn for that reason, where the epithet *secundos* makes it clear enough that *proventus* only means the same as *eventus* or *exitus*. But this process began long before. In Plautus, *Most*. 414 ('*id virist opus, quae dissignata sint et facta nequiter,*) *tranquille cuncta et ut* proveniant *sine malo*'. The text hardly lets us say whether we have a *vox media* or not. Cf. Lorentz on this passage: 'proveniant "progress, result", an unusual meaning of the verb (more frequent is the pregnant "make good progress", "succeed")', and he compares Lucil. 667 M '*denique adeo male me accipiunt decimae et* proveniunt *male*'. In its proper sense the substantive *proventus* occurs for instance in Vergil, *Georg.* 2, 518, 'proventuque (*annus*) *oneret sulcos*'.

This had to be said first before we could investigate the real meaning of Aemilius' phrase *in maximo proventu felicitatis nostrae*. It is realized at once that *proventu* cannot possibly here have a medial sense since of course the addition of the epithet *maximo* makes that impossible. Therefore it either means the same as *successu*, 'success', or it is used in its proper, primary sense of *fructu*, 'fruits'. The choice does not seem to me so difficult. For either *felicitas* is a sort of favour of the gods—as Erkell thinks—or it is *fecunditas*, 'fertility', understood in the metaphorical sense, that is, a certain power of magical origin, as I think. But if *proventus* were to be understood as *successus*, neither of these alternatives would do, as the favour of the gods cannot be said to 'succeed', since it would be like a reiteration of the word. Against that if we understand *proventus* as 'fruits', 'increase', and *felicitas* as 'fertility' we have a transparent meaning given by the nature of the words. Therefore '*in maximo proventu felicitatis nostrae*' is to be understood as '*cum in summo staremus culmine vigoris*'—'when we stood at the peak of our strength'—or literally 'when the fruits of our innate strength were at their greatest'.

L. Aemilius Paullus was a highly cultivated and humane man, one 'in whom old Roman ability had been ennobled by Greek education' (Klebs, *RE* I, 578). It is most probable that he would have abhorred any magical frivolities. But just as nobody will take us for devotees of astrology if we say that somebody was born under a lucky star, though undoubtedly that is the superstition in which the saying originated, neither shall we be accusing that excellent man of magical beliefs when we maintain that his distant ancestors speak through his mouth and that the primary sense of *felicitas imperatoria* shines from his words as clear as day.

After careful examination of three very ancient testimonies I am forced to conclude that the word *felicitas* in early times signified fruitfulness or an efficacious power innate in human beings. It follows that there is nothing strange in its being closely associated with *virtus* (I); or included in an enumeration of properties of the same kind (II); or in the fact that *'proventus felicitatis'* speaks for itself (III). Besides that, we have come to realize that the questions raised above (pp. 62ff.), and in my opinion not answered by Erkell, have lost all their point. It stands to reason that the *felicitas* in question was preeminently a quality of an *imperator* or commander-in-chief, as has been briefly explained above and at more length in the book referred to. We are no longer offended at the attribution of this *felicitas* not only to Romans but also to strangers, and even to enemies. Finally this kind of magic did not suddenly and surprisingly raise its head in the imperial age—it was totally different of course from the Oriental kind with its revolting absurdities—but from the earliest times had been native to the soil of Italy. I have made it abundantly clear how it came step by step to retire into the background. It remains for us to recognize its few surviving traces in the literature. In doing so we shall notice how much more easily the progression of changing meanings can be discerned than if we follow Erkell's suggested sequence (pp. 127f.): '*Felix* no longer meant "fruitful" but signified what from a sacral point of view was "usable", "acceptable", for the gods ... From the meaning "usable in cult, acceptable to the gods" there evolved quite easily the meaning "loved by the gods, blessed" '. I frankly confess that such transitions of meaning seem very strange to me. Against that I propose: *felicitas* was a primitive notion arising from the comparison of excellence in a man with the gifts of the earth and the attribution to both of a certain magic power. And since they were accustomed to award the supreme command to the very men thus endowed—I pass over for now the fact that in my opinion *imperium* and *felicitas* are almost synonymous (so that *imperium* was not so much awarded as acknowledged; in historical times the title of *imperator* was actually only awarded by acclamation of the soldiers to the general who had won a great victory)—it went without saying that the *felicitas* was preeminently that of an *imperator*. In more cultivated times, however, the Romans—the more educated they were, the further removed from the ideas of a more primitive age—did not properly understand the ancient word and gave it a new aspect. Partly, under the influence of Greek philosophy, they assimilated it to εὐτυχία and not infrequently described it as received from the gods, partly they equated it with the Greek τύχη and interchanged the notions of *fortuna* and *felicitas*. That the custom of attributing it principally to commanders-in-chief none the less survived so long was due to the tradition of centuries, to ancient annals, and especially to ancient inscriptions conspicuous everywhere. The authors, when they speak here and there in such a way as to give us the impression that we are catching an echo of that early meaning—several examples of which I have quoted above—were undoubtedly no longer conscious of it. Against that, I am not convinced that ideas of this kind had altogether vanished from the minds of the common people, as I now attempt to show by a few examples.

Among the maxims of Publilius Syrus, who lived about the middle of the first century B.C., we find (C 36), '*Contra felicem vix deus vires habet*'. Erkell himself (p. 54) is obliged to concede that these words are 'at the furthest removed from the "divine blessing" '. And yet you will look to him in vain for an explanation. To me it seems that we have here a sort of unmistakable echo of the ancient ideas. I add in passing that several passages can be found which are hard to reconcile with the notion of *felicitas* as given by the gods, as Liv. 30, 30, 23 '*Inter pauca felicitatis virtutisque exempla M. Atilius quondam in hac eadem terra fuisset, si . . .,; sed* non statuendo felicitati modum . . . *eo foedius corruit*'. For how could anyone limit his own *felicitas* if it depended entirely on the gods? (cf. Sen *Dial.* 6, 14, 3). I wish we knew what Servius' sources were for writing (*ad Ecl.* 5, 65), '*deos enim vel felices vel infelices ex rebus, quas praestant, vocamus*'. Such a sentence is altogether more intelligible on my view of the word than on Erkell's.

A writer's words sometimes give the impression that the ancient association of the words *virtus* and *felicitas* is interpreted to mean that *felicitas* is peculiar to youth and shows itself most clearly in the successful conduct of affairs by a young man. Erkell (pp. 60ff.) has already pointed out that *felicitas* and *prudentia* are often opposed to one another. I can only not follow him in declaring that by this *prudentia* the writers have wanted to indicate 'in what way this divine blessing works'. I had rather believe they had retained some inkling of what is certainly a very ancient notion, that just as the earth bears its fruits of its own accord so the *imperator felix* is a good general more by natural disposition than by judgment and prudence. It was not a far cry from there to the *imperator* making use of blind fortune with *felicitas*, and a position about midway between the two was occupied by the youthful *imperator* wonderfully fortunate in war. Cf. e.g. what Plutarch writes about Octavian, with whose *felicitas* we shall become more closely acquainted below, *Cic*. 45, 3: νέον ἄνδρα καὶ τύχῃ λαμπρᾷ κεχρημένον, or Livy 30, 30, 11 '*tuam et* adulescentiam *et perpetuam* [16] felicitatem *metuo*'.

Felices arbores, trees which were *felix*, were without doubt originally 'fruitful trees' but we have already noticed above (p. 65) that here too a notion of magic soon crept in. Fronto for instance, a fairly late author, says (pp. 195, 6ff.). '*Leges pleraeque poenam sanciverunt, ne quis* arborem felicem *succidisset*'. *Quaenam est* arboris felicitas? *Rami fecundi et frugiferi, bacis pomisque onusti*.

In my opinion both Fronto and Maius, his worthy annotator, have wrongly interpreted the purport of these early laws. Maius (I follow Naber in this edition) refers us to *Dig*. 47, 7, 2 '(*Gaius libro primo ad legem duodecim tabularum*): *Sciendum est autem eos, qui arbores et maxime vites ceciderint, etiam tamquam latrones puniri*'. Yet there is no mention of *arbores felices* either here or in any other place concerning the felonious cutting down of trees. Cf. Bruns, *Fontes Iuris Rom. Ant*. p. 31 ad Leg. XII tabb. (tab. 8, 11) where

[16] Here a more recent idea of *felicitas* has the consequence that it has become 'temporary'. The idea that *felicitas* 'constantly' accompanies a man as it would if innate is no longer conveyed by usage, so that 'constant' *felicitas* has to be expressed in words. Several places are quoted by Erkell as clear examples of temporary *felicitas*, as Liv. 38, 48, 15 (Erkell p. 56), 38, 51, 7 (p. 65); 42, 59, 8 (p. 68); and many others (cf. also Cic. *Brut*. 4).

you will find several passages concerning it, and see especially Gai. 4, 11 '*quod lex XII tab. ex qua de vitibus succisis actio competeret*, generaliter de arboribus *succisis loqueretur*'. Since laws seem certainly to have existed which forbade by name the cutting down of any *arbor felix* (otherwise Fronto would not have mentioned them in this context) we must suppose that the prohibition concerned some religious scruple, almost a case of sacrilege. This is confirmed by Tarquitius Priscus, an author of the beginning of the first century B.C., who tells us (*ap. Macr. Sat.* 3, 20, 3) '*arbores, quae inferum deorum avertentiumque in tutela sunt, eas* infelices *nominant . . . sentesque, quibus portenta prodigiaque mala comburi iubere oportet*'. It is noteworthy how constantly the authors contradict one another and themselves on these questions.

I quote one out of many examples, Plin. *N.H.* 16, 108 '*Fructum arborum solae nullum ferunt, hoc est ne semen quidem, tamarix scopis tantum nascens, populus, alnus, ulmus Atinia, alaternus, cui folia inter ilicem et olivam.* Infelices *autem existimantur damnataeque religione quae neque seruntur umquam neque* fructum ferunt'. (cf. also 24, 68). And yet against that Tarquitius in the passage quoted, '*arbores . . . infelices . . ., quae . . . bacam nigram nigrosque fructus ferunt*'. Yet Tarquitius is a great deal earlier than Pliny! The confusion in which Ladewig & Jahn flounder is thus excusable, in their note on *Aen.* 6, 230, '*felices arbores* are fruit-bearing trees, *infelices* wild ones'. Nevertheless the service tree (*sorbus*) e.g. is *felix* (Veranius *ap.* Macr. 3, 20, 2), whereas black fig and *Pyrus sylvatica* (pyraster) are *infelices* (Tarquitius ibid. § 3).

In view of these and similar passages can we wonder that the adjective *felix* has diverged into a synonym of the adjective *salutaris*, while *infelix* on the other hand has begun almost to mean the same as *funestus*, 'deadly'?

Compare the following:

> Verg. *Ecl.* 5, 65 '*Sis bonus o* felixque *tuis*'.
> Verg. *Aen.* I, 330 '*Sis* felix *nostrumque leves, quaecumque, laborem*'.
> Liv. 3, 54, 9 '*Ibi* felici *loco, ubi prima initia inchoastis libertatis vestrae, tribunos plebi creabitis*'.
> Verg. *Aen.* 2, 245 '*et monstrum* infelix *sacrata sistimus arce*'.
> Verg. *Aen.* 3, 246 '(*Celaeno*) infelix *vates*' (cf. Serv. *Dan. ad l.*).

Erkell has well shown that *felicitas* was often attributed by the Romans to the favour of the gods. At the same time nobody reading him carefully can fail to see how many difficulties they had to contend with in this question. If, as I noticed above (n. 16), *felicitas* in later times was usually temporary rather than permanent, and if then the gods gave it to anyone they liked, how could a man give himself credit for it, so that in titles and eloges it was not only closely associated with *virtus* but again and again took precedence of it (as in Cic. *Phil.* 4, 15; Liv. 22, 58, 3; 30, 30, 23; 39, 32 4)? The question indeed was one with which Cicero concerned himself (*de Or.* 2, 343ff.). After a full treatment of a passage on the praise of *virtus*, he goes on (§ 347), '*Neque tamen illa non ornant, habiti honores, decreta virtutis praemia, res gestae iudiciis hominum comprobatae; in quibus etiam* felicitatem ipsam deorum immortalium iudicio tribui laudationis est'. Such a reply does of course touch the heart of the matter, but it does not remove the difficulty. Other writers have been no more successful, for it seems that this was already a subject for disputation in schools of rhetoric when Cicero was a young man—compare:

> Rhet. ad Herenn. 4, 28 '*Hominem laudem egentem virtutis, abundantem felicitatis?*'.
> Cic. *de inv.* 1, 94 '*Si non ad id, quod instituitur, adcommodabitur aliqua pars argumentationis, horum aliquo in vitio reperietur: si...*, *aut* si qui, cum aliquem volet laudare, de felicitate eius, non de virtute dicat'.

If you ask me therefore how those difficulties arose I reply without hesitation: because at that period the Romans no longer understood what the ancient term *felicitas* which they saw every day in old monuments and inscriptions really meant. Of course even for later generations the same term had uses which betrayed its origin. Erkell (p. 67) himself quotes Sen. *contr. 3 praef 8* '*Ciceronem eloquentia sua in carminibus destituit; Vergilium illa* felicitas ingenii *in oratione soluta reliquit*'; Veget. *mil.* 2, 18 'huius felicitatis ac provisionis est perennitas tua, ut . . . nova excogitet'. Here Erkell thinks *felicitas* means 'a certain power of invention' but how such a meaning could arise from the one he generally proposes he does not explain. Yet he comments on the first passage, 'In modern times too it has been possible to speak of a poet as "happy" (*glücklich, heureux*) in this sense'. 'In this sense'? Never, in my understanding. Such epithets, if I am not mistaken, can properly be used of single poems or words but not of a brilliant poetic personality, and I am afraid it will cost E. considerable trouble to adduce a testimony which talks of 'poet's luck', *du bonheur d'un poète* 'vom Glück eines Dichters'. Against that, if *felicitas* from the beginning was a sort of force innate in men, it is hardly surprising that it was later transferred to other fields.

It remains to say a few words about *Sulla Felix*, dealt with at considerable length by Erkell. In particular, his objections to Carcopino,[17] though sometimes pressed too hard, do seem correct on the whole. I can be much briefer, because of course Sulla himself, if asked whether there was any magical significance in his epithet, would have sworn that there was not. But it is a completely different question what a man of the people more tenacious of older religious beliefs might have thought of it. We can see this very clearly thanks to Plutarch (*Sull.* 35, 6), at least if in such matters we may legitimately put a woman, even though a patrician one, on a level with a man of the people. In fact at that period she would often have been not much better educated. Plutarch relates that Valeria, the daughter of Messalla and sister of the orator Hortensius, was sitting not far from Sulla in the amphitheatre, watching a gladiatorial show. He goes on: Αὕτη παρὰ τὸν Σύλλαν ἐξόπισθεν παραπορευομένη τήν τε χεῖρα πρὸς αὐτὸν ἀπηρείσατο καὶ κροκύδα τοῦ ἱματίου σπάσασα, παρῆλθεν ἐπὶ τὴν ἑαυτῆς χώραν. Ἐμβλέψαντος δὲ τοῦ Σύλλα καὶ θαυμάσαντος, Οὐδέν, ἔφη, δεινόν, αὐτόκρατορ· ἀλλὰ βούλομαι τῆς σῆς κἀγὼ μικρὸν εὐτυχίας μεταλαβεῖν.[18]

The word for 'good luck', εὐτυχία, is certainly a translation of the Latin *felicitas*. Now consider Erkell's comment (p. 110): 'In this case the good luck is conceived quite materially, as a sort of '*Kraftfluidum*'! I can spare the labour of recalling all that I have written more than once about Roman opinion on this question,

---

[17] J. Carcopino, *Sylla ou la monarchie manquée*, 1931.
[18] She walked past behind Sulla and pressing her hand against him plucked at the nap of his cloak, then returned to her seat. Then when Sulla stared at her in surprise she said, 'No harm meant, dictator, I only want a small share of your luck for myself'.

in the book I have quoted so widely and so often. There (p. 138, 1) I also gave examples of the transmission of strength through contact with clothes and could easily add further ones. Erkell has rightly compared with this reference another from Plutarch (*de fort. Rom.* 7) where we read that when Octavian and Anthony played at ball or dice or even staged cockfights against each other Octavian usually won, wherefore one of Antony's friends urged him to avoid Octavian: ὁ σὸς δαίμων τὸν τούτου φοβεῖται· καὶ ἡ τύχη σου καθ' ἑαυτήν ἐστι μεγάλη, κολακεύει δὲ τὴν τούτου· ἐὰν μὴ μακρὰν ᾖς, οἰχήσεται μεταβᾶσα πρὸς αὐτόν.[19] (cf. Plut. *Ant.* 33). A more transparent example of the contact which I have called *contagio enervans*, (*R.D.* p. 138) could not be imagined. 'In both cases' says Erkell 'the force fluid passes over into another without any act or knowledge of its possessor. It is remarkable, however, that in Octavian the stronger luck so to speak magnetically attracts the weaker'. Very true, and I am little less than flabbergasted, that is, as long as I try to follow Erkell's trail. For these wonders are here offered without explanation; on the other hand, they agree perfectly with my own interpretation. Let us only remember, what cannot be often enough repeated, that returning to the surface in such stories are survivals long deeply submerged in the minds of men of civilization and refinement. Therefore when Erkell (p. 88) writes, 'What I have said here about *felic-* in Livy and in this Chapter about Sulla's interest in divine revelations, signs, prophecies, and manifold obeisances to the gods should be enough to refute the magical hypothesis', the question that really matters is wrongly put. We must distinguish between the considered and careful meditations of Sulla himself and ideas current among the common people. Furthermore, we must even distinguish between the thoughts thought by the dictator when in complete solitude and those which may have taken him unawares with a sudden rush. To me what he himself wrote in his memoirs (Plut. *Sull.* 6, 6): ὅτι τῶν καλῶς αὐτῷ βεβουλεῦσθαι δοκούντων αἱ μὴ κατὰ γνώμην, ἀλλὰ πρὸς καιρὸν ἀποτολμώμεναι πράξεις ἔπιπτον εἰς ἄμεινον [20] seems

[19] 'Your Genius is afraid of his, and while your Luck is strong on its own, it fawns on' (is subservient to) 'his. If you do not keep away from him, it will leave you and go over entirely to him'.

[20] 'That among his apparently good decisions the actions taken not with forethought but on the spur of the moment had turned out better.'

to have nothing in common with any sort of divine favour, but to betray some vague conception of the ancient *felicitas imperatoria*.

The same seems to hold for the passage *Diff. gramm.* 7, 521, 19. Certainly the source is of doubtful authenticity—we do not know where it 'got its water'. All the same it rings remarkably true: 'felix ita natus est, *fortunatus cum opibus nomen accipit; ita* felix naturae bono fruitur, *fortunatus commodo temporis*'.

VI

CUPID AND PSYCHE *

Apuleius' 'Cupid and Psyche' *Märchen*, so to call it for the present, has had a great impact on the world's literature and art. The number of translations and free adaptations is very extensive. From France I need only mention Molière, Corneille, and La Fontaine, from England Spenser and William Morris, from Germany Wieland and Robert Hamerling. Since the Renaissance painters and sculptors have found rewarding themes there. Raphael used them for his frescoes in the Villa Farnesina, Thorvaldsen embossed several of them, and in the Louvre there is Canova's famous Cupid and Psyche group, of which the Villa Carlotta, near Cadenabbia on Lake Como, possesses an excellent copy. It is therefore a text deserving special study both for its own sake and for the great number of questions it raises.

An account of Apuleius' life and work and a summary of the content of the 'Cupid and Psyche' tale, well-known as they are, can both be omitted here. I only observe that the actual narrative of the *Metamorphoses* in which this tale occurs, and which itself was taken over by Apuleius from a Greek source, is repeatedly interrupted by very erotic and spicy interpolations. Short stories, or novellas, like these were widely popular in late Hellenistic times. They were called 'Milesian tales' (*fabulae Milesiacae*) because Miletus or its neighbourhood was their original scene of events. The most important and least improper of the interpolations is the tale of 'Cupid and Psyche' itself. It is also much longer than the others. While the whole work comprises 11 books, 'Cupid and Psyche' takes up two of them, the last quarter of Book IV, the whole of Book V, and three quarters of Book VI.

It has been previously observed by others that the tale itself consists of different sections. At V 24 there seems to be a clear hiatus. Before it the goddess Venus does not know Psyche at all.

* Abridgement of a lecture given by H. Wagenvoort on 20 March 1954 at the Congress of the United Departments of Royal Netherlands Academy of Sciences.

After it Psyche is suddenly a runaway slave of Venus. A second piece of evidence has not been noticed by anyone. It concerns the scene of events. At the beginning, IV 29, we read that the fame of Psyche's beauty had spread 'over the neighbouring islands, a great part of the mainland, and several provinces'. This formulation in my opinion can only apply to the coast of Asia Minor. Furthermore, Psyche's elder sisters live across the sea, for they can only visit her by ship. Perhaps they are thought of as resident in the Peloponnese, where Psyche, before later going to Taenarum, also visited the cities in which her sisters were queens. If I am met with the objection that it is methodically incorrect to look for geographical references in such a tale, then I refer to the passage V 24, on the dividing line between the first and second sections, where Apuleius makes Psyche hang on to Cupid's leg in order to get away from the place. How did such a strange idea occur to him, rightly described by Purser in his *Commentary* (1910) as absurd and ridiculous? As if he could think of no other way of transporting Psyche where he wanted her to be. The real reason in my opinion was that Apuleius or his original model could not or would not cut themselves loose from their principal sources of which one had its scene of events in Asia Minor, the other in Greece.

Is it then a *Märchen*, an allegory, or a myth which we have here? All three views have enthusiastic supporters, and there is a lot to be said about each one of them. The opening alone seems to confirm that it is meant to be a *Märchen*. 'Once upon a time there were a king and a queen who had three beautiful daughters...' A still stronger argument is that from Norway to Sicily, from Iceland to India we find countless folk tales constructed in a similar form. Its detailed discussion must be postponed till later. I remark only that the girl usually has three tasks to perform before being reunited with her lost lover. In Apuleius there are four. But many have already assumed correctly that the third task (the fetching of water from the Styx) and the fourth (the fetching of the beauty ointment from the underworld) are duplicates. In both cases what was to be fetched was originally the water of life. A folk-tale of Indo-European origin, to judge from the version in Apuleius and some others, has been influenced from a hitherto unknown quarter.

An *Allegory* too has been suggested. No wonder, because the principal figures, Cupid and Psyche, besides many really allegorical figures, seem to point in this direction. But so far no explanation based on this idea has stood up to criticism.

The view that it might be a *Myth* was enthusiastically and expertly put forward by Richard Reitzenstein. He did in fact prove that there was an Iranian goddess Psyche. She was the soul who entered into matter. This gave rise to a myth. Psyche's father the King of Light handed her over to the Prince of Darkness, before whom he and his whole kingdom trembled. This myth is said to have been re-worked into a Greek adaptation in Alexandria, which then in circumstances of which we are ignorant became the source of Apuleius' novella. This explanation too leaves many problems unsolved, the most conspicuous of which is that in the Iranian myth Eros/Amor/Cupid does not occur at all. Reitzenstein then has to admit that in the Greek world a connection between Eros and Psyche was in fact known already and that this conception became fused with the Iranian myth.

Let us return to the text. At the beginning Psyche's marriage is called a funeral wedding (IV 33). It is indeed more of a funeral than a wedding procession which follows her (IV 34) and she is mourned like a dead girl (V 5; 7). This fact has received little attention. Apparently Apollo's oracle is regarded as a sufficient explanation—she is to marry a dangerous monster. But that she must marry this monster only to be killed, of that we read no word. There is another thing, however, which has provoked speculation, Cupid's long, serious illness, caused by nothing more than a drop of hot oil on his shoulder. From this it is inferred by Reitzenstein and others that Psyche herself had wounded him, perhaps even killed him with her knife, and that is why the water of life had to be fetched from the underworld. Earlier Liebrecht had even dared to assert that in an older version Psyche herself had gone to her death. So far as Cupid is concerned I believe there can be no possible doubt, first because of several indications scattered through the text, secondly because of numerous traces in closely related folk-tales, thirdly and quite especially because of a remarkable separate section in Apuleius' story. When Venus at the beginning has instructed her son to inspire Psyche, her rival in beauty, with the love of some worthless man, she dives down to the floor of the ocean with her retinue to swim there (IV 31). She swims there (on the sea-floor!) for days, weeks, even months. And when a separation between Cupid and Psyche has finally come about, the news has to be brought to her in the deeps by a sea-bird, a *gavia* or diver. (That this is done by none other than a *gavia* I find significant. But let me here pass over the question). It is strange that nobody has commented on the incongruity of this story! There has been just as little comment on the strange reproach addressed to the goddess by the bird (V 28) 'that Venus and her whole household were getting a bad reputation from a spate of gossip and scandal about Cupid having gone off for a love affair in the mountains while she herself was having a seaside holiday. The result is that there is no longer any pleasure, grace, or delight. Everything on earth has become wild and desolate and ugly. No marriages are being held, no friendships formed, no children petted, nothing but boundless decay and filth of corrupt relationships.' The whole section gives the impression of having been squeezed into this context. It occurs to me, however, that we know the theme well enough, but from a quite different cultural sphere.

The hymn sung by Ishtar's procession to the realm of the dead has been translated (among others) by Zandee in the *Jaarbericht No. 6* (1939) of *Ex Oriente Lux*. I quote: 'After Ishtar the Queen had descended to the land from which nobody returns, the bull ceased to mount the young cow, the ass no longer impregnated the she-ass, the young man lay in his room, the young woman lay on her own side.' Here we have the same plaint as in Apuleius, but now in its proper organic context. And when we further read in Aristides, Apuleius' younger contemporary, (*Apol.* 11, 3): 'It is told of Aphrodite that she descended into Hades to ransom Adonis from Persephone'—where Aphrodite has already taken the place of Ishtar, and Tammuz has been replaced by Adonis but not yet by Eros/Amor/Cupid—then it is almost a certainty that in an earlier version of Apuleius' story not only Eros but also Aphrodite/Venus herself visited the underworld. Reitzenstein himself incidentally must already have been thinking of the Ishtar myth when he wrote (*Das Märchen von Amor und Psyche bei Apuleius*, 1912, p. 23): 'Like Psyche the Babylonian goddess

Ishtar descended to the underworld, realm of the dead, and obtained from its queen the water of life.' It is indeed true that new texts about Inanna/Ishtar and Dumuzi/Tammuz have given us an entirely new view of what really happened in the original Ishtar myth. I shall not go into that here, but will later show that our line of thought need not be affected by it.

But now another question presses for an answer. It is no surprise to anybody that Aphrodite should have continued the series Inanna/Ishtar/Astarte. But how is it to be explained that Eros-Cupid should have become a term in the series Dumuzi/Tammuz/Adonis? What has the god of love to do with death?

When the satirist Lucian speaks of the 'double god Eros', the one frivolous, the other 'the father of time immemorial' (*Amor.* 37; cf. *de Salt.* 7; *Dial. Deor.* 2, 1; 1. 4), he is describing two very different forms of the god, the second of which is far the most ancient. The cult of this Eros spread hardly at all in Greece and was of importance only in the Boeotian city of Thespiae, where Eros was worshipped in the form of a stone. Furtwängler thinks it probable that this cult was already practised by the pre-Aeolian population, while von Wilamowitz based it on Thracian influence. In fact everything does point to Thrace. While Homer does not mention Eros, Hesiod in his *Theogony* calls him 'the most beautiful of the immortal gods who relaxes the limbs of all gods and men and enters into them to conquer their mind and understanding'. Here, in his *Theogony*, the poet is under the influence of Orphic mysticism, which had its origins in Thrace. Though Eros is better known to us as a divine good-for-nothing who plays a mischievous game with gods and men, he did in the contemplation of mystics through the centuries carry out his ancient task and in the Egyptian magical papyri is still the 'first cause of all Creation'.

Of his attributes in art, wings, bow with quiver of arrows, and torch, it is the torch which calls for attention here. Often he holds it aloft, but often too he lowers it. We notice that in this case he usually has some connection with death, on numerous tombstones, for instance. Yet another connection between Eros and death? In fact this has been felt as so bizarre that many have sought to separate this figure altogether from Eros and called it Thanatos. Consequently in the interpretation of ancient monuments we constantly meet with a vacillation between Eros and Thanatos. Thus Carl Robert for instance wrote (*Thanatos*, 39. Winckelmannsprogr. 1879, p. 32): 'The familiar winged boy with lowered torch which is so frequent on Roman tombstones can hardly be given a Greek name and must be ... described as the mourning Genius of the dead man.' And yet the connection of Eros with Death is in any case very old. For instance a terracotta votive relief in Italy, dated by Furtwängler (*Roschers Lex*. 1. 1, 1357) to the 5th century B.C. shows him as the servant of a chthonian goddess with the attributes of Persephone. It has in my opinion been an oversight to disregard the link connecting Eros and Thanatos. I mean Hesperus, the evening star.

On numerous Mithras reliefs (e.g. that from Heddernheim) the bull-slaying god is flanked by Cautes and Cautopates, one with raised, the other with lowered torch. It is usual to see in these the rising and setting sun. But Cumont thinks it possible that they originally personified the morning star (Phosphorus, Lucifer) and the evening star (Hesperus, Vesper). The origins of this iconographic invention, so Dr. Vermaseren informs me, date from the 4th century B.C. Even Greek art is acquainted with almost the same idea, only then the morning and evening stars are usually winged. Thus Rehm (*R.E.* 8, 1254) writes: 'In the type just described we have an especially frequent case, the morning and evening stars confronted as winged torch-bearers, the one usually with raised, the other with lowered torch.'

It is Hesperus who interests us here, for he was gradually identified with Eros. Both were admired as beautiful boys, both winged, and both carrying torches (even though Eros originally had his raised, Hesperus lowered). A more particular reason was that the evening star accompanied every wedding-procession, since they always took place in the evening, and as Rehm remarks, Hesperus and Eros could often not be distinguished. We may for example compare the well-known relief of the wedding of Peleus and Thetis from the Villa Albani in Rome. But Hesperus belongs to the west, to night, to the realm of the dead. He sinks beneath the sea, to rise again out of it later as the morning star. It is revealing here to recall Diodorus' story (3, 60) about the death of Hesperus, who climbed to the peak of Mt. Atlas and was whisked off it by a gust of wind. Can it be quite by chance that this scene shows such a striking similarity with the manner in which Psyche, borne by Zephyrus, is wafted from a mountain peak to her palace in the underworld?

The identity of the morning and evening star was already known to the ancient Assyrians. The Greeks knew of it since Pythagoras or Parmenides. The identity is often referred to in the literature, although the ordinary people were not conscious of it and they remained separate in legend and poetry. It would be of the greatest importance if the frequent conjecture were to be confirmed, that the Ishtar myth originally had an astral meaning. We speak of the planet Venus, Romans and Greeks spoke of 'the Venus star', 'the Aphrodite star', and the Assyrians of 'the Ishtar star'. The relation of Ishtar to Tammuz may originally have been the same as that of Aphrodite to Hesperus. In new texts the theme of underworld deputies plays an important part. It could very well have some connection with the alternating rise and fall of the morning and evening Star.

I must draw attention to one remarkable circumstance. Waser (*RE* 6, 516ff.) knows of 97 cities which minted coins on which Eros appeared, in many different forms and in a variety of company. Of these cities 57 were in Asia Minor, 14 in Thrace and Moesia, 10 in Greece, 11 in Italy, 3 in Syria and Palestine. Far the greatest interest taken in this god seems to have been in Asia Minor, followed by Thrace and Moesia, with a relatively slight proportion in Greece and Italy. But if we consider only the special type of Eros with lowered torch, the proportions are quite different. He is found eight times in Thrace and Moesia, five times in Asia Minor, and nowhere else. When we further note that of the five cases in Asia Minor three come from Bithynia, that is, in the country bordering Thrace, in my opinion we are justified in inferring that there was a close connection in Thrace between Eros and the realm of the dead.

So what can have induced the Thracians to reproduce such a melancholy figure on their coins? I cannot be sure, but I can guess. And here I come finally to the theme of the funeral wedding. Only one region is known to me in which the custom of the funeral wedding has survived from antiquity to the present day, or even where 'love in the afterworld' has remained a very serious matter for its inhabitants. This region again has Thrace as its core, including Bulgaria and part of Yugoslavia, but also extending across the Danube over Rumania, Galicia, and White Russia, perhaps as far as Lithuania and in the east as far as southern Russia. I know of one monograph by Otto Schrader, *Totenhochzeit* (1910), another by Muslea, 'La Mort-Mariage: a peculiarity of Balkan folklore' in *Mélanges de l'École Roumaine en France* (1925) p. 3ff.; besides that, for South Russia, Uno Holmberg, *Die Religion der Tscheremissen*, FF Communications 61 (1926). Among all these people it is the custom, whenever a young man or young woman dies unmarried, to constitute the funeral procession entirely as a bridal procession. There are all sorts of variations. Generally however it takes the following form. Not only is the dead man or woman escorted with singing and fife-playing, wreaths and bridal finery, but there is also a living bride or bridegroom, accompanied by bridesmaids and 'best men'. In many cases he or she counts as widower or widow from then on and calls the parents of the dead person father and mother. The obvious inference that originally a young man or woman followed the dead person into the grave is confirmed by the account of the 10th-century Arabian traveller Ibn Fadhlan, who among a Slavonic tribe north of the Danube attended the funeral of a young warrior for whom a young woman in bridal attire was killed as wife. We can also go still further back, at least if Schrader is right in attaching the quotation to this context, as I think he is, and remember how in Euripides the ghost of the murdered Achilles demanded Priam's daughter Polyxena, who was thereupon sacrificed to him—on the coast of Thrace!

I am far from thinking that the whole course of development of Apuleius' novella has been cleared up. There are other important aspects of the problem which can only be considered in a detailed treatment of the whole work. Putting together what we have learned, we have the outcome that the story in the main results from a fusion of an Indo-European *Märchen* or folk-tale with an oriental myth which can clearly be traced back to Ishtar and Tammuz. It is very possible that it was an astral myth, arising from the kinship between Ishtar-Aphrodite and the evening star. Even if this is not the case, a fusion of Hesperus and Eros is very understandable, so that the myth of the evening star which sinks and therefore dies, but then rises again to a new life as Lucifer, can also be associated with Eros. In Thrace a dead youth received by the custom of the country a bride. It would be thinkable that in the land of origin of Orphic mysticism she might even have been called Psyche. In this case she would not have been fused with the oriental goddess Psyche until later—unless the two were originally in fact the same. That would be inevitably yet another hypothesis. But in conclusion I must point out that in Apuleius it is an old woman who tells this story of love in the underworld and its ultimate reward, to comfort a girl who fears she has lost her bridegroom just before their marriage.

VII

THE GOLDEN BOUGH

1. *The golden bough in Virgil*

The reader is acquainted with the plot of Book VI of the *Aeneid*. Before his death Anchises (vs. 115; cf. V 731ff.) has told his son to visit him in the underworld with the assistance of the Cumaean Sibyl. The Sibyl says she is ready to help Aeneas, but points out that it is easier to get into the underworld than to get out of it again (126-129). This can only be done if Aeneas first fetches the golden bough from a grove dedicated to Proserpina in order to present it to the queen of the underworld (136-148). The task was far from simple: how was that particular bough to be found amid the thickets of a wood? But (190) two doves sent by his mother Venus-Aphrodite show Aeneas the way and alight on the tree from which he can tear off the bough. When he reaches the Styx with the Sibyl, and Charon obstinately refuses to ferry them across, Aeneas only has to show the bough (406) for Charon, marvelling at the sight of the 'venerabile donum fatalis virgae', to abandon all resistance. After they have wandered for a long while through the melancholy abode of shadows they come to the palace of Pluto and Proserpina. They do not actually enter it, but Aeneas fastens the bough to the entrance 'adverso in limine' (636), after which, 'perfecto munere divae', they both pursue their journey to the Elysian fields.—It should, incidentally, be pointed out that the words 'ramumque adverso in limine figit' do not mean 'he lays the bough on the threshold', as Norden and other commentators will have it (why, in this case, would it be *figit*?), but 'he fastens it to the cross-beam above the door'. This is a common meaning of *limen*; the rite can be illustrated with numerous classical quotations and a mass of folkloristic material, but this is not of essential importance to my argument.

What is important, however, is that we should look closer at the passages where the bough is mentioned. To start with there is vs 137, which immediately presents us with an enigma: 'aureus et foliis et lento vimine ramus'. As far as *aureus* is concerned we have a choice between the translations 'made of gold' and 'golden coloured'. But that the poet actually means 'made of gold', even if he speaks of 'auricomos fetus' in vs 141, emerges clearly in vs 195, where the bough is called 'dives', and still more clearly in vs 209, where we read: 'leni crepitabat brattea vento'. For, if the leaves on the bough are here termed *bratteae*, a word which is only used of thin metal discs, the leaves must have been fine sheets of gold. Indeed, were they otherwise they could hardly *crepitare*. But now we come to the enigma: how can this golden bough have 'lenta vimina', as we read in vs 137? *Lentus* is a common epithet of branches, especially of willow branches, and means that they are tough and bend easily without breaking. Can this apply to a golden bough as well? The commentators, including Norden, say nothing about this. It would seem to me that Virgil is immediately emphasizing with this single word the magical character of the golden bough, which has something essential in common with a normal bough. If this were not so the leaves would not be able to 'crepitare', tinkle in the breeze. The magical character is still further accentuated in the succeeding verses: when the bough is broken off (143) a new one appears, a second combination between the anorganic and the organic. And in the third place the bough can only be torn away (146f.) by someone called by Fate. We now see why the bough is called 'fatalis virga' in vs 409.

This still leaves us with the remarkable verses 205ff., where we read: 'As in the winter cold the mistletoe, a parasite which surrounds the slender stems with yellow growth, is green with young leafage, such was the sight of the leafy gold on the thick foliage of the holm-oak, so did the gold foil tinkle in the gentle breeze'. Here we have *two* problems, the first of which has not been pointed out in any commentary. The poet is comparing not only the external aspect of the golden bough with that of a mistletoe, but also the sound of the leaves tinkling in the wind. Can there be any question of this in the case of the mistletoe? It does not seem so. It could be objected that my translation of *crepitare* as 'tinkle' is too suggestive. Does not the word also signify noises like creaking, screeching, clanking, chattering, etc., so why can it not mean the rustling of leaves too? However, the Thesaurus Linguae Latinae only cites one passage for the *crepitare* of leaves (Pliny *Nat. Hist.* 16, 91), and there we read that it only happens in the case of poplars. Furthermore, I believe that the best parallel is to be found in Ovid, *Metam.* 10, 647, where the poet writes of a miraculous tree bearing golden apples: 'medio nitet arbor in arvo, fulva comas, fulvo ramis crepitantibus auro'. It is almost certain that Ovid was influenced here by our passage in Virgil, for he also follows the golden bough episode elsewhere, as we shall see. And when, in his tragedy *Agamemnon* (vs 855), Seneca, after speaking of the golden apples in the garden of the Hesperides, goes on to talk about the 'sonitus crepitante lamna' (*lamna* or *lamina* is synonymous with *brattea*), he may well be recalling both passages. In short, I have the feeling that the *vimina* had to be *lenta* for the *crepitare* to be possible, and that the poet must have had a reason, albeit an incidental one, to allude to the *crepitare*. I shall return to this point later.

The second problem, on the other hand, has been pointed out on numerous occasions and has perhaps even been solved. I shall repeat briefly what can be found in a more extensive version in, for example, Steier's article 'Mistel' in Pauly-Wissowa's *Real-Encyclopädie* (15, 2063ff.)—unless, that is, the reader prefers to plunge into Tubeuf's *Monographie der Mistel* (1923), a book of over 700 pages. Well, what Virgil tells us about the mistletoe is all wrong: the real mistletoe does not have a *croceus fetus*, but green sprigs and leaves and white berries. Or this, at least, is true of the mistletoe which we know, the *viscum album*, the mistletoe which has such a charming function at Christmas in England. Here in Holland we only encounter it in South Limburg, particularly on apple trees and Canadian poplars, and it is on these same trees that it grows elsewhere in Europe, including Italy and Greece. It is seldom found on oaks, however—and the golden bough grew on a holmoak (209). Only isolated cases have been reported in France and England, and in France an oak mistletoe was even presented to a museum. But there is also another type of mistletoe which does not appear in Western Europe, but which can be found in South Eastern Europe and Asia Minor, the *loranthus europaeus*, called 'Riemenblume' in Germany, where it has been found in the south-east. It frequently grows on oak trees and has yellow berries. The reader might now say: Ah, the whole matter is quite simple: this, of course, is what Virgil meant. But the matter is actually not so simple: the 'Riemenblume' is bare in winter, and this does not fit in with the 'brumali frigore fronde virere nova' in Virgil. The solution, which is accepted quite generally and to which I cannot provide a better alternative, is that the poet confused the two types.

We must now keep in mind that Virgil only compares the golden bough to mistletoe. Even if it appears that the golden bough is not an invention of Virgil's—and that is what my argument is about—we must still take into account the possibility that the comparison with mistletoe was indeed of his own devising. This should make us a little wary of connecting the entire folkloristic tradition concerning mistletoe with our subject, although this *has* been done. The folklore of the mistletoe is rich—and this is hardly surprising when we think how this curious parasite must have worked on people's imagination. An illustrative example springs to mind in the Celtic religion. In a well-known passage Pliny tells us (*Naturalis Historia* 16, 249ff.) that the Celts regarded the oak mistletoe as particularly sacred and as a cure of all ills. It had to be present at every religious ceremony. Only a priest in white vestments could cut it with a golden sickle, after which two white bulls had to be sacrificed. It was regarded as especially auspicious for fertility.

Another element, that constantly crops up in the same connection, is the death of the Germanic deity Balder, who was miraculously wounded with a sprig of mistletoe. Whoever wants to read a brief account of the event in a broader context will find one in the standard work by Tubeuf which includes a chapter, 'Die Mistel in der Sagendichtung', written by the highly competent Gustav Neckel. A more extensive account is given by Frazer in his *Balder the Beautiful* (1913), by the aforesaid Germanic philologist Neckel in *Die Ueberlieferungen vom Gotte Balder* (1920), and by F. R. Schröder in his *Germanentum und Hellenismus* (1924). More recent works, such as those by the Dutchman Jan de Vries, contain criticisms of the last two studies on points of detail, but accept the main ideas—ideas which are quite enthralling and which the classical philologist can hardly afford to neglect. I cannot go into this more deeply here, however, since there is no direct connection with my subject as it stands at the moment. Nor shall I deal with the folkloristic material on the mistletoe, as long, that is, as there is no definite deeper link between the mistletoe and the golden bough.

The passage in Virgil which now deserves our special attention is VI 408ff. When Aeneas has shown Charon the golden bough we read:

Ille admirans venerabile donum
fatalis virgae longo post tempore visum
caeruleam advertit puppim ripaeque propinquat.

What we are primarily concerned with are the words *longo post tempore visum* which have puzzled many commentators. Had Charon already seen the golden bough in the distant past? 'Certainly not,' says the straight philologist, 'if he had I would have known about it.' The ancients had also reasoned thus. Cornutus observed (in Macrobius 5, 19, 2) that Virgil 'adsuevit poetico more aliqua fingere, ut de aureo ramo'. To begin with Norden could not agree and sought another way out, but in his commentary he states that there was no literary precursor. He bases so peremptory a conclusion on a remark by Kroll, viz. that the poet only added the words 'longo post tempore visum' to persuade the reader that Charon acknowledged the validity of this passport to the underworld! It may seem surprising that Norden should have yielded to such an argument. Apart from the fact that Charon was a daemon and obviously knew more than a common mortal, the passport was clearly valid, and that is something a passport official would have realized even if he had never seen it before. Besides, what do we then do with vs 138, where the bough is called 'Iunoni infernae dictus sacer'? Was this only because the bough appeared in a grove dedicated to Proserpina? But it does not follow from this that (142) 'hoc sibi pulchra *suum* ferri Proserpina *munus* instituit'. Be this as it may, we are here dealing with an existing institution and, in the poet's mind, Charon must have been acquainted with it.

Ovid does not seem to have known what to make of all this. Let us take *Metam.* XIV, where he obviously has Virgil's example before his eyes, although he summarizes briefly and occasionally deviates drastically from it. In vs 113, after the Sibyl has imparted her instructions to Aeneas, he says simply: 'Dixit et auro/ fulgentem ramum in silva Iunonis Avernae/ monstravit iussitque suo divellere trunco'. The ancient commentator Servius was puzzled by the matter too. He provided a long note to vs 136, obviously compiled from still earlier commentaries which included a great deal of fruitless fantasy (Frazer based the title of his rightly famous work *The Golden Bough* on these same fantasies: we cannot go into this here, however.) But Servius begins by saying that those 'qui de sacris Proserpinae scripsisse dicuntur' have seen 'quiddam mysticum' in the tale of the bough. The significance of these words did not escape Norden. He points out that *instituit* (143) is the technical term for the establishment of feasts and rites, and concludes: 'In die Literatur hat erst Vergil das Motto vom goldnen Zweige eingeführt. Er entnahm es einem Brauche in gewissen Mysterien der Persephone (Kore). Ob er die Kenntnis dieses Brauches aus dem Leben oder aus Büchern bezog, lässt sich nicht bestimmt entscheiden; aber da es über alles was Religion und Kultus betraf, gelehrte griechische Werke gab, so ist es das Wahrscheinlichere, das Vergil . . . sein Wissen aus Büchern entnahm und dann die Gelehrsamkeit in Poesie umsetzte.'

Norden's theory is bold indeed. For one thing we are too unfamiliar with Greek-Hellenistic literature—not to mention earlier literature—to be able to state for sure that Virgil did *not* have a literary source. And besides, there is both literary and archeological evidence which I believe to be pointing in a different direction. This will be the subject of the next section.

2. *Evidence outside Virgil*

Let us start with a literary element which did not escape Norden's notice, but whose full significance Norden does not seem to have appreciated. Over a hundred years ago a German scholar pointed out a gloss in Hesychius. When treating the expression χρυσορραγὲς ἔρνος Hesychius explains it as follows: ἀπερρηγμένον ἢ ἀπεστραμμένον ἀπὸ του δένδρου. The German, Schmidt, brought this expression into connection with the golden bough (ἔρνος means 'shoot', 'spray') and, since it forms the end of a hexameter, he thought that it was taken from a poem. Norden flinched from concluding that we here have one of Virgil's literary sources, and so do we. Yet the possibility is somewhat greater than Norden realized.

Hesychius only explains the second component of the compound χρυσορραγές and says 'broken or torn from the tree'. Well and good, but what does the whole compound mean? Liddel and Scott translate the expression as 'a golden branch plucked off'. This, of course, is wrong: just as χρυσοβαφής and χρυσογραφής mean 'embroidered with gold', and χρυσομιγής means 'mixed, interwoven with gold' (of hair), so χρυσορραγής must mean 'broken off with gold'. Do we know of a branch which was broken off with gold? Not, to the best of my knowledge, in the Greek or Roman world: Aeneas breaks off the golden bough with his hand in Virgil (210). Yet we have indeed already come across a similar case: the Celtic priest had to cut off the consecrated mistletoe with a golden sickle. Might the Celts not have brought the rite from their Indo-Germanic land of origin, and were the Greeks also acquainted with it? The question remains open. Be this as it may: we can consider it likely that Hesychius contains a fragment of Greek poetry connected with the sacred mistletoe. What is purely hypothetical, however, is that the golden bough developed from this concept of the mistletoe. And even if it could be proved to have done so, we would still be a long way from the golden bough as a passport to the underworld—which is what we are actually trying to get at.

Perhaps certain archeological data will bring us a little closer to our object. We should first observe that in 1911, in Kolonos Hippios, just north of Athens, where Sophocles' *Oedipus Coloneus* is set, a grave was brought to light in which the deceased was entrusted, amongst other things, with a golden bough. We must keep in mind at this point that Colonus was supposed to contain an entrance to the underworld through which Theseus and Pirithous are said to have descended according to a local tradition, as well, perhaps, as Oedipus at his mysterious death and even Persephone herself when she was abducted by Hades: we need only compare the end of Sophocles' play. But here too we must beware of overhasty conclusions. The golden bough of Colonus has never been described—or at least I have never found a description of it. Consequently we do not know what sort of a branch it was. This is an important point since various branches play a part in connection with death and the underworld, especially in the mysteries— the myrtle branch, for example, the laurel branch and the olive branch. They each have their own particular significance, but it is always different to that of the golden bough in Virgil. According to Diels (*Sibyllinische Blätter*), for instance, the olive branch was the symbol of the *pax deorum* and was consequently especially propitious for putting the gods of the underworld in a conciliatory frame of mind.

This same difficulty appears in two sarcophagus reliefs to which Carl Robert devoted an article entitled 'Der goldene Zweig auf römischen Sarkophagen' in the *Sitzungsberichte der preussischen Akademie* of 1915. This article, a mere three pages long, can hardly have been known to Norden when he published the second edition of his commentary in the same year. Robert identified the golden bough on both coffins. Whoever, without having read the article, jumps to the conclusion that the Roman representations obviously go back to Virgil, would appear to be quite wrong. They have nothing to do with the sixth book of the *Aeneid*. The first case is that of the famous Adonis sarcophagus of the Lateran (Plate I). The relief contains many figures, and I cannot discuss them all here. What interests us is the farewell which Adonis bids Aphrodite on the far left when he is about to fight the boar represented on the right—a fight which will be fatal to him. Aphrodite does try to restrain him from his purpose, but in vain. There is, however, a remarkable detail: in his right hand, which rests on Aphrodite's knee, Adonis holds a leafy branch. Robert sees this as the passport which will enable Adonis to return from Hades to the world of the living. And Helbig, in his *Führer*, cannot suggest a better solution. One might object that this is not a true golden bough since it would seem to be reposing too easily on the bended knee. Yet Virgil has taught us not to underestimate the possibilities of such a bough, and there are indeed certain factors in favour of Robert's hypothesis: I have in mind above all the parallelism between this relief and the second which Robert cites which is also reproduced in Overbeck, *Kunstmythologie Atlas* Taf. XVII, 22). It is a sarcophagus from Vienna on which Pluto's abduction of Persephone is depicted. Pluto has lifted the girl onto his four-in-hand which is led by Hermes. The entrance to the underworld is indicated by the fact that Charon and Cerberus raise their heads among the horses. In addition to this two goddesses are present: Aphrodite and Athena. According to a well-established tradition Aphrodite was on Pluto's side. She holds up a pomegranate, an evil omen since the pomegranate is the symbol of marriage, and it was to be by eating a pomegranate in the underworld that Persephone bound herself to Pluto for ever. Athena, on the other hand, who was well-disposed towards Persephone, is holding up a bough before her which closely resembles the bough on the Adonis sarcophagus. Robert's interpretation—and I cannot think of a better one—is that she is prophetically presenting Persephone with the magic bough 'der ihr die Rückkehr auf die Oberwelt wenigstens für einen Teil des Jahres ermöglicht'.

To these representations we can add an Etrurian gem in Berlin to which Prof. de Waele draws our attention in his dissertation 'The magic staff or rod in Graeco-Italian antiquity'. In Roscher's *Lexikon*, s.v. Psyche, Otto Waser writes next to a not altogether clear reproduction: 'Der unbärtige Hermes ... trägt in der Rechten das Kerykeion, auf seiner Linken eine kleine nackte menschliche Figur, einen Jüngling, der die Rechte adorierend erhebt und in der gesenkten Linken einen Zweig hält.' De Waele again connects this representation with the golden bough, and the chances are high that he is right. Unfortunately, however, we cannot be certain: it could also be an olive branch, for example, and on neither of the sarcophagi would one be immediately inclined to think it was mistletoe. The same applies to a vase from Leningrad, about which Kuhnert wrote in an article on 'Unteritalische Nekyien': 'sie zeigt uns... einen bekränzten Jüngling mit Chlamys, der in der rechten einen grossen Zweig hält, durch den er als flehend den Gottheiten nahend charakterisiert wird; er blickt der Entscheidung harrend auf die mit ihrem Gemahl und dem Seelengeleiter Hermes beratende Persephone'.

I believe that this material should not be ignored, although, admittedly, it does not provide any *certain* information. We have a literary indication that a magic mistletoe very probably appeared in a Greek poem, but we do not know whether it had anything to do with a journey to the underworld. Ancient art provides a number of examples of how someone doomed to die carried a bough in his hand, but since, in antiquity, there were also other boughs which had a religious and, frequently, a magic significance (de

Waele's work is informative on the subject) we are not entitled to equate them with the golden bough without further investigation. We must not forget that both Circe and Hermes possessed an *aurea virga*, and although we cannot dismiss the possibility that they both have the same origin as Virgil's golden bough, it still remains an unfounded hypothesis.

Are we therefore 'au bout de notre Latin'? I do not believe so, but in order to prove this I will have to reach far afield.

Norden, obviously, wondered which mythological figures had gone down to the underworld before Aeneas. Could one of them, he asked himself, have shown Charon a golden bough as a passport? The answer was no. Heracles, Theseus and Pirithous cannot be taken into consideration since they forced their way into Hades. We could think of Orpheus and arguments have sometimes been advanced for regarding an Orphic 'catabasis' as Virgil's source. But we must agree with Norden that these arguments do not hold good. Does this mean that the series of visitors to Hades who then returned to the world of the living is exhausted?

Five years ago I spoke before the Academy about 'Apuleius' tale of Amor and Psyche'.[1] The theory that I then put forward is the basis of what follows, but I can obviously only repeat what is indispensable for my argument.

The tale is well enough known. A royal couple has three daughters. The two eldest marry kings; the youngest, Psyche, is fabulously beautiful but remains unmarried for a long time: nobody dares approach her. Venus is violently jealous and orders Amor to make sure that Psyche marries someone vile. After this she goes for a swim on the bed of the Ocean. In accordance with an oracle of Apollo Psyche marries a mysterious being in a subterranean palace where she is served by invisible hands. She cannot see her husband either: he only appears at dead of night. Rumour has it that he is a serpent. Her marriage is repeatedly described as a wedding of death, although the reader can never really understand why. When Psyche can no longer control her curiosity she lights a lamp at night and, in order to protect herself, she has armed herself with a ... razor. A drop of oil falls on the shoulder of her

[1] Cf. above p. 84-92.

husband, whom she now recognizes as lovely Amor himself. But he resents this breach of trust and leaves Psyche who, in the meantime, has conceived a child. A waterbird, a sort of gull, now plunges to the depths of the Ocean and gives an account of the events to Venus, who is still swimming around after what appears to have been a period of months. Just as remarkable as this fact is the reproach which the bird makes to the goddess, viz. 'that Venus and her whole family have fallen into disrepute owing to their long absence, Amor making love in the mountains and Venus swimming in the sea. Everything on earth has consequently been neglected and has gone to rack and ruin: no marriages are being made; friendship and love for children have disappeared; all that remains is a state of utter squalor and warfare between opposing factions.' Venus then rises from the Ocean, indignant about her son whom she finds in her chamber, grievously ill because of the drop of oil.

Meanwhile Psyche, after a long journey, reaches Venus who covers her with scorn and mockery and gives her four impossible tasks: amongst other things she has to draw the water of life from a spring of the Styx and visit the underworld to get Proserpina to fill a jug with beauty cream for Venus. Fortunately animals help Psyche to perform the labours and there is a 'happy end': Amor and Psyche are united in matrimony on Olympus.

In my paper before the Academy I remarked that the curious and unmotivated reproach of the bird reminded me strongly of an earlier element. In the Sumerian hymn which sings of the journey that Inanna-Ishtar, the prototype of Astarte-Aphrodite-Venus, made to the underworld in order to fetch her beloved Tammuz whom she herself had killed on an impulse, we read: 'After Ishtar, the ruler, had descended to the land from where there is no return, the bull no longer covered the young cow, the male ass no longer mated with the she-ass, the young man lay in his chamber and the maiden lay turned away'.

The similarity did not seem to me to be a mere coincidence. It was once frequently assumed that Amor was killed by Psyche's razor in an earlier version of the tale. Various ancient representations have been found which suggest this, and there are hints of it in Apuleius: the subterranean palace, Amor as a serpent, the theme of the wedding of death, Amor's long and deadly illness after the drop of oil, the quest for the water of life. We can now add that the parallel with the Ishtar myth is still more indicative: just as Ishtar killed her beloved Tammuz and tried to bring him back to life again, so Psyche killed Amor. Indeed, we can even go a step further. For it is not Psyche who really replaces Ishtar, the goddess of love and fertility, but Venus herself. Admittedly she is not said to have gone to the underworld to fetch the water of life: she is said, rather, to have swum on the bed of the Ocean. Surely we see what has happened: a Hellenistic poet has introduced the figure of Psyche into the Ishtar myth. How he got round to doing this will appear in due course. But he found the lament about the desolation of nature too beautiful to be left out, and since Venus herself did in this version not go to the underworld he relegated her for a period of time to the bed of the Ocean. An unfortunate device—but by no means the only one in Apuleius' tale.

Before I take my argument any further, I should make an observation. I can well imagine that one of my readers is thinking: 'I'm not going to let myself be fooled: it is much too far-fetched to believe that a writer like Apuleius—and, we'll soon see, like Virgil—should have anything even remotely to do with Sumerian hymns'. I shall therefore quote three competent scholars who disagree with this view, a German philologist, a classical philologist, and an Orientalist. As early as 1920, in his book *Die Ueberlieferungen vom Gotte Balder*, Gustav Neckel, who had sought a connection between our Virgil passage and a Persian legend on the one hand, and a Norse legend on the other (a connection which I do not regard as impossible, but which is insufficiently relevant for me to go into it here) wrote as follows: 'Der literargeschichtliche Zusammenhang der drei Quellen, insbesondere derjenige Vergils mit den beiden andern, kann im grossen Ganzen nicht zweifelhaft sein. Vergil dürfte den Stoff seines sechsten Buches grösserenteils einem griechischen Dichter, vermutlich der hellenistischen Zeit, verdanken, und dieser hat unter starken 'Orientalischen' Einflüssen gearbeitet, ebenso wie z.B. Aristeides von Milet, der Vorgänger des Apuleius. Die orientalischen Einflüsse aber kamen aus denselben Quellen, die auch die persische und die nordische Dichtung gespeist haben. Welches diese Quellen des genaueren gewesen sind, sehen wir

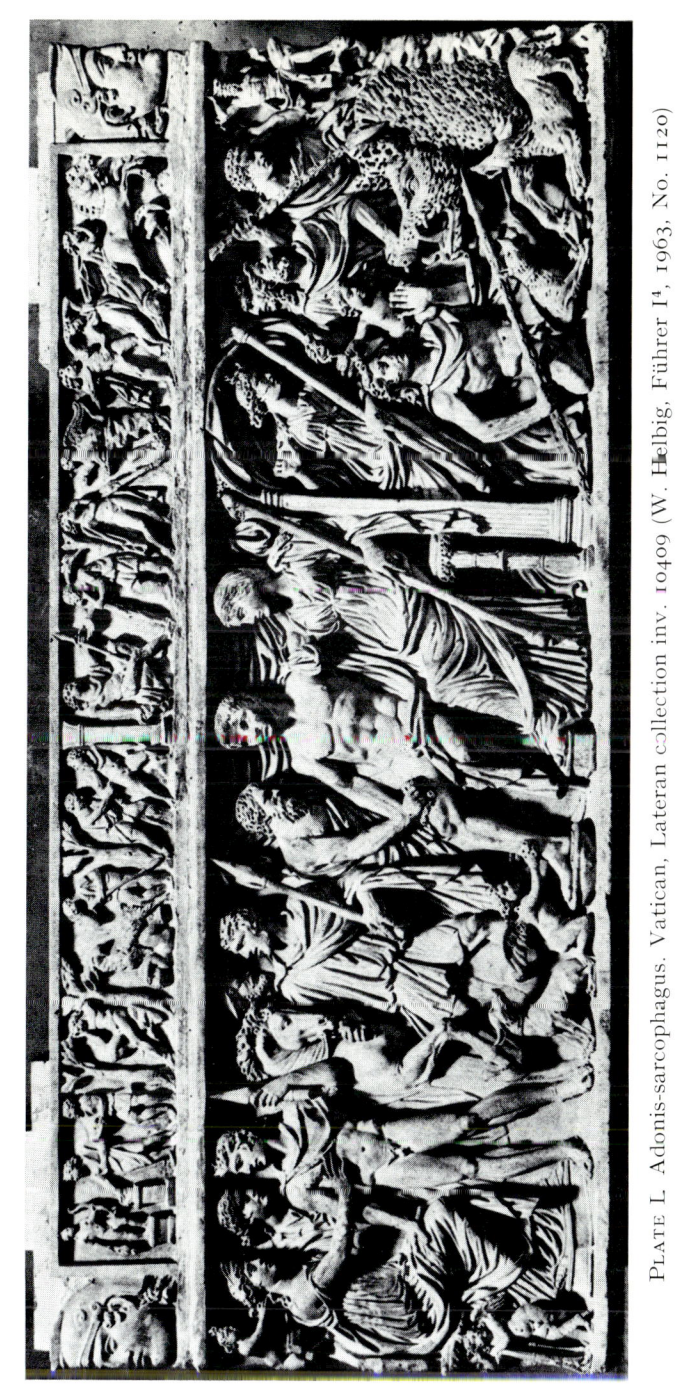

PLATE L. Adonis-sarcophagus. Vatican, Lateran collection inv. 10409 (W. Helbig, Führer I⁴, 1963, No. 1120)

vorerst nicht. Hier grössere Klarheit zu schaffen, ist eine gemeinsame Angelegenheit der germanischen und der klassischen Philologie, die zu ihrer Bewältigung ebensosehr auf einander angewiesen sind wie auf die Hilfe der Orientalisten'. What is interesting is that he later points to Thrace as the land where the link must lie between East and West: that was the same conclusion which I reached myself some time ago by following completely different lines.

Now, in the above quotation there is no specific mention of Babylon and Ishtar. But when, in 1936, Jackson Knight wrote his *Cumaean Gates*, he referred to a connection with the epic of Gilgamesh and, in his *Roman Virgil* (I quote from the second edition of 1944) we read: 'The Sumerians had other literature which, by whatever way, affected Greek poetry, especially the *Epic of Gilgamesh* and the *Descent of Ishtar*. Saga, which consists of stories of fact and true myth, developed normally from cult and plain fairy tales also, all affect each other; and certain favourite forms are found which attract into themselves new material. The *Iliad* of Homer, perhaps finished in the eighth century B.C., reflects the siege of Babylon that occurred before 2000 B.C.; and the *Odyssey* of Homer the stories, earlier still, about journeys of both Gilgamesh and Ishtar to the world of the dead, stories that were originally cult-myths, designed to secure happiness after death'. (Compare here Norden's commentary, p. 168, n. 8: he too sees a striking analogy with the golden bough in the epic of Gilgamesh). In 1939 there appeared the book by my compatriot, the late lamented Orientalist Frankfort, entitled *Cylinder Seals*, where he writes, on the subject of plants which sprout from the Babylonian graves: 'They may either signify in a general manner the connection between the god and the life of vegetation, or they may represent the "golden bough" which Aeneas had to break before he was taken across the Styx, just as Gilgamesh had to fetch something from a nearby grove before his boat journey'—and he here quotes Jackson Knight's *Cumaean Gates*. Now, in my view the plants on graves have nothing to do with our own subject, and although the story of Gilgamesh perhaps does, the connection is so remote that we can let it rest. My intention was simply to illustrate that to establish a link between the catabasis of Aeneas, that of Psyche and that of Ishtar is not as ludicrous as one might think.

Where, in the meantime, does this get my argument? Does the golden bough play a part in Apuleius or in the fragments of the Ishtar hymn known to us? No, it does not. Yet there are indications that, in the course of time, it did find its way into the Ishtar myth. These indications will be the subject of the third and last section.

3. *Reminiscences in fairy tales*

We find a vast quantity of fairy tales throughout Europe, as well as in certain areas outside Europe, which have some, and frequently many, traits in common with Apuleius' tale of Amor and Psyche (if I consider that story a fairy tale this must not be regarded as a partisan choice in the discussion of the true character of the episode—that would be a subject in itself). Of course, in their peregrinations through the centuries they have undergone every sort of change and have sometimes been mutilated beyond recognition. Five years ago I maintained that they ultimately went back to a contamination of two stories: one was the story of Ishtar and Tammuz, and the other an Indo-Germanic fairy tale in which a witch tries to impede the marriage between two young people by assigning the girl, who is in her power, all sorts of impossible tasks. A year later, in 1955, there appeared the work of the Swedish folklorist Jan-Öjvind Swahn, entitled *Cupid and Psyche*. With admirable perseverance the author spent ten years gathering all kindred fairy tales and obtained 1,137 variants. He did not, of course, publish the entire text of each, but, after giving a survey of all the themes, he lists the fairy tales in 160 pages according to country of origin, and he notes the source, and, when possible, the exact locality, finally to devote a special column to recurrent motifs.

The second part of the book consists of interesting observations which are, however, of no direct relevance to our subject. I believe I am right in saying that Virgil's name does not appear. But in my view the first part points to a number of conclusions which have escaped Swahn's notice. We immediately see not only that the journey to the underworld appears in many of these fairy tales, but that there are numerous reminiscences of the dead husband. The snake theme, which we also get in Apuleius, is fairly common. In Hungary, moreover, the girl marries a black man, in Arabia,

Greece (Crete, Myconos, Melos and Chios), in Turkey, Italy, Spain, Portugal and Mexico a negro, in Crete and in Italy also a Moor (the negro and the Moor often represent a dead man); in Georgia in the Caucasus it is specifically a dead youth whom she marries. What is very striking is that this theme appears exclusively in the Mediterranean countries, while there is no known example in Germany, Scandinavia and other Western European countries, in spite of the fact that most of the fairy tales are indigenous there. This strongly suggests that the theme of the marriage of death was not a part of the Indo-Germanic fairy tale. Nor, on the other hand, does if fit in with the Ishtar myth. It belongs, rather, to that later insertion, the Psyche episode. Here I can only say a few words on a subject treated at greater length in the year-book of the Academy. Ishtar herself had killed Tammuz; originally it was Aphrodite-Venus who must have killed Eros-Amor and went in person to fetch the water of life for him—we found a reminiscence of this in her protracted stay on the bed of the Ocean. A later adapter then gave the dead youth Amor a bride, thanks to a tradition to be found above all in the Danube countries and which is as alive today as it was in remote antiquity.

The theme of the water of life appears in at least twenty variants from the whole of Scandinavia, including Finland, from France and Italy, from Russia, Turkey and Persia. We do not find it, however, among the 110 German or the 55 English ones. Although this motif spread across Scandinavia (from Finland?) it is primarily indigenous, like the death theme, in the East and the South. It is always the girl who is sent to the underworld—a clear parallel with Psyche—and it should be pointed out that we also possess some remarkable links aside from the fairy tales reminiscent of the older tradition according to which the goddess of love herself went to the underworld. In the 41st Orphic hymn we read that Demeter descended in person to Hades when her daughter was abducted by Pluto. Another Orphic tradition ascribes this role to Hecate. A still more explicit example is in Aristides, Apuleius' younger contemporary, who assures us that Aphrodite was also said to have descended to Hades 'to redeem Adonis from Persephone', whereby Aphrodite (Venus) would already have taken the place of Ishtar, while Tammuz would have been replaced by her beloved Adonis, but not yet by Eros-Amor. We get the impression, too, that the contamination of the fairy tale by the old myth cannot have occurred so very early, although we cannot tell even approximately when the Psyche figure was adopted in this context.

But now we must at last return to the golden bough. Here, too, I believe, the fairy tales have something to tell us.

When the girl embarks on her adventures and her journey she often asks—usually of her father—for something to take with her. This theme appears in some 400 variants. In almost half of them it is a rose, sometimes another flower or a flower in general. In the other half she asks for other things, which include, as Swahn puts it, 'some exceedingly queer objects'. He does not give an actual explanation of the girl's frequently curious request; he only assumes that it was originally for a rose, but that this was later found to be too simple and that other, more fantastic or expensive presents were devised. I admit that this might have played a part, as, for example, when we read of a golden rose or a diamond flower (see column II of the table attached to this article). But when, from France to Finland, from Flanders to Hungary, we get dozens of variants (column V; N.B. continued under IV)—a singing or a speaking rose, singing or speaking leaves or fruits, a singing or speaking bough, etc.—it is most unlikely, in my mind, that the same arbitrary fantasy was at work in the most distant areas. We should rather assume a common source.

In the table I have included all the variants which seem worthy of notice for one reason or another. In the cases in column I the number 3 plays a part. It does not seem to be limited to a particular area—we find it in the South, in Spain and Italy, in the North, in Sweden and Norway, in the East, in Hungary, Croatia and Slovakia. We cannot conclude that this theme is connected with a golden bough which would then have had three leaves, but we are tempted to think of Hermes' golden staff which is called τριπέτηλος, 'three-leaved', in the Homeric Hermes hymn. That the golden staff has been considered—and is still considered—puzzling because of this is evident, for example, in de Waele. I shall not go into this here, but I only wish to point out that even if Hermes' magic staff was made of gold, it originally had an organic life: the number three in these fairy tales would then constitute yet another basis for the hypothesis that the golden staff of Hermes, who led the dead into the underworld, was once identical to Aeneas' golden bough.

The second column is dominated by the gold motif. I have already said that we must exercise caution here, but it is interesting to see that (under d) we even have the 'golden bough', which will be singing under Vb 6. The bough, it must be emphasized, appears in every column.

The bough theme prevails in column III. After boughs with roses or other flowers, we get different boughs, including the olive branch which I have already discussed and the hazel branch, which still plays a leading role in folklore, if only because it is used by preference as a divining rod. Finally we get the magic staff. For that matter, magic comes into play elsewhere too, as we see from Vb 9 where we have 'a blue singing plant which breaks iron', and which is reminiscent of the mistletoe which opens all locks in modern folklore—something which could well be an extension of its function as passport to the underworld.

The midwinter-theme in column IV is poorly represented and I do not wish to attribute too much weight to it. Yet it is sufficiently widespread not to be wholly negligible, and Virgil also mentions the mistletoe which 'brumali frigore viret' (205).

Column V is particularly remarkable. From the singing or speaking rose it passes on to the singing, playing, tinkling leaves (or bough or plant or tree), and from suchlike fruits to heterogeneous objects—obviously devices whose purpose is somehow to rationalize the more incomprehensible side of the matter—in order to lead, via ringing golden bells, to 'something that is heard and not seen' in Finland.

Whoever views these variants objectively will, I feel, be convinced that it is quite impossible that they all developed out of the plain rose. As a prototype I see before me—odd though this may sound—a bough, probably golden, with (three?) moving leaves, which are saying something, possibly with a metallic tinkle, and are consequently reminiscent of bells (cf. not only e 1 and 2 in Germany, but also c 3 in Hungary). I admit that this is strange, but is it not exactly what Virgil also says: a golden bough *lento vimine*, with leaves which tinkle in the gentle breeze (*leni crepitabar brattea vento*)? There is, however, this difference: the bough seems to be saying more than a mere tinkle. What can that be? It is hardly a problem. We are acquainted with speaking leaves from elsewhere, and every reader will surely remember Dodona and the oracle in the oak. Aeschylus speaks of αἱ προσήγοροι δρῦες, Sophocles of ἡ πολύγλωσσος δρῦς—in the singular, and indeed, there was only one ὑψίκομος δρῦς which Homer also mentions. How the oak originally delivered its oracles is something we do not know; Kurt Latte (art. 'Orakel' in Pauly-Wissowa) says: 'unsere Nachrichten über die Form, in der das in ältester Zeit geschah, schwanken seltsam'. It has usually been assumed from what evidence we have that men listened to the rustle of the leaves as the wind passed through them. This does not seem impossible: a writer of the ninth century, Moses Choronensis, who wrote a history of Armenia, says that there the priests delivered oracles according to whether certain cypresses were swayed violently or gently by the wind, and the Old Testament also alludes to such tree oracles (2 Sam. 5, 24). Ovid, as usual, gives a taller story when he tells us that an oak stood on Aegina 'de semine Dodonaeo', and that, after a prayer was pronounced, 'intremuit ramisque sonum sine flamine motis alta dedit quercus': it was therefore the oak which made a sound, since the boughs moved 'sine flamine', without the wind passing through them. If someone asks whether it is possible that what is said of a tree can also be applied to a lopped-off branch, the answer must be yes, for Apollodorus tells us that when the ship the Argo was built, the goddess Athena attached to the prow a φωνῆεν φηγοῦ τῆς Δωδωνίδης ξύλον, 'a speaking piece of wood from the Dodonean oak'.

I believe that the chief character in Apuleius' source, whether direct or remote, must have been equipped with such a magic bough—of mistletoe or something else. Is the origin to be sought in the Ishtar myth or in the Indo-Germanic fairy tale? This is a difficult question since a trip to the underworld appeared very probably in both sources—and that was one of the causes of the contamination. From what can this be deduced? From another peculiarity in Apuleius' story. In Apuleius, as we have seen, Venus assigns four labours to Psyche. This has attracted a great deal of attention because, in all the fairy tales, the witch only gives three. Now, everyone agrees that the third and the fourth form a doublet.

The third time Psyche is sent to the top of a rock where she finds a spring of the Styx in order to fill a jar with the water of life. The fourth labour is to ask Proserpina in the underworld to fill a casket with *formonsitas*, 'beauty cream'. There is unanimous agreement that the first trip was only to the summit of the rock because the author could hardly let Psyche go twice to the underworld. In my view we are here dealing with the confluence of two sources: in the Oriental myth the journey was to the underworld to fetch the water of life for the dead lover, and in the fairy tale the witch dispatched the girl to fetch a beauty aid (a Finnish variant speaks of eye-ointment) from below.

So much for the journey to Hades. But does the golden bough come from the Ishtar myth or the tale of the witch? One can argue in favour of either view. As far as the former is concerned, we saw that similar concepts were alive in Babylon. But to my mind there can be little doubt that we should here prefer the Indo-Germanic fairy tale. Precisely the description of Ishtar's visit to her sister Ereshkigal, the Babylonian Persephone, has been extensively preserved, and there is no mention of a bough. But let us look at columns III and V of our table. While the theme of the dead bridegroom, as well as that of the journey to the underworld, appears especially in the countries situated on the eastern basin of the Mediterranean, we do not find the theme of the bough (which is by no means uncommon) either in Greece or in Italy, in Turkey or in Russia. My conclusion, therefore, is that the Hellenistic poet responsible for the contamination of both sources, found in the fairy tale the magic bough which he gave to Psyche (whom he introduced), but which Apuleius omitted.

Yet Apuleius was familiar with the poem and imitated it freely (I speak of a poem on the unproven assumption that a fragment of it survives in the Hesychius quotation; it could equally well have been a fabula Milesiaca, however.) Whether that poet already mentioned a mistletoe is something we do not know with any certainty. A striking fact is that, as far as we can see from Swahn, the mistletoe is never mentioned in the fairy tales. On the other hand it is perfectly conceivable that in ancient times, when the fairy tale originated, the name of the sacred mistletoe was taboo and had to be paraphrased. Something else struck me too in this connection. According to Jacob Grimm, in his *Deutsche Mythologie*, the Welsh call the mistletoe *pren puraur*, 'the tree of pure gold'. This is all the more remarkable since only the green mistletoe with white berries is known in Wales. Does the term 'golden bough' for the mistletoe have a prehistory? Or is this Welsh name a reminiscence of Virgil?

However this may be, the golden bough itself certainly has a long prehistory. That Virgil took it from a Greek manual on ancient cults is something I cannot believe, any more than I can believe that he invented it himself. I have not been able to prove that he had a literary precursor at this point, but I hope to have made it plausible.

THE GOLDEN BOUGH

(204 of the c. 400 cases in which the young woman obtains something to take on her journey)

Holland, Flanders, England, Ireland, Denmark, Norway, Sweden, Latvia, Lithuania, Estonia, Finland, Germany, Tyrol, Hungary, Rumania, Bulgaria, Czechoslovakia, Croatia, Poland, Russia, France, Spain, Portugal, Italy, Greece, Turkey.

I	II	III	IV	V
a 1. three roses (Germany, Hungary, Croatia, Spain, Italy, Porto Rico)	a 1. golden rose (Germany)	a 1. bough with roses (see I c 1)	a rose in midwinter (Germany, France, Poland)	a 1. singing rose (Holland, Tyrol)
2. white ribbon with three roses (Denmark)	2. golden carnation (Italy)	2. bough with 100 flowers (Rumania)	b 1. bough with buds in midwinter (Hungary)	2. speaking rose (France)
3. red ribbon with three dancing golden roses (Sweden)	3. golden wreath (Norway)	3. bough with nuts (Germany)	2. 3 red apples in midwinter	b 1. singing, ringing leaf (Germany, Norway)
4. three garlands of roses in flower (Sweden)	4. diamond flower (Sweden)	2. olive branch (Germany)	c flower that never dies (Finland)	2. singing, dancing, playing leaves (Latvia, Tyrol)
5. rose with 3 buds (France)	b 1. golden grapes (Flanders, Germany, Turkey)	3. bough which strikes the head (Germany, Hungary)	d 1. dancing, singing bird (Germany, Lithuania, Berber)	3. playing leaves, singing grass (Germany)
b 1. three nuts (Norway)	2. golden apple (Norway, Iceland)	4. hazel branch (Germany)	2. bird of gold and silver which can sing and speak (France)	4. leaf of singing laurel (France)
2. three red apples (Sweden)	3. golden tree (Germany)	c 1. magic olive branch (Fr. Canada)	3. speaking violin	5. bough of singing tree (France)
3. three singing leaves (Sweden, France)	c 1. golden bird (Poland)	2. magic staff (Finland, Sweden)	4. speaking book (Norway)	6. golden, ringing bough (Germany)
c 1. bough with 3 roses (Germany, Slovakia)	d golden bough (see V b 6)		e 1. golden bells (Germany)	7. singing, tinkling tree (Germany)
2. bough with 3 acorns (Germany)			2. ringing bells (Germany)	8. singing, frisking lily tree (Flanders)
			f something that is heard and not seen (Finland)	9. blue singing plant which breaks iron (France)
				c 1. singing pear (France)
				2. ringing peach, laughing apple (Hungary)
				3. speaking grapes, laughing apples, peaches tinkling like silver bells (Hungary)

8

VIII

THE GODDESS CERES AND HER ROMAN MYSTERIES

France continues to enrich us with books, *doctos, Iupiter, et laboriosos*, on the history of Roman religion and dealing with individual gods and goddesses. We have had in succession A. Bruhl on *Liber Pater* (1953), J. le Gall on *Tiberinus Pater* (in the second part of his work *Le Tibre, fleuve de Rome dans l'Antiquité*, 1953), R. Schilling on *Venus* (1954), J. Gagé on Roman Apollo (1955), and now H. le Bonniec has joined them with a book of nearly five hundred pages on the goddess Ceres.[1] And it is no wonder that with such men as Jean Bayet and Georges Dumézil leading the way, to name only those to whom this particular author owes so much, many young French classicists should have been stirred to study the history of Roman religion. It is a phenomenon of which we outsiders gratefully reap the fruits.

Now I had good reason indeed to read this book with special interest. Twelve years ago I investigated the real meaning of the expression *Initia Cereris* and devoted eighteen pages to what I thought was the answer.[2] Le Bonniec repeatedly refers to this short article,[3] with the purpose it seems of refuting it, as it befits a disciple of Dumézil, of course because I had dared in this 'étude très suggestive' (p. 28) to attribute the origin of the goddess Ceres to some *numen* of fertility. 'Il n'est pas de thèse plus fausse', so we read at the conclusion of the first part,[4] 'que celle qui prétend rendre compte, à partir de *numina* spécialisés, de la genèse des grandes divinités romaines.' Here I must point out, or rather repeat, that I have nowhere maintained that all the Roman gods

---

[1] Henri Le Bonniec, *Le Culte de Cérès à Rome* (*Études et Commentaires* XXVII), Paris, Klincksieck, 1958.
[2] *Meded. Kon. Vlaamse Akad. v. Wet., Lett. en Schone Kunsten v. België*, Kl. der Lett. 10 No. 4 (1948); English version in *Studies in Roman Literature, Culture, and Religion*, 1956, pp. 150ff.
[3] pp. 28-33; 182f.; 209; 251; 392; 395; 425-430.
[4] p. 209; cf. p. 30.

derived from such *numina*. I have denied this again and again.[5] But how far this author has really proved what he set out to prove we shall see later.

I should be failing in a pleasant duty if I did not make it quite clear not only that several parts of this work seem to me worthy of everyone's attention but also that here and there it offers what I find decisive solutions of difficult questions. First I should like to observe that Le Bonniec (pp. 60ff.) against Wissowa and others seems to me to have effectively made the point that the festival of the *feriae Sementivae* lasted only one day. Thus Lydus was wrong, Varro and Ovid right. He has hit the mark, if I am not mistaken, with his interpretation of Vergil's lines *Georg.* I, 338-350 (pp. 134ff.), where Ceres plays such a large part. He is very probably right in thinking that the poet in this passage after a brief mention of the *Cerialia*, passes on to a description of the *Ambarvalia*. Though perhaps the arguments he adduces on pp. 218ff. in defence of Dionysius of Halicarnassus' account (*Ant. Rom.* 6, 17, 2-4, cf. 6, 94, 3) of the temple of Ceres, Liber, and Libera are not such as to convince everybody, they are important and not easy to reject. Rather easier to accept is his discussion (pp. 266ff.) of the site of the temple. Against Huelsen and most of the archaeologists he proves by valid arguments that the site of the temple was the same as what is today that of the Church of St. Maria in Cosmedin, a view which was put forward some decades ago by R. Lanciani and G. B. Giovenale. Very clear too is his account (pp. 312ff.) of the actual games of the *Cerealia* except indeed in those pages (328-330) where he discusses the religious significance of these games. There he gets into difficulties, uncertain what to make of the interpretation proposed by Piganiol, who had written: [6] *Le grand problème est de savoir comment s'exerce l'efficacité religieuse des jeux. Dirons-nous que les dieux y prennent plaisir comme les hommes? ou bien s'agit-il d'une opération magique agissant directement, pour les ranimer, sur les énergies naturelles ou divines? Cette dernière solution est celle vers laquelle nous orientent ces recherches.'* Even according to Le Bonniec (p. 330) it may be that this interpretation,

[5] E.g. *Mnemos.* 4a Ser. 5, 1952, pp. 305f.; *Historia Mundi* 3, 1954, pp. 488ff. Which of us can be accused of 'généralisations' (p. 30)?
[6] A. Piganiol, *Recherches sur les jeux romains*, 1923, avant-propos p. V.

'qui se fonde sur les résultats des enquêtes menées chez les peuples "primitifs" ', may be valid for some archaic phase of Latin superstition. But, so he consoles us, 'c'est l'exception...' Doubtless it is the foxes let loose about the circus, 'their backs aflame with burning torches', which disturb our author. In other respects, however, he has to admit that it is *no* exception. For in dealing with the nuts strewn at the Cerialia (p. 115, 5), he confesses, 'il ne s'agit pas d'un "symbole"' (as A. Pestalozza had urged) 'mais d'un rite magico-religieux',[7] and again, p. 142, 'il n'est pas douteux que ces rites' (performed in the rustic Ceres cult) 'soient d'origine magique', or cf. p. 209. On pp. 337ff. I find his reasoning persuasive in connection with the festival twice celebrated in Sicily in honour of Ceres and her daughter, where he shows that τὴν καταγωγὴν τῆς Περσεφόνης (Diod. Sic. 5, 4, 5) is not to be interpreted, as Nilsson and Bayet would have it, as her descent to the underworld, but rather as her return from exile. Finally, to mention only the most important points, I was much impressed by Le Bonniec's pages (381ff.) about the Greek rites of Ceres, where he seeks to show that mysteries of Ceres did not exist in Rome before the end of the third century B.C. How far he has succeeded in demonstrating this will be considered below. But it may be granted at once that he has rightly objected to the manner in which many other scholars including myself have assumed that Greek priestesses took part in the Ceres cult at Rome at a much earlier date, without producing clear evidence. Hence, in what follows it will be necessary to examine this question more closely.

All the same anyone who thinks that all the questions have been solved by these voluminous and accurate investigations is in my opinion mistaken. First, I cannot but think that Le Bonniec, after his careful investigations of individual points and separate formulation of their results, has not taken the time to compare them with one another. For how otherwise could it have happened that they often do not agree with one another and that Le Bonniec seems to be in dispute with himself? I must give some examples.

[7] I wonder that Le Bonniec should make so much (p. 117) of 'la *course* des renards, non pas au hasard, mais en circle, puisqu'ils sont lâchés dans le Cirque', where their 'race' (p. 119) 'est comparable au cercle rituel de la lustration'. As if there would be any rhyme or reason about the course taken by the wretched animals, scattering about the Circus, tortured by the flames!

First example:

p. 82: 'On peut supposer, sans avoir le moyen de le démontrer, que le sacrifice du porc par les mariés, attesté par Varron (*R.R.* 2, 4, 9f. '*nuptiarum initio antiqui reges ac sublimes viri in Etruria in coniunctione nuptiali nova nupta et novus maritus primum porcum immolant. Prisci quoque Latini, etiam Graeci in Italia idem factitasse videntur*') pour l'Étrurie et l'ancien Latium, était offert à Tellus et à Cérès. La victime conviendrait particulièrement à ces deux déesses.' [N.B. The words here quoted from Varro are in the original preceded by: '...*quod initiis Cereris porci immolantur, et quod initiis pacis, foedus cum feritur, porcus occiditur, et quod nuptiarum*...etc.']

p. 428f. (against me!): 'D'autre part le masculin qu'utilise Varron: '*initiis Cereris porci immolantur*' est un argument de poids en faveur d'Eleusis' [that is, Varro is not considering the mysteries of the Roman Ceres but of the Eleusinian] 'où on immolait des porcs à Déméter, alors que le rituel romain, toujours attentif á approprier le sexe de la victime á celui de la divinité, n'a jamais immolé que des truies à Cérès. Sans préjugé, si on ne connaissait pas par les textes des Lois l'existence des mystères de la Cérès romaine, aurait-on jamais pensé, en lisant cette phrase, à d'autres mystères qu'à ceux d'Eleusis?'

Who, I ask, in such a context would not have written '*sans préjugé*'? The same author who on pp. 428f. claims that the pigs sacrificed at the *Initia Cereris* could not have been sacrificed to the Roman Ceres, for whom only sows were appropriate, nevertheless elsewhere in the same book (p. 82) sees no objection to supposing that at a wedding a hog was sacrificed to this same Roman Ceres. And that even when the words quoted in both places form part of the same passage of Varro's. Besides, hardly anyone will fail to notice that the whole question is wrongly discussed, for the obvious reason that *porca*, which time and again stands for a *porcus femina* or female pig,[8] can even more simply be represented by *porcus* used as feminine gender.[9] This, for instance, is how we must understand Horace's words,[10] '*Tellurem porco, Silvanum lacte piabant*', for Tellus' victims too were usually sows. In any case the argument against me completely falls to the ground. But I will be coming back to this.

[8] E.g. Cic. *Leg.* 2, 57, a passage quoted by Le Bonniec himself p. 104; cf. also Cato *agric.* 134, 1.
[9] Cf. Festus p. 364 L.: '*Etiam in commentariis sacrorum pontificalium frequenter est hic ovis, et haec agnus, ac porcus. Quae non ut vitia, sed ut antiquam consuetudinem testantia, debemus accipere.*'
[10] *Ep.* 2, 1, 143. Cf. Wissowa, *Rosch. Lex.* 5, 333, 42ff.

Second example:

p. 71 (he is discussing the *sacrum Cereale*): 'Qualifié de *Cereale*, le rite semblerait appartenir en propre à Cérès, dont le flamine officie. Pourtant Tellus y participe, et, comme toujours dans les rites communs aux deux déesses, elle est nommée la première, revendiquant ainsi la primauté. D'ailleurs le sacrifice n'est peut-être qualifié de *Cereale* que parce que le prêtre en est le flamine *Cerealis*. Tellus emprunte les offices du prêtre de Cérès, mais cela ne veut pas dire qu'elle passe au second plan.'

p. 129 (he is discussing the same *sacrum*): 'Rien n'oblige d'ailleurs à comprendre que l'adjectif marque l'appartenance à Cérès: si on l'écrit avec une minuscule, il signifie tout simplement "relatif aux céréales": on traduirait alors' [i.e. Serv. *Georg.* 1, 21: *Fabius Pictor hos deos enumerat, quos invocat flamen sacrum Cereale faciens Telluri et Cereri etc.*] 'Le flamine célébrant, en l'honneur de Tellus et de Cérès, le rite céréalien,...'

Nobody will blame the author for wavering between two different interpretations. What causes me some disquiet, however, is that on p. 129 he seems to have forgotten what he had said not long previously. Such things happen not infrequently in this book. Often they are of minor importance, and I shall not enumerate them all, but they are signs of a work too little pondered and with its parts badly balanced. There are two more examples, however, which I cannot pass over, since they concern my own line of discussion.

Third example:

In my article (*Meded.* pp. 12ff.; *Studies* pp. 157ff.) I had put forward a conjecture about the possibility that for political reasons the *Initia Cereris* as they were called were moved after a certain time from one day to another. I prefaced my conjecture with these words: 'I would point out emphatically that this is indeed based on a combination of facts which are still hypothetical and that the remainder of my argument by no means stands or falls with this hypothesis.' Listen to Le Bonniec's refutation:

p. 427, 'Que dire du changement de date des *initia Cereris*, absolument contraire au conservatisme religieux des Romains? Une fête se transforme, prend à la longue une signification nouvelle, mais garde

p. 449 (he is writing about the *Ieiunium Cereris*): 'Ainsi donc cette fête, d'abord célébrée seulement tous les cinq ans, était devenue annuele. En l'absence de tout autre renseignement, il est impossible

sa place dans le calendrier. M. Wagenvoort serait en peine de citer un autre example dans la religion romaine, peut-être même dans toute autre religion d'un changement de date aussi surprenant.'

de préciser à quelle date se fit ce changement et pour quelle raison. Il faut remarquer qu'on n'a pas seulement modifié la périodicité du rite, mais aussi la date de sa célébration.'

Who would not be baffled at reading and comparing these two passages? First I am virtually challenged to produce a single example of such a change from any of the world's religions. (Will it not immediately occur to anyone that Christmas Day was celebrated at first on 6 January and later on 25 December? [11] Secondly, the author himself quotes a shining example from the Roman religion itself. I should like to know what purpose is served by such type of argumentation. Add to this that my conjecture, not certain but by no means without a semblance of truth, does much less violence to the traditional continuity of feast days than (on the testimony of M. Le Bonniec himself) was done to the *Ieiunium Cereris* when it was transferred from the beginning of the year to 4 October. For here it is a question of days thus casually changed, but if my conjecture is correct, the *Initia Cereris*, when they became public, were indeed transferred from 19 April to the *Sacrum Cereris*, an annual summer celebration, but the holiday in the month of April continued to be held as sacred to Ceres. Almost the same procedure, so far as the change of day was concerned, is to be seen in most temple birthdays, which were transferred to other dates after the restoration of the temples.[12]

My fourth example of inconsistency plunges us into the middle of things, being concerned with the very proposition mentioned above, in which this book contends that no theory could be more false '*que celle qui prétend rendre compte, à partir de* numina *spécialisés, de la genése des grandes divinités romaines*'. Again and again the author returns to this point. But look at the difficulties he gets into, how he wavers and vacillates:

p. 209: 'Cérès n'*est* pas un *numen*, mais elle *a* un *numen*. *Cereris numen*, dit Ciceron'.

p. 206: "Cérès peut se définir comme un pouvoir de Tellus, un *numen Telluris*".

[11] Cf. e.g. E. Norden, *Die Geburt des Kindes*, pp. 33-40.
[12] Cf. Wissowa, *R.u.K.*² 106; 123; 155; 197, 4; 202; 227; 295, 5.

p. 150: '...dans le rituel le plus ancien que nous possédions, Cérès nous apparaît bien comme une puissance personnelle, comme une vraie déesse. Ce n'est en aucune façon un *numen* émetteur de *mana;* ce n'est pas une force que le paysan chercherait à capter par des pratiques d'une efficacité automatique.'

p. 461... 'La divinité ne se confond pas avec l'objet: elle déploie son activité dans l'objet. On peut concevoir que son mode d'action soit animiste ou dynamiste, sans en conclure qu'elle même n'est qu'un *mana* ou un *numen* impersonnel. Cérès n'est pas une force magique puisqu'elle reçoit un culte proprement religieux.'

p. 252 '...la puissance secrète de la Terre qui donne la vie gagnait, à n'être pas réduite aux dimensions de l'homme, une véritable grandeur: cette force créatrice universelle avait quelque chose de vraiment divin.'

p. 330 'Il est possible que cette conception' [evidently of M. Piganiol, according to whom in the *Ludi Cereales* '*il s'agit d'une opération magique agissant directement, pour les ranimer, sur les énergies naturelles ou divines*'] 'qui se fonde sur les résultats des enquêtes menées chez les peuples dits "primitifs", rende compte de croyances latines très archaïques...'

I could quote more but this will be enough. What does it tell us? First, Tellus is a goddess and possesses a *numen*. This *numen* is Ceres, but Ceres too is a goddess and possesses a *numen*. And this *numen* undoubtedly is a goddess—and so on *ad infinitum*. Whence the confusion? From Le Bonniec's constant failure, and not his alone, to distinguish between the origin of a goddess to be traced back to the earliest antiquity and her status as attested in history by written evidence. When he declares that Ceres is not some magic force for the very reason that she is worshipped religiously, I entirely agree, so long as it is understood between us that we are discussing the period of recorded history. What was before that can be reached only by conjecture. And the conjecture is not a frivolous one, since it is based not only on the etymology of the noun but also on certain analogies both Roman and foreign. On which point we shall see below that there is a really remarkable likeness between our respective opinions.

In the second place the passages quoted show Le Bonniec as one of those for whom the word *mana* is like a red rag to a bull, though that other word *tabu* derived from the same areas of anthropology is more kindly received by him (p. 421). So let us dismiss that poor little word, since it is right to spare another man's religious scruples, and speak of the secret force of Terra ('la puissance secrète de la Terre'), since it means exactly the same. One thing Le Bonniec can be charged with, though, is that he more than once gives a distorted account of my views, as when he writes (p. 31), 'Pour obtenir un sens acceptable, il faudrait parler d'un *numen* de genre animé, mais *indéterminé*. Ce ne peut être le cas du *cerus neutre de M. Wagenvoort; ce ne serait pas le cas du *ceres neutre de K. Brugmann qui, pour être promu déesse, devrait lui aussi faire son stage de *numen* inerte et sans vie, ce qui est inconcevable.' Numen inerte? Numen *inerte?* Where I ask in all my work is there any word of an 'inert' *numen?* No, *numina* are never inert, which is more than can be said of gods and goddesses. Following Pfister I explained (*Rom. Dyn.* p. 74) that *numen* properly means 'motion', and added, 'As *numen* is known only by its effects and manifestations, i.e. by "movements" in the most general sense, so *numen* in its original meaning is the particular power and force which is manifested in any movement whatsoever.' Thus if every *numen* is not always moving (compare what I wrote about the spears of Mars [13] this is not to be put down to inertia but to a certain restraint. For certain *numina* are sometimes spoken of as acting only during short moments.

But neither is a *numen* animated with a divine intelligence ('une puissance personnelle, comme une vraie déesse') nor do I understand how it could be. Let Ceres for instance be 'la force créatrice de la Terre' (p. 26) or '*vis creatrix Telluris*' (p. 34), or '*vis seminis*' (p. 38), 'la puissance secrète de la Terre' (p. 252); 'une force vague, mystérieuse, insaissable bien que concrète' (p. 457); 'la force de croissance immanente aux fruges', 'une force

---

[13] *Rom. Dyn.* pp. 75ff. To quote only one other example, Pliny (*N.H.* 34, 137) relates: 'The Servilius family, distinguished in our Annals, possesses a bronze *triens* which it 'feeds' with gold and silver, both of which the coin consumes. I have been unable to discover its origin or nature. I put down the actual words of the elder Messala about it: "The family of the Servilii have a sacred *triens* to which they every year offer attentive and magnificent sacrifices. They say that it is sometimes seen to have grown and sometimes to have shrunk, and from this they are able to foretell honour or decline for the family" '. The nature of numen could hardly be more clearly described, though the word itself is not used. The bronze coin is carefully tended, it grows and shrinks of its own accord, and is certainly not motionless. Yet not even Le Bonniec could maintain that a god or any really 'personal' force was hidden in it.

intérieure aux récoltes'—I have nothing against it, provided we both agree that we are talking about a fairly remote antiquity. Had not I myself written that Ceres got her name 'as growth-producing' (*Studies*, p. 162)? Was it not in support of this very 'vegetative power of nature' that I quoted Cicero's words (*Tusc.* 5, 37, in *Rom. Dyn.* p. 129)?—: '*Itaque et arbores et vites et ea quae sunt humiliora neque se tollere a terra altius possunt, alia semper virent, alia hieme nudata verno tempore tepefacta frondescunt, neque est ullum quod non ita vigeat interiore quodam motu et suis in quoque seminibus inclusis, ut aut flores aut fruges fundat aut bacas*' [14]— and added, 'a more striking expression of the old *mana*-idea' [*sit venia verbo*] 'than this *vigere interiore quodam motu* would be hard to find in classical Latin'. And what of Le Bonniec? He quotes the same passage (p. 37ff.) and concludes (p. 39), 'Ce *motus interior*, c'était Cérès pour les anciens Romains'. I should applaud once more if I could possibly conceive how an 'internal motion' could be a goddess. Yet in historical times Ceres was a goddess, not a *numen*, not 'une force sécrète', not '*motus interior*', although not only in the age of the Republic but even in the imperial age there were abundant modes of speech and sometimes actual rites to show that the Romans of that time still had some idea of the origins of the goddess. Therefore, as I understand it, this author contrary to all his denials and objections is in absolute agreement with me, except that he is ready to advance rather further than I along the road which today is called 'dynamistic'.

I have already referred above to the great importance of his discussion on pp. 381ff. of the rites of Ceres at Rome. With great care he has collected everything concerning these and after correctly refuting, at the beginning of his work (pp. 14ff.), the arguments of those who have thought that the Roman cult of Ceres right at the outset was taken from Greece, he deals with those Greek rites which between the years 249 and 218 'mais sans doute ... plus près de 218 que de 249' (p. 393) were instituted at Rome as

---

[14] 'Thus both trees and vines and lower-growing plants which cannot rise to a great height above the earth are either evergreen or become bare in winter and put out leaf again in the warmth of spring. And there is nothing which does not thus grow with a kind of inner motion, contained in its very seeds, so as to put forth flowers or fruits or berries.'

public rites. He produces much that needs consideration. The only serious point I would make is that he does here and there use a line of argument which I find less convincing. His book abounds with conjectures. We constantly read, 'Simple hypothèse' (p. 55); 'nous pouvons supposer (sans avoir la possibilité de le démontrer)' (p. 67); 'on pressent, sans pouvoir le démontrer' (p. 73); 'Il est naturel de supposer. . . . Mais ce n'est là qu'une hypothèse' (p. 75); 'on peut supposer, sans avoir le moyen de le démontrer' (p. 82); 'hypothèse invérifiable, mais non pas invraisemblable' (p. 122), and so on and so on. Nor would any sensible person blame him. He is right to complain again and again 'que nous soyons si mal renseignés' (p. 294) and gives as an excuse 'l'insuffisance de notre documentation' (p. 335); 'la pénurie des documents' (p. 413). It appears however, that such excuses are valid only for Le Bonniec himself. When G. Wissowa for instance—not to mention myself— conjectures that Ovid *Amor.* 3, 10, has in view a day sacred to Demeter in Greece, not the Roman festival, the matter is disposed of with the words 'supposition invérifiable' (p. 409). When U. von Wilamowitz, seeing on the one hand that the Sibylline books, originating in Cumae, had at the beginning of the 5th century B.C. ordered the Romans to institute a cult of Ceres and Liber and Libera, and on the other that both a cult of the Greek Ceres and of Dionysus had been peculiar to Cumae, conjectured that the three deities there were artificially linked—in my judgment a probable enough conjecture—Le Bonniec objects, 'c'est justement ce qu'il faudrait démontrer' (p. 290)!

For the rest, there is not much of relevance that the author has omitted. Nevertheless he has overlooked one passage which seems to me of considerable importance. I refer to Gellius 11, 6, 5f., where we read: '*M. Varro adseverat antiquissimos viros neque per Castorem neque per Pollucem deiurare solitos, sed id iusiurandum fuisse tantum feminarum ex initiis Eleusinis acceptum; paulatim tamen inscitia antiquitatis viros dicere 'edepol' coepisse factumque esse ita dicendi morem, sed 'mecastor' a viro dici in nullo vetere scripto inveniri.*'

Three questions arise:

1. What Eleusinian mysteries is he referring to?

2. How could women be accustomed to swear a definite oath in mysteries?
3. What have the Dioscuri themselves to do with Eleusinian mysteries?

As for the first question, it cannot be doubted that Varro is talking about mysteries celebrated at Rome. The women he refers to were certainly Roman, because of course Eleusinians could never have learnt to swear by Castor and Pollux. Moreover it is clear that Varro meant mysteries open only to women. We are immediately led to think of the annual feast of Ceres. But at this point we are faced with a considerable difficulty. Could those Greek rites possibly have been called 'Eleusinian'? Did not Le Bonniec rightly declare (p. 422), 'Le *sacrum Cereris*, qui n'est absolument pas éleusinien, n'est donc pas non plus pleinement thesmophorien'? Was Varro then making a mistake, though otherwise 'une bonne source' (p. 90)? Not at all, in my opinion, for we are very well acquainted with Eleusinian rites which perhaps had nothing at all to do with Eleusis itself. I condense briefly what has been discussed at greater length elsewhere.[15] In Laconia and Arcadia right from the earliest times a goddess was worshipped whose name was (Demeter) Eleuthia or Eleusinia and whom several authorities have regarded as the same as Eleutho, Eileithyia. In her honour festivals were held, called *Eleusinia*, to which only women were admitted, so that 'they are distinct from the Eleusinian mysteries and come closer to the distinctive fertility festivals celebrated only by women' (Nilsson, 335). It is true that Hesychius' gloss Ἐλευσινία· ἀγὼν θυμελικὸς ἀγόμενος παρὰ Λάκωσιν can only refer to a theatrical contest.' But there is some doubt about this text. Wide (pp. 119f.) thinks it complete as it stands but there is a further corrupt section which seems like a continuation of it (τριήμερος· Θεσμοφόρια ὑπο † Λάκωνες).[16] According to Herodotus

[15] Cf. A. Rutgers van der Loeff, *De ludis Eleusiniis*, 1903, p. 19ff.; S. Wide, *Lakonische Kulte*, 1893, pp. 170ff., 374; Jessen, *RE* 5, 2356; M. P. Nilsson, *Griech. Feste* pp. 334ff.; O. Kern, *RE* 16, pp. 1269ff.

[16] Cf. Wide p. 178. His observation on p. 180 about the connection between the Andanian and Eleusinian mysteries is not relevant here. It is fairly well agreed that they were not the Eleusinian goddesses worshipped there but certain 'Great Gods' (cf. O. Kern, *RE* 16, pp. 1267f.).

(2, 171) these *Thesmophoria* were celebrated actually by the Pelasgian women, and Wide remarked seemingly with justice (p. 181), 'The worship of the Laconian Demeter flourished especially in the Pre-Dorian (Achaeo-Minyan) settlements—Therai, Amyklai, Helos, Tainaron, Hippola, Aigila, Mistra(?). By contrast this goddess is not much in evidence in cult at Sparta.... Her Laconian cults point incidentally to Pre-Dorian connections with Arcadia, Messenia, Hermione, Troizen, Eleusis, and Attica.'

'But' you ask 'what are you after? What has Rome to do with Laconia and Arcadia?' Quite right, right indeed, but wait.

It was from 'Eleusinian' rites like these celebrated at Rome according to Varro that the Roman women learned to swear by Castor and Pollux. There is no doubt what oath Varro had in mind. In all mysteries the initiates had to bind themselves by an oath not to disclose the secrets of the ceremony. '*De nombreux témoignages attestent que les mystes juraient de ne rien divulguer de ce qui leur était révélé dans le télestérion.*' [17] Thus our second question was not difficult to answer.

Against that, in dealing with our third question we seem to find ourselves at once in the same difficulty as with the first. Many commentators have warned us that of all the Greeks only the Laconians were accustomed to swear by the Dioscuri,[18] so that Aristophanes for instance in his comedies has his Spartan women using this very same oath. But nobody as far as I can see has a clear reply if you again ask: What are you after? What

---

[17] F. Cumont, *Harv. Theol. Rev.* 26, 1933, p. 158; cf. R. Reitzenstein, *Hellen. Mysterienrel.*³, 1927, p. 195: 'it is generally assumed that where there is a rite of initiation an oath is taken too'; Foucart, *Mystères d'Eleusis*, pp. 358ff. Cf. the accounts of Orphic mysteries: Reitzenstein, *op. cit.* 225; of Dionysian-Bacchic rites: A. Bruhl, *Liber Pater*, 1953, p. 91; J. Leipoldt, *Dionysus*, 1931, p. 47; Liv. 39, 15, 13; of Mithraic mysteries: Cumont *op. cit.* ('*Un fragment de rituel d'initiation aux mystères*', which was published in *Papiri della Società Italiana* 10 no. 1162, where we read, vs. 4ff.: ἐπόμνυμαι / [ἦ μὴν ἐκ πίστεω]ς ἀτρεκ]οῦς συντηρήσειν / ἐν ἀπορρήτοις τὰ παραδεδομένα μοι μυστήρια; the missing portion of text is as supplied by Cumont; before ἦ μὴν ἐκ πίστεως Wilcken, *Arch. f. Papyrusforsch.* 10, 1932, thinks the name of a *mystes* has dropped out; Momigliano, *Aegyptus* 13, 131ff., believes the fragment should rather be assigned to the mysteries of Serapis).

[18] Passages in support of this have often been collected; cf. Ziebarth, *RE* 5, 2077; Deubner, *N.Jbb.* 9 (1902) 386; Wide 307; Ziehen *RE* 3A, 1479; Altheim, *Griech. Götter im alten Rom* (1930) 39.

has Rome to do with Laconia? The answer to this question will become all the more important to us below, when it will be asked for the third time in connection with Mackauer's conjecture (*RE* 18, 1, 923) regarding the so-called Wedding of Orcus. There it is put by Le Bonniec himself (p. 442), 'M. Mackauer n'a pas réussi à jeter un pont entre la Laconie et Rome; il lui faudrait montrer comment le rite du mariage sacré entre Déméter et le dieu des Enfers a pu se transmettre jusqu'à Rome.'

Certainly Deubner had no doubts on this point, at least in regard to the cult of the Tyndaridae. He wrote (*P.C.* p. 387), 'The cult of the Dioscuri migrated from Laconia to Lower Italy, from there to Central Italy and probably by way of Tusculum to the Romans'. Altheim [19] was little more accurate, 'The way of their origin from the Greek South, especially from Tarentum, has long since been demonstrated'. Later (p. 268) he speaks of 'Greek Gods, adopted like Mercurius and the Dioscuri by way of Etruria'. The actual part played by Tarentum in transferring the cult of Castor and Pollux to Rome and establishing it there is still in question. But it is agreed that it did play some part, as correctly demonstrated by P. Wuilleumier among others. He wrote (*Tarente*, 1939, 1, 680), '*Parmi les héros, les Dioscures ont passé d'Étrurie ou plutôt de Locres à Rome dès le début du Ve siècle, associés à une déesse qu'on ne rencontre pas à Tarente. Cependant, leur image à été gravé au IIIe siècle sur des monnaies d'argent à l'imitation du type tarentin*'.[20] The same author has summarized (*op cit.* pp. 677ff.) the contribution of Tarentum to the establishment of the religions and cults of the Romans. His conspectus, though it does not seem to me to find the right answer in every case—in particular I do not believe the games called 'Tarentine' at Rome were really borrowed from

---

[19] *Hist. of Rom. Rel.* (1938) 40. A little later he adds that the Dioscuri did not originate only in Tarentum, 'but also from the exactly opposite quarter, over the Timavus'—a point less relevant here.

[20] Cf. p. 519: '...le culte des Dioscures est bien attesté à Tarente. Héros prédoriens...ils ont passé de Laconie à Locres et à Tarente. Leur culte présente des analogies dans les deux cités; mais il est plus ancien dans la première, plus répandu dans la seconde, où la cavalerie jouait un rôle prépondérant....Ils portent sur un fragment de vase le titre de Σωτῆρες sous lequel on les invoquait en Laconie'. Cf. E. Petersen, 'Dioskuri in Tarent', *Röm. Mitt.* 15 (1900) 3ff., esp. 39ff.; G. Giannelli, *Culti e Miti della Magna Graecia* (1924) 33.

the Tarentines (cf. *Studies*, 197ff.)—makes it plain enough how important Tarentum was in shaping and composing the Roman religion. At any rate it is by no means difficult to understand the route taken by the Laconian Dioscuri in reaching Rome, that is, by way of the Dorian colonies in Magna Graecia. The choice is still open at the moment between Tarentum and Locri, where also the Dioscuri were prominently worshipped, provided we do not give too much weight to the arguments on this point of J. Bayet. In what is otherwise a learned and useful book, *Les Origines de l'Hercule Romain* (1926, e.g. p. 172 n. 1) this writer seems to have set out to show that the authority of Tarentum in matters of religion is on the whole much exaggerated. Against him Wuilleumier, though recognizing that his opinion is not completely worthless ('sa réaction, parfaitement justifiée, contre les excès de la théorie favorable à Tarente') none the less again himself defends the authority of Tarentum.[21]

The facts seem to be no different in the case of the Eleusinian Ceres. Above we saw that she was worshipped especially in Laconia. But we see the same at Tarentum. For although the cult of Demeter does not in general seem to have been popular there, yet Wuilleumier (p. 512), relying primarily on the researches of Wide, has declared, 'D'après Hésychius, le nom d'Ἐπιλυσαμένη, equivalent d'Ἐλευθώ, désignait l'une des Ilithyies et Déméter à Tarente et à Syracuse. Ce rapprochement des deux villes incite encore à chercher *une origine commune à Laconie*' (my italics); 'Déméter y était invoquée sous le nom d'Ἐλευθία, et sous celui d'Ἐλευσινία elle jouait à Therai, auprès de Léto, le même rôle qu'Ilithyie à Délos'. Therefore since in those words of Varro's there are two points which have attracted attention, the Eleusinian rites celebrated at Rome and the oath there sworn by Castor and Pollux, and since these things occur both together, so far as we know, only in Laconia and nowhere else, it is natural to infer that that was their origin, and that they were transmitted by way of a Laconian colony in Magna Graecia. To me it seems most probable that this was Tarentum.

---

[21] Not only p. 680, where the subject is Hercules, but especially p. 679, where he is speaking of Damia, whose rites were transferred to Rome, where she was worshipped under the name of Bona Dea.

Evidently it would interest us very much to know which celebration Varro had in mind. Perhaps at first sight it seems not an absurd conjecture that he meant the annual Greek Feast, because of course like the *Thesmophoria* it was nearer and more closely related than the actual Mysteries celebrated at Eleusis. But we are soon forced to discard this idea. For first we must wonder what could have induced an author, experienced if anybody was in these matters, to call the festival by a name not occurring anywhere else. And this all the more since Cichorius (*Römische Studien* 198ff.) has proved by strong arguments that Varro himself was one of the *Quindecimviri Sacris Faciundis*, so that you would expect him to have been careful to choose words with due regard to religion in general and the Greek rite in particular. But in the second place there is a really decisive argument at hand.

In respect of the swearing of the oath by Castor and Pollux Varro distinguishes three periods: 1. In ancient times such an oath was completely unknown at Rome. 2. After the introduction of the *initia Eleusinia* the women learned to swear by Castor and by Pollux. 3. Little by little the men too began to say '*edepol*', but they allowed only the women to say '*mecastor*'. The question at once arises how long these stages of time lasted. Nobody will doubt that to begin with the women will have learnt to swear, say, *me Castor iuvet*, and especially '*e deive Pollux*' (or *Pollūcē*). But these full forms no longer occur anywhere, or rather with the passage of time have become so worn that *edepol* especially, let alone *pol*, can hardly be recognized. Will anyone deny that for words to be worn down to that extent, and sacred words at that, an interval not of years, not of decades, but of centuries would be needed? This I have been able to confirm on the authority of people much more highly specialized in such matters than myself. But if this line of reasoning does not yet seem sufficient, I would ask you to consider what follows.

Undoubtedly the third of Varro's periods mentioned above must have been long before the end of the third century. The phrases *pol* and *edepol* are found in common use about the year 200 B.C., and that promiscuously by men and women. *pol* already occurs among the few Livius Andronicus fragments still surviving (*Frgm.* 25R), though it is otherwise uncertain whether spoken by a man or woman. But Ennius has *pol* twice,[22] once definitely given to a man. Naevius' comic fragments have both *edepol* (*Frgm. com.* 55V) and *pol* (*Frgm. com.* 60V), but in neither case can we tell the sex of the speaker. Against that, Plautus without hesitation gives both *edepol* and *pol* to men.[23] Statius Caecilius follows the same rule.[24] From *Fragment* III R of Titinius, it is true, the words '*an quia "pol edepol" fabulare, "edi medi" meministi*' (where according to Charisius (p. 189P.) a 'soft' young man talking effeminately is being taken off) show clearly that even at that period *pol edepol* was still more frequent in female than in male mouths. All the same my quotations do show clearly enough that around the year 200 B.C. men were not at all unwilling to use such an oath. Consequently it is difficult to say when Varro's third period may be supposed to have begun, that is, when men started to say '*edepol*' in ignorance of the past. What we can for certain conclude is that at that date the adoption among women of the oath 'By Pollux!' from the *Initia Eleusinia* must already have been ancient. Hence it follows from Varro's testimony that the institution of the *Initia Eleusinia* was very ancient indeed.

Le Bonniec[25] however thinks, rightly in my opinion, that the annual Feast of Ceres was instituted at Rome between the years 249 and 218, and at that 'undoubtedly ... nearer 218 than 249'. It is hardly necessary for me to conclude that this festival could not possibly have been the same as the *Initia Eleusinia* recorded by Varro. Well, perhaps the good Varro just nodded off for once! You might well ask why the oath by Castor and Pollux could not simply have been introduced with their cult at the beginning of the fifth century. But I shall never be brought to believe that a man so learned in things divine could have casually invented those 'Eleusinian mysteries' together with an oath by Castor and Pollux' in which its women initiates swore to keep its secrets inviolate.

[22] *Trag.* 354 V (Thyestes speaking): *Ann.* 99 V (it is very probable that here too a man is speaking).

[23] *Edepol* said by a man e.g. *Amph.* 182, 271, 282, 371, 399; *Aul.* 215; *Cas.* 354; *Merc.* 126, 127, 140; *Mil.* 988; *Most.* 766, 1077; *Pers.* 8, 23, 26; *Pseud.* 337; etc.; '*pol*': *Amph.* 371; *Bacch.* 1010; *Capt.* 840; *Men.* 1064; *Merc.* 6; *Pers.* 50, 89 etc.

[24] '*Edepol*' said by a man: *frgm.* 173 R.; less obviously *frgm.* 135 R.: 'pol' *ibidem frgm.* 190 R.

[25] I myself (*Studies* p. 155) had proposed the year 217; I am now convinced by Le B.'s contrary argument.

Thus Varro informs us: 1. There existed at Rome 'mysteries' of Ceres much more ancient than the annual Feast of Ceres in which only women were initiated; 2. The women there learnt to swear by Castor and Pollux; 3. These 'mysteries' originated in Laconia and it was very probably through the intermediary of a Tarentine cult that they reached Rome; 4.—Something I now add—it is an obvious conjecture that the Roman women were instructed by priestesses from Tarentum, assuredly Greek. Otherwise, how are we to suppose that the women learnt to swear by Castor and Pollux, and by no other gods? As I have already admitted above, (p. 116), before I had taken account of Varro's words as transmitted by Gellius, I once wrongly assumed as a matter of course that Greek priestesses already officiated at religious ceremonies at Rome before the middle of the third century. My mistake is rightly pointed out by Le Bonniec (p. 395). What is not so right, however, is his subsequent argument, when he says (p. 397), 'Il est notable que les divinités grecques introduites à date ancienne sont venues à Rome sans leurs prêtres: ainsi les "décemvirs paraissent s'être toujours occupés directement du culte et du temple d'Apollon sans jamais faire appel à de vrais prêtres d'origine non romaine" (J. Gagé, *Apollon* p. 54)'. He forgets, however, that this is not a reference to mysteries. It is hard to imagine how mysteries could have been transplanted to another country without some native help from their place of origin. It is all the more surprising that the same author only a little further on can write, 'C'est seulement en 291 av. J.-C. que les Romains, adoptant le culte d'Esculape, ont recours pour la première fois à des prêtres étrangers', as if we had a single document in evidence of any such thing. With little more prudence Wissowa (pp. 307f.) makes the same assertion, in these words, '*Wenn wir auch direkte Zeugnisse dafür nicht haben, so unterliegt es doch keinem Zweifel...*' Undoubtedly if both are right Valerius Maximus (1, 8, 2) is wrong in his account of the invitation to Aesculapius by the Roman envoys at Epidaurus; '*Tum legati perinde atque exoptatae rei conpotes, expleta gratiarum actione cultuque anguis a peritis excepto laeti inde solverunt...*' [26] But

---

[26] 'Then the envoys as soon as they had achieved their aim, having offered their thanks and received the snake cult from its competent officiants, joyfully set sail...'

whatever the case here, matters are seen to be completely different when it comes to the mysteries. When in the year 396 B.C., as attested by Diodorus (14, 77, 4), the Carthaginians decreed πάντι τρόπῳ τοὺς ἀσεβηθέντας θεοὺς ἐξιλάσκεσθαι,[27] this is what they did: οὐ παρειληφότες δ' ἐν τοῖς ἱεροῖς οὔτε Κόρην οὔτε Δήμητρα, τούτων ἱερεῖς τοὺς ἐπισημοτάτους τῶν πολιτῶν κατέστησαν, καὶ μετὰ πάσης σεμνότητος τὰς θεὰς ἱδρυσάμενοι τὰς θυσίας τοῖς τῶν Ἑλλήνων ἔθεσιν ἐποιοῦν καὶ τῶν παρ' αὐτοῖς ὄντων Ἑλλήνων τοὺς χαριεστάτους ἐπιλεξάντες ἐπὶ τὴν τῶν θεῶν θεραπείαν ἔταξαν.[28] Of course we cannot rely on a Carthaginian observance for evidence to illustrate a Roman one. I would only point out that the Carthaginians too, though they were not even putting on a proper mystery celebration, still could not do without Greek officiants. In Rome what we read about the Annual Feast itself bears this out. Valerius Maximus (I, I, I) relates that a Greek priestess was summoned from Velia when the Feast was instituted, 'ne deae vetustis ritibus perita deesset antistes'.[29] And no wonder, since the rites, on Cicero's evidence (Verr. 5, 187), 'longe maximis atque occultissimis caerimoniis contine-(re)ntur'.[30] It is therefore most probable that there were Greek priestesses helping the Roman women also in those more ancient Eleusinian mysteries recorded by Varro, even though the correctness of this conjecture cannot be inferred for certain, as I have explained above, simply from the fact of the oath by Pollux.

What I have argued up to this point is in great part corroborated by another author, Dionysius of Halicarnassus, who wrote (Ant. Rom. I, 33, of the Arcadians who had settled at Rome under the Palatine): 'Ἱδρύσαντο δὲ καὶ Δήμητρος ἱερόν, καὶ τὰς θυσίας αὐτῇ διὰ γυναικῶν τε καὶ νηφαλίους ἔθυσαν, ὡς Ἕλλησι νόμος, ὧν οὐδὲν ὁ καθ' ἡμᾶς ἤλλαξε Χρόνος.[31]

[27] 'that everything should be done to propitiate the gods who had been sinned against'

[28] 'Having never received Kore or Demeter in their temples, they appointed the most distinguished citizens as their priests, and having set up the statues of the goddesses with all solemnity they performed the sacrifices to them according to the Greek rite and seeking out the most cultivated of the Greek residents they put them in charge of the goddesses' service.'

[29] 'so that they might not be without a high priestess qualified to perform the ancient rites of the goddess'.

[30] 'consisted of far the most considerable and most secret ceremonies'.

[31] 'They dedicated a temple to Demeter, and instituted sacrifices to her performed by women and without wine, according to the Greek custom, nothing of which had been changed by our times.

Le Bonniec refers three times to this passage. The first reference if I am not mistaken must have been written later than the second. It is (pp. 250f.): 'Un curieux texte de Denys d'Halicarnasse peut fournir un indice de la présence de Déméter, à date ancienne, sur le sol romain. Il affirme qu'au temps du roi Évandre les Arcadiens lui avaient fondé un sanctuaire sur le Palatin et qu'ils lui rendaient un culte féminin, excluant les offrandes de vin. Laissons de côté la mention de ce culte particulier, qui constitue une évidente anticipation. Ne retenons pour le moment que la donnée de la consécration à une époque légendaire d'un sanctuaire à Déméter au cœur même de la Cité. Bien entendu, l'autorité de ce texte est très faible: il s'explique par la thèse "arcadienne" de l'auteur et par sa manie d'attribuer des origines grecques à tout ce qui est romain. Il suffit de renvoyer sur ce point à l'étude approfondie de M. J. Bayet, qui a expliqué la genèse de l'*Arcadisme romain*.[32] Pourtant cette affirmation légendaire, qu'inspire un hellénisme intempérant, peut conserver le souvenir déformé d'une antique présence à Rome de Déméter, le Palatin transposant simplement l'idée de la Cité. Un noyau de vérité se cache peut-être sous les élucubrations savantes de Denys.' A little later (p. 254), however, the same passage is again referred to, this time in only a few words, and rather contemptuously dismissed ('un texte dont le caractère légendaire est évident'). None the less the author recognizes that Dionysius seems to have been right in his dating of the foundation of the Ceres temple (p. 255). The passage is then quoted once more on p. 416, where Le Bonniec has a much better opinion of it. We are indebted to it, he now thinks, for 'une particularité intéressante du culte féminin de Cérès, valable par conséquent pour le *sacrum anniversarium*.... Faisant abstraction de l'"arcadisme" de Denys, retenons l'existence au temps d'Auguste d'un rite grec d'offrandes féminines, dont le vin était proscrit.' It will not escape the reader that the author is rather wavering in his judgment nor will he fail to note the cause. Though he gives great credit to other passages from Dionysius, indeed he uses him here and there (esp. pp. 213ff., 271ff.) as a primary source, what piques him about this author is not so much his readiness to derive all Roman institutions from an Arcadian origin—and I have no difficulty in

[32] *Mél. Rome* 38 (1920).

agreeing with him there—as the fact of his asserting the great antiquity of the festival of Ceres. For Le Bonniec has set out to prove that before the annual Feast of Ceres no mysteries of Ceres existed in Rome. I for one do not deny that Dionysius' words contain 'une particularité intéressante', for he maintains that up to his own time nothing had changed in that very ancient rite. The significance of this deserves our closest attention. However, we must first discuss two other passages from Varro which are relevant to this question.

Varro in fact twice refers to the mysteries of Ceres, and it is already twelve years (cf. *Studies*, pp. 150ff.) since the two passages furnished me with grounds for concluding that the mysteries were to be dated to the first century of the Republic, on which point of course Le Bonniec has contradicted me. Here is the first:

> Varro *r.r.* 2, 4, 9: '*Sus graece dicitur* ὅς, *olim* Θῦς *dictus ab illo verbo quod dicunt* Θύειν, *quod est immolare. Ab suillo enim genere [pecore] immolandi initium primum sumptum videtur, cuius vestigia quod initiis Cer<er>is porci immolantur, et quod initiis pacis, foedus cum feritur, porcus occiditur, et quod nuptiarum initio antiqui reges ac sublimes viri in Etruria in coniunctione nuptiali nova nupta et novus maritus primum porcum immolant.*' [33]

The author seems—so I considered at the time—to be making a deliberate connection between the term *initia*, and *initium* as well, and the notion of beginning. This judgment is clearly confirmed by the second passage:

> Varro *r.r.* 3, 1, 5: '*Nec sine causa terram eandem appellabant Matrem et Cererem, et qui eam colerent, piam et utilem agere vitam credebant atque eos solos reliquos esse ex stirpe Saturni*

---

[33] '*Sus*' in Greek is ὅς, which was once θῦς from the verb θύειν, that is, '(animal) sacrifice'. For it seems that animal sacrifice had its beginning with pigs, and traces of this are seen in the sacrifice of pigs at the "beginnings" of Ceres (as her mysteries are called), in the killing of a pig at the "beginnings of peace", when a treaty is concluded, and at the "beginning" of marriage when the weddings of the kings of old and leading men in Etruria were preceded by the new bride and new bridegroom first sacrificing a pig.'

regis. Cui consentaneum est, quod initia vocantur potissimum ea quae Cereris fiunt sacre,' [34]

From these I had inferred, to put in a few words what I then worked out at greater length, that according to Varro the mysteries of Ceres were very ancient, more ancient certainly than the mysteries of Bona Dea, which it is very probable were introduced in Rome in the year 272 B.C. Now Le Bonniec (p. 428) says: 'nous serions fort embarrassés pour expliquer les textes de Varron, dont le second implique bien que les mystères de Cérès sont très anciens, ou les plus anciens, si M. Wagenvoort avait raison d'y voir des allusions au culte *romain*'. In which he thinks I was wrong—in both passages he thinks Varro was talking about the Greek mysteries celebrated at Eleusis!

Let us have another look at them. The first is part of a prolix article on Roman pig-keeping. It has matter both preceding and following the passage quoted. The author's idea is that among livestock the pig was in some way considered sacred by the ancestors of the Romans. From the sacrifice of the pig, indeed, almost all the Roman sacred ceremonies began—mysteries, treaties, weddings. He thinks this borne out by the very name itself, *sus*, which in its derivation from the Greek contains the notion of sacrifice. But I ask, would it readily occur to anybody that Varro in this context was combining Roman treaties and Roman weddings with the mysteries celebrated at Eleusis? The whole of this passage is concerned with Rome, or rather Italy. Where the Greeks are named, they are expressly said to be Greeks in Italy. Moreover, we have already seen above (p. 117) that what was claimed to be 'un argument de poids en faveur d'Éleusis' in fact had no weight.

The case is no different with the other passage. This is preceded by the words, '*Itaque non sine causa maiores nostri ex urbe in agros redigebant suos cives, quod et in pace a rusticis Romanis alebantur et in bello ab his † alebantur*'.[35] So once again the subject of discussion

---

[34] 'Nor was it without reason that they called the one Earth 'Mother' and 'Ceres' and believed that those who worshipped her led a good and useful life and that they alone were of the surviving stock of King Saturn. In accord with this is the fact that the rites of Ceres are the very ones to be called "beginnings".'

[35] 'So it was not without cause that our ancestors forced their citizens from the city back into the fields, because it was the Roman countryfolk who both fed them in peacetime and' (? defended) 'them in time of war.'

is the ancestors of the Romans, so many of whom practised agriculture that they believed the tilling of the soil to be the test of a good and useful life. And to illustrate this, Varro appealed to mysteries held in Greece? Let him believe it who will.

In my judgment it cannot be doubted that in both passages Varro meant the same *initia Cereris* which elsewhere (see p. 123 above) are called the *initia Eleusinia* and in the Gellius fragment and *r.r.* 2, 4, 9 are shown to have been very ancient. I think the four passages quoted have enough weight to demonstrate that Le Bonniec was wrong in arguing that there were no mysteries of Ceres at Rome before her annual Feast.

Nor have I any grounds to withdraw my previously published (*Studies*, pp. 155ff.) conjecture, to which I refer the reader, that the name *initia Cereris* originated in quite a different meaning of the words, and that it started as *initia cereris*, with a nominative **cerus*, which later became obsolete, and meant much the same as *vis creandi*, 'creative force', with which Le Bonniec too would regard the goddess Ceres as equivalent. I am not in the least convinced by what he says against my suggestion. He continues (p. 430), '*Mysteria* et *initia* s'emploient comme synonymes, mais le mot latin avec la nuance d'"initiation" (aux mystères)'. Must we accept the implication: *Initia* from *initiare*? No. Whatever the case, I think all Latin linguists will grant that the early Romans had the greatest difficulty in designating things remote from the senses. This is what the authors of later times, Lucretius, Cicero, Pliny, Seneca, mean when they complain of '*patrii sermonis egestas*', this is the gap which Cicero among others devoted all his efforts to filling. I am convinced it would not have been possible for the Romans, before the 3rd century B.C. at that, to venture beyond an attempt to interpret the Greek term as literally as possible. Perhaps we detect a trace of such an attempt in Paul's gloss '*conivola occulta*'.[36] But Cicero's words (*Leg.* 2, 36) which were quoted at me by Le Bonniec (p. 430), '*nihil melius illis mysteriis, quibus ex agresti immanique vita exculti ad humanitatem et mitigati sumus, initiaque ut appellantur, ita re vera principia vitae cognovi-*

---

[36] P. 53, 21 L. Another gloss, *Fest.* p. 422, 31, 'seclusa sacra *dicebantur, quae Graeci mysteria appellant*', may more probably refer to things contained in a *cista mystica*.

mus' [37] reveal a man steeped in Greek philosophy and as remote as possible from that 'rustic life' into which we now know for certain that those very ancient mysteries dropped as it were from heaven.

I now return to the words of Dionysius of Halicarnassus, who has told us that up to Augustus' time nothing was changed in the rite of the Ceres-mysteries. If we believe him we have to suppose that the ancient *initia* were the same, if not in every detail (for he speaks only of νηφάλια or wineless offerings made only by women) at least in great part, as the annual Feast. And there are reasons in favour of this conclusion. Chief of these is that we were obliged to recognize above (p. 124f.) that both occasions, the ancient and the more recent, were similar to the *Thesmophoria* and thus had some resemblance to one another. But there are many objections to supposing that one festival was a mere continuation of the other. First there is that passage of Arnobius (2, 73), where he is defending the Christians from the charge of having introduced a new cult and throws the same charge back at the pagans, saying among other things: '*Quid, Phrygiam matrem non, cum Hannibal Poenus res Italas raperet et terrarum exposceret principatum, et nosse et scire coepistis et memorabili religione sancire? Sacra Cereris matris non quod vobis incognita essent, adscita paulo ante, obtentum est ut Graeca dicantur, novitatem ipsam testificante cognomine?*' [38] This passage is evidence, as Le Bonniec has rightly maintained, that the Greek festival was not instituted before the middle of the third century. And if anyone asks us, perhaps not without reason, whether it is quite certain that Arnobius could have ascertained the truth about things which happened five centuries before his time, we can reply with our French scholar that there is other evidence to hand in confirmation of Dionysius' words (pp. 390ff.)

---

[37] 'there is nothing better than those mysteries by which we have been mellowed into humanity and civilized out of a rustic, savage life, and just as they are called "beginnings" we recognize them as truly a beginning of life'.

[38] 'What, did you not, when Hannibal the Carthaginian was devastating Italy and trying to establish his supremacy, begin to know and cultivate the Phrygian Mother and sanctify her worship in a striking manner? Did you not arrange for the Feast of Mother Ceres, with which you had just become acquainted, not having known it before, to be called Greek, proving its novelty by this very name?'

But there are in my opinion other more serious objections. We will now see whether they can be overcome. There are two unavoidable difficulties which immediately present themselves, and the first of these, which is indeed closely bound up with the other, seems to me to be this. The culmination of the annual Feast is agreed by all authors, ancient as well as modern, to have been the finding of Proserpine. (cf. Le Bonniec, pp. 412ff.). But it is no less agreed by all recent scholars that before the institution or renewal of the *Ludi Saeculares* in the year 249 B.C. Proserpine played no or next to no part in Roman religion.[39] Against this everybody knows and nobody has more clearly explained than Le Bonniec that the cult of Ceres herself was already popular in the fifth century, first of all with the *plebs*. How then can we suppose that the finding of Proserpine was celebrated at those earlier ceremonies, even though we are not absolutely sure when they were instituted? It is quite unthinkable. But if we consider Dionysius' words more closely, he only declares that both in ancient times and in his own the women alone took part in the rites and sacrifices θυσίας νηφαλίους. The purpose of the rites he does not tell us. But since they must necessarily have belonged to Ceres and not to Proserpine there remains as far as I can see only one solution to the puzzle. *In ancient times a Wedding of Orcus and Ceres was celebrated at a secret religious ceremony in Rome.*

I realize that I have here come up against a crux of interpretation. In only one place is there a mention of a Wedding of Orcus.[40]

[39] Wissowa, *R.u.K*[2] 310; Carter, *Rosch. Lex.* 3, 2, 3143. 3147; Cichorius, o.c. p. 47; Altheim, *Hist. of Rom. Rel.* 287.

[40] Servius, *Georg.* 1, 344: '*Superfluum est quod quidam dicunt, contra religionem dixisse Vergilium, licere Cereri de vino sacrificari: pontificales namque hoc non vetant libri. Quod autem ait Plautus in Aulularia* (vs. 354), *cuius illi utuntur exemplo, "Cererin nuptias facturi estis, qui sine temeto huc advenitis?" non est huic loco contrarium: nam aliud est sacrum, aliud nuptias Cereri celebrare, in quibus re vera vinum adhiberi nefas fuerat quae Orci nuptiae dicebantur, quas praesentia sua pontifices ingenti sollemnitate celebrabant.*' 'It is an uncalled-for remark by certain commentators that Vergil was going against religion when he said it was permissible to sacrifice to Ceres with wine. The pontifical books have no such prohibition. What Plautus says in his *Aulularia* (l. 354), which they use as an example, is nothing to the contrary. 'Are you preparing a wedding for Ceres, that you've come without wine?'—these are the words. But it is one thing to celebrate a feast of Ceres, quite another to celebrate Ceres' wedding, in which it was really impious to introduce wine. That was called the 'Wedding of Orcus,' and it was celebrated with great solemnity by the *pontifices* in her presence.'

Almost always till now it has been assumed that the bride was Proserpine, and Le Bonniec (p. 442), listing the authors who have accepted this view, rightly includes my name, although even then, when I treated the question only in passing (*Studies*, p. 106, 1), I gave a clear indication of my considerable doubts. Since then there have been others who thought that Ceres ought to be substituted for Proserpine (cf. Le Bonniec, p. 441), prominent among them Mackauer (RE 18, 924). Nobody can fail to notice that the phrase *nuptias Cereri celebrare* can hardly, if at all, mean anything else, so that the burden of proof is with those who want it to be the daughter not the mother who put on the red bridal robe. Le Bonniec, for instance one of those who is sure Proserpine was the new bride, at first seeks support (p. 439) from Macrobius (*Sat.* 3, 11, 1, 9): 'D'abord il est troublant de constater que Macrobe discute ce même vers de Virgile, en utilisant la même citation de Plaute, à propos de l'interdiction du vin dans le culte de Cérès, sans souffler mot des *Orci nuptiae*, qui pourtant lui fournissaient un excellent example, puisque, selon Servius, le vin en était proscrit. S'il ne les mentionne pas, n'est-ce pas parce qu'il avait conscience que cette cérémonie n'appartenait pas à proprement parler au culte de Cérès?' I am not impressed by this argumentation. At the beginning of the chapter Macrobius had posed the question: '*si eventu excusantur inlicita, dic quaeso, quod erat monstrum secuturum et cum Cereri libari vino iuberet, quod omnibus sacris vetatur.*' [41] There was no need, as far as I can see, to name the wedding with Orcus expressly, at least not if he wished to include that ceremony too among all the others, which we can neither affirm nor deny.

Then Le Bonniec offers his own interpretation of the line of Plautus quoted by Servius. Following the example of M. Schuster [42] he regards it as nothing but a joke. 'Plaute et ses spectateurs savent fort bien que le vin est interdit dans le culte de Cérès (tout au moins dans celui de Cérès hellénisée),.... C'est donc Cérès qui par bouffonnerie est censée se marier, mais on ne dit pas à qui...

---

[41] 'if an unlawful act may be excused by its outcome, what terrible consequences could follow, I ask you, even if he does prescribe a libation of wine to Ceres, just because it is forbidden *at all her Feasts?*'

[42] *Quomodo Plautus Attica exemplaria transtulerit*, diss. Greifswald. 1884 p. 39.

et toute précision serait ridicule.' Does this line of argument carry conviction? At any rate nobody who believes that a wedding of Orcus and Ceres, to which *'temeti nihil allatum'*, (*Aulul*. 355), was celebrated at Rome will credit that the poet had anything else in mind, particularly as the joke would otherwise be hardly intelligible, since in the whole really Roman worship of Ceres libations of wine were permitted.[43] It is my belief that the ban on wine at the Wedding of Ceres had become proverbial, just as in Greece the saying νηφάλια θύειν τῷ Διονύσῳ.[44]

Now let us consider Mackauer's view. He points out with good reason that a wedding of Ceres with the lord of the underworld is by no means an unknown ceremony. In Laconia, in southern Arcadia, 'the god of Hades is wedded to Demeter (not to Kore) and this marriage bond is certainly more ancient than that of Hades and Kore' (thus quoted by Wide, *Lakonische Kulte*, 245, who has collected all the relevant passages). In Sparta and Hermione the god of the underworld on this occasion bears the name Klymenos. But in the Samnite cult at Agnone there appears as associate of Ceres-Demeter an Eyklos, who has been equated, no doubt correctly, with Εὐκλῆς, an Orphic name for the lord of the underworld from Lower Italy (Altheim, *Röm. Religionsgeschichte* II 120). This looks like a bridge from Greece to Rome ... It therefore emerges into the realm of possibility that alongside the young *Graeca Sacra* of Ceres there was another religious celebration, felt as primordially Roman and developed under 'pre-Homeric' Greek influence, in which the god of the underworld, who took the name of the Roman Orcus, was abductor and husband of Ceres herself, not of her daughter.' I must point out how he has been brought to the same conclusion by a completely different route from the one we took above (p. 127) when we supposed that an ancient feast of Ceres had existed in Rome, of Laconian origin.

Let me repeat the words used by Le Bonniec (p. 440) after establishing a much less striking correspondence, 'Cet accord est indice de vérité'. I have already argued above the likelihood that

---

[43] Cf. Cato *agr.* 134; Verg. *Georg.* 1, 344; Hor. *Sat.* 2, 2, 125; Serv. *Georg.* 1, 344 (*'pontificales hoc non vetant libri'*).

[44] Plut. 2, 132 E; cf. Liddell & Scott s.v. νηφάλιος, 'proverb of a frugal meal'.

the Tarentines transmitted this feast to Rome. But if you ask when this happened I frankly confess that owing to the sparsity of tradition I do not know. If we believe Dionysius it must go back to very early times. On Varro's testimony it was certainly older than any other feast, and for that reason I would not venture to suppose that it was instituted in the year 272 B.C., having crept into Rome after the conquest of Tarentum, if only because in this case the mysteries of Bona Dea could boast of the same antiquity. Nor can I think of any other reason against their antiquity.

Now we must consider the second question raised on p. 137. Servius says that 'by their presence *pontifices* celebrated the wedding with Orcus with very great solemnity'. But what have *pontifices* to do with mysteries of Ceres? Surely only women were admitted? There have been varying opinions on this point. Wissowa (R.u.K². 301, 4) declares that Servius' words were *'gewiss ungenau'*, and yet he writes elsewhere (pp. 517f.) 'Their participation in sacred rites performed by other priests is attested on many occasions, and that not only in those of ancient Roman priests, like the Salii and Luperci, but later too in those of the *graecus ritus*, as when in the procession of the *Argei* probably the whole college took part, or when the night celebration of the Bona Dea was performed by the Vestal Virgins.' Thus it is not the Greek rite but the male sex which seems to be the difficulty in the way of *pontifices* being present. Owing to the lack of evidence no definite conclusion can be reached. It seems we have one of two alternatives. Either the ancient festival was open in part to women alone, in part to men (or to men as well) and this part included the Wedding of Orcus—as we know happened at Phlius [45]—or the whole festival was open only to women. Anyone who considers that here was a goddess

---

[45] Pausan. 2, 11, 3: Ἐκ Σικυῶνος δὲ τὴν κατ' εὐθὺ ἐς Φλιοῦντα ἐρχομένοις. . . . Πυραία καλούμενόν ἐστιν ἄλσος, ἱερὸν δὲ ἐν αὐτῷ Προστασίας Δήμητρος καὶ Κόρης. Ἐνταῦθα ἐφ' αὑτῶν οἱ ἄνδρες ἑορτὴν ἄγουσι, τὸν δὲ Νυμφῶνα καλούμενον ταῖς γυναιξὶν ἑορτάζειν παρείκασι· καὶ ἀγάλματα Διονύσου καὶ Δήμητρος καὶ Κόρης τὰ πρόσωπα φαίνοντα ἐν τῷ Νυμφῶνί ἐστιν. The fact that on the evidence of Statius (*Silv.* 4, 8, 50) men too were initiated into the mysteries of Ceres at Naples and took part silently, each brandishing a votive torch, would fit very aptly here, particularly if in Rome too they attended with torches the solemn wedding-procession of Orcus and Ceres.

marrying a god and is aware that often in mystery celebrations such weddings were presented either as a spectacle or to the imagination, so that the priest of the god had intercourse with the high priestess of the goddess,[46] will hardly admit the thought that men could be excluded from such a rite. We do however know of such a ceremony being performed without a man being present, presumably with a simulated intercourse between the high priestess and some image of the god (Fehrle, 10; Klinz, 73).

Nor, whatever the case here, can the tangle be unravelled by reference to the second question I mentioned above—the actual presence of the *pontifices*. Le Bonniec, it is true, judges differently (p. 444): 'Il n'y aurait donc pas d'impossibilité théorique à la participation des pontifes. Mais les prêtresses sont tout de même sous la dépendance directe des décemvirs, dont la présence serait beaucoup plus justifiée.' A true judgment, if only we suppose that the Wedding of Orcus was instituted after the decemvirs began to function as a separate college for the management of religious services. Wissowa (*O.G.*, p. 535) has pointed out that probably the duumvirs, who originally performed their duties, were appointed to the priesthood merely at intervals for supervising particular religious services, until the college of decemvirs was instituted in 367 B.C. Before that, however, all private religious services were in charge of the *pontifices*, whose office was *beratender Art* ('advisory'—cf. Geiger, *RE* 1A, 1659, 59). Whether the Wedding of Orcus was a private ceremony or not is a matter of dispute. Le Bonniec has quite rightly argued that the Ceres-ceremonies were only made public when the annual festival was instituted. In any case we cannot expect that the *pontifices* would have transferred this charge to the decemvirs once it had been assigned to them. Therefore if it were certain, which it is not, that the Wedding of Orcus existed before the year 367 B.C., we should not see any difficulty in the presence of *pontifices* even if we knew that only women took part in it. These uncertainties are tiresome but inevitable.

I must say a few words about the annual Ceres-Feast itself

[46] Cf. K. H. E. de Jong, *Das antike Mysterienwesen*, 21; L. Deubner, *Attische Feste*, 40; E. Fehrle, *Kultische Keuschheit* (RVV 6) 105; A. Klinz, Ἱερὸς Γάμος (diss. Halle 1933) 73, 116.

Le Bonniec has examined in great detail the question at what time of year it was held. Livy (22, 56, 4f.) relates that after the disaster of Cannae the whole city was filled with mourning, to such an extent *ut sacrum anniversarium Cereris intermissum sit.* The Battle of Cannae is recorded as having taken place on 2 August (Gell. 5, 17, 5), and the Feast of Ceres is generally assigned to the beginning of August. Le Bonniec, however, rightly points out that the dating system had gradually fallen into confusion and had not yet been corrected, so he follows F. Cornelius (*Klio, Beiheft* 26 (1932) 1ff.; Le Bonniec, p. 404) in holding that the battle really occurred in the middle of June. In this he could also have consulted Mommsen, who sixty years earlier (*Röm. Gesch.* I [6], 602) had written that the battle of Cannae was fought 'in the grey of the morning of the 2 August according to the uncorrected, in about June according to the correct, calendar'. Le Bonniec in my opinion proceeds less happily when he tries to fix more precisely the days on which the Feast was celebrated. 'Tite-Live dit exactement' he contends (p. 401), que la fête a été interrompue: *sacrum.... intermissum sit* (et non pas totalement omise, ce qui se dirait *omissum,* ou *praetermissum)*'. Wrong. I wonder how he would explain Curtius' words (4, 3, 23): *Sacrum quoque, quod equidem dis minime cordi esse crediderim, multis saeculis intermissum, repetendi auctores quidam erant.*[47] Then we have Plutarch's express words (*Fab. Max.* 18, 2): Ἑορτῆς τε Δήμητρος εἰς τὰς ἡμέρας ἐκείνας καθηκούσης βέλτιον ἐφάνη παραλιπεῖν ὅλως τάς τε θυσίας καὶ τὴν πομπὴν ἢ τὸ μέγεθος τῆς συμφορᾶς ὀλιγότητι καὶ κατηφείᾳ τῶν συνερχομένων ἐλέγχεσθαι.[48]

This passage has not been overlooked by Le Bonniec (p. 402, 2) but he refrains from quoting the actual words. παραλείπειν, however, means the same as *omittere, praetermittere,* not *intermittere* in the sense of interrupt. Finally Livy's own actual words should have given him pause for doubt. According to Le Bonniec the

---

[47] 'There were also some who favoured reviving the Feast, interrupted for many centuries, which I should hardly have thought was dear to the gods.'

[48] 'And as the Feast of Demeter was then due it seemed better to pass over the sacrifices and procession entirely than to expose the greatness of the disaster by the fewness and misery of the participants'.

Feast of Ceres consisted—and I know no reason against it [49]—of nine days of abstinence followed by the *Inventio Proserpinae*. Consequently if the day of the battle of Cannae really interrupted

[49] Although some points still remain obscure to me and Le Bonniec has not satisfactorily explained them either. I think I have shown that he was wrong when he wrote (p. 404), 'Nous avons tiré du texte de Tite-Live l'indication que les cérémonies de la fête annuelle de Cérès-Déméter devaient durer plusieurs jours'. Nor is the argument (p. 408) from Ov. *Amor.* 3, 10, 1 much more convincing. The line has '*annua venerunt Cerealis tempora sacri*', 'the yearly season' (lit. 'times') 'of the Ceres-Feast has come', and Le Bonniec comments, 'l'expression *tempora annua*, indéterminée, mais impropre à désigner une seule journée'. But Ovid frequently uses plural *tempora* with a singular meaning (cf. S. G. Owen *ad Trist.* II, 484), e.g. about the spring equinox, '*tempora nocturnis aequa diurna*' (*Fast.* 3, 878). So there remains only that one passage of Ovid, *Met.* 10, 434, '*perque novem noctes venerem tactusque viriles / in vetitis numerant*', which though the context is one of Cyprian rites is by almost universal consent thought to refer to the Annual Feast. I cannot quote anything better, but there is something to wonder at. Dealing with the *castus Cereris* Le Bonniec writes, 'Nous nous proposons de montrer que pendant neuf jours les adoratrices de Cérès devaient faire pénitence, pour s'associer aux souffrances de la déesse'. But in Festus (p. 144 L) we read: '*Minuitur....luctus....privatis...., cum liberi nati sunt, cum honos in familiam venit, cum puerens aut liberi aut vir aut frater ab hoste captus domum redit, cum puella desponsa est, cum propiore quis cognatione quam is, qui lugetur, natus est, cum in casto Cereris est, omnique gratulatione*'. 'Mourning for private people is remitted when children are born, when honour comes to the family, when a relation or children or a husband or brother made prisoner by the enemy returns home, when a girl is betrothed, when a baby is born more closely related than the person who is mourned, *when it is during the castus Cereris*', or at any public thanksgiving'. When every instance breathes joy and hilarity, what, I ask, can have moved Verrius Flaccus to insert an 'Abstinence' of Ceres full of grief and repentance? Did he refer only to the day of the Finding and quietly overlook the nine days of the actual *castus*? As Le Bonniec himself, perhaps forgetting these words of Festus, a little later tells us (p. 408), 'Le *sacrum anniversarium* est une fête d'allégresse'. Then there are those other words of Ovid (*Am.* 3, 10, 43ff.) '*Quod tibi secubitus tristes, dea flava, fuissent, / hoc cogor sacris nunc ego ferre tuis. / Cur ego sim tristis, cum sit tibi nata reperta / regnaque quam Iuno sorte minore regat?*' 'What were sad and lonely nights for you, golden goddess, I now am compelled to bear at your Feast. Why should I be sad, when your daughter has been found and rules a domain second only to Juno's?' So Proserpine has been found and yet the Abstinence is still in force? Could it have been that apart from the priestesses themselves the women observed continence only on the day of the Feast, as was the custom in the ancient *Thesmophoria* (cf. Fehrle 158, 'The ἀντλήτριαι only have to abstain for three days. For the rest of the women chastity was probably prescribed only on the feast days, as in the ancient cults generally, where a term is seldom indicated')? In that case, however, Ovid's nine days would not be explained.

the Feast even if on that precise day the celebration of the Feast had just begun, there were not more than nine days remaining on which the Feast could be interrupted in the sense desired by Le Bonniec. To any attentive reader of Livy's account it will be quite plain that several days must have passed before it became known at Rome who had fallen and who were the survivors of the battle. For it was some time, some days at least (cf. Dio Cass. frgm. 57, 29), before a despatch arrived from the consul C. Terentius Varro (Liv. 22, 56, 1) informing them among other things that he 'was at Canusium collecting the survivors of the great disaster'. Thus it was not even then known for certain who were the dead for each woman to mourn. It follows that when we read (Liv. 22, 56, 4) *'tum privatae quoque per domos clades volgatae sunt'* ('then too the private disasters began to spread from house to house'), the *tum* does not mean 'at that moment of time' but 'from then on' and, as the subject itself indicates, 'in the following days'. The strongest argument in support of this interpretation is the words that follow: *'adeoque totam urbem opplevit luctus, ut sacrum anniversarium Cereris intermissum sit, quia nec lugentibus id facere est fas, nec ulla in illa tempestate matrona expers luctus fuerat'*.[50] The significance of this pluperfect did not escape Weissenborn-Müller *ad loc.*, where one reads: 'nicht in Trauer versetzt war, *als man das Fest feiern wollte*' (my italics W.). All this evidence is enough and more than enough to show that the Feast of Ceres had not yet been celebrated when the battle of Cannae was fought, but was due some days later, near the beginning of July.

Finally from the great abundance of my notes on this book there are certainly a few worth producing here. How it could have happened that Le Bonniec in interpreting the name *Proserpina* (p. 189) has adopted Varro's etymology,[51] 'Proserpine, déesse de la végétation qui rampe', which all qualified judges known to me have long since dismissed,[52] is beyond my comprehension. A little

[50] 'And the whole city was so overwhelmed by mourning that the Annual Feast of Ceres was passed over because it was forbidden to those in mourning to participate and the calamity had left no married woman out of mourning.'

[51] *Ling. lat.* 5, 68: '*Dicta Proserpina, quod haec ut serpens modo in dexteram modo in sinisteram partem late movetur*'—'called Proserpina because she moves from side to side like a serpent now to the right and now to the left'.

[52] Cf. Ernout-Meillet and Walde-Hofmann on the name; Carter, *Rosch. Lex.* 3, 2, 3142; Wissowa 310.

earlier (p. 183) he put a question to which I must reply, because he was right to ask it. It concerns the three days on which the *mundus Cereris* was open. I once (*Studies* 167f.) quoted the scholium Bernense on Verg. *Ecl.* 3, 104: *Apud antiquos fuit altissimus puteus, in quo descendebat puer ad sacra celebranda quo cognosceret anni proventus*. Following other authors I took this as an allusion to the *mundus Cereris* and I proceeded to write: 'This is therefore a case of a magic rite for the purpose of "examining" and probably stimulating growth in the soil. The part played by boys in antique magic and religious ceremonies is well-known. It is not surprising that this magic should be applied just before sowing; it seems to our ideas less self-evident that they should do so as early as on the 24th of August but it is not absurd.' On this Le Bonniec observes, 'M. Wagenvoort auralt dû dire pourquoi cette interprétation "n'était pas absurde".' Here now is my reply. When we speak of 'the sowing' it is almost universally agreed that it is the sowing of grain which is meant. But there were also other crops at that period most necessary to human survival. The most useful of these were covered by Cato (*Agr.* 134, 1) in these words: '*Cereri porca praecidanea porco femina, priusquam hasce fruges condas*: *far, triticum, hordeum, fabam, semen rapicium*'.[53] Thus he deliberately combines beans and turnips with corn grains. But these crops were sown towards the end of August.[54] For this reason my conclusion above did not seem to me absurd, nor does it now. I have a note in passing (*ad* p. 197) on Paulus' gloss (p. 81 L.) '*Florifertum dictum quod eo die spicae feruntur ad sacrarium*';[55] for *Florifertum* in my opinion *Floriferium* should be substituted, for that is how a series of such compounds were formed: *florilegium, spicilegium, sacrificium, fordicidium, tubilustrium, lectisternium*, etc.[56]—'Au milieu de ces vieilles divinités agraires' writes Le Bonniec (p. 190) 'se rencontre le culte singulier de *Iuppiter Arborator*. Il ne nous est connu que

[53] 'The preliminary sacrifice to Ceres is a sow, before harvesting spelt, wheat, barley, beans, and rape'.
[54] Theophr. *Hist. plant.* 7, 1 (cf. Orth, *RE* 7, 1122ff.); Colum. 11, 3, 59; Pallad. 9, 1, 1.
[55] 'It is called '*Florifertum*' because that is the day on which ears of corn are brought to the shrine'.
[56] Equally tentative, though in my opinion vain, is Walde-Hofmann's attempt (1, 484) to defend the received form.

par le texte de la *Notitia*, qui mentionne pour la XIe région (Grand Cirque) une *aedem Matris Deum et Iovis Arboratoris*....Bien que le mot *arborator* semble relativement récent—mais c'est peut-être une forme rajeunie—ce culte doit être archaïque'. I wonder who will believe in this 'early' god. It occurs once, in the *Notitia Regionum* of the fourth century, and that together with the Phrygian Goddess —a point Le Bonniec does not even hint at. But here perhaps the splinter can be extracted from the wound if, as Aust supposes (*Rosch. Lex.* 2, 1, 661), they were two neighbouring temples. However, there are other reasons why we should not accept Le Bonniec's notion that *Jupiter Arborator* was a guardian and caretaker of trees and of vines above all! Aust again has justly written, 'The word formation *"arborator"* shows that the drawing out of this special function from the universal concept of a nature deity cannot have occurred before the Imperial Age. None of the *cognomina* derived from substantival verbs (*Fulgurator, Serenator, Sospitator, Tonitrator, Tutator*) are attested earlier.' If the *cognomen* '*Arborator*' has come down to us correctly—there is a more recent reading *Arbitrator*, equally without parallel—it can hardly be supposed that the country people of early times would have given it to Jupiter, since '*arborator*' is a rustic term meaning a 'lopper' or 'tree surgeon'. I had rather believe—but this is a mere guess—that we here have some 'Hellenistic' god, possibly from Greece itself, where on the island of Rhodes at any rate a Ζεὺς Ἔνδενδρος was worshipped.[57]

To conclude: as I said at the beginning, Le Bonniec in his handling of this material has put in a wonderful amount of hard work and I am sure he has not wasted his time. All the same, led astray perhaps by certain prejudiced opinions, he has been frequently entangled in error, and the last word in Ceres research is a long way from having been said.

[57] On the epithets Ἔνδενδρος and Δενδρίτης cf. Jessen, *RE* 5, 2553 and 215.

IX

ON THE MAGICAL SIGNIFICANCE OF THE TAIL

From time to time, often at long intervals, I used to come across representations in literature or the visual arts in which the tail of an animal, almost always a bull or a horse, played a significant part. At first I could not explain them, but little by little vague impressions began to cohere and the various details formed themselves into what I thought was a satisfactory synthesis. I concern myself, at least in this article, exclusively with the Indo-European cultural sphere. Things outside it will be treated only incidentally. So far as I know the topic has not received more than an occasional mention, although Eitrem did observe quite rightly, in his *Beiträge zur Griechischen Religionsgeschichte*:[1] 'The important role of the tail in religion and superstition can be established in many ways among the Greeks and Romans as well.' He then refers to the Roman 'October Horse', which first started me thinking about the question. Perhaps it would be best first of all to examine the three cases which specially aroused my curiosity and base my further examination on that.

Let us begin then with the October Horse. It is well-known that among the time-honoured rites which the Romans kept up through the centuries was a ceremony on the 15th October in honour of the god Mars. On the Campus Martius chariot races were held. When they were over the strongest horse of the victorious team, which was always the right-hand one, was sacrificed to Mars, after its head and tail had first been cut off. Then there was a fight for the head between the residents of two quarters of the city, the *Via Sacra* and the *Subura*. The victorious party was allowed to fasten the head to a wall in its own quarter. But the bleeding tail had to be taken by a fast runner at full speed to the Regia and the blood made to drip still warm on the sacred Hearth of State. According to Verrius Flaccus (in Paul. ex Festo 246 L.) this was done *ob frugum eventum*. But whether this means 'in thanks for

[1] *Skrifter Videnskapsselskapet i Kristiania. II Hist.-filos. Kl.* (1919) 28.

the completed harvest' or 'for the sake of the next harvest' scholars are not agreed. For my purposes only one thing is important, that an old source connects the blood from the tail with the promotion of fertility. Wissowa (*R.u.K.*² 145), it is true, writes to contest Verrius' explanation: 'This explanation is ruled out by the association of the rite with the Equirria in the middle of the War Festival of Mars, especially as there is a much plainer one. The champion steed ... is sacred to the war god (Plut. *Qu. Rom.* 97) and therefore sacrificed ... to him.' However, Verrius had seen this too: in Paulus the immediately following words are, *et equus potius quam bos immolabatur, quod hic bello, bos frugibus pariendis est aptus.* But this in no way explains the ceremony with the horse's tail. We must add, moreover, that there exist strong indications that the original function of Mars was that of a fertility god and at the same time of an underworld god.²

We shall return to the October Horse, but now direct our attention to the second occasion for my researches, a well-known feature of the illustrations of the Mithras-cult. Numerous reliefs show the Persian god killing the cosmic bull at the command of Ahriman. With his left hand he grips his nostrils and with his right plunges the dagger in his neck. To left and right usually stand Cautes and Cautopates, the one with raised, the other with lowered torch, to personify the morning and evening stars. The death of the bull will bring fertility on earth and summon men, beasts, and plants to existence. Several reliefs symbolize this in such a way that ears of corn are seen growing from the tip of the animal's tail (Plate II). Why the tail? Would it not be more natural if they came out of the head, or, even more intelligibly, out of the wound? This last does in fact occur exceptionally, once and no more among hundreds of illustrations, on a relief in the British Museum (Plate III). In another way too this relief makes an exception, since it puts

² Cf. Wagenvoort, *Studies in Roman Literature, Culture, and Religion* (1956), 193ff. What another passage in *Paulus* (50 L) actually refers to is unfortunately not clear. But the words '*Caviares hostiae dicebantur, quod caviae pars hostiae cauda tenus dicitur, et ponebatur in sacrificio pro collegio pontificum quinto quoque anno*' seem to show that the tail was cut from other sacrificial animals as well. We do not know for what purpose. The passage cannot refer to the October Horse, since that was an annual festival. Cf. Walde-Hofmann s.v.

Cautes and Cautopates both behind the bull. Unfortunately their heads are missing, together with the tip of the bull's tail. Vermaseren [3] after a study of the relief itself wrote: 'Cautopates points his torch downwards with both hands; Cautes with his right hand grasps the bull's tail, holding a torch with his upraised left hand.' Thus we do not know whether the tail ended in ears of corn here too, but another detail deserves attention, the grasping of the tail by Cautes. This too is rather unusual, though not altogether unique. On a relief in the Vatican Museum [4] for instance it is Cautopates who grasps the bull's tail with his left hand. And Vermaseren [5] has published 'an important monument in the Reiss-Museum in Mannheim' (Plate IV) representing Mithras the bull-slayer. The relief is distinguished by a remarkable configuration of the god and unusual details which I cannot here go into. But the figure which holds the tail—Vermaseren is inclined to call him Cautes—deserves special notice. V. writes, in my opinion quite correctly, 'It (the figure) desires ... immediate participation in the magical force of fruitfulness issuing from the bull.' But I shall return to this. What does the posture signify? Is he trying to prevent the bull escaping? It hardly looks like it. In both cases the bull is already pressed to the ground. So that is our second question. Let us pass to the third.

This time the scene is not Italy or Persia but Thrace. There the Thracian Rider was worshipped, often under the name Heros or Heron. Numerous reliefs are evidence of his cult. Professor Kazarow in his standardwork *Die Denkmäler des thrakischen Reitergottes in Bulgarien* (1938) [6] can vouch for many more than a thousand of them from Bulgaria alone. They pose several questions which can be answered either not at all or only in part. We do not know, for instance, how far the god went under different names in different places. There are different views on the relationship between the name Heros and its Greek homonym. But most of these questions have no bearing on ours. Kazarow divides the reliefs into three

---

[3] Vermaseren, *Corpus Inscr. et Monum. Relig. Mithr.* p. 225, n. 593 and Fig. 168.
[4] Vermaseren, ibid. p. 216, n. 556 and Fig. 159.
[5] *Mannheimer Hefte* 1958, 2, 16ff.
[6] *Dissertationes Pannonicae*, Ser. 2 fasc. 14.

groups,[7] as follows: a) the Rider keeps his horse stationary or at a walking pace: sometimes there are accessory figures, which are found also in other groups; b) the Rider is hunting, on a galloping horse; c) the Rider, still galloping, is returning from the hunt with his game. Accessory figures, common to all three groups, are principally: a hound, under the horse, chasing a wild boar; a female figure in front of the Rider with a cloak drawn over her head, who at the same time raises her right hand in adoration or holds a goblet in it; and a third figure which I propose to consider more closely. Of course we must not forget that these reliefs are all from the 2nd or 3rd century A.D., that is, rather late, and that they are obviously much under the influence of Greek tomb reliefs dedicated to the memory of the illustrious dead. These already bore the honorary title *Heros*[8] at an early date and were for preference depicted as riders, and probably hunting at that. I shall have more to say about the relationship between the Thracian and Greek representations.

The third accessory figure I have mentioned is a man who stands behind the horse and usually holds its tail (Plate V). The Rider is in his usual costume with flying cloak; in front of him two women, behind him the servant—for that is how he is usually designated—who holds the horse's tail. The servant is called by Kazarow a *piqueur*, or whipper-in. Ernest Will too, (*ad* fig. 306) who dealt with all of this material together with the Mithras-reliefs some years ago [9] speaks of an *écuyer*, or 'squire'. Whether groom or squire, the prevailing view seems to be that the subordinate uses this method of stopping the horse from galloping away against the Rider's will. And I do not doubt that the sculptor from the imperial age had some such idea. But is it always the case? It would still be conceivable in the case of one relief (Kazarow Fig. 403), in which three youths are standing behind Rider and horse, and the foremost among them holds its tail. Anybody, or a god in any case, might have three grooms or stable-boys. It is a different matter in my opinion on a relief (Plate VI), the description of which I quote from Kazarow (Fig. 301, cf. p. 103) because some of the details are

[7] Pp. 6f.; cf. Will, *op. cit.* (n. 9 below) 66ff.
[8] Cf. S. Eitrem, *RE* 8, 1138.
[9] *Le Relief cultuel Gréco-Romain* (1955) 67.

unclear on the reproduction: 'Rider facing right, thick hair with headband, belted chiton and chlamys partly flying backwards, right hand outstretched to receive the gift; before him a female figure with hair parted, in long belted chiton with mantle the left hand lowered, offering the Rider a fruit (?) in the right: behind the horse a similarly clothed woman holding the horse's tail with her right hand.' Has the god female stable-hands? The only earlier treatment of this question I have been able to find was that of Georges Seure.[10] But the solution he offers is in my opinion not very convincing. It is, he suggests, a woman, perhaps one of the Nymphs: *'C'est une femme, peut-être une des Nymphes, qui joue auprès du Cavalier ce rôle de suivante à pied.'* Certainly a solution that will not satisfy everybody. But though this case is something of an exception it is not altogether unique. There are two figures standing behind the Rider on another relief. Kazarow (Fig. 47, cf. p. 36), after first describing a figure in front of the Rider as 'female form front face, with chiton and mantle covering the back of the head, the hands apparently crossed under the breast', continues: 'Behind the Rider two figures in the same posture and costume who hold the horse's tail.' Given that these figures are indistinct, yet there can be no doubt that they have drawn their mantles over their heads. In the reliefs this occurs regularly with women, never with men. So here we have actually two women who hold the horse's tail, and if we are unwilling to suppose that the god generally preferred female stable-hands, a third tail problem presents itself. I believe that between the amputated tail of the October Horse, the corn-bearing tail of the Mithras-bull, and the horsetail-holding worshippers of the Thracian Rider-God a certain connection can be proved. Let us take the three points one by one, the October Horse first.

In contrast to the other two problems the October Horse's tail has interested many. First let us take Mannhardt, who in his *Mythologische Forschungen* adduced parallels from other lands and other times. He himself does not doubt, any more than most later scholars, that it is a case of fertility magic, though of course not everybody agrees with him when he immediately introduces the

[10] 'Étude sur quelques types curieux du Cavalier Thrace', *REA*. 14 (1912) 158.

vegetation *daemon* (cf. p. 159, 2; 183), as Frazer does too,[11] calling the October Horse 'an incarnation of the corn-spirit'. Onians, too, in his excellent work *The Origins of European Thought* (1951) seems to agree with this point of view.[12] I want to express myself more carefully and with Eitrem (o.c. 29) allow it as probable that the tail has a direct connection with the corn harvest. Of the parallels cited by Mannhardt I make special mention of two or three. In the neighbourhood of Alençon in Normandy as soon as the threshing is ended they bring the farmer's wife a 'straw-man', who offers her his heart. She answers it with the gift of a ram or a wether. It is immediately slaughtered and a banquet prepared, but first the tail is cut off, roast separately, and cut into as many pieces as there are young girls in the party, each of whom is given a piece. It cannot be doubted, Mannhardt (p. 186) rightly says, that 'the tail here... is distributed with the obvious meaning of future fertility.'

In some districts of Germany the bride at her wedding gets the roast pig's tail. These examples have been repeatedly quoted but nobody seems to have remarked that the folk-custom must go back to classical antiquity.[13] How else can we explain that in the *Testamentum Porcelli*, the witty but in some places rather coarse burlesque which the Church Father Jerome [14] twice uses as an illustration of what his contemporaries find more interesting than devotional books, the 'porker' sets out a long list of bequests of particular parts of his body to different groups of people, including *mulieribus lumbulos ... puellis caudam*? When the first barley is sown in Kurland, they boil a back of pork, according to Mannhardt (183), cut off the tail, and stick it upright in the baulk of the ploughland. The corn stems will grow as tall as the tail is long. When in East Prussia, so Frazer records (*Golden Bough* 7, 272), the peasants see a wolf running across their fields, they watch carefully to see whether

---

[11] *The Golden Bough*, 8, 49.

[12] P. 126. Cf. also J. J. Meyer, *Trilogie altindischer Mächte und Feste der Vegetation* 3 (1937) 237.

[13] It is discussed in quite a different context by Ludwig Radermacher, 'Beiträge zur Volkskunde aus dem Gebiet der Antike' (*SBB. Wien, phil.-hist. Kl.* 187, 3 - 1918); he quotes variants from Köhler's *Kleine Schrifte*, which in part too are comparable with our theme here.

[14] *Praef.* XII *Comm. Isai.* 493 V (XXIV 425 M); in Rufin. 1, 17 (XXIII 430 M). The text of the *Testamentum* is also in Buecheler's edition of Petron., p. 243f.

PLATE II. Marble relief from the Esquiline. Vatican, Mus. Chiaram. XIV 1 (M. J. Vermaseren, Corpus inscriptionum et monumentorum religionis Mithriacae I, 1956, No. 368, Fig. 106)

PLATE III Marble group from Rome. London Br. Mus. 1721 (Vermaseren I, No. 593, Fig. 168)

PLATE IV. Sandstone relief from the valley of the Neckar. Mannheim, Reiss Museum
(Vermaseren II, 1960, No. 1275, Fig. 334).

PLATE V. Thracian rider-god. Sofia inv. 3100 (G. I. Kazarow, Die Denkmäler des thrakischen Reitergottes in Bulgarien, 1938, Pl. LII 306)

PLATE VI. Thracian rider-god. Sofia inv. 2953 (Kazarow Pl. LII 301)

PLATE VII. Rock-paintings from Tanum, Sweden (O. Almgren, Nordische Felszeichnungen als religiöse Urkunden, Frankfurt a.M. 1934, p. 122, Abb. 80)

PLATE VIII. Corinthian pinax from Penteskouphia. Berlin F 865 (Antike Denkmäler II, Pl. 23, 11)

PLATE IX. Rock-painting from Val Camonica (F. Altheim, Italien und Rom, Amsterdam-Leipzig 1941, Abb. 14)

PLATE X. Potnia Theron, fragment of a 'Melian' amphora. Berlin F 301 (D. Papastamos, Melische Amphoren, 1970, 65, Pl. 14a)

PLATE XI. Marble relief from Tanagra. Athens N. M. 1386 (J. N. Svoronos, Das Athener Nationalmuseum, 1908-37, Pl. 52)

PLATE XII. Thracian rider-god with cornucopia. Sofia inv. 1322 (Kazarow Pl. XLV 265)

it is holding its tail up or trailing it close to the ground. In the first case they try to kill it, but if it is trailed over the ground they thank the animal for the blessing it brings and offer it dainties to eat. And to switch from West to East, in an ancient Indian animal sacrifice, when the victim was dismembered the tail was put aside as a special offering for the gnās, the wives of the gods. 'This custom' writes Johansson (*Über die altindische Göttin Dhiṣaṇa und Verwandtes*) [15] 'is analogous with the folk-customs mentioned by Mannhardt and related to them.' And he adds: 'The tail in fertility rites sometimes represents the male member.' He adds some references which could very easily be added to, because it had been noticed often enough that in almost all languages the words for the two members are often interchanged. I say 'interchanged', for it is not the case, as it is often made out to be, that the *membrum virile* is only called 'tail' for decency's sake. Not only is this out of the question at periods when phallus images played an important part in all kinds of cults and were carried around in solemn procession, but the tail itself could just as well be called *penis*. Thus Cicero informs us (*Ep. ad. Fam.* 9, 22, 2) *caudam antiqui penem vocabant, ex quo est propter similitudinem penicillus. At hodie penis est in obscenis.*[16] It is clear that *penem* is a predicative substantive. According to Cicero the word in his day was regarded as indecent, but the diminutive *penicillus* ('paint-brush', cf. modern German *Pinsel*), that was still in general use, really meant 'little tail'. He may be right there, because a tail was generally used as a whisk or feather duster. See for instance what von Negelein says about the use of a horse's tail for cleaning purposes.[17] Cicero's information is confirmed by other writers. Festus (260 L.) for instance not only makes the same observation but also adds that a sacrificial offering consisting of a piece of pig's tail was called *offa penita*. That other factors are involved here than a mere similarity of form is hardly to be doubted. Onians (126, 3; 149ff.; 207f.; 213) dealt with this question in a different context. I briefly give his views. The tail is

---

[15] *Skrifter kongl. human. Vetenskaps-samfundet i Uppsala* 20 (1917-1919) 117; cf. H. Oldenberg, *Religion des Veda* ², 358.

[16] Cf. *Paul.* p. 231 L. *Peniculi spongiae propter similitudinem caudarum appellatae. Penes enim vocabantur caudae.*

[17] *Das Pferd im arischen Altertum* = *Teutonia* 2 (1903) 9.

the continuation of the spine. This contains the bone-marrow, which according to Pliny and other sources consists of the same substance as the brain and is the seat of all the vital force. In ancient literature the marrow (Gr. μυελός, Lat. *medulla*) is constantly considered as the seat even of feeling and the emotions. It goes so far that bone-marrow is even supposed to contain semen, which is why Plato in the Timaeus [18] speaks of γόνιμος μυελός 'reproductive marrow'. Connected with this must be the fact that to this day we call the rumpbone the sacrum, from the Roman *os sacrum*, just as the Greek was ἱερὸν ὀστοῦν.[19] This is more or less parallel with Eitrem's line of thought (29, 32), that for the Greeks and Romans 'tail was phallus'. He cites the scholiast on Aeschylus *Prom.* 496f., who says the tail was sacrificed to the gods σπέρματα ἔχουσα 'containing semen'.[20]

It was natural here that some [21] should feel reminded of the passages in the *Avesta*,[22] referring to the primal bull killed by Ahriman, from whose marrow sprouted fifty-five different sorts of

[18] 77 D. Cf. Cels. 5, 2 *ex medullis profluere semen videtur*; 7, 18. 1 *testiculi simile quiddam medullis habent*.

[19] Onians, *op. cit.* 119. Cf. Eitrem, *op. cit.* 32, 5: 'According to the Schol. ad Ar. *pac.* 1053 the servant must not touch the lower part of the spine (ὀσφύς, ὀσφὺς ἄκρα in Men. *Dysk.*, Athen. IV 146e, fr. 129 K.) with the skewer because it is used for soothsaying.' *Etym. m.* 468, 24: ἱερὸν ὀστοῦν· τὸ ἄκρον τῆς ὀσφύος· οὕτω γὰρ κέκληται. . . . ὅτι ἱερουργεῖται τοῖς Θεοῖς. —E. Stemplinger, *Antiker Volksglaube* (1948) 123 (no source quoted): 'When bulls refuse to mount, a stag's tail is burnt and the bull's testicles brushed with the ashes. . .; if he-goats' or rams' tails are tied in the middle, they refuse to mount.'

[20] The passage was also considered by Eitrem, op. cit. 32, but differently interpreted. On μακρὰν ('one would expect ἄκραν, Eitrem) ὀσφὺν πυρώσας the Scholiast remarks: εὐκίνητος γὰρ οὖσα καὶ σπέρματα ἔχουσα θύεται τοῖς Θεοῖς (ἀφ' οὗ καὶ κλόνις [ἱερὸν ὀστοῦν] ὀνομάζεται διὰ τὸ ἀεικίνητον). E. comments: 'Thus the Scholiast too was quite familiar with the equivalence ὀσφύς or κέρκος (οὐρά) = *Phallos*.' Indeed he may have been, but that cannot in my opinion be inferred from this passage. κλόνις is the *os sacrum*, which can more readily be equated with the tail than with the phallus. According to H. Lommel, 'Mithras und das Stieropfer' (*Paideuma* 3, 1949, 214) the bull's semen is the life-giving *Haoma*. So far as I can judge (not very far I fear) that may be right, I would then be inclined to regard this view as an Iranian specialization of an older Indo-European belief.

[21] Among others Wilh. Koppers, 'Pferdeopfer und Pferdekult der Indo-germanen', *Wiener Beitr. z. Kulturgesch. und Linguistik* (1936) 378.

[22] *Bundehišn* 10, 1; 14, 1; 27, 2 (Tr. West); *Datastān-i-dēnīk* (Tr. Zaehner in Turvan), kindly supplied by my colleague Professor Kohlbrugge.

grain and twelve medicinal herbs. There is in any case a direct recall of the Mithras bull with the ears of corn sprouting from its tail, even though the two are not quite the same.

I must deal very briefly with a phenomenon on Greek soil which at once calls the tail affair to mind. The popular fancy there was crowded with satyrs and sileni. Originally they all had horse's tails, often too horse's ears and feet, or at any rate hoofs. Later, under the influence of the Dionysus cult this was changed to a goat figure, which however occurs nowhere in the art of the archaic period (Hartmann, *RE* 3 A, 37, 34). Many of these figures are ithyphallic. I have the impression, though I could not prove it, that originally two forms could be distinguished. First there was the horse-spirit, the personification of extraordinary strength and of other horse attributes. According to Wiesner's researches it was the Thracians, Germans, and Celts who first became acquainted with these from the twelfth century B.C. onward, while the Greeks and Romans did not come into contact with them till much later (*ARW* 37 (1941/42) 36). If I am right, it is generally believed that from this time onward the bull had to yield its pride of place to the horse as a specially sacred animal. But beside these horse-spirits we must in my opinion think in particular of people who for cult purposes had fastened to themselves a horse's tail, so as to absorb the horse's magic force. Scandinavian rock drawings of the Bronze Age seem to me evidence of this original situation, for instance a drawing from Tanum in Sweden (Plate VII) taken from Oscar Almgren's book, *Nordische Felszeichnungen als religiöse Urkunden* (Fig. 80; cf. p. 122). Of course the interpretation is not quite certain, but it is natural to suppose that the tall figure in the middle with a battle-axe in his hand is a god and, in the opinion of Almberg and others, a fertility god. The figure on the right with bow and arrow is taken, no doubt correctly, to be the winter god who is being driven off his ship by his assailant. He occurs also in other rock drawings, and in the Finnish epic *Kalevala* there are passages which clearly refer to such a ritual combat between summer and winter and in which a ship also plays a part (Almgren, 326, 2). It is further noticeable that here (and in many other representations) both the god and several mortals are shown not only ithyphallic but also wearing tails. In my opinion there can be no doubt of this. Strangely enough, there was previously a notion of a sword in a scabbard, but A. W. Persson, as quoted by Almberg, was the first (1936) to come down in favour of the tail, and Almberg too supports this interpretation.[23] Since these are fertility ceremonies—as convincingly argued by the same scholar [24]—we may probably venture in this case too to consider the tail as a magical instrument of creative force. As I have said I cannot here spend time on the supposition that the Greek satyrs are closely related to these Scandinavian figures, which is rather corroborated than refuted by their later association with Dionysus.[25]

Another representation of which the interpretation is disputed can best be inserted here (Plate VIII). An Old Corinthian *pinax* shows a rider on horseback. On the rump stands a dwarfish spirit holding its phallus with both hands. According to Weniger (*Rosch. Lex.* 5, 99) this must be the demon Taraxippus, who in popular belief used to strike terror into horses. Apart from other reasons for doubt, the horse shows no sign of agitation. Roscher [26] thought it an incubus or 'nightmare', and explained its ithyphallic form by the character traits of the 'nightmare' demon. It would not be clear from this, however, what it was doing behind the rider. But Herter in his comprehensive treatise on the phallus (*RE* 19, 1695, 22) comes to the following conclusion: 'I for one would rather regard it as a helpful spirit and explain its ithyphallic state by the apotropaic force of the phallus rather than with Roscher by the erotic features of nightmares.' This seems correct to me. I only wonder whether there is not a closer connection between this protective character and the special meaning attributed to the horse's tail. In other words, is not this demon perhaps the personification of the force inherent in the tail on which he stands?

There is yet another function of the horse's tail in the ancient

---

[23] So too Ferd. Herrmann, 'Zu einem verbreiteten Verwandlungsrequisit europäischer Kultbünde', in the *Jahrbuch des Linden-Museums* 1951, 102ff. He also brings the satyrs into his account. (Reference supplied by my colleague Professor von Koenigswald).

[24] Cf. Jan de Vries, *Altgerm. Religionsgesch*[1]. 1, 114ff.

[25] According to Eitrem, *op. cit.* 31, both the horse's and the goat's tail of satyrs and sileni were a survival of their original animal form. That is correct in my opinion for the goat's tail but only partly so for the horse's tail.

[26] *Abh. Sächs. Ges. d. Wiss., phil.-hist.* Kl. 20, 2 (1903) 74f.

Greek world to which I must refer. That is the κόρυς (τρυφάλεια, κυνέη) ἵππουρις (ἱππόκομος, ἱπποδάσεια, ἱππόλοφος). Why did the prehistoric warriors wear a horse's tail on their helmets? Only for ornament? That is the usual verdict, and for historical times it may be the right answer. We have it on the authority of no less a source than Alcaeus (*Frgm.* 15, 2f.): λάμπραισιν κυνέαισι, κατταν λευκοὶ κατύπερθεν ἵππιοι λόφοι νεύοισιν, κεφάλαισιν ἀνδρῶν ἀγάλματα. All the same, Homer for one puts more emphasis on the terrifying than on the ornamental effect of the helmet plume (e.g. *Il.* 3, 336; 6, 467ff.) and Vergil follows him: Mezentius (Aen. 8, 620) wears *terribilem cristis galeam*. According to Herodotus 1, 171, the plumed helmet is of Carian origin and the same is testified by Strabo (14, 660) and Pliny (*N.H.* 7, 200). But Strabo's own citation of a fragment of Alcaeus (22) λόφον τε σείων Κάρικον (and nodding a Carian crest') may rather refer to a particular kind of helmet plume. This is how How and Wells [27] read the passage: 'He may be referring to the later form of crest which fits right on the helmet, as opposed to the earlier form which was raised on a κύμβαχος (*Il.* 15, 536). In my opinion this is probably connected with the fact that the tail was replaced by a plume of red feathers which was stuck into a sort of 'horn' (*rubrae cornua cristae*, Verg. *Aen.* 12, 89). However that may be, it seems to me not too bold a guess that the tail was originally bound to the head (ἐπιδέεσθαι, says Hdt. 1, 171), in order to fill oneself with the horse's strength in battle.

Now I return to the Mithras-bull. Two of its aspects must be considered, but one of them finds a strict analogy in the Thracian Rider, so it will be better to discuss it later. I shall consider the other now.

Many writers have asked themselves where the idea of the bull-slaying Mithras comes from, in the form known to us from the reliefs and mysteries, since it does not occur in the Avesta. Cumont still started from the standpoint that the Hellenistic Mithras worship had its real origins in Babylonia but on its way westward was subjected to strong influences in Asia Minor and the surrounding regions which determined its further development. The usual mode of representation as encountered on the reliefs is to be traced back to the work of the Pergamum School of the second century B.C.

[27] *Commentary on Herodotus* I, 132.

Many scholars have been content to follow Cumont. Yet his authority has been questioned,[28] with the result that for instance Will in the 1955 work already referred to disputed his view and gave it as his own opinion that the Mysteries and the cult-image of the bull-slayer had nothing to do with the East and had arisen about 100 B.C. at the earliest in a western cultural sphere. It is not within my competence to offer a view of this question. But perhaps I can contribute a phenomenological argument which, if I am not mistaken, entails the consequence that the bull-slaying Mithras-idea contains elements of very great antiquity. Its significance for my own thesis will be obvious. We may rule out from the start any possibility that entirely new cult-themes with a magical tendency could have arisen in the Hellenistic Greek cultural domain.

As far as I know, nobody has yet quoted an exact parallel for the corn ears growing out of the bull's tail. Yet, if I am not mistaken, such a parallel picture does exist.

About 25 years ago it is well-known that a considerable number of rock drawings were found in northern Italy not far from Brescia on the rock shelf of the Val Camonica. They have been well published and interpreted by Altheim and Trautmann.[29] The drawings originated with the Camunni, who gave their name to the valley and who, as the language of the inscription shows, belonged to the Latino-Faliscan tribe. There are striking correspondences with the south Swedish rock paintings already referred to, which still belonged partly to the Bronze Age. The similarities are often particularly striking in the case of cult representations, figures of gods, sacred ships, sun symbols, and so on. On the basis of these correspondences Altheim has dated the Italian rock pictures to the ninth or eighth century B.C. They include the Rider-figure (Plate IX)[30] which demands our attention. Of this and similar representations Altheim and Trautmann write (*Italien und Rom* 39): 'The Riders are represented legless as on the *hällristningar* and the Sub-Mycenaean *Crater* from Muliana. They carry a shield

[28] Cf. Wikander, *Études sur les mystères de Mithras I* (1950) 46; H. Lommel, *op. cit.* 207ff.; Duchesne-Guillemin, *Ormazd et Ahriman* (1953).
[29] F. Altheim-E. Trautmann, *Vom Ursprung der Runen;* id. *Italien u.d. dorische Wanderung* = *Albae Vigiliae* (1940); Altheim, *Italien und Rom* 1 ², 16ff.
[30] *Italien und die dor. Wand.* Fig. 4; *Italien und Rom* Fig. 14.

and a cut-and-thrust weapon.' Probably we have here the figure of a god, even though we cannot prove it. Gods with spear or axe are of frequent occurrence in the Val Camonica. About the horse Altheim and Trautmann say not a word. Obviously its form, including the remarkable appearance of the tail, are quite familiar to them. What I wonder is, what the striking extensions can mean. I have heard the opinion expressed that they are merely a primitive attempt at rendering the tuft. That can be ruled right out, especially by comparison with similar rock drawings, for instance the 'Rider Combat' (*Italien und Rom*, Fig. 15), where the horses' tails have no such development. I can think of no other explanation but that the tail is sprouting. If this is the case, it looks as if the horse had taken over the bull's magic realm in this respect too. It would follow that the bull's tail which generates sprouting corn-ears could hardly be a late Hellenistic invention.

Finally we turn our attention to the Thracian Rider, or more correctly to the figure holding his horse's tail. It reminds us of the figures who grasp the tail of the Mithras-bull. We have seen that these are usually men but that women too are sometimes shown in this posture. I want to offer grounds for believing that originally its purpose was contact magic, of which I have quoted numerous examples in my *Roman Dynamism*. If this view is correct, the tail was grasped in order to draw strength from it.

Next, we must notice that other examples are known from the literature. In the ancient Indian Asvamedha ritual a horse sacrifice, which has reminded many of the Roman October Horse, when the horse was being conducted to the place of sacrifice the priests had to hold its tail.[31] Similarly those taking part in a burial service on their return had to grasp the tail, not of a horse this time but of a bull (von Negelein, 407). Even the dying person too would have had to lay hand on the tail of a cow. I find this case instructive. Initially I thought that this was again a typical case of contact magic, and then I changed my mind and decided I was combining things

---

[31] Johansson 112; Sources in J. von Negelein, *Das Pferd im Seelenglauben und Totenkult*, 406. There we find (*Apastamhaçrautasutra* 13, 4, expounded by *Taittiriyabrahmana* 3, 8, 22, 1: 'For men did not know the way to the world of heaven but the horse knew it. Thus it conducts them to the world of heaven.' This is no doubt the fruit of later speculation: the priests did not make the journey to heaven.

which did not belong together, and finally I was obliged after all to return to my first thought. 'To this very day' von Negelein writes 'a cow with her calf is led to the bed of a dying person. She is richly adorned. She is brought right up to the bed so that the patient can hold her tail, while at the same time the *Purohita* recites a *mantra* (liturgical formula) to ensure that she conducts the patient safely to the other world.' On the face of it this account seemed to me plausible. On the one hand, the ancient Indians believed in a river of death called Vaitarani in which bad people sank and were carried off to hell while a blessed after-life was reserved for the good. On the other, we know the custom among shepherds and others when crossing a river or brook of holding the tail of a horse or a cow. Only, just because this was so wellknown, I thought it must be a later interpretation and was inclined to believe that the holding of the tail served just the same purpose as with the sacrificing priests. I gave up this idea when I found in Koppers (294) the remark that in Slovenian the rainbow is called *mavra*, 'brindled cow', while in Low German the Milky Way has the name *kaupat*, 'cow path'. He continues: 'Is it too bold an inference from these names for the rainbow and the Milky Way, in a territory that is early attested as a region of very strong belief in a Mother Earth, that in pre-Slavonic times cattle were once given as companions for the dead on their last journey?' This observation, which clearly had no reference to the Indian parallels, seemed to be convincing. The rainbow and the Milky Way have always stirred the popular imagination as possible ways of communication between the worlds of gods and men. The Indians themselves called the Milky Way 'Way of Gods' (*devayânam* or *suravîthi*),[32] while the custom of using animals, cattle for preference, to 'show the way' to a new settlement or to the right place for building a temple or church is well-known in many European countries and was observed till far into the Middle Ages.[33] Further clues, however, made it clear to me that Koppers by a roundabout way must have been drawing on a century-old treatise by Kuhn (311ff.). This however discusses the words *mavra* and *kaupat* in

[32] A. Kuhn, *Ztschr. f. vergl. Sprachforschung* 2, 316; R. Eisler, *Weltenmantel und Himmelszelt.* 2, 432, 5; Gundel, RE 7, 561ff.
[33] Wagenvoort, *Hermeneus* 9 (1937) 61ff.; 88ff.

the actual context of the Indian parallel and besides that quotes many other sources. In particular he quotes a passage from the *Yajurveda* according to which on the twelfth day after a person's death a cow was sacrificed and a formula read containing the assurance that the soul which until then had dwelt in the earthly sphere was being led by a cow across the red bloodstream Vaitarani, with which aim the dead person in the hour of death grasped the tail of a cow. If this is so, we have every reason in the first case to think of a safe-conduct into the afterlife and in the second of a piece of contact magic.

We must of course beware of subjective interpretations. Without any doubt this danger exists in the case of the Thracian Rider, which lacks any literary supporting material, so that we are entirely dependent on visual representations. The same applies incidentally to the closely related Danubian Rider-Gods, as they are called, which were worshipped not in Thrace but in Pannonia, Dacia, and Moesia. On the monuments, also dated to the 2nd-4th centuries A.D., they occur mostly as a pair. But here too the figure holding the tail is occasionally present.[34]

Of course it would be going too far to credit every case of tail touching with magical intentions. It could be some involuntary gesture, the conductor of the animal might want to stop it or guide it in a different direction. In every case where such an explanation is unforcedly appropriate it would be wrong to look for others more far-fetched, though against that it must be remembered that the feeling for magic in course of time was greatly weakened until in the end people had quite forgotten the original meaning of many customs. We shall have to consider the question more fully. But here let me give one example, the Πότνια Θηρῶν on a Melian vase of the 7th century B.C. (Plate X).[35] She was the nature goddess worshipped under different names over a great part of the ancient world as mistress of wild animals. Here she is accompanied by a lion on whose head she lays her left hand and

---

[34] See e.g. D. Tudor, 'I cavalieri danubiani', *Ephem. Dacoromana* 7 (1937) 302 mon. 20 Fig. 21; 344 mon. 121 Fig. 79 (where one hand holds a snake, the other clearly the horse's tail).

[35] Cf. Studniczka, *Kyrene*, 162; RE 2, 1, 1751. Studniczka in fact identified the figure here represented with Kyrene. This was rightly disputed by Malten, *Kyrene* (1911); cf. Broholm, RE 12, 155.

whose tail she grasps with her right. The gesture is no doubt to be regarded simply as a symbol of intimacy, perhaps too as a feeling of power. Altogether, I think there is here a broad field open for research. A few instances, for some of which I am indebted to Dr. Vermaseren, will suffice. Recently there was found in the ruins of the temple of Poseidon at Corinth a lustral water basin (*perirrhanterion*) of blue-grey marble. Though it is far from being complete a restoration was possible.[36] Four caryatids stand each on the back of a reclining lion and hold a leash in the right hand and the lion's tail in the left. The type is known. Also from Corinth is a stone tripod, now at Oxford,[37] from the first half of the 5th century. Here too three female figures stand each on a lion and hold the tail in one hand. Fragments of a similar tripod were found at Olympia (Treu, *Olympia* III, 26). So far as I have been able to discover the meaning of these figures is not certainly known, nor have the postures been explained. Perhaps the leash gives an immediate pointer in the same direction as the attitude of the Πότνια Θηρῶν. What I find surprising is their similarity with a picture from an entirely different domain. On the island of Java have been found numerous stone figures of the goddess Durgā. Some of these are in the possession of the Rijksmuseum voor Volkenkunde at Leiden. I take the following from the description of a particularly large and fine example: [38] 'The scene depicted is the victory of Durgā, the *śakti*, the energy personified as a woman of the god Siva as destroyer and creator of this world, over the mighty Asura or Devil who for this occasion has changed himself before our eyes into a buffalo (*mahiṣa*). This well-known representation from Indian mythology is to be interpreted symbolically as the victory of good over evil, of light over darkness ... The eight-armed Durgā with the foremost of her right arms is energetically twisting the buffalo's tail.' It escapes me what she is supposed to intend by this—the animal is fatally wounded (in the throat, just like Mithras' bull). But it must strike anyone how completely Durgā's attitude on the buffalo, with its tail in her right hand, coincides with that of the Corinthian caryatids on their lions, with their

[36] Reproduced in *The Illustrated London News*, 15.9.56, p. 431.
[37] Percy Gardner, *JHS* 16 (1896), 275ff. and Table XII.
[38] J. J. Boeles, 'Het groote Durgā beeld te Leiden', in: *Cultureel Indië* 4 (1942) 37-49; cf. Jessy Blom, *The Antiquities of Singasari*, Diss. Leiden, 1939.

tails in their right hands. We are bound to ask whether they have some primeval prototype in common. And though it must remain a matter of doubt whether such a prototype did have a magical meaning, I cannot refrain from referring to another illustration, from yet another quite different domain, which seems, though rather more remotely, related to the two others. A Hittite statuette [39] represents a goddess standing on a lion and suckling a child. She holds the lion's tail tightly pressed between her knees. The very strangeness of this theme lends force to the supposition of some magical transfer of strength. Onians has devoted a separate section to the significance of the knee (o.c. 2, Ch. 4, pp. 174ff.), on which he has collected extensive material and among other things thrown new light on the Homeric γουνάζεσθαι, γουνοῦσθαι. But I cannot go into that here.

On the other hand I must say a word on the relation between the Thracian Rider-reliefs and the representations of Greek heroes. On the soil of classical Greece magic had long lost all significance, at least among educated people. So if the type of the Thracian Rider with his retinue was modelled on that of the Greek heroes, as there are good reasons for supposing, would not that automatically disqualify any attempt to invest him with magical motifs? Let us consider this in conclusion.

The correspondence between the two groups is indeed striking. Only the Thracian Rider goes from left to right, the Greek Hero from right to left. On a relief from Tanagra, for instance (Plate XI), a female figure with a goblet in her left hand and a wine jug in her right is waiting on the Rider to offer him a drink.[40] It is undoubtedly the dead man's wife, whom we often meet with in Thrace too. In addition we have the man, in this case undoubtedly the servant, who holds the horse's tail. He is clearly identified as a servant by the fact that he carries a hare over his shoulder. But this too

[39] See Haas, *Religion der Hethiter*, Fig. 7 a and b; O. Weber, *Die Kunst der Hethiter* (n.d.) Pl. 8 and 9).

[40] We may compare the well-known tomb-painting from Paestum, where we meet among others with these same figures, only the servant carries no game but does hold the horse's tail (illustrated in Springer, *Hb. d. Kunstgesch.* I 350; Ducati, *Etrusk. italo-hellenist. u. röm. Malerei* p. 34) and in addition Olga Elia, *Pitture murali e mosaici nel Museo Nazionale di Napoli* (1932) p. 126 Fig. 45. Also a relief in the Museum Barracco in Rome, see Bruckmann-Barracco-Helbig, *La Collection Barracco* (1892) 40f. and Table XLIX.

is a usual theme in Thrace, so usual that Will among others (105) draws the conclusion: '*En Thrace et en Asie Mineure, pays de grandes plaines fertiles en chevaux, les seigneurs allaient à cheval; on s'imaginait donc les dieux à cheval*' and adds '*C'est en qualité de chasseur que le Héros thrace est représenté en cavalier.*' This formulation is of course incorrect. There can hardly be a doubt that one of the two groups was influenced by the other. If the hunting theme were originally Thracian we should be forced to suppose that the Thracian reliefs influenced the Greek, whereas there are some hundreds of years older. The true state of affairs is the opposite. In Greece hunting was a favourite sport and the dead man was gladly shown not only as a rider but also as a hunting man. The Thracian sculptor, required to make a portrait of his Rider-God, took such reliefs as a model. But in many cases the servant who held the tail acquired a different meaning. This is proved by the women who sometimes replace him. The gesture was interpreted magically and transformed into a religious rite. This indeed is proved not only by the women in the case but also by the analogy with the reliefs of Mithras Tauroktonos, where Cautes and Cautopates have sometimes caught hold of the badly wounded bull's tail.

There is one more link missing from the chain of proof. If it is justifiable to assume that the act of holding the tail may in both cases, not only of the Mithras-bull but also of the Thracian Rider's horse, be associated with fertility magic, it must still be proved that the Rider was in fact a fertility god.

And among all the Thracian reliefs there is indeed one (Plate XII), to which Kazarow [41] has drawn attention and which is worked with special care. It does represent the god with a horn of Plenty in his right hand and thus in fact marks him as a promoter of fertility. It would no doubt be risky to draw far-reaching conclusions from a single exceptional case. But the evidence is in fact not quite so meagre as that, for we possess representations of the Rider-God which are at least three centuries older than the oldest relief. These did not, it is true, escape the attention of earlier scholars,[42] but in my opinion they did not attach enough importance to them. Coins of the Thracian city of Odessos (today Varna on the Black Sea), the earliest of which date from the 4th century B.C.,

[41] Kazarow, *Denkmäler*, Mon. 518, Fig. 265.
[42] Kazarow, *RE* 15, 226f.; Wiesner, *op. cit.* 43; Will, *op. cit.* 63f.

bear the portrait of a μέγας θεός, who was mostly anonymous but also worshipped as Derzelas, a name which was also conferrred on the Thracian Rider. Generally he is regarded as identical with the Rider,[43] although he is not on horseback but on the oldest bronze coins is shown lying down, while on silver coins of about 200 B.C. he appears as a 'bearded god in a long robe and mantle standing and facing left, in his right hand the bowl and on his left arm the horn of Plenty'. So here too we have the cornucopia, that is, at least since the 4th century B.C. Thus the original character of the Thracian Rider as a god of vegetative fertility—and therewith probably also of the underworld—is sufficiently established. It need cause us no surprise that with it all he was a lover of the chase—we have only to think of Artemis.

If my view is correct, the circle is beginning to close. Originally it was the bull, later the horse that had the power—perhaps through being identified with a god—of promoting fertility and strength. This was specially concentrated in the tail, which was more or less equated with the phallus. This explains why in Rome a man ran with the bleeding tail of the 'October Horse' to the Hearth of State, why in the Mithraic bull sacrifice it was the tail from which ears of corn sprouted, and why to all appearances in the Val Camonica too it was the tail of the horse ridden by the Rider-God which sprouted new life. It explains why in India both the sacrificing priest and the dying patient held the tail of a cow, to draw strength through contact magic—just as Cautes and Cautopates occasionally also do—and why in the countries of the Indo-European domain people for cult purposes attached horses' tails to themselves. Finally it explains the fact that in Thrace both men and women on the Hero reliefs hold the horse's tail. Undoubtedly this was connected with an age-old rite, but we do not know what it was. Had the god perhaps an earthly deputy, a priest on horseback, and did the believer try to grasp the horse's tail? That I fear will remain for ever hidden from us.[44]

[43] Will, e.g. p. 64; '*Le personnage des monnaies est indubitablement le dieu cavalier thrace.*'

[44] For instruction of all kinds I am indebted to my Utrecht colleagues H. T. Fischer, J. Gonda, and J. H. Jongkees; also to Professor F. B. J. Kuiper at Leiden, and especially Dr. Vermaseren at Amsterdam.—Time and space do not allow me in this treatise to hunt around for parallels outside the Indo-European domain and in later periods.

X

THE ORIGIN OF THE GODDESS VENUS

A discussion of R. Schilling, *La religion romaine de Vénus depuis les origines jusqu'au temps d'Auguste*. Paris, E. de Boccard, 1954.

Already ten years have passed since the appearance of Schilling's book, and never till this day has it been mentioned in these pages. *Mea culpa, mea maxima culpa*. A work distinguished at so many points deserved better treatment. It is impressive not only in wealth of matter but also in clarity and frequent persuasiveness of argument. It is wonderful how much material Schilling has collected from all sides to establish and vindicate the place of Venus as a truly Roman goddess in the history of religion. I have long considered these discussions, many passages I have read again and again, I have looked up ancient and modern works, and having at last finished my reading (the book has nearly 400 pages, not counting the indexes) I asked myself whether every doubt, every obscurity had been completely removed, or whether perhaps I was deceived by an author's 'amiable insanity'—because it is easy to fall in love with his Venus. I wanted to postpone my reply for a while and think the thing over. But there was another reason for delay. Not long after, I received a bulky dissertation on the goddess Venus written by Karl Koch (*RE* VIII A 1, 828ff.) and appearing at almost the same time as Schilling's book, so that neither could have known the other's work, unless Koch had read the article of Schilling which preceded his book. (*REL* 20 (1942), 44ff.). Since it was not possible for me to ignore the opinions of either—often enough there were considerable differences between them—to do justice to both would have required me to write a book rather than a review. Thus it has come about that with all my other different occupations the years have slipped away more rapidly than expected, until now at last I have decided what to do. Having become convinced that the first part of the book, dealing with the origins of Venus, is more open to objections than the rest, I shall deal only with this, leaving the second much longer part alone, and hoping it will be clear enough that the little I have to offer in no way detracts from my genuine admiration of the whole work.

Schilling starts by repudiating the arguments by which Wissowa tried to show that Venus to begin with was a goddess of the sweetness inherent in blossoming nature. Wissowa's line is remarkable in offering almost no handle for contradiction. But it is at once apparent how much importance Schilling attaches to the etymology of the word *venus* with all its derivatives when he writes (p. 25), 'Vénus protectrice des jardins est aussi hellénique que Minerve protectrice des olivettes' (and that with reference to Varro's words *r.r.* 1, 1, 6). 'Trait piquant: Varron a transmis dans la même formule l'héritage authentique de la Vénus latine; il n'est pas là où croyait Wissowa, il n'est pas dans l'affabulation hellénique de la déesse des jardins, mais dans le verbe *adveneror*....' Then he soon passes to the consideration of the word *venus* and its relatives, prefacing it, by way of fundamental principles, with two general remarks. This is the first (p. 30): 'D'abord les recherches de la linguistique n'ont pas prétendu faire une étude exhaustive des mots de la famille de *venus*: elles ont indiqué les rapprochements principaux *venus, venia, venerari, venenum*, négligeant des termes plus particuliers tels que *venenatum, venerium*. L'historien des religions ne saurait se contenter du simple rapprochement de mots groupés au nom de leur parenté étymologique: il se doit d'établir un inventaire aussi complet que possible des mots dérivés de la même racine'.

'Un inventaire aussi complet que possible'—Here I am brought to a stop, almost struck dumb with astonishment. How many hundreds of times in preparing this book must the author have been confronted by the words *venustus, venustas*—even occurring in passages he himself has quoted (*venustus* p. 34, *venustas* p. 33). Nevertheless he passes them over in deepest silence; περὶ δ'αὐτῶν οὐδεὶς λόγος. Why so? I have thought and thought about this strange fact, but no probable reason has occurred to me. Is he perhaps taking his lead from Latte,[1] who comments: 'Venustus

[1] *Röm Religionsgesch.*, 183, 4.—And yet in the same passage he gives a correct enough interpretation of the verb *venerari* (see below), without discussion, however, and not, it seems, aware that his opinion conflicts with Schilling's.

and its derivates need not be older than the third century; the formation from the nominative (in contrast with *funestus*) points to a more recent date. It is apparently a semantic loan-word on the model of ἐπαφρόδιτος'. This is an addition by Latte to Schilling's arguments, which he quotes briefly with approval. It seems that he noticed the lacuna and sought to close it on his own account. But first, if this was also the opinion of Schilling himself, he should not have concealed it from us. Secondly, as we shall see later, Latte's reasoning was mistaken. I did think of another possible motive for deliberate reticence but discarded it at once. The words themselves, *venustus, venustas*, and what we may call their semantic history are less favourable as I see it, to the interpretations proposed by Schilling or at least to some of them. But the book offers instances of such acumen, such ingenuity, that I have no difficulty in rejecting this less creditable notion. We are left then—with an enigma.

It is today an almost general opinion that the goddess's name evolved out of a neuter noun *venus, veneris*, indicating some sort of occult force. Schilling thinks no differently. With prejudgment he translates it '*charme*', noting—a point which he afterwards makes repeatedly—a certain magical quality about the word. I can only applaud. It is not often that the French school, which has otherwise made exceptional contributions to the history of Roman religion, can be persuaded that magic once flourished at Rome, not the absurd and tedious magic which was much later to invade Italy (like other places) from the Orient, but simple, almost natural magic, without much actual scientific content but still here and there in some way bearing the seeds of science.

In the first passage he quotes, dealing with the word *venerari* Schilling derives *veneror* from *věněs-o(r), rightly in my opinion, though it would have done no harm to spend a few words in support of this etymology. For the view put forward by Wackernagel (*Festschrift Thomsen* 1912; 134, 1) is by no means absurd. 'With *van*, "beg, do homage to"', he writes, 'belongs Latin *venerari*, which has as little directly to do with Venus as *generare* with *genus*. Both verbs, like e.g. also *tolerare, recuperare, lamberare*, seem to be pure *deverbalia*.' So far as concerns the verb *generare* I agree. So far as concerns *venerari*, it will immediately become apparent why, after long hesitation, I think otherwise. This verb is translated by Schilling 'exercer la *venus*', 'pratiquer le charme religieux'. But if you ask how, if the verb is thus translated, it then comes, to govern an object in the accusative, you get no proper reply. After he himself has quoted several such examples, like Plaut. *Rud*. 305 '*Nunc Venerem hanc* veneremur *bonam* ut *nos lepide adiuerit hodie*', id. *Poen*. 950f. '*Deos deasque* veneror *qui hanc urbem colunt* / ut *quod de mea re huc veni rite venerim*', and so on, he proceeds (p. 36), 'Dans toutes ces expressions, on est porté à traduire l'expression *veneror ut* (*ne*) par "je demande la grâce que (ne ....pas)"', and a little further on, 'Il est probable que le verbe avait à l'origine une valeur plus magique que révérencielle. *Veneror ut:* "J'use de charme religieux pour obtenir" (note that so far the accusative has not been explained), "Je cherche à gagner", "Je cherche à me rendre propice", "Je vénère": le verbe a dû traduire des nuances successives depuis l'appel magique primitif jusqu'au ton de la pure prière'. This last is the most correct. But nobody will fail to notice that in his later translations a way is prepared for the accusative of the object (e.g. 'Je cherche à gagner' sc. *le dieu*) only in such a way that the magic force of the verb completely disappears. If I am not altogether mistaken, the origin of the word has to be explained otherwise.[2]

Venerare (*-ri*)[3] in its formation can be compared with such verbs as *animare* (i.e. 'to equip with a mind', 'to impart a mind' or 'cause it to grow'), *coronare, figurare, onerare*, and many others. Therefore *venero*(*r*) is not, as Schilling would have it, 'I exercise my *venus*,' but 'I increase the *venus* of the god', 'I fill the god with *venus*'. It means almost the same to begin with as *mactare* (*mactare deos extis*).[4] For in early times the Romans were convinced that not only sacrifices but also prayers had this function. Later, as is usual, almost all understanding of such a notion disappeared. All that remained were some vague memory traces, as when among ourselves highly educated people have the habit of saying 'bless you!' to those who sneeze and know no more than Pliny (*N.H.* 28, 23)

---

[2] After studying the point afresh I feel obliged to correct what I wrote in *Rom. Dynam.*, 82.

[3] On the significance of the middle cf. Schilling, 35, 1.

[4] Cf. what I wrote after quoting other passages in *Roman Dynamism*, 46, 3.

what we are really saying, or when there is a ringing in our ears and we say jokingly just as they did in ancient Rome (Plin. *N.H.* 28, 24; M. Aurel. 2, 2 i.f. Nab.; *Anthol. Lat.* 452 R.) that somebody is talking about us, we are quite unconscious that in its origins this manner of speaking is tinged with magic (cf. e.g. Apul. *Apol.* 48 and Butler & Owen's *Commentary*). The situation is similar, if I am not mistaken, when we read in Valerius Flaccus (2, 336) 'give wine and prayers' so that we are told to make a present of our prayers to the god together with our sacrifice, or again when we read in Vergil (*Aen.* 8, 60) *'Iunoni fer rite preces'*, where Servius Danielis notes: *'fer preces'* just as we say *'sacra ferri'*![5] Pfister (*Die Religion der Griechen und Römer*, 195) summed the matter up correctly: 'The energetic purpose of prayer originally consists in the fact that a good deed is being done to the deity, whose being is thereby fortified'. Thus when Accius (*fr.* 5f.) writes:

Te sancte venerans precibus, invicte, invoco,
portenta ut populo patriae verruncent bene

the verbs *venerans* and *invoco* (to both of which *te* functions as object) do not repeat one another. He could have written *'venerans donis'* or some such phrase.[6] Whether he was actually conscious of the point is a very difficult question for us to decide, because

[5] I think it worth referring to the devotional formula transmitted by Livy (8, 9, 6): '*Iane, Iupiter, Mars pater, Quirine, Bellona, Lares, divi, Novensiles, di Indigetes, divi quorum est potestas nostrorum hostiumque, dique Manes, vos precor, veneror, veniam peto feroque uti populo Romano Quiritum vim victoriamque prosperetis...*' Thus the *codices* and also Schilling (p. 42), though Weissenborn-Müller and others follow Forchhammer's conjecture and substitute *oroque* for *feroque*, on the ground presumably that the transmitted reading is meaningless. I, however, do not doubt that Schilling was right to keep it. I only do not understand why he did not think such an invaluable *locus* was worth an interpretation. It has not yet been understood by recent writers or even by Romans of classical times. Macrobius at any rate (*Sat.* 3, 9, 7) in a formula of evocation uses the same words *'precor venerorque veniamque a vobis peto'* but has preferred to omit the following *'feroque'*. This in my opinion makes quite evident the mutual force and nature of *venia*. Though *venus* and *venia* do not mean the same in all particulars, a point which I shall deal with below, yet the passage quoted seems to me a clear illustration of the very ancient mode of thought they represent.

[6] Cf. e.g. Verg. *Georg.* 4, 547 '*placatam Eurydicen vitula venerabere caesa*', *Aen.* 5, 745 '*farre pio et plena supplex veneratur acerra*'; *Cir.* 18 '*non ego te talem venerarer munere tali*'.

there is no doubt he was using (see below) an ancient and fixed formula.

With the lapse of time the zeal to strengthen prayer by the accumulation of words meaning almost the same, together with the gradual fading of magical ideas, brought it about that *venerari* came to mean almost the same as *precari*. It is relevant too (contrary to Schilling p. 54) that the words *preces* and *precari* were always in use not only in mutual conversation between human beings, but also in addressing the gods. Schilling writes: 'Alors que *veneror* est réservé au culte divin, de toute antiquité, l'emploi de *precor* appartient encore dans le théatre de Plaute, presque exclusivement au domaine profane. Par la suite, l'emploi de *precari* s'est étendu aux demandes adressées aux dieux'. Yet on the contrary it seems obvious to me that the only difference between *venerari* and *precari* in Republican times was that *venerari* was rather more elevated in style. Thus it is no surprise to find that *precari* was much more commonly used in everyday speech than *venerari* and of seven Plautine examples only one had a religious force. But Schilling himself (p. 42) quotes formulae of consecration (Liv. 8, 9, 6) and evocation (Macrob. 3, 9, 7). In both of these we read *vos precor, veneror, veniam peto*, an accordance which testifies to a tradition which had remained intact since very early times. See further e.g. Pacuv. *fr.* 296 R.: '*precor veniam petens, uti quae ⟨ego⟩ egi ago axim verruncet bene*'; Enn. *Ann. fr.* 52 V ²: '*Te sale nata precor Venus*'; Cato, *agric.* 134, 2 in a very old hymn: '*Iane pater, te hac strue ommovenda bonas preces precor, uti...*' (almost the same, 139); L. Afran. *fr.* 83 R.: '*Deos ego omnis ut fortunassint precor*'; Varro *ap*. Non. p. 480 M.: '*Ego medicina Serapii utor: quotidie precantor*'; Lucil. *fr.* 206 M.; '*divos ture precemur*' where *precari* seems to me to have been construed on the model of the verb *venerari*, as I mentioned above).

But if we have rightly decided that *deum venerari* properly meant 'to provide the deity with *venus*, to increase the deity's *venus*', the question arises whether this **venus* was attributable solely to gods or also to men. It seems that the second alternative was that adopted by Schilling because of course in his opinion the original sense of the verb was 'operate the *venus*'. I do in fact agree with him but for a different reason. The adjective *venustus*, which we have already noted is passed over in complete silence by Schilling, is undoubtedly very ancient. Yet it cannot be denied that adjectives with the -*ustus* termination seem more recent than those in -*estus* (*funestus, modestus, scelestus, faustus* < *faves-tos, iustus* < *ioves-tos*, and so on). But if this is the case it must still be that what we have to do with here are suffix formations which diverged long before human memory.

We conclude, first that the primitive nouns ending in -*us* on which such adjectives are formed were declined partly in such a way that in all cases but the nominative the original -ĕ- of the stem was retained (*genus-genĕris, scelus-scĕleris*), but partly with the substitution of -*o*- for -*e*- (*decus-decoris, corpus-corporis*). Moreover from the beginning, as it seems to me, there occurred a mixture, or ambiguity, between the two, as *fēnus*, -ŏris beside -ĕris; *pignus*, -ŏris beside -ĕris. And it must have been a similar ambiguity which rang the changes as in *tempus*, -*oris* beside *temperies, temperare, tempestas, tempestivus*, adv. *temperi; facinus*, -ŏris, beside *facinerosus* (cf. Lindsay, *Latin Language*, 355f.: Sommer, *Handbuch*, 395). Exactly the same kind of process seems to me to have been at work in the adjectives above-mentioned, formed by a -*to*- suffix. Secondly, the adjectives *angustus, augustus, confoedustus* (Paul. Fest. p. 35 L.), *fidustus* (ibid. p. 79 L.), *onustus, subverbustus* (Fest. p. 402 L.), *venustus, vetustus* they too in a different way can lay claim in the majority of cases to high antiquity. Of them four are derived from substantives which in classical times were no longer in use, that is, beside *venustus*, also *angustus*,[7] *augustus*,[8] *vetustus*.[9] Two others have their origin in nouns known later but slightly changed, one in its stem vowel, *fidustus* from *fidus*, -*eris*,[10]

---

[7] *Angustus* < **angos-to-s* from a noun **angus*, -*eris* or -*oris* beside *angor*, -*oris* (cf. *decus*, -*oris* beside *decor, decoris*); cf. the adjective **ang(e)s-ios* > *anxius*. See Walde-Hofmann s.v.; Leumann-Hofmann, 246; Wagenvoort, *Mnemos.* Series 3 Vol. 9 (1941), 251ff. (= above p. 21-24); *Rom. Dyn.* 82, 1.

[8] Augustus: on **augus*, -*eris* cf. Walde-Hofmann s.v.; Wagenvoort, *Rom. Dyn.*, 12ff.

[9] Vetustus: on a subst. **vetus*, -*eris* (Gr. τὸ Ϝέτος) cf. Walde-Hofm. s.v. However, Leumann-Hofm., p. 228, doubt whether *vetustus* could have meant the same as *annosus*, and therefore conjecture that it was formed on the analogy of *vetustas*, but on the evolution of its meaning cf. Skutsch, *ALL* 15, 35ff. = *Kl. Schr.* 312; Benveniste, *Rev. Phil.* 22 (1948), 124. Szemerényi, *Glotta* 34 (1955), 276 takes a different view.

[10] According to Varro (5, 86) Ennius had *fidus*, -*eris* for *foedus*, -*eris* as accepted up to his own time.

the other in its number, *subverbustus*.[11] But as for *venustus*, it cannot have been formed after **venus* itself, the neuter substantive, had become obsolete. We are not helped by a conjecture that it was formed on the analogy of the word *vetustus*, because that must assume that not only **venus* but **vetus* were still current in their principal sense. Therefore *venustus* and the substantive *venustas* (*venus-ti-tāt-s*) are well worth careful consideration in this context.

Schilling (p. 61, 3) notes: 'Certains érudits s'obstinent à poser l'équation "*venus*=charme de femme" au point de départ. Cette restriction de sens est tout aussi arbitraire que l'équation formulée par Wissowa "*venus* = charme de la nature" '. First of all I would point out that among these 'erudite people' it seems to me that Cicero was to be numbered. In *de Off.* 1, 130 he offered the following opinion: '*Cum autem pulchritudinis duo genera sint, quorum in altero venustas est, in altero dignitas, venustatem muliebrem ducere debemus, dignitatem virilem*'. 'Since there are two kinds of beauty, in one of which is grace, in the other dignity, we ought to consider grace womanly and dignity manly.' I grant at once that such a saying must be received with caution. It may be that *venustus*, *venustas* are easily associated in thought with the name of the goddess Venus (cf. as early as Plautus, *Poen.* 255f. '*Diem pulchrum ob oblobrum ob venustatis plenum, / dignum Venori pol, quoi sunt Aphrodisia hodie*'; [12] ibid. 1176ff. '*lepidissima munera meretricum, digna diva venustissima*' (i.e. Venus)).[13] Further while women are very often said to be *venustae* (e.g. Plaut. *Poen.* 1113; *Rud.* 320; *Truc.* 714; Ter. *Andr.* 119f.) there is on the contrary nowhere talk of a man who is *venustus*, that I can find, before Cicero *Pis.* 70, and that of an effeminate man. And while the goddess Venus herself is called *venusta* (Plaut. *Poen.* 1177), nowhere is a true god *venustus*. Here and there, however, not only is *venustas* attributed to human beings more generally, without discrimination of sex (as in Plaut. *Poen.* 255) but more than once too it appears that a certain *venustas* of behaviour can exist in men (Plaut. *Mil.* 651. 657; Ter. *Hec.* 848. 858).

[11] **verbus*, *-eris*, plur. *verbera*.
[12] 'a beautiful, distinguished day, full of *venustas*, right worthy of Venus, whose festival it is'.
[13] 'a most delightful parade of courtesans, worthy of the most *venusta*' (charming) 'of goddesses' (i.e. Venus).

To the question asked above, then, whether *venus* was peculiar to the gods (the verb *venerari* is evidence that it was attributed to the gods) or belonged to human beings as well, it seems we must reply: if we believe the literary tradition, we must decide that it really was common to men and gods, but in such a way that women somehow had a greater share of it than men. But let us never forget how hazardous it is to put too much trust in the state of affairs to be met with in classical times, when men no longer had even the vaguest notion of early magical thought. Let me show what I mean by an example. I have already observed that there is nowhere talk of a '*venustus*' god. But do not suppose the gods were lacking in that *venus* quality. The verb *venerare(-ri)* is evidence enough to the contrary, and there is other evidence too which may be added.

I mean the goddess whose name is *Venus Iovia*. Schilling (pp. 92f.) takes the name as meaning 'une liaison étroite entre Vénus et Jupiter'. Koch (col. 837) gives almost the same interpretation, 'Venus in the sphere of Jupiter'. I am far from venturing to deny that in two inscriptions, one from Capua (*CIL* 10, 3776=I², 675=Dessau 3185), the other from Abella (*CIL* 10, 1207=Dessau 3186), the name is to be understood in that sense. For one thing, neither is very ancient. The Capuan inscription was dedicated in 108 B.C., while the Abellan is in all probability more recent, from the name of a priestess Avillia on it. Moreover, nobody will deny that there are many points of association between Venus and Jupiter (cf. Schilling, 91ff.). Nevertheless, in my opinion it was Latte (p. 183) who gave the correct answer: [14] 'In Capua we meet with a Venus Iovia, which indicates that she was once a "force" in the sense I have discussed above'—where he should have referred the reader to pp. 55ff. He was there discussing those general supplications of the immortal gods according to the Roman rite listed by Gellius (13, 23, 2), such as the *Lua Saturni*, the *Salacia Neptuni*, and the rest, and argued: 'Every interpretation must start from the fact they are all feminines meaning a force or will. When the god's name is added in the genitive, it is the effective

---

[14] I only wonder at his adding (N. 2), 'We are indebted to R. Schilling for having recognized the original function of Venus'. For in this particular, as I see it, Schilling scarcely improved on his predecessors.

will of the god which is important not his form'. Nor did he fail to notice that the genitive could be replaced by an adjective derived from the god's name. Alongside *Heries Iunonis*, he points out, we find *Heres Martea*. The Iguvii sacrificed to *Ahtu Iuviṗ*. and *Ahtu Marti*, i.e. *Actui Iovio* and *Actui Martio*.[15] Unless I am quite mistaken, we shall see below another similar case concerning Venus herself. It is not surprising, however, that such associations of names should later have come to be misunderstood, when the epithet *Iovius* was attributed for instance to Hercules (cf. R. Drexler, *Rosch. Lex.* 1, 2, 2946). Thus we can take it as established—and already indicated, I have shown, by the use of the verb *venerare(-ri)* —that the early Romans believed Jupiter too was imbued with that 'force', that *venus*.

But if *venus* was 'a certain mysterious force', as Schilling says— and I do not disagree with him—something to some extent common to men and gods—whatever can we suppose it to have been? What was the *impetus* which those early Romans thought they detected in the nature of the gods, which they were conscious also of being innate in their own selves? A very difficult question if we consider it carefully. Yet at first glance we might perhaps think it easily answered. If it is certain, and I know of no expert who has questioned it, that *venus* is related to the Sanskrit root *van-*, which is usually translated 'desire', even 'procure', we can hardly doubt that it originally meant 'goodwill', 'favour', 'grace'. But the slippery slopes on which we then find ourselves are shown first of all by the word *venēnum venes-no-m*, which Schilling dealt with on pp. 42f., giving the following opinion: 'Le nom *venenum* paraît à première vue aberrant. Très souvent, il est foncièrement péjoratif et doit se traduire par "poison"...." Cet emploi ne doit pas nous donner le change sur la valeur véritable de *venenum* qui...s'est employé aussi bien en bonne qu'en mauvaise part.... Le mot a primitivement le sens de "charme": il peut donc traduire aussi bien l'action mystérieuse du poison que l'ensorcellement du philtre'. This is quite cleverly argued, especially as the French

---

[15] *Tab. Iguv.* II A 10f. But on this point I think he is mistaken: *Iuviṗ*. cannot be anything but the dative, for *Iuvi p(atre)*, and thus the same holds of *Marti*, though Buck, *Grammar*[2] (1928) p. 338 s.v. doubts it. Otherwise Actus and Venus can suitably be compared with one another.

word 'charme' has the two meanings of 'possessing charm, persuasive' and 'instrument of sorcery, φάρμακον'. All the same, it is not yet clear to me how an ancient people came to inscribe such an ambiguous notion among the gods. All the less so when account is taken of another noun, *venia*, which Schilling discusses at length (pp. 39-42). It is the general view that this too is derived from the same root as *venus*, and I have no objection to make, though the formation of the noun does seem to me rather unclear.[16] Certainly whoever reconsiders the use of this word in classical literature will be unable to avoid the conclusion that in contrast to *venenum* it was a word of good omen. Perhaps appearances may be deceptive as usual. It is to allay this fear that I have given the matter so much further thought.

Scholars have often noticed that the words *venia* and *pax* often have much the same meaning. Schilling e.g. (p. 41) quotes the following: Cic. *Rab.* 2, 5 '*Ab Iove Optimo Maximo ceterisque dis pacem ac veniam peto precorque.* . . .'; Liv. I, 31, 7 '*unam opem aegris corporibus relictam si* pax veniaque *ab dis impetrata esset credebant*'; Serv. *Aen.* I, 519' Orantes veniam pacem *propter incendium navium. Et proprie verbum pontificale est: unde est* 'tu modo posce deos veniam' *et paulo post* 'pacemque *per aras exquirunt*'; Verg. *Georg.* 4, 534ff. '*Tu munera supplex tende* petens pacem *et facilis venerare Napaeas: namque* dabunt veniam votis'. I myself add Prop. 2, 25, 4 '*Calve, tua* venia, pace, *Catulle, tua*'.

[16] Hofmann in *Walde's Lexicon* gives his lemma to the word *venia*, where he immediately notes 'Zu *venus*', yet does not venture as usual to include the noun in the lemma to *venus* and its relatives. The one who has to my knowledge touched on the formation of the word, F. Muller (*Altit. WB.* s.v.) writes: 'From *ven-iā* either "the seeking to win" or (looked at from the opposite side) "friendliness" '. In my opinion the former conjecture is preferable to the latter. A noun of action is derived from an obsolete verb *venere*. It is true that very few such words or none at all are found in Latin. *Fluvia, pluvia* are properly adjectives, with *aqua* understood. *Furia* is thought to be a 'back formation from *furiosus* (Leumann/Hofmann, 231; which I find hardly credible). There is silence about *effigia* but it must be allowed as possible—on account of *effigies*—that it was formed on the analogy of words like *materies-materia*. Whatever the case, the formation is adequately corroborated by cognate languages, the suffix *-ia* either indicating the action itself (Sanskrit śam-ī śam-iə—'work', śam- 'to work', 'to labour'; Greek φύζα < φυγ—ια 'fleeing') or the result of the action (Sanskrit vep-ī vep-iə- 'inspired work', vip- 'to inspire'; Greek μᾶζα < μαγ—ια 'dough' from a root μαγ—'to knead').

This *pace tua* is already found in an inscription by L. Mummius [17] put up after the capture of Corinth (146 B.C.). Also *pacem petere* was a fixed formula in religious speech (cf. *CIL* I², 1805 = 9, 3569, which includes 'te orat: tu es [sanctus] deus, quei tou[am a te] pacem petit, [eum] adiouta'. Nevertheless, however great the similarity of meaning attributed to the words *venia* and *pax*, there remains evidently a difference between the two, which is in some way relevant to our enquiry. Often the Romans were not content to ask for *venia*, they asked for *bona venia*. As Ter. *Phorm.* 378 'primum abs te hoc bona venia peto'; Cic. *N.D.* 1, 59 'bona venia me audes'; *de Orat.* 1, 242 'bona venia huius optimi viri dixerim'; further Liv. 6, 40, 10; 7, 41, 3; 29, 1, 7. 17, 6. Against that *bona pax* nowhere occurs in such a context. It is true we already have from Plautus *Pers.* 189 'Bona pax sit potius', but as all the other passages clearly show, this phrase was with special reference to a war already concluded and used metaphorically by a poet.[18] Here it is always a question of concluding an honourable peace, excluding all penalty, revenge, or indemnity. The contrary is always said to be a *mala pax*, cf. Val. Max. 6, 21: (*Priverno capto princeps Privernatium a consule Romano interrogatur*) 'qualem cum eis Romani pacem habituri essent inpunitate donata. At is constantissimo vultu "si bonam dederitis", inquit, "perpetuam, si malam, non diuturnam". Qua voce perfectum est ut victis non solum venia, sed etiam ius et beneficium nostrae civitatis daretur'.[19] But when *pax* really pertains to the benevolence, clemency, and favour of the gods, no Roman thinks it necessary to use such a phrase as 'bona pace tua dixerim'.—'speaking by your good favour'. In such an apology the word *pax* seems to convey a fixed notion. But since on the contrary the word *venia* often has the epithet *bona* added to it, it seems to make sense to ask, even though there

---

[17] *CIL* 1, 542 = 9, 4672; cf. *CLE* büch. 248; Ernout, *Recueil de Textes Latines*, 74.

[18] Liv. 1, 24, 3; 8, 15, 1; 21, 24, 5; 28, 37, 4; 32, 6.

[19] (After the capture of Privernum the Chief of the Privernates was asked by the Roman consul) 'what sort of peace the Romans could have if they granted impunity. But he with a bold face answered, "if you give us a good peace, for ever, if a bad, not for long". This speech obtained not only pardon for the conquered, but their rights and the boon of our Roman citizenship'.

is nowhere a reference to *mala venia*, whether there was a time when *venia* too, just like *venenum*, was ambiguous in meaning.

However that may be, at least the word *venenum* itself compels us to enquire what the root $u̯en$- properly meant. For Meringer (*IF* 16 (1904), 180) has rightly observed: 'All attempts to bring the many forms under which the Indo-European root *$u̯en$- occurs together in one complex of meaning have hitherto failed'. This question, unless I am badly mistaken, takes on a more serious aspect when we ponder in our minds what on earth could have induced the Romans to associate Venus with Mefitis, Libitina, and Cloacina. It is no wonder that the commentators have got into severe difficulties over this point. Let me recapitulate the sources, including some recent attempts at solving the question.

I shall deal first not with Venus Mefitis but with *Venus Libitina*. About *Libitina* herself, a funerary goddess of Etruscan origin, I have nothing new to offer. Both Schilling [20] and Koch (col. 851) have given the right answer about the other name *Venus Libentina* or *Lubentina*; it was invented by Varro or one of his predecessors in a vain effort to elucidate the link between Venus and Libitina. The name *Venus* Libitina (Libentina, Lubentina) is used by the following authors: Varro (6, 47; *ap.* Non. p. 64 M.); Cicero (*N.D.* 2, 23), Dionysius Halic. (*A.R.* 4, 15), Plutarch (*Q.R.* 23). There is the further fact that a temple of Venus had been founded in the Grove of Libitina, situated almost certainly in the Esquiline Hills, on the evidence of Festus (p. 322 L.) and again Dionysius. It seems that the 'treasury of Aphrodite' mentioned by Plutarch in that grove must have belonged to it: (θησαυρός) τῆς Ἀφροδίτης τῆς ἐν ἄλσει καθιδρυμένης ἣν προσαγορεύουσι Λιβιτίνην.

Schilling (p. 8) rightly records 'la perplexité des anciens dans leur effort pour élucider les raisons de cette assimilation' and a little further on quotes the expedients devised by later authors (Lactantius Placidus, *in Stat. Theb.* 4, 527, Plutarch, *Numa* 12 & *Q.R.* 23) for solving the puzzle, too fanciful to convince us moderns. No more enlightening is Schilling's own rather vague conclusion (p. 167): 'Vénus a eu l'occasion d'"absorber" une divinité funéraire, dont la personnalité demeure mystérieuse. . . .Nous aurons à nous

---

[20] Cf. Schilling 204f. Latte gave a different opinion, *RE* 13, 113; and *Röm. Rel. gesch.*, 185, 2, wrongly in my opinion.

demander si les "affinités" funéraires de Vénus ne s'expliquent pas par une contamination étrusque'. Later he seeks to strengthen this conjecture with arguments which I again find unconvincing, and concludes, 'Telle paraît être la conclusion la plus vraisemblable, qu'un examen objectif permet de tirer d'une situation religieuse qui n'était rien moins que limpide pour les anciens.'

Koch is no less troubled by doubt (*RE* VIII A 1 col. 851): Venus at some unspecified time found her way into the grove of this Libitina, which was probably on the Esquiline. The *dies natalis* of Venus proves that the event was sanctioned by the state. We do not know the reason why Venus gained her foothold here, certainly not the etymological play with the word *libido*, which caused Varro or his predecessor to change the name into Libentina....It is possible that a subordinate non-erotic function of Aphrodite was here brought to the fore with deliberate state connivance.'

We note therefore that not even the most recent commentators have understood why the early Romans associated Venus with Libitina.

It is no easier to comprehend how *Venus Cloacina* found her way into the Roman religion. The cult of Cloacina was very ancient. According to Seneca (ap. Augustin. *C.D.* 6, 10) 'Tatius dedicated the goddess Cluacina'. Plautus (*Curc.* 471) knew her sanctuary and several authors [21] mention her, but it must be noted that only two of them speak of Venus Cloacina (or Cluacina, on which point the reader is referred to an etymological dictionary). These are Pliny and Servius, so that there is not even sure evidence that Venus was associated with Cloacina from the beginning. Nevertheless coins struck in 42 B.C. by L. Mussidius Longus, one of the *quattuorviri auro publico feriundo*, bore the inscription CLOACIN and showed two statues of Venus clothed. So there is no doubt that the association had taken place at least as early as the first century. Schilling (pp. 210ff.) has given a striking account of the manner in which learned Romans of classical times conceived of the goddess. She was a goddess of purification, as is natural in view of her name, taken from *cloaca*, which itself was a word

---

[21] Liv. 3, 48, 5; Plin. *N.H.* 15, 119; Min. Fel. 25, 8; Tertull. *de pallio* 1; Augustin. *C.D.* 4, 8, 23; Serv. *Dan.* 1, 720, and other church authors.

derived from the verb *cluere*, i.e. purify. At the same time she was a goddess of union and reconciliation, according to Pliny (*N.H.* 15, 119), who tells of the meeting of "Romans and Sabines with myrtle branches", instead of "the battle they had been about to fight because of the ravished maidens, laying down their arms and purifying themselves in the place where the images of Venus Cluacina now stand", and adds that Venus was a goddess of union as also of myrtle.

Do we then conclude that Venus Cloacina was an invention of the first century B.C.? Not at all, though any opinion to the contrary is equally lacking in solid grounds. Matters would be different, in my opinion, if there were any proof of the view put forward by Latte (*RRG*, p. 186), that 'another Venus sanctuary, of unknown age, was situated at the spot where the drainage canal of the *Cloaca Maxima* intersected the *Novae Tabernae*, and was called after it'. But all that we know for certain is this: near the Cloaca Maxima stood a Cloacina sanctuary of unknown but very great antiquity, in the northern part of the Forum between the Basilica Aemilia and the Comitium. When Pliny in the passage quoted above refers to '*eo loco qui nunc signa Veneris Cloacinae habet*', the general opinion is that this was the sanctuary referred to,[22] while the coins of Mussidius are evidence that the 'images' were actual statues of Venus.[23] But we really do not know when these statues were put up in the shrine. It is therefore possible that they were to be dated as late as the first century B.C. It is true that Iulius Obsequens (*Prodig.* 8 62) is authority for the fact that in the year 178 B.C. a temple of Venus near the Forum was burnt to the ground, leaving no trace, and that we do not know of any

---

[22] Wissowa, *R.u.K*², 245; Schilling 211; Koch, col. 868; Latte, *RRG*, 186.
[23] Cf. Ch. Huelsen, *Das Forum Romanum*², 126: 'The so-called *parabasis* from Plautus' *Curculio* mentions the *Cloacinae sacrum* between Comitium and Basilica Aemilia. Its position is further indicated by the story of the death of Verginia, daughter of Verginius (449 B.C.). To judge from the coins there must have been two female statues on the circular building, the left-hand one of which had a flower in its hand. Beside each was a low pillar on which was a bird with folded wings. Flower and dove were characteristic attributes of Venus'. Of course the Verginia story tells us nothing about the antiquity of the Cloacina temple—it is put together from nothing, cf. Gundel, *RE* 8 A2, 1530ff.—except perhaps Livy's opinion that it was exceedingly ancient.

other Venus sanctuary having existed there, but it would not be permissible rashly to identify the two sanctuaries.

I shall return to this question later. Meanwhile let me warn the reader against certain mistakes made by scholars. Wissowa (*RE* 4, 59) in his account of the *Cloaca Maxima* wrongly calls it 'the most important and oldest of the drainage canals by which the original low-lying swamps between the Seven Hills were first made habitable'. Clearly the very name is evidence that being the greatest it was *not* the oldest, unless the epithet *Maxima* was added at a later date, which seems very unlikely. Livy for instance thought there were lesser canals before the 'greatest' (cf. 1, 38, 6 with 1, 56, 2). I find Latte (*op. cit.* 186, 3) just as mistaken in arguing that 'the Romans, who named this chapel of Venus' (evidently referring to the Cloacina sanctuary) 'after its situation by the drainage culvert of the Forum, could really not have guessed what an evil meaning *cloaca* would later acquire in its own and modern languages. But we should stop drawing conclusions from it about the nature of the goddess'. Is that really so? When in Plautus (*Curc.* 121) a cup of unmixed wine is handed to a drunken old woman with the words, 'Come on, quickly, clear this back into the abyss, give the drains (*cloaca*) a good clean', were these 'drains' (*cloaca*) to be understood as a receptacle of pure water? When Livy (1, 56, 2) is talking about a covered *cloaca* he calls it a receptacle for all the purgings of the city. At Pompeii in the period of the Roman Republic there were few public lavatories but all public slops were emptied into the *cloacae*. Would Rome have been any better? [24]

I shall presently attempt to show that the point is of no small importance for the understanding of the original nature of Venus Cloacina.

But first we must consider *Venus Mefitis*. Whether she ever had a cult at Rome is uncertain and extremely doubtful, and it is not long since we knew for certain that gifts were dedicated to her at least in Lucania. E. Vetter in the year 1942 first published [25] an Oscan inscription extant in the Museum at Potenza, by which a gift had been dedicated to Ϝενζει· μεfιτι 'Veneri Mefiti', and

[24] Mau. *Pompeji* ² p. 232; A. W. van Buren, *RE* 21, 2033.
[25] *Glotta* 29 (1942), 226 sq. = *Handb. d. ital. Dial.* 1 (1953), 182.

fully realized its importance. It is all the more regrettable that this inscription was overlooked by Schilling, as he of course dealt extensively (pp. 383ff.) with the epithet *'fisica'* as applied in inscriptions not only to the Pompeian Venus but also to the goddess Mefitis. If he had not, he would undoubtedly have had occasion to modify his views somewhat. Koch (*op. cit.* col. 835) by contrast did know the inscription and gives an excellent demonstration of the value he set on it. I cannot avoid quoting him in part, first where I agree with him and then where I must differ. The inscription, he writes, 'teaches us that there is no justification for excluding the name Venus from the Oscan dialect, as is often done, or to take the Herculanean inscription *Herentatai Herúkinai* as our text for deducing that wherever in Oscan territory there is a tradition of Venus worship originally independent of Rome, as for instance in Pompeii, it must have been preceded by a cult of Herentas. Matters are not quite so simple. The pre-rhotacist consonantism (z-stage) shows that if this were a case of adoption from the Latin it must have occurred before the completion of rhotacism in Latium, that is, about two centuries before the colonization of Pompeii.' I am less ready to agree with him a little further on, where he proceeds, 'the deity was undoubtedly an original Mefitis, like that worshipped in Grumentum and near-by Potenza. Her special interest methodologically speaking, is to document, in a manner so strange to modern minds, how disparate the ideas can be which in such superimpositions coalesce to a single entity—a goddess with the name "Grace" adulterated with the demon of sulphurous earth exhalations!' First, the name Venus did not initially mean the same as the English 'grace' (German *'Anmut'*), and secondly, I shall try to show that the *'numina'* concerned in this case were not altogether strange to one another.

'Mephitis', writes Servius (*Ad Aen.* 7, 84), 'is properly speaking a foulness of earth arising from sulphurated waters. . . .We know however that such foulness originates only in the pollution of the air, just as a good smell comes from pure air, *so that Mephitis is a goddess of a very bad, that is foul-smelling, odour.*' We note that the bad smell is emitted continuously, as in Heges. 1, 35, 3 *'antrum, per quod graveolentis praecipitii profundum saevam exhalat mefitim'*— 'a cave from which the depths of a foul-smelling abyss emit a noxious exhalation' (for *'saevam mefitim'* cf. Verg. *Aen.* 7, 84); or Plac. *gloss.* IV M 6 *'huius deae fons est, ex qua gravissimus odor redditur sulphureus'*—'it is the source of the goddess who exhales a very foul sulphurous odour' (cf. also Serv. *Aen.* 7, 563; Pease *ad Cic. Div.* 1, 79). The ancients always wondered what force could be the cause of these exhalations and alleged that it was divine. Vergil (*Aen.* 7, 568ff.) called it Erinys: '*Hic specus horrendum et saevi spiracula Ditis | monstrantur ruptoque ingens Acheronte vorago | pestiferas aperit fauces, quis condita Erinys, invisum numen, terras caelumque levabat*' [26]—he is talking of Lake Ampsanctus. But most Italians called it the goddess Mefitis. There are some, however, who with more perspicacity dispute the divine origin of such exhalations and would deny them the actual name of a god or goddess. First of these I quote Pliny (*N.H.* 2, 208), whose words seem to me most worth recording. The passage is too long to be given here in full, but it all turns on the wonders of the earth, which he lists in some variety—the wealth of metals, precious and semi-precious stones, medicinal springs, mountains burning with perpetual fires, then '*deadly vapours in some places either issuing from orifices or causing death on the spot*, in other fatal only to flying creatures'. . . .(geographical examples follow) . . .'in others again oracular caves where those intoxicated by the exhalations foretell the future. . . .In such cases what reason could any mortal give than a *numen, or divine force, naturally diffused through all things and* constantly *bursting forth* in one way or another?' There are three main points to which I should wish to draw special attention. First, the *numen* is as powerful for good as for bad. It may do good with prophecy or harm with deadly vapours. Secondly, it pertains both to external things and to the inborn mind of man. Third and last, it is a force which bursts out, it is violent and impetuous, it boils over, cf. Schol. Stat. *Theb.* 1, 91 *'Sulphur terrae ebullientis spuma est*' 'Brimstone is the foam of the earth boiling over'.

Pliny's words are aptly matched by those earlier written by

---

[26] 'Here you may see the grim cave and breathing vents of cruel Dis and the monstrous chasm through which Acheron erupts here opens its deadly jaws, inside which the invisible *numen* of Erinys hides, so that earth and sky are rid of her.'

Cicero (*Div.* 1, 79). The immortal gods, he says, 'do not present themselves personally to our view, but *they diffuse their force far and wide, filling the caves of the earth with it and instilling it in the constitutions of men. For the force of earth inspired the Pythia at Delphi, the force of nature the Sibyl.* Well, then. Do we not see how various are the lands and soils of earth? Some part of which is fatal to life, like those we have seen, Lake Ampsanctus in the land of the Hirpini and Plutonia in Asia, and in the country some fields are pestilent, some healthy, some breed sharp wits, others dull—*all of which comes about through the changes in the sky and the varied breathing of the earth*'. In the same way a little further on (*Div.* 2, 29), 'and certainly if there is in entrails a force which foretells the future, it must necessarily be either bound up with the nature of things or *in some way moulded by the numen of the gods and the divine force. Since the nature of things great and splendid as it is and spread over every part and motion* may have some common element...' He cannot be treated lightly, this is not the language of a man given to primitive superstition. On the contrary, as Pease has rightly put it,[27] 'the *De Divinatione* stands forth as a vigorous rationalistic protest'. As primary source in Book 1, here and there too in Book 2, Cicero seems to have used Posidonius.[28] Moreover there are coincidences of language between Cicero and Pliny in almost the same context which may perhaps show that Pliny drew on the same source, e.g. *rerum natura in omnis partis motusque diffusa* ~ *diffusae per omne naturae numen*, and similarly where the coincidence is in the examples quoted, *Ampsancti in Hirpinis et in Asia Plutonia* ~ *in Hirpinis Ampsancti ad Mephitis aedem locum, Hierapoli in Asia*. Nevertheless, in such statements on religious topics by Roman writers there is often (the point needs more careful study) some vague memory of ancient fact. A. Grenier (*Les Religions étrusque et romaine* (1948), 151) very rightly observed: 'Entre la religion des penseurs, variable comme la pensée elle-même, et le culte officiel qui concerne l'État, subsiste en effet une religion

[27] Intro. to *comm. De Divinatione*, part 1 p. 12.
[28] Cf. Pease, 24; 'We may say that the first book of the *De Divinatione*.... was apparently derived from a work of Posidonius, probably his περὶ μαντικῆς, though possibly his περὶ θεῶν; p. 25, 'The occasional allusions to Posidonius in the second book are best regarded as direct additions by Cicero himself, not using any Greek source'.

populaire, faite des imaginations simples de la tradition ancienne, nourrie des émotions naturelles à l'homme devant l'inconnu et de la ferveur de ses besoins de protection. Cette couche religieuse profonde affleure toujours, chez tous, en quelque point'. Cicero indeed, in keeping with his subject, though he does not overlook the caverns of the earth, pays less attention than Pliny to those deadly vapours, though both are agreed that the toxic exhalations no less than the divine madness of prophecy are caused by some numinous force. The only difference between the two accounts is that Pliny speaking simply of *numen* is a little closer to the thoughts of their remote ancestors than Cicero attributing to a '*numen* of the gods' those accepted effects.

Yet if anyone asks me what particular noun was used in classical times to describe mephitic effects, I should have to reply, the noun '*aestus*'. Lucretius (6, 806f. and 816f.), for instance, after asking, '*Nonne vides etiam terra quoque sulphur in ipsa / gignier et taetro concrescere odore bitumen. . ?*' [29] he proceeds '*Hos igitur tellus omnis exaestuat aestus / expiratque foras in apertum promptaque caeli*'.[30] Thus it happened in digging wells that if there was a danger of sulphurous exhalations arising, channels were made to draw them off on the other side and called *aestuaria* (Plin. *N.H.* 31, 49; cf. Lucr. 6, 1138 '*mortifer* aestus'). I later seek to prove this *aestus*—without regard to its etymological meaning—had almost the same sense as the original *venus*, so that after *mefitis* had put on a divine semblance and a goddess Mefitis had emerged, then too a *venus Mefitis* became a goddess and *Venus Mefitis* came into existence. If I succeed in convincing the reader of this, I shall then hope to bring out *Venus Libitina* and *Venus Cloacina* into the clear light of day from the mists hitherto surrounding them. The foul smell is characteristic of the abodes of both these goddesses and both are full of *aestus*. This can hardly be better illustrated than by the fragment of Pacuvius (*frgm. trag.* 102 R.) '*ossuum inhumatum* aestuosam auram'.[31] However, the names V. Libitina

---

[29] 'Do you not see too how brimstone is generated and foul-smelling pitch congeals in the very earth. . . ?'

[30] 'The boiling earth ejects all these vapours and breathes them out through holes into the open expanses of sky'.

[31] 'the fetid air of unburied bones'.

and Cloacina do seem to differ from V. Mefitis in being slightly more recent. For if the name Venus Mefitis really originated in this way, from *venus mefitis* to *venus Mefitis* to *Venus Mefitis*, so that the genitive case of a common noun gradually moved over into the nominative of a proper noun, *Libitina* (cf. Walde-Hofmann s.v.) and *Cloacina*, being adjectives, would clearly not have arisen until after Venus had been received among the gods. Whether this in fact happened on the analogy of Venus Mefitis we cannot say, for lack of definite evidence.

If I am asked why I do not adopt the apparently more direct explanation of the name Cloacina, that it was given simply because of the proximity of the *Cloaca Maxima* (as e.g. Latte, *RRG*, 186), I reply first, that not even the Roman authors themselves have ventured to put forward such an idea. They seem to have been convinced that the Cloacina cult was of very great antiquity, having been instituted by King Tatius after the Romans and Sabines, as Pliny (*N.H.* 15, 119) has it, had laid down their arms and purified themselves in that spot, actually adding 'for the ancients used a verb *cluere* in the sense of purify'. It seems to me clear as daylight that the figure of Cloacina and her union with Venus came to give very great difficulty to the Romans, who proceeding from the correct etymology of the word *cloaca* concocted a learned but fictitious explanation, to which Schilling (p. 210) has given too much credence, though he begins well enough: 'Le nom de la déesse ne peut guère nous éclairer sur sa nature fonctionelle; il s'agit sans doute d'une désignation secondaire, suggérée par le voisinage de la Cloaca Maxima'. Secondly, hardly anyone will suppose that it could have happened by chance that a temple of Venus was dedicated in the actual Grove of Libitina. She was not called Venus Libitina because they were neighbours, but they became neighbours because of a certain bond of kinship. Why should we not assume that the same reason caused the Romans to found a temple to the goddess near the *Cloaca Maxima*? Thirdly, and this is the further point which I have already anticipated and undertaken to explore more closely, there really was such kinship. Neuburger (*Antike Technik*,[2] 448; cf. Altheim, *HRR*, 283) has explained, in my opinion rightly, that the *Cloaca Maxima* consisted of a stream with tributary canals dug for drainage of the land, but that later, so he says, 'the sewage was directed into it and the whole system eventually covered over because of the smell. That is how the *Cloaca Maxima* gradually took shape as the main sewer.'

At this stage of my investigation it occurred to me that there was something in common not only between Mefitis, Libitina, and Cloacina themselves but also between them and *Venus* the goddess of love. This common thing, I say, was *aestus*. It must be understood of course in a special metaphorical sense to signify the erotic stimulation of the mind.³² We find *amoris aestus*, for instance, in Cat. 68, 108; Ov. *Am.* 3, 5, 36; cf. further Varro *Men.* 204; Ov. *Her.* 16, 25; Prop. 2, 33, 43; Val. Fl. 3, 572. I do not deny that here and there the proper etymological sense, of *ardor*, heat, preponderates, as in Nemes. *Ecl.* 2, 14 '*ardentes flammati pectoris aestus*'—'the blazing heat of his inflamed breast'. Elsewhere, however, it is hardly to be discerned at all, as in Ov. *Her.* 16, 25 '*ut pelagi, sic pectoris adiuvet aestum*'—'may Venus cause commotion in the heart as she does at sea'. Having come this far, it seemed necessary to recapitulate what we have learned hitherto and then to enquire what relation the outcome of my efforts has to the root **ven* and its known derivatives.

The verb *venerari* showed us (pp. 3ff.) that the magic force called *venus* is attributed to the gods and that men exert themselves to increase it with gifts and prayers. Then the adjective *venustus* left no doubt that the same force could be possessed also by man himself (pp. 6ff.). Consequently we interpreted the goddess's name *Venus Iovia* as *venus Iovis*, the 'magic force of Jupiter'. But the noun *venenum* prevented us from considering that 'magic force' as solely of good omen. It could do harm, it seemed, as well as good. *Venia*, although a word of the same stock as *venus*, evolved differently. It conveys a much gentler, less violent notion, which though perhaps not always felt as good may have some analogy

---

[32] Here, if I am not mistaken, we must also put *Venus Calva*, known only from a single note by Servius (on *Aen.* 1, 720), about whom both ancient and modern commentators have dreamed wonderful dreams. Yet there have been those who realized that this was not a goddess despoiled of her hair and therefore pitiable but that the *calva* was connected with a verb *calvor*. However, I do not believe that either the adjective or the verb had the sense of 'deceiving', but that we here find traces of the same meaning as in the cognate Greek verb κηλέω, so that it would mean 'bewitching'.

with the word *venus*. However, the names of the goddesses, *Venus Libitina, Venus Cloacina, Venus Mefitis*, at once seemed to represent another aspect of the same notion. It is no longer a case of stimulation or commotion of mind but the impetus or commotion of natural phenomena. Or, to speak differently, and complete the picture with Venus the goddess of love, we have a great variety of functions clothed in divine form.

Now let me try an experiment to see whether my explanation fits. The Sanskrit *vanas* occurs only once in the literature that has come down to us.[33] The text is difficult but probably concerns the morning gods and begins by invoking the goddess Uṣas or Aurora in these words: '*ā́ yāhi vánasā, sahá gāvaḥ sacanta vartanim, yád ū́dhabhiḥ*', i.e. 'Come hither with your *vanas*; at the same time cows follow in (your) tracks with full udders'. What does the *vanas* really mean? It is usually translated 'longing' (presumably for love); Walde-Hofmann after '*Verlangen*' ('longing') adds '*Lieblichkeit*' ('loveliness'), but all these suggestions to me sound too feeble. It is some violent force, an internal stimulation of love for which the English with the approval of other peoples have coined the phrase 'sex appeal'.[34] I do not think Uṣas approached with longing alone. We read elsewhere how she came to her lover the sun (*Rgv.* 1, 124, 7) 'like a wife beautifully clothed who bares her breast in desire for her husband'. Did not Afranius rightly exclaim (*frgm.* 380f. R.) '*Aetas et corpus tenerum et morigeratio, / haec sunt venena formosarum mulierum*' 'The time of life, a delicate body, and winning ways, these are the magic spells of beautiful women'. If we do not take enough notice of this boiling over of instinct how are we to understand the fact that Sanskrit *vánati, vanóti*, Old Saxon *winnan*, Dutch *(ge)winnen*, verbs meaning 'to win over', can come from the same root? *Vēnāri* too, a Latin verb

---

[33] Rgv. 10, 172, 1. For the Sanskrit my grateful thanks are due to my colleague J. Gonda.

[34] Less useful for us are the oft-quoted compounds *gīrvaṇas* and *yajñávanas* which are translated by Ernout & Meillet (as epithets of gods) 'hymn-loving' and 'sacrifice-loving'. Their general sense is clear, but it cannot be made out for certain whether they mean 'desirous of singing hymns', '...of making sacrifices' or 'loving hymns sung', '...sacrifices made'. The second translation, which is adopted also by Schilling (p. 31)—'qui agrée les hymnes, les sacrifices'—seems to be the one preferred above.

which Schilling did not deal with but which Meillet decided, without objection from Hofmann, must also belong to this family, gains its force not from mere longing but from some effective impulse of capture. And when Varro (*r.r.* 2, 10, 6) writes, '*Quod ad feturam humanam pertinet pastorum, qui in fundo perpetuo manent, facile est, quod habent conservam in villa, nec hac* venus pastoralis *longius quid quaerit*',[35] he is speaking of a sexual urge which is both vulgar and commonplace.[36]

Simply in order to give some illustration of what *venus* originally meant I earlier suggested as a synonym the word *aestus*, without in any way disguising the fact that it often betrayed its etymological sense and included the notion of heat. But all the same the comparison does seem to me preeminently apt, since both nouns express a violent and spontaneous agitation of mind as well as the effervescences and exhalations occurring in nature. Nor does it seem that the comparison was far from the minds of the ancients themselves. We may compare for instance (Dir. 22f.) '*Hinc aurae dulces, hinc suavis spiritus agri / mutent pestiferos aestus et taetra venena*'.[37]

Finally, the same comparison, if I am not mistaken, makes it easier to understand why *venus* and its derivatives were thought to pertain more to goddesses than to gods, more to women than to men. There was a conviction that woman's nature was more liable than man's to violent impulses. It is true I have already admitted the possibility of a man's being called *venustus* or of *venus Iovis* turning into Jovian Venus. For anyone who called out

---

[35] 'As for a human stud of shepherds who never leave the farm, it is easy, because they have a girl-slave in the farmhouse and the pastoral sex-urge need look no further'.

[36] Cf. Ov. *Met.* 4, 258; Tac. *Germ.* 20.

[37] 'Hence let the sweet breezes, hence let the gentle breath of the countryside drive off the noxious vapours and fetid poisons.' Cf. Lucr. 6, 818ff.

> *Sic et Averna loca alitibus summittere debent*
> *mortiferam vim, de terra quae surgit in auras,*
> *ut spatium caeli quadam de parte venenet;*
> *quo simul ac primum pennis delata sit ales,*
> *impediatur ibi caeco correpta veneno,*
> *ut cadat e regione loci, qua derigit aestus*

'Thus too the region of Avernus must assail birds with a deadly force rising from the ground into the air so as to poison a certain part of the sky. And the moment a bird is borne there by its wings, it is arrested and seized by an invisible poison and falls straight down where the emanation directs it.'

in prayer *'Mars vigila!'* ('Mars awake!') or *'Enos Lases iuvate!'* ('Lares, help us! help!') or the like was not so much praying as stimulating, as 'venerating', i.e. trying to increase and stir the god's *venus*. Nevertheless the ancient Romans had a long-standing fear of every kind of instinct, and especially of 'the loves of women, to which nature has granted greater licence' according to Cicero (*Tusc.* 4. 71). Or as Servius (*Aen.* 7, 456) put it, *'in mulieribus semper viget venenum'.*—'there is a strong magic potency always in women'. I should not wonder if this would provide the context for Livy's account of an episode in 217 B.C., when Q. Fabius Maximus ordered the decemvirs to consult the Sibylline Books about the means of expiation required to appease the wrath of the gods. The prescription they brought back to the Senate after inspecting the books included the dedication of a temple to 'Venus Erycina and Mens'. Why should Mens (Mind) be associated with Venus? That is the question, which others besides Schilling have tried to answer at some length. Schilling (p. 251) takes refuge in Klausen's suggestion (*Aeneas und die Penaten* 1, 282f.) and writes 'Klausen a eu le mérite de suggérer que le culte de Mens pouvait s'expliquer en fonction de la légende troyenne (on s'étonne que sa remarque ait été perdue au profit de discussions oiseuses sur la nature de Mens). En effet, si Hector passait pour le "bras des Troyens", Énée était considéré comme "leur tête", les Grecs estimaient que "la sagacité d'Énée leur donnait plus de mal que la fureur d'Hector' (Philostr. *Heroica* 14 p. 723 = p. 302, ed. Didot, 1849). 'Homère n'avait-il pas appelé Énée βουληφόρος et Lycophron ne prêtait-il pas les mêmes qualités à Énée, en lui conférant le titre de βουλαῖς ἄριστος?' I have to confess that I cannot follow this lead. It seems to me too obscure. I had rather believe that the advice to found a temple of Venus was felt by those early men to be in conflict with traditional morals, and that it was to honour these that a temple of Mens was added as if for protection. But, someone may ask, are you not forgetting that this temple was dedicated on the instructions of a Sibylline oracle? No, but it seems to me very probable that here Tacitus' words apply (*Ann.* 6, 12; cf. Suet. *Aug.* 31), *'multa vana sub nomine celebri vulgabantur'* —'much idle nonsense was circulated under cover of a famous name'. Latte rightly observes (*RRG*, 240), 'The dedication of a temple for Mens was ordered according to Livy by the Sibylline books, but it is not easy to find a Greek equivalent'. Wissowa (*R.u.K.*[2], 537) considered these, what he called 'forgeries fabricated with a definite political purpose', to be restricted to the more recent collection, but I do not in the least see why we need assume that the earlier magistrates and priests would have shunned such tricks.

Perhaps nowhere is the conflict between judgment and love more clearly stated than in Vergil's lines (4, 448f.) where Aeneas '*magno persentit pectore curas, / mens immota manet*'—'his great heart was deeply troubled but his mind remained unmoved'. Pease here rightly notes, 'It may be said that if any one line is the key to the tragedy of the Fourth Book it is this'. Ovid (*Am.* 1, 2, 29ff.) in love wrote, '*Ipse ego, praeda recens, factum modo vulnus habebo / et nova captiva vincula mente feram; /* Mens Bona *ducetur manibus post terga retortis / et Pudor et castris quidquid Amoris obest*'.[38] Against that Propertius (3, 24, 17ff.), altogether despairing of Cynthia's love, has it

Nunc demum vasto fessi resipiscimus aestu,
 vulneraque ad sanum nunc coiere mea.
Mens bona, *si qua dea es, tua me in sacraria dono.*[39]

Once again we have the word *aestus*, and strange as it may seem, it gives me an opportunity to say a few words about the epithet *Frutis* applied to Venus. Cassius Hemina, according to Solinus (2, 14), wrote that Aeneas dedicated in a field of Laurentum an image which he had brought with him from Sicily to 'Mother Venus, who is called Frutis'. At Lavinium therefore a temple of this goddess does seem to have existed, and is undoubtedly referred to by Paulus' gloss (p. 80 L.) '*Frutinal templum Veneris Fruti<s>.*' Many have laboured to explain this name, and some of them have sought its origin in Etruria, claiming that *Frutis* in Etruscan is a

---

[38] 'I too, a recent prey, shall have a wound just inflicted, and bear new bonds with a captive mind. Mens Bona' (Conscience) 'shall be led past with her hands tied fast behind her back, and Modesty, and all who are hostile to Love's camp'.

[39] 'Now at last exhausted by the great passion I am coming to my senses and my wounds are healing. Mens Bona, if a goddess you are, receive me into your shrine.'

corruption of Ἀφροδίτη. Schilling (p. 76) moreover rather boldly states that 'Aujourd'hui, cette explication linguistique est admise par la plupart des savants'. Which I deny. Hammarström (*Glotta* 11 (1921) 216) thinks, with some hesitation, that the conjecture is defensible. Wissowa rejects it in emphatic terms (*R.u.K*,[2] 290, 2; *Rosch. Lex.* 6, 186). Ernout and Meillet put a question mark. Walde-Hofmann *s.v.* and Bömer (*Rom und Troia* (1951), 33; 63f.) are in favour. Koch (*RE* 8 A1, col. 845f.) hesitates but is willing to let it pass. Latte (*RRG*, 184, 2) argues against it.

I prefer to recall Krogmann's account (*Glotta* 20 (1932), 175ff.). He too rejected an Etruscan origin for the name and offered an alternative approach. He considers that it is a -*ti*-noun from an Indo-European root **bhereu-*: **bheru-*: **bhreu-*: **bhrŭ-* which he translates 'to move violently, *wallen*' ('boil' or 'surge'). As Latin derivatives of the root he lists *ferveo, -ēre, fervo, -ĕre* 'to boil, surge' and *defrŭtum* 'boiled must'. To be brief, I quote from his remaining examples taken from other languages only those which best illustrate the view I myself am about to offer: Old Indic *bhurvaṇi-ḥ*, 'restless, wild'; *bhurván-*, 'restless movement of water'; Greek φρυάσσομαι 'behave impatiently', 'be boisterous'; Old Irish *bruth* 'live embers, anger'; Old Welsh *brut* 'mind'; Lithuanian *briáujus, brióviaus, briáutis* 'advance with brute force'; Icelandic *breyma* 'on heat', 'ardent'; Middle High German *brüsen*, 'effervesce, rage' *brūs*, 'effervescence, roar'. In case I should be straying outside my province I put this question to my colleague J. Gonda, who kindly replied, first, that he was highly dubious of the proposal to identify the names *Frutis* and *Aphrodite*, and secondly, that Krogmann's etymological solution did not seem to him to raise many doubts and he found it indeed preferable to the other attempted explanation provided it was borne out by arguments from semantics and the history of religion.

I have not overlooked Hofmann's (Walde-Hofm. *s.v.*) warning reproof: 'the meaning "*Brunst, brünstig*"—"passion, on heat" —is only once represented in this family'. In my judgment this is of no significance. This very transparent etymology indicates that *frutis* is a preeminently Latin word, and nobody will have failed to notice that it shows the same variations of meaning which we have already noted one by one in the word *venus*. Both combine the notions of natural effervescence ('*wallen*', Krogmann) and stimulating the mind ('to advance with brute force', 'animus', 'to behave impatiently', Krogm.). The fact that not even the 'heat' of bodily love is missing from the series ('*Brunst*', Krogm.) only confirms my opinion. Certainly it is not for me to object if we explain the word *Frutis* in such a way that *Venus Frutis* is a reiteration of the same idea. The same, though in a rather different way, would hold for *Venus Frutis = Aphrodite*. Probably the same *numen* was *venus* in one place, *frutis* in another. Afterwards, when Venus had assumed the primacy, the Laurentes, by then ignorant of the original sense of the word, called her *Venus Frutis*.

Finally—for even this discussion must come to an end, however inconclusive—something may be added about the epithet *Fisica*, applied both to Mefitis and to Venus. It is astonishing how much trouble this word too has given scholars. Schilling (pp. 383ff.) devotes a first Appendix of his book to it and gives a useful conspectus of different views. After rejecting the view,[40] based on Oscan words of similar appearance, that *fisica* has the same meaning as *fida* and thus like Ribezzo (*RIGI* 18 (1934), 149ff.) defending the conjecture that *fisica* is to be referred to the Oscan **futri-* which corresponds to the Latin *genetrix*, Schilling associates himself with those who think the word is simply the Greek φυσική. According to him 'le mot exprime un concept philosophique, qui implique une théorie de la φύσις—théorie de la nature, telle qu'elle existe par exemple dans la théorie épicurienne. L'épithète *fisica* peut donc convenir aussi bien à la déesse tellurique des exhalaisons méphitiques...qu'à la Vénus naturaliste de la philosophie grecque'.

To a certain extent, but not altogether, this seems to me correct. Let me recapitulate the material. *Venus fisica* is twice named in inscriptions from Pompeii (*CIL* 4, 6865; 10, 928 = Dessau 3180), and once we have *Venus Fisica Pompeiana* (*CIL* 4, 1520). Additionally there is an inscription found at Grumentum, a city of Lucania (see above p. 182), which is dedicated to *Mefitis fisica*. I refrain from repeating everything that has been published in course of time on these inscriptions. Both Schilling and Koch have studied

---

[40] Zangemeister, *C.I.L.* 4, 1520; A. Sogliano, *Atti R. Acad. di Archeol. Napoli* (1932), 361ff. Latte, 184, accepts a connection with Umbrian *Fisios*, but regards the puzzle as unsolved. So does Koch, col. 841ff.

them with the required care and I am satisfied to refer the reader to them. I should just like, however, to put my own thoughts in a few words. First of all, I think it obvious that *Venus Fisica Pompeiana* and *Mefitis Fisica* were closely connected with one another and that Koch has correctly observed (col. 836, 24), 'We must therefore be prepared to assume that there were once material contacts between the V. Pompeiana and the Mefitis cults of Lucania, about which we have no exact information'. But even shrewder and of more importance for solving the problem is Latte's remark (p. 184) in dealing with the Oscan inscription quoted above (p. 181), which both turned up in Lucania itself, near Potenza, and bears the name *Venus Mefitis*. 'As Venus' he observes in passing 'is otherwise unknown in Oscan, it must probably be regarded almost as a common noun'. I can only applaud: *venus mefitis* (genitive) > *venus Mefitis* (genitive) > *Venus Mefitis* (nominative)! I am convinced the other Venuses had a similar origin. I refer to what I said above (p. 174) about *Venus Iovia*. Moreover several cities and towns had sanctuaries of Mefitis, of which the following are known (cf. R. Peter, *Rosch. Lex.* 2, 2, 2520): in Cisalpine Gaul one outside the gates of Cremona, another in the canton of the Boii called Laus Pompeia, situated between Mutina and Bononia; in Latium one at Rome on the Esquiline, one at Atina of the Volsci; two in Samnium, at Aequum Tuticum and near Lake Ampsanctus, both in the territories of the Hirpini; finally in the Lucanian city of Potenza.

Although the word *mefitis* is not absolutely clear, I think that by common consent it can hardly mean anything but 'the personification of the foul-smelling, noxious, sulphurous vapours which in certain places issued from the volcanic earth' (Peter ibid. 2519). Moreover I think there can be hardly any doubt that little by little the word came to have a less definite sense. Peter himself (col. 2520, 2) warned us that there was nothing in the historical writers to suggest that the Esquiline area at Rome was troubled with sulphurous exhalations, and added, 'the altar to Febris in the same district testifies to the unhealthiness of the air in that part of the Esquiline'. Elsewhere the point is generalized by Koch (col. 835, 60): 'However, many of the cult territories of Mefitis have no ground exhalations; the character of Grumentum, for instance, is determined by its water and swamp'. Indeed, the Romans do not seem to have made a sharp distinction between sulphurous exhalations and those heavy, pestilential vapours occurring in marshland as for instance in the Pomptine marshes and mentioned by Vitruvius (1, 4, 12). Porphyrio (*ad Hor. Od.* 3, 18) referring to Vergil's lines on the Albunean Spring writes, 'he shows that he (Faunus) had his sacred grove near a *Mefitis*, a marsh with a pestilential smell'. To say briefly what I think, from the similarity of meaning between the words *mefitis* and *febris* a gradual confusion grew up between them, all the easier to understand from the fact that the force and effect of both was in part the same, because the fever, or *febris*, which today we are accustomed to call "malaria" continually plagued a great part of Italy. Perhaps this may give us a clue to the meaning of the epithet *fisica*.[41] I have no doubt whatsoever that it is a Greek word. It is not by chance that it is found only in the southern part of Italy. If I am right it cannot mean anything but 'induced externally by natural causes', the opposite of *aestus* which is induced internally. This opposite if applied to *mefitis* makes no sense, but if to fever the case is different. But we have already seen that at Grumentum where the inscription containing the words '*Mefiti fisicae*' was found, in a marshy region that is, it can hardly be a case of a true *mefitis*—a volcanic exhalation—it must be a question of fever. On the contrary the *Venus fisica* worshipped at Pompeii seems to me to have been a very ancient goddess of a city always exposed to *mefitis*. Later, however, in the time of Sulla, when possibly nobody any longer knew what *fisica* meant, the adjective was differently interpreted as signifying the mother and mistress of all

[41] Valerius Maximus, 2, 5, 6, lists the three temples of Febris standing in Rome and thus continues: '*in eaque remedia, quae corporibus aegrorum adnexa fuerant, deferebantur. Haec ad humanae mentis aestus leniendos cum aliqua usus ratione excogitata*'. 'And the remedies which had been attached to the bodies of the sick were deposited in them. This practice was devised with some idea of its usefulness in calming the agitations of the human mind.' From this it appears that not even in this context did *aestus* always pertain to the heat of the blood. Often too *febris* and *aestus* are distinguished, cf. Cic. *Cat.* 1, 31; Plin. *Ep.* 10, 17, 1; Oros. *Hist.* 6, 12, 2; Cels. 3, 5 p. 82 D. Pliny makes a clear distinction between them, but at the same time he adds *N.H.* 2, 208 (above p. 183), where we read 'deadly vapours either issuing through orifices or causing death on the spot'.

nature. I have no wish to labour the point. Schilling and others have sufficiently illustrated this figure. I would only recall what Eisler (*Weltenmantel und Himmelszelt* 1 (1910), 67) wrote in connection with the fresco found in the building called '*Casa dei Dioscuri*', where Venus is clothed in a sky-blue mantle sprinkled with golden stars, describing her 'as a cosmic Venus and ruler of the three domains of the universe—Heaven, Earth, and Sea—as she seems to have been worshipped by Sulla and his people, certainly in accordance with the temple doctrine of some oriental cult.'

But here I conclude. It is time at last to say goodbye to Venus. If anything of what I have written is found useful, part of the credit must go to the impact of Schilling's book.

XI

ORARE, PRECARI

Writers on prayer among the Romans, numerous as they are, seem to be in general agreement on one point. Perhaps it was Pease (ed Cic. *Div.* 1, 129) who most succinctly expressed the common view when he wrote: 'Ancient prayers were usually uttered aloud rather than silent....Silent prayers were in the early period chiefly for magical purposes or for the attainment of wishes which the worshipper was ashamed or afraid to mention aloud, but later, especially in Christian usage, were far more generally employed (perhaps under the influence of such passages as Matth. 6, 6)'. All the same it does seem to me worth while to look into this question once more. I am far from being persuaded that the opinion just quoted is based on solid enough grounds. First of all, if I am not mistaken, it will be useful to spend a little time on the meaning of the verbs *orare* and *precari*.

The principal force [1] of the verb *orare* is 'to make words', to speak, and that almost always with some authority. And certainly they were not just anybody's words. In ancient times the Roman farmers and herdsmen were a rough, hard lot who, like most simple rustics to this very day, had unbounded admiration for the man with a ready and eloquent tongue who could express his thoughts clearly and fluently. We shall scarcely find a more striking example of this wonder and reverence than in Homer (*Od.* 8, 170ff.), where he makes Ulysses paint a portrait of the orator speaking eloquently in the assembly and conclude with the

---

[1] The etymology of the word is not very clear. According to Varro, *l.l.* 6, 76 *oro* is from *ore*, but Ernout-Meillet, supported by Walde-Hofmann, argue on the contrary that though the ancients thought so (cf. Enn. *Trag.* 306 *quam tibi ex ore orationem duriter dictis dedit;* I add Enn. *Ann.* 303 V² *additur orator Cornelius suauiloquenti ore;* Plaut. *Merc.* 176 *Tu quidem ex ore orationem mi eripis*) this was undoubtedly a piece of popular etymology, '*car nulle part ailleurs le mot correspondant à ōs n'a fourni rien de pareil*'. I doubt whether such an argument can lead to the truth, but the question is not within the scope of this article or within my province.

words ἐρχόμενον δ'ἀνὰ ἄστυ θεὸν ὡς εἰσοράουσι ('They stare at him like a god as he walks through the town'). Of Roman authors I quote Pacuvius,[2] who sang: '*O flexanima atque omnium regina rerum oratio!*' ('O moving eloquence queen of all things'). We may suppose they frequently needed such an orator both in their public life and in divine matters, to the extent that as early as the laws of the Twelve Tables *orare* meant *agere in iudicio*, 'to plead a case at law', and *orator* was equivalent to *causae patronus*, or 'defence counsel'; or that envoys sent to other peoples were called *oratores*,[3] including the *fetiales* or 'diplomatic corps' (cf. Varro *De Vita Populi Romani Libro II* in Nonius p. 529 M, *fetiales legatos res repetitum mittebant quattuor, quos oratores vocabant*—'they sent four diplomatic envoys, whom they called *oratores*, to demand satisfaction') Finally, the *pontifices* and other priests, magistrates too, who addressed the gods in prayer on behalf of the people, were said *orare*.

Right at the start there are some points to be noted. First, *orare*, as one might expect from its meaning 'to speak', was in its very nature an intransitive verb. Secondly, it must necessarily have acquired little by little the sense also of praying. And it seems to me not irrelevant also to ask how this development occurred—my intention will appear in due course.[4]

It is not infrequently made clear that the earliest authors were conscious that the sense of prayer in the verb *orare* was really required, when they either added *prece* or *precibus*: as Enn. *Ann.* 20 V[2] '*tum face vero quod tecum precibus pater orat*'—'then do as your father with prayers implores you'; or Hor. *Sat.* 2, 6, 13, *hac prece te oro*—'with this prayer I beg you'; or *per precem*, Plaut. *Capt.* 244 *nunc te oro per precem*—'now I do beg and pray you'.

[2] *Fr.* 177 ap. Cic. *de Orat.* 2, 178: Quintil. 1, 12, 18.
[3] Cf. *Fest.* p. 218 L: *Orare antiquos dixisse pro agere testimonio sunt et oratores et i qui nunc quidem legati, tunc vero oratores, quod reipublicae mandatas partis agebant;* Varro *op. cit.* 7. 41, after quoting Ennius, *Ann.* 207 V[2] (*orator sine pace redit regique refert rem*), goes on, *Orator dictus ab oratione; qui enim verba haberet publice adversus eum quo legabatur, ab oratione orator dictus.*
[4] Cf. *oraculum;* Sen. *Contr. Praef.* 9, *Quid enim est oraculum? Nempe voluntas divina hominis ore enuntiata.* But also, and indeed primarily according to E. Benveniste, *Rev. Phil.* 22 (1948) 120, it was the name of a place of prayer.

Or they may add another word of asking, as Plaut. *Asin.* 662 *hanc.* . . .*petere atque orare mecum*—'bid her beg and pray with me; and similarly vs. 686. *Curc.* 432, *tecum oro et quaeso, ut.* . . .—'I pray and implore you to'. . . .; Ter. *Hec.* 686, *egi atque oravi tecum uxorem ut duceres*—'I urged and prayed you to take a wife.' But there are other points deserving our attention in these examples. Three times already we have seen the verb *orare* not construed with an accusative but instead the expression *orare cum aliquo*, which we may assume to have been the construction in common speech used from the beginning.[5] A certain transition is shown by *orare* construed on the analogy of the verb *petere*, as in Pacuv. fr. 125 R '*primum hoc abs te oro,*. . . .' ('first I pray of you. . .'). Finally on the analogy of the verb *rogare* it is beginning to take an accusative (see below p. 201f. and n. 12). Moreover we can establish that in none of the passages quoted is it priests or magistrates who are said '*orare*'. It is always a question of private people asking something of private people. Meanwhile, and by a different route, if I am not quite mistaken, *orare* diverged into the meaning of *precari*, 'pray'. For in the public cult, when prayers were offered, the priests 'led' the words, that is, they dictated certain formulae. At that stage, I think, a father might have said to his young son who chattered, 'Quiet, the priest *orat*, (is speaking)', and it would be no wonder if by this route *orare* came to mean the same as *precari*.

All the same, it is of great importance to us to observe the relation that existed between *orare* and *precari*. For they do not have the same significance in all contexts. At a later date and not, as I have found, before the Christian period, a person who prayed silently was said *orare*. Against that, *precari*, like *poscĕre* < *porc-scĕre* from the root **p(e)rek-*, is related to Dutch '*vragen*', German *fragen*. Therefore although in course of time both verbs began to mean the same, there was necessarily less of the sense of 'speaking aloud' in *precari* than in *orare*.

This preliminary is intended to open the way to a treatment of the question I have briefly outlined above. On this topic it will be necessary to separate public cult from professions of private piety just as clearly as magical transactions from true religion.

[5] Cf. Plaut. *Cas.* 324; *Pers.* 117; *Rud.* 773; Ter. *Hec.* 686.

About the prayers encountered in public cult I can be brief. Many have dealt with them in detail and there is scarcely anything new I could add to their arguments. The point which I think it important to make first of all is that too often public and private cult are treated alike. Thus when Wissowa ($R.u.K^2$ pp. 396f.) writes, 'prayer according to Roman ideas is not so much an independent act of piety as the necessary oral accompaniment of every sacral procedure and performance, which from the mortal side legalizes and perfects the sacral transaction and, if uttered in correct form, at the same time compels the deity too to enter into it', and in what follows rather freely expands on the magical force and nature of prayers, he altogether fails to warn us that all that is valid for the public cult but not for the private. Nor must we forget that matters concerning Roman public worship have been handed down to us in much more detail than the religious life of citizens, humble and rustic as they originally were. For the same reason I am not willing too rashly to put my trust in assertions such as we find in Appel [6] among others, e.g. 'the Romans do not think the gods demand of people praying, as Christian opinion does, that they should be emotionally absorbed, they think it enough that the actual prayers they offer should be correctly framed.' He rightly adds that certain rules arose about the rite and gesture to be observed in prayer, the neglect of which would always make the whole prayer ineffectual, while their observance, so the Romans thought, actually obliged the deity to grant them. But neither here nor in what follows does he make it sufficiently clear that while the public prayers of priests and magistrates did indeed have this character and it must moreover have been the case that public rites of prayer were to some extent carried over into private use, none the less it must also have happened quite frequently that a sincere state of mind would cause a man, even one expert in those time-honoured rules, to address his god, or all the gods, in extempore silent prayer.

Previously Sudhaus [7] had already laid it down—and his views made many converts—that 'quite often we find ... mention of silent prayer among the ancients, but it always forms an exception.

[6] G. Appel, 'De Romanorum Precationibus', *RVV* 7, 2 (1909) 184.
[7] S. Sudhaus, 'Lautes und leises Beten', *ARW* 9 (1906) 187.

It was in the first instance public prayer that as a matter of course was spoken aloud, but private prayer too, which I shall be discussing almost exclusively in what follows, was not silent except for very special reasons.' I cannot write at length about these special reasons for silent prayer, in such a short essay. But the main reasons were of three kinds—shame at something dishonourable, such as anyone might want to conceal from others,[8] something with a magical purpose, such as might prove ineffectual if concealment were lifted,[9] and the fear of rivals or enemies, who if they heard someone's prayers might be able to harm the author by more powerful spells (Sudhaus, 194). Nor would I want to press the arguments used by Rohde[10] in support of his view that: 'Unfortunately almost nothing has come down to us about loud or silent prayer in the Roman state cult.' He is right to insist on the fact that the priests too might utter their prayers silently[11] and in this connection it must always be remembered that in such a context *tacite*, 'silently', could not infrequently have the sense of a 'quiet or low murmur' (Appel, 210)—but the instances he mentions are associated with such special conditions that they can easily be regarded as exceptions. Undoubtedly *orare* from the beginning meant 'to speak aloud'. In course of time this sense was weakened, so that Ovid, (*Ex Ponto* 2, 9, 65) for example, could write *ad vatem vates orantia branchia tendo*—'as poet to poet I stretch my praying arms'. Above, I guessed that *orare* may have begun to acquire the meaning of *precari* by a double route. Whatever the truth, the actual origin of this affair must lie in the mists of earliest antiquity, for though *orare* governing the accusative[12]

---

[8] Cf. H. J. Rose, *The Roman Questions of Plutarch* (1924) p. 87 n. 89; J. Balogh, 'Lautes und leises Beten' *ARW*. 23 (1925) 345.

[9] Rose *ibid*. 88; F. Pfister, *Relig. d. Gr. u. Röm.* (1930) 194; E. E. Burriss, *Class. Philol.* 25 (1930) 48.

[10] G. Rohde, *Die Kultsatzungen der röm. Pontifices* (1936) 84.

[11] 'At a lightning funeral the pontifex maximus prays silently (*quadam tacita orans prece*, Schol. Juv. 6, 587) and at the burial of a Vestal guilty of incest it is said of the *pontifex maximus* (Plut. *Numa* 10, 12) εὐχάς τινας ἀπορρήτους ποιησάμενος... "after some unspoken prayers"'.

[12] On the analogy, if I am not mistaken, of a verb such as *rogare*. Indeed, *petere* too is thus construed. *Ita peto vos, manes sanctissimae, commendatum habeatis meum carum...*' (CIL 6, 18817, 9 sq.; it is the prayer of a wife for her dead husband; cf. Appel *op. cit.* 39).

is very rarely found before the first century A.D. it does occur in Livius Andronicus.[13] All the more remarkable then is it that so far as we know the verb *orare* was never used by the priests and magistrates themselves in their fixed formulas and solemn prayers. They never said *vos, deos, oro* but *vos quaeso precorque* or *precor quaesoque*,[14] or *vos precor venerorque* or *vos precor veneror veniamque peto*,[15] or more simply *precor*.[16] And as it is most probable that these formulas of prayer, prescribed by the priestly books, are very much older than the whole literary tradition, I am all the more led to believe that far from *orare* being a more solemn word than *precari*—as many have supposed [17]—the reverse is the case.[18]

But though the priests and magistrates in their prayers were accustomed to 'speak aloud' and use fixed formulas, the question now arises whether they were so bound by the solemn rules of their books as not to be able to adopt any prayers but those of which the words were sanctioned by ancient authority. I know of nothing which has been handed down in clear terms on this point, but such a rigid restriction seems hardly worthy of credence. I would rather believe that the general run of prayers were extempore provided that the rites accorded with the rules. A further point is that in cult too emotional reactions more and more asserted themselves. Latte himself (p. 245) correctly drew attention to the influence exerted in this connection by the introduction of *suppli-*

---

[13] *Od.* fr. 19 R. *utrum genua amplectens virginem oraret. Cf.* Enn. *com.* 9; L. Calp. Piso *fr.* 19P.; *CIL* I, 1290, of uncertain date, but before the middle of the 1st century B.C.

[14] Twice in the *Acta fratrum Arvalium*, ed. Henzen p. 122f.; The *Fratres Arvales* are speaking. In addition Liv. 9, 8, 8; 29, 27, 1 (the consul Sp. Postumius and the imperator L. Scipio pray one after the other); six times in the *Acta Sacrorum Saecularium* for 17 B.C. (*CIL* 6, 32323), where Caesar Augustus invokes individual gods.

[15] *Imperatores* in a hymn of dedication (Liv. 8, 9, 6) and in a hymn of evocation (Macr. *Sat.* 3, 9 7); cf. Tac. *Hist.* 4, 58.

[16] Liv. 5, 21, 3 (M. Furius Camillus the dictator is praying); Plin. *Paneg. Trai.* 94 (the author is speaking as consul).

[17] It was a different question raised by Löfstedt, *Peregr. Aeth.* 41 (cf. *Syntactica* 2, 463), where he thinks the Christians deliberately restored words like *orare, oratio* in earlier passages after they had gone out of use with the passage of time.

[18] Vergil so far as I can discover was the first to use the word *orare* where it was a question of private individuals addressing the gods in prayer (as *Aen.* 4, 205; 9, 24).

cationes. 'The participation of the whole people in a religious act, the intensification of feeling thus produced, had been up till then unknown in Roman religion. Instead of prayers every word of which was fixed, in which it is usually wishes which are laid before the gods, we have a "pleading" which found words in the mood of the moment'. Valerius Maximus (4, 1, 10) tells a story about the vigour and good sense of P. Scipio Africanus Minor. As censor he held a lustration and at the sacrifice of the *Solitaurilia* repeated the hymn of prayer after the scribe, who was solemnly leading the prayer as he read from the public tables. Then, at the point where the immortal gods were prayed to bestow more success and greatness on the affairs of the Roman people, Scipio himself added, 'They have success and greatness enough, I pray therefore that their success and greatness may be maintained always'. Valerius Maximus seems more to have admired than been disturbed by this liberty, and not he alone but Scipio's colleague as well, for he proceeds, 'and he at once gave orders that the hymn should be corrected in the public tables to this effect. From then on the censors observed a like modesty in the wishes they expressed to the gods when holding lustrations'. For brevity's sake I shall not quote what Fowler (*Rel. Exp.* 184ff.) has published on these questions, rather incautiously in my opinion but with shrewd insight on the whole.

What holds good about the public cult applies all the more to the private. First indeed it appears that the Romans themselves soon became conscious that it was of less concern to the gods that the exact words of a prayer should be adhered to than that it should come from a righteous heart. As early as Plautus (*Rud.* 26f.) we read

*facilius si qui pius est a dis supplicans
quam qui scelestust invenient veniam sibi.*

'A man who is righteous when he prays to the gods will sooner get a favourable hearing than one who is wicked.' It is a probable conjecture that these words came by a roundabout route from a Greek source,[19] but they do not seem to have been translated from Diphilos' Greek comedy. For F. Marx (*ad. loc.*) has revealed that

[19] Cf. the passages quoted by Orelli on Hor. *Od.* 3, 23, 17-20.

these verses were inserted from another author in a second, revised version of about B.C. 177. It cannot be proved that this had in some way become a common sentiment, shared even by those Romans who had learned to cast doubt on the principle of their inherited religion. Few men, least of all Romans, are accustomed to speak out their minds on such matters. But at least it is a conjecture supported by a good deal of evidence. Cicero for instance declares openly, and that not in a book of philosophy but in a legal speech,[20] that 'the minds of the gods are to be appeased by righteousness and religious observance and correct prayers, not by vile superstition nor by victims killed to procure crime'. It was the Stoics who first preached such an attitude to the Romans. Seneca [21] for instance wrote, 'do you not think God is to be worshipped with a pure mind and good, honest intentions...rather than by sacrifices and a welter of blood?' And if it was the Greeks especially to whom the Romans were indebted for notions like these, we must not forget that the growth of such teaching in Rome was of much earlier date. We already read in Terence (*Ad.* 704f.) of a young man telling his adoptive father, 'Better you pray to the gods than me, I'm sure they'll give you more of a hearing, you're a better man than I am'. No doubt these are Menander's words, but Terence, when translating his comedy into Latin, neither could nor would leave them out. *'Rien n'est plus étranger au formalisme précis du culte romain'* said P. Lejay (*Plaute*, p. 183). But if you agree with me, the stubborn fetters of ritual had already begun little by little to be broken.

It is not surprising that the public cult should strongly influence the private. 'The whole public religion of the state', says Warde Fowler (p. 286), 'and to some extent also the private religion of the family, became a mass of forms and formulae, and never succeeded in freeing itself from these fetters.' Never? These words seem to me a trifle exaggerated, unless we only consider those prayers hallowed by tradition which a son would learn from his father or would be offered at table to the Lares and Penates,[22] to some extent

---

[20] *p. Cluent.* 194; cf. *Leg.* 2, 24.
[21] *Fr.* 123 H. = Lact. *Inst.* 6, 25, 3. On this point the Christian authors agree: Tert. *de Orat.* 17, 3, *Deus autem non vocis sed cordis auditor est;* cf. Cypr. *de dom. Orat.* 4; Cassian. *Conlatio* 9, 35.

comparable perhaps to such modern prayers as the 'Our Father' and the 'Hail Mary'.[23] Certainly the Romans were tenacious of opinions handed down from ancient times, but those fixed formulae of the priests in no way sufficed to express all the intimate needs of their hearts. We know too little of religious life in country homes, but even Vergil's first Eclogue can tell us what piety of heart it was proper to feel for the family hearth. Nor was this only true of the countryfolk. I ask, how could the wife of Ovid when she '*ante Lares sparsis prostrata capillis/contigit extinctos ore tremente focos,/ multaque in adversos effudit verba Penates/pro deplorato non valitura viro*'[24] have used solemn words handed down from ancient times? How could any sensible person discover any such thing in Ovid's own prayer just before that very same passage? Gellius (13, 23, 1) rightly wrote: 'General supplications of the immortal gods held according to the Roman rite are published in the Roman people's priests' books and in a number of ancient speeches', but it often seems wrongly to be inferred from this that all Roman prayers were said according to the Roman rite. Thus on Ovid's words (*Met.* 7, 953) '*dum vota sacerdos concipit*' Ehwald in his revision of Haupt's commentary observes, '*Concipere vota, preces*, Gelübde, Bitten in bestimmten Formeln (*verbis conceptis*) aussprechen' ('to utter vows, prayers in definite formulae'). In this passage, where it is the priest speaking, his observation is in fact correct, but when on *Met.* 8, 682 *concipiunt Baucisque preces timidusque Philemon*[25] he only notes 'See on 7, 594', he is wrongly inducing the reader to believe that this humble couple had at their command a large repertoire of fixed formulae. No different was the case of those Roman mothers of whom Livy[26] wrote, *Stratae passim*

[22] Cf. Verg. *Aen.* 8. 279; Quint. *Declam.* 301 p. 187, 16 R.

[23] As an example of a tradition preserved we may take: in private cult Acc. *frgm. praet.* 5 R. *precor veniam petens, / uti quae ⟨ego⟩ egi axo axim* VERRUNCET BENE; in public worship Liv. 29, 27, 2, *divi divaeque...vos precor quaesoque, uti ea...mihi populo plebique Romanae...*BENE VERRUNCENT; cf. Acc. *frgm. praet.* 36 R.; Pacuv. *frgm.* 296 R.

[24] *Trist.* 1, 3, 43ff. 'prostrate with scattered hair before the Lares she touched the extinguished fire with trembling lips and poured out to the Penates opposite a stream of unavailing words on behalf of her lamented husband'.

[25] 'both Baucis and shy Philemon offer prayers'. Cf. Sen. *H.F.* 926.

[26] 3, 7, 8. 'everywhere prostrate mothers sweeping the temple floors with their hair implore mercy of the angry heavens and an end to the pestilence'

matres crinibus templa verrentes veniam irarum caelestium finemque pesti exposcunt, or the unhappy mother for whose sick son *nec valuere preces, quas funderat anxia caras.*[27] It would be easy but hardly useful to put together a long series of such prayers, there is one however which I prefer not to omit.

In the *Corpus Tibullianum* (3, 11 = 4, 5) there is an ode which we are uncertain whether to attribute to Albius Tibullus himself or to another poet who was a friend of his. It is about the birthday of a young man, Cerinthus by name, and his love. A girl is introduced who is herself fired with love for him and utters prayers and vows on his behalf. Then we read

Optat idem iuvenis quod nos, sed tectius optat:
  nam pudet haec illum dicere verba palam.
At tu, Natalis, quoniam deus omnia sentis,
  adnue: quid refert, clamne palamne roget? [28]

Where there is talk of love, recent commentators too will acknowledge that even the Romans were ready to expose their most intimate feelings in prayer to the gods and did so silently. For instance Sudhaus (195) thus reasons in his treatment of another passage, 'Ariadne's prayer in Catullus 64.104 does not pass the maiden's lips, *tacito suscepit vota labello*. . . .But beside these mute harmless lovers' prayers are other *tacitae preces* which equally get pressed back into the subconscious by αἰδώς but are not so harmless', and he proceeds to discuss the magical prayers previously mentioned above. Why then, I ask, does he suppose that only love could have driven people not to *orare* in the primary sense of the word, to pray aloud, but to pray silently, and that grief, anxiety, and other emotions did not do so?

Thus the very order of discussion has brought us back to the question how far the Romans, though accustomed in general, we agree, to pray aloud, and I refrain from adding to the number who have quoted evidence of this, did all the same often pour out

---

[27] 'nor did the prayers poured from a loving heart avail'.
[28] 'The boy wants the same as me but doesn't openly pour his heart out. He's too shy to say such things in public. But you, his birth-god, a god from whom nothing is hidden, hear our prayer. What does it matter whether he says it to himself or openly?'

their prayers in silence without any intention either of harming anybody by magic or of concealing for some reason from others what they were asking for.

First let us hear Seneca: '*Vota homines parcius facerent, si palam facienda essent; adeo etiam deos, quibus honestissime supplicamus, tacite malumus et intra nosmet ipsos precari.*'[29] Not even Sudhaus (200) could fail to concede that 'the passage is all the more remarkable for recognizing unmistakably a universal tendency to pray silently to oneself.... The reason according to Seneca is a sense of delicacy, making a person reluctant to stand out as a petitioner even before the gods. However, the expression he chooses, *deos... tacite malumus et intra nosmet ipsos precari*, seems to betray a quite different, much more modern feeling which revolts against the intrusion of a third person into one's personal dealings with deity.' His observations are altogether right, though we have to proceed cautiously where it is a matter of prayers among Stoics, who of course teach, to use Seneca's own words,[30] that 'the hands are not to be held up to heaven nor the temple attendant begged to let us get close to the image's ear', for *prope est a te deus, tecum est, intus est*—'God is near you, with you, in you.'

But it is not necessary to interrogate only Seneca on this point. Cicero (*De Div.* 1, 129) too assures us of it when he writes, 'just as the minds of the gods without eyes, ears, or tongue are mutually aware of what any of them feels or thinks so that men even when they wish or vow something silently have no doubt of being heard, in the same way too the minds of men....' It seems to me probable [31] that the same kind of prayer was generally felt as appropriate for the Lares and Penates—'meaning by Penates all those gods and goddesses who were worshipped by individual Romans at home'.[32] We are not very well informed on this subject. The pieces of evidence surviving here and there are too scarce. I would not believe that everyone was so indifferent in the choice of a divine patron as

---

[29] *De Ben.* 2, 1, 4. 'People would not be so free with their wishes if they had to be spoken aloud. It is in pleading to the gods especially, with whom we are at our most honest, that we prefer to pray in silent self communion.'

[30] *Ep.* 41, 5. Cf. W. J. Richards, '*Het Gebed bij Seneca, die Stoïsijn*', diss. Utrecht, 1964.

[31] Cf. Plaut. *Merc.* 834ff.; Ov. *Trist.* 1, 3, 43 (above p. 205).

[32] Cf. Wissowa, *Rosch. Lex.* 3, 2, 1887, 9.

Apuleius,[33] who asked the craftsman to make him 'an image of some kind' . . . 'of any god he liked to whom I might pray after my fashion.' Even Epictetus the Stoic philosopher, not himself a Roman but for a very long time practising in Rome, kept the images of the gods at his home with a stone lamp hanging before them.[34] Though he may not speak of prayer in this context, it is hardly to be believed that he did not worship his gods by the light of that lamp.

Finally I quote a passage which seems to me most deserving of the reader's attention. Ovid in the sixth book of his *Fasti*, dealing with the feast-days of the month of June in line 249, begins his account of the Vestalia with these words:

> *Vesta, fave! Tibi nunc operata resolvimus ora,*
> *ad tua si nobis sacra venire licet.*
> *In prece totus eram: caelestia numina sensi,*
> *laetaque purpurea luce refulsit humus.*

Who will not be astonished to read these lines? Latte (41) wrote: 'The feeling of bliss and rapture in the presence of deity is lacking in the Roman as opposed to the Greek', but rarely can a Greek poet under an almost divine inspiration have described that blessedness with such rapture as Ovid in these lines. Moreover if we take in the rest of this poet's work in one glance, such religious feeling seems to have a significance remote from his normal disposition. Did not Wilamowitz (*Glaube der Hellenen*, 2, 338) pass judgment in the words, 'of religion hardly a trace remains'? I shall be writing further about this elsewhere. Here there is a third noteworthy point which I want to press. The poet does not so much pray as be absorbed in prayer ('I was wrapt up in prayer'—Frazer; *'ich war ganz im Gebet (vertieft)'*—Bömer). Though Peter and Frazer and Bömer all in their commentaries observe profound silence about this passage—how inscrutable are the minds of commentators!—nowhere that I know in the whole of Latin literature before Christian times could we find another example of a man thus riveted in prayer. Nor can it possibly be that Ovid

---

[33] *Apol.* 61 (*supplicassem* for *supplicarem:* cf. Butler and Owen *ad. loc.*).
[34] Epict. *Diatr.* 1, 29, 21; Lucian. *adv. Indoctos* 13, 3 (p. 146).

means he prayed aloud (*oravit*). A man riveted in prayer was certainly silent.

In short, I conclude. In the public cult both priest and occasionally magistrates were accustomed *orare*, that is to lead the prayers word for word aloud. Individual words were repeated by the citizens. Thus they '*orabant*', but they themselves called it '*precari*'. Even in private cult there were many solemn phrases and fixed formulae which were carefully observed and clearly pronounced aloud by those praying. But in the course of time many Romans had learnt to address the gods in prayer, and this they did sometimes aloud, sometimes silently.

XII

AUGUSTUS AND VESTA

A passage of Ovid's *Fasti*, VI 249-252, which has not in my opinion yet received the attention it deserves, has caused me to examine more closely the relations between Augustus and the goddess Vesta. Before describing the Feast of Vesta on 9 June Ovid addresses the goddess with great veneration in these terms:

Vesta, fave! Tibi nunc operata resolvimus ora,
  ad tua si nobis sacra venire licet.
In prece totus eram: caelestia numina sensi,
  laetaque purpurea luce refulsit humus.

That is:

'Vesta, be gracious. To you I open my lips now in prayer, if I am permitted to take part in your holy Feast. I was entirely absorbed in prayer. Then I felt the presence of a heavenly *numen*, the joyful earth shone back with empurpled light'.

Now, the question I ask myself is the following. Who would expect of a Roman in general, and a poet like Ovid in particular, such words as 'I was entirely absorbed in prayer'? Does not Bömer (Comm. Ov. *Fasti* (1957), 14) altogether agree with Wilamowitz (*Glaube der Hellenen* 2, 338) in his verdict on Ovid, 'Of religion there remains hardly a trace'? Besides, is not this opinion shared by almost the whole world, whether, like Émile Ripert in his charming book *Ovide, poète de l'amour, des dieux, et de l'exil*, we are full of admiration for Ovid's poetry but describe the poet's religiosity in the words (p. 106), 'La religion de la Beauté, voilà celle, somme toute, qu'Ovide *pratiquait*', or like René Pichon,[1]

---

[1] *Hist. de la litt. lat.*, p. 425. Cf. Paul Brandt on *Am.*, 3, 3, 23. I am happy, in return, to agree here with what was written recently by J. Carcopino in the essay he devoted to Ovid's exile in *Rencontres de l'histoire et de la littérature romaines* (1963), where we read: 'Two men cohabited in Ovid, the libertine and the philosopher, a sensualist and a mystic.' Although to my great regret I have not yet been able to become acquainted with this

highly critical of the *Fasti* and thinking that 'ils sont bien près d'être la parodie *du culte latin*'?

However, even when we do not stop at Ovid himself but turn our attention to the religious feelings of the Roman in general the passage I have quoted must in my opinion cause us astonishment. It will be worth-while considering it carefully, with special attention to any light it may throw on the Roman practice of prayer.

We observe first of all that there are other respects too in which Ovid's verses seem almost incredible. According to Kurt Latte (*Röm. Religionsgesch.*, 1960, 41), 'the feeling of blessedness or enthusiasm induced by the presence of the godhead was lacking in the Roman by contrast with the Greek'. As for me, however, I should hardly know where to find in Greek literature a more striking example of the blessedness induced by the divine presence than in '*caelestina numina sensi...*'

There is a complete literature of prayer among the Romans. But the tendency has been almost always to overlook the fact that our Latin authors are nearly all intellectuals under the influence of philosophy, so that it is dangerous to draw conclusions about the religious life of the Roman in general. Above all, the growing influence of Stoic teaching becomes more and more manifest. I shall not linger over this question.[2] The generally accepted view is roughly as follows.[3] In the beginning a Roman's prayer was exclusively magical. It was offered to the deity as a sacrifice, not only stimulating the god to act, to come to man's help, but also to increase by the sacrifice the power of the god, *mactare* the god.[4] To achieve this *verba certa* are needed. Anyone straying from the text renders the prayer ineffectual. Only the priest knows these proper terms.

book—I owe the quotation to the good offices of M. Heurgon—so that it is not possible for me to associate myself in anticipation with the great scholar's thesis, which goes much further than I do in this article and deals more with the religiosity of Augustus than with that of Ovid, there are certainly some points of contact.
 [2] It is unfortunate that the thesis of W. J. Richards, '*Gobod bij Seneca, die Stoisijn*' Diss. Utrecht, Groningen, 1964), is accessible only to those who understand Afrikaans.
 [3] E.g. Warde Fowler, *Religious Experience of the Roman People*, 185ff.
 [4] Pfister, *R.E.*, 11, 2154ff.; Wagenvoort, *Roman Dynamism* (1947), p. 46.

This was extended to the public cult. But little by little an evolution occurred in the practice of prayer, to which a good deal was contributed by the *supplicationes*, days of prayer during which men and women circulated from temple to temple, praying at each.[5] The question arises, however, whether these men and women of the people who till then had only known prayers in a prescribed wording were not embarrassed by such a *supplicatio*. Moreover, when we consider the material as a whole, for instance by consulting Appel's book *De Romanorum Precationibus*, we observe that people so often ask for all kinds of things in their prayers for which there could not have been fixed formulae that we must in my opinion allow a good deal of room for 'open prayer'. Thus it seems to me that Saint Augustine's prayer as a child (*Confess.* I, 14) that he might not be beaten at school, *ne in schola vapularet*, could just as well have been addressed by a peasant's son to his *Lar familiaris*. We already read in Plautus (*Rudens*, 26ff.), *facilius si qui pius est a dis supplicans quam qui scelestus inveniet veniam sibi*, 'A man who is good will more easily win the favour of the gods when he prays to them than one who is bad.' Friedrich Marx in his commentary maintains that these lines were only added at the revision of the comedy in 177 B.C. That only makes them more important, because it would then be probable that they were not borrowed from the Greek original. It seems hardly likely that the prayers referred to here were of fixed formula type. At any rate it is no longer the words that matter so much as the mentality of whoever pronounces them.

But there is something more. It is fairly generally agreed that the Romans prayed aloud.[6] If they departed from this practice it was for one of two reasons. Either they were asking the god for things they were ashamed of, or they were practising magic. In

---

[5] Latte, *op. cit.*, p. 245; 'The participation of the whole people in a religious act, the intensification of feeling thus caused, was hitherto unprecedented in Roman religion. Instead of prayers fixed word for word, in which it is usually wishes which are laid before the gods, we have a supplication finding words in the mood of the moment'.

[6] Sudhaus, *ARW.*, 9 (1906), 185ff. Schmidt, 'Veteres philosophi quomodo indicaverint de precibus', *RVV.*, 4, 1 (1907), pp. 55ff.; Appel, *op. cit.*, p. 210; H. J. Rose, *Roman Questions of Plutarch* (1924), 87ff.; Balogh, *ARW.*, 23 (1925), 345.

either case it was not permissible for anyone else to hear. I do not believe this theory is correct. Apart from other arguments already detailed above (p. 197ff.), I refer again to the lines from Ovid. There it is even a case of being 'absorbed in prayer'. So there can be no question of reciting a formula of prayer aloud. Van der Leeuw (*Phänomenologie der Religion* (1933), 405) has written: 'The man at prayer must be like a burning candle and consume himself with love. Thus this prayer finds its highest form in absorption.' Is it not very remarkable that the sole place in all profane Latin literature where this form is mentioned should be in the work of a Don Juan like Ovid? And is it not equally remarkable that neither Peter, nor Frazer, nor Bömer in their commentaries bothered themselves even for an instant to linger on this passage?

This is the problem I have considered, with the following result.

It is impossible to put an exact date on the lines of Ovid already quoted. When he was exiled to Tomis in A.D. 8, half of the work, comprising Books I to VI, was provisionally ready. He did not succeed in finishing it in his place of exile. Circumstances were too unfavourable and he had not got his library with him. If, however, he did none the less try to continue it, his sketches have not come down to us.[7] Meanwhile the death of Augustus in A.D. 14 had compelled him to revise his first part, for he had dedicated the *Fasti* to Augustus and he now wanted to replace this dedication by one to Germanicus. But he was able to rework only the first book. In the rest it is exceptional to find a passage which has been altered or inserted. On the other hand the poet must have begun this work some years before his departure for Tomis in the last months of the year 8 and it may be useful to recall what had happened at this period in matters of cult, with especial reference to Augustus himself. For it is he whom the poet addresses and to whom he dedicates his book, thereby attempting to regain the favour of the *princeps* by convincing him that the scandal he had caused by his eroticism *errorem, non scelus esse*, 'was an aberration not a crime' (*Fast.* I, 90). So when we encounter a passage which must have been ridiculed by his friends and other readers—'Imagine our Ovid absorbed in prayer!'—we are bound to ask whether it is

---

[7] According to *Trist.*, 2, 549, we may conclude with virtual certainty that these projects did exist; cf. W. Kraus, *R.E.*, 18, 1, 1950.

possible that he deliberately risked their mockery, knowing that his words would give great pleasure to Augustus. To my mind the reply to this question can only be affirmative.

The celebration of the *ludi saeculares* in 17 B.C. and Horace's *Carmen saeculare* had clearly shown, if indeed it was at all necessary, that for Augustus henceforward Apollo was the great protector of Rome. The reasons for this choice have often been examined. The main one, it seems to me, was that he considered Jupiter as the god of a past age, a god who had not intervened in the crisis of the civil wars. The new age, the *aurea aetas*, was to be presided over by Apollo, the god of peace and civilization. Vergil had already declared in the *Fourth Eclogue*, '*iam regnat Apollo*'. About this development there is an abundant literature. But the sequence of events so far as cult was concerned has on the contrary not received sufficient attention.

P. Lambrechts [8] has the distinction of having made a profound study of this period. He was led to the conclusion that little by little Augustus's 'Apollinism' lost its vigour. Jean Bayet [9] has agreed with him, and the correctness of his theory seems to me indisputable, at least in principle.[10] It seems to me doubtful that the process had already begun in 27 B.C. as Lambrechts seeks to show but that is a point we can here pass over.

The date 6 March 12 B.C. is again critical. Augustus became *pontifex maximus*. He could, as he relates in the *Monumentum Ancyranum* (Ch. 10), have assumed this office earlier, but then Lepidus his fellow triumvir would have had to resign it and that he did not want. Lepidus meanwhile had died. There are several indications how impatiently he had awaited this moment and what importance he attached to his election.[11] It is shown by the boastful

---

[8] P. Lambrechts, 'La politique apollinienne d'Auguste et le culte imperial', *La Nouvelle Clio*, 5 (1953), 65ff.; 'Augustus en Apollo', *Gentse Bijdragen tot de Kunstgeschiedenis*, 15 (1959), p. 97, n. 28; 117.

[9] J. Bayet, 'Les sacerdoces romains et la prédivinisation impériale', *Acad. Royale de Belgique, Bull. Classe des Lettres*, 5e série, t. II (1955), 508.

[10] The observation of Elisabeth H. Haight, *A.J.Ph.* 39 (1918) 360, that in the *Fasti* the relation between Augustus and Apollo is less obvious than in the *Métamorphoses*, is correct and agrees with Lambrechts' reasoning.

[11] Cf. Bayet, *loc. cit.*, p. 506. Previously Gagé ('Les sacerdoces d'Auguste et ses réformes religieuses', *Mél. d'Archéol. et d'Hist.*, 48 (1931), p. 105) had thus argued: 'His election (i.e. of Augustus to the supreme pontificate) in 12

tone of his own words (loc. cit.): *Quod sacerdotium ... suscepi ... cuncta ex Italia ad comitia mea coeunte tanta multitudine, quanta Romae numquam antea fuisse narratur*. Moreover, he must have taken his measures in advance. It is known that he did not move into the official residence of the *pontifex maximus*, but as he was actually required to reside *in loco publico*, he declared a part of his palace on the Palatine national domain and there dedicated a chapel to Vesta, which in contrast to the goddess's temple in the Forum, contained a statue of her. When we learn that its consecration took place only seven weeks after his election, on 28 April 12 B.C., we can hardly doubt that his plans had been made some time ahead.

Undoubtedly Ovid concerned himself with the question of the *princeps'* motives. There is nothing inherently strange about his having repeatedly emphasized the close relations between the Supreme Pontiff and Vesta. When he reaches 15 March, the day of Caesar's murder, he says (*Fast*. 3, 697) 'I had no intention of speaking about the swords which pierced the body of Caesar when suddenly from her chaste hearth Vesta thus spoke "Do not hesitate to name them. He was my priest and it was I at whom the weapons in those sacrilegious hands were aimed."' Similarly he imagines Venus praying the gods in heaven (*Met*. 15, 777), 'Stop them' (the conspirators) 'avert the crime and let Vesta's flames not be extinguished by the murder of her priest!' Elsewhere he makes Augustus himself speak of his adoptive father as 'Vesta's priest' (*Fast*. 5, 571).

An explanation of Ovid's preference is not far to seek. On 6 March, the date of Augustus' election as *pontifex maximus*, he writes (*Fast*. 3, 417), 'Whoever you are you who pay homage here at chaste Vesta's sanctuary, congratulate her and lay incense on her Trojan hearth. To Augustus' numerous titles of honour (and what title could have pleased him better?) that of Supreme Pontiff has been added. The everlasting divinity of Augustus has been

---

was fateful and necessary. But we need not suppose that he had looked forward to it with much secret impatience, nor indeed that he had long felt the want of it.' In my opinion, in this account—which is otherwise of great value—too little attention is paid to certain psychological factors to which I shall return later.

put in charge of the everlasting fire. Here you see the pledges of empire united. You, gods of ancient Rome, worthy spoils for him who carried you, under whose weight Aeneas ran no risk in face of the enemy, a priest descended from Aeneas gives all his care to gods who are his kin. Vesta, protect your kinsman'. Two themes are strongly emphasized here, the everlasting divinity of Augustus in relation with the everlasting fire as a guarantee of the survival of Rome, and the Trojan origin of Vesta which makes the *princeps*, descendant of Aeneas, her kinsman. The two themes deserve to be treated separately, but I must confine myself to a few remarks. Not long before, Horace (*Od.* 4, 14, 3) had asked himself how the Senate and People of Rome could immortalize (*aeternare*) the glorious actions of Augustus by means of inscriptions and records. But Ovid's intention was quite different. Carl Koch [12] has thus expressed his opinion: 'Ovid has taken up a special position. Obviously what he wanted was to call the Emperor *aeternus*. The description of the close relation between Augustus and Vesta in the Palatine palace ... gave the poet the idea of making the *aeternitas Vestae* stream over on to the Emperor.' What remains a little unclear to me is his later remark: 'A striking passage however is *ex Pont.* 2, 2, 47, in which the *princeps aeternus* occurs without any immediate connection with Roman deities. Can this be a case of oriental notions working on the banished Ovid? For Rome such a combination of titles is decades too early.' For eternity implies divinity. Even to a Roman that is quite obvious.[13] Well, it is true that Ovid did not insist on the divinity of Augustus until later, especially after his exile.[14] Then (*Ex Pont.* 1, 4, 56) he even attributes it to Livia. It goes without saying that there is an element of flattery here, but flattery does not explain everything. For he was already writing before his exile (*Met.* 15, 868ff.): 'All of you, gods, ... delay, postpone beyond the end of my life the day when Augustus, having left the world he governs, shall ascend to heaven and answer from afar the prayers of mortals'. To which

[12] 'Roma aeterna', *Gymnasium*, 59 (1952), p. 24.
[13] Cf. Cic., *Fin.*, 2, 88; *N.D.*, 2, 62.
[14] *Trist.*, 5, 2, 35; 5, 10, 52; 5, 11, 20; *ex Pont.*, 1, 2, 73; 1, 4, 44; 1, 4, 56; 10, 42; 2, 2, 43-111-124; 3, 6, 16; 4, 13, 26. Previously only *Fast.*, 1, 530, cf. *Met.*, 15, 860.

Burdach [15] rightly replied, 'Thus Ovid deifies the savers of the tottering Roman state and the peace of the world. Thus he confers on them, together with this Imperium, immortality.' If we consider the gods addressed by the poet in his prayer, the Penates, Quirinus, Mars, Vesta, Apollo, and Jupiter, we are surprised to find Vesta occupying a pre-eminent place in the list. We read, *Vestaque Caesareos inter sacrata Penates / et cum Caesarea tu, Phoebe domestice, Vesta.* In the first place, it seems to me quite clear from these words that Apollo—though it is true that the *domus Palatina aeternos tres habet una deos* (*Fast.* 4, 954), i.e. Apollo, Vesta, and Augustus—in Ovid's estimation is inferior to Vesta. Secondly the Trojan origin of Vesta and her kinship with Augustus are strongly underlined. Of course this kinship depends, as the context alone indicates, on their common Trojan origin, since as was well-known [16] in the Augustan period since Vergil (*Aen.* 2, 296) Vesta herself was regarded as a native of Troy. But it would be wrong to think this explains everything. Bayet (519) remarks very justly: 'When Augustus assumed the office of Supreme Pontiff it gave him a unique superiority, in a religious and mystical sense.' Only I would go further than he in describing the mystical relation between the goddess and this Supreme Pontiff. What is most striking—and the passage quoted is a good illustration—is that a god figures as the priest of a goddess. Moreover, the fact that he is related to her is not always formally linked to her Trojan descent. In *Fasti*, 4, 949, we read: 'This day is yours, Vesta! Vesta has been received on her kinsman's' (*cognati*) 'threshold, thus the senators have rightly decided. Phoebus has one part; the second has been assigned to Vesta; that which remained, the third, is occupied by himself' (Augustus). 'Endure, Palatine laurels, and may the oak-wreathed dwelling endure. This single house contains three eternal deities!' The fact that the poet so sharply brings out this relationship is all the more remarkable in that it must have been rather obscure to his contemporaries. We could say with Frazer (*ad. Fast.*, 3, 425) who tries to draw up a genealogy: 'The flattery of Augustan poets did not stick at trifles', but it is inconceivable that Augustus, whom Ovid was addressing, did not realize the poet's intention.

---

[15] Quoted by Korn-Ehwald, ad loc.
[16] Wissowa, *Rosch. Lex.*, 6, 250, 41.

Moreover, when Ovid speaks of the Vesta cult of this period we meet other views which seem to testify to a new Vesta theology. Thus it is striking that according to Ovid prayers were addressed in the first place to Vesta (*Fast.*, 3, 604ff., . . . *precando/ praefamur Vestam, quae loca prima tenet*), while, according to Cicero's testimony (*N.D.* 2, 67), it is she who has the last place, the first being reserved for Janus.[17] If, like many commentators, we are content to observe that Ovid is here following the Greek usage in respect of Hestia, we overlook his decided tone (*praefamur*) and do not take account of the possibility that we here have yet another symptom of the dominant position occupied by Vesta in the ideas of the aging Augustus.

This exceptional position is psychologically understandable. It rests on what Koch (1757, 64) rightly describes as 'the connection (of the goddess) with the ruler's family, whose Trojan origin was impressively demonstrated.' In this context we must remember the succession of blows suffered by the house of the *princeps* with advancing years. After the death of his nephew and well-loved son-in-law Marcellus in 23 B.C., his two grandsons Lucius and Gaius Caesar were successively snatched from him by death in A.D. 2 and 4. In the year 7 he had to exile his youngest grandson Agrippa Postumus and in the following year his daughter Julia. All these domestic tragedies were aggravated by the ever more urgent need to choose a successor. Superstitious though he was, the emperor, at least in his younger years, showed very little religious feeling. All the same we must be cautious in our judgment. For Augustus was characterized by a strong 'secondary function' which prevented him from expressing himself spontaneously. In everything he weighed his words maturely. His private conversations, even those with Livia, when they were of any importance, were written down by him word for word and read subsequently (Suet. *Aug.*, 84, 2). Such an excess of caution may be beneficial from one point of view but from another it is paralysing. He took

[17] Cicero's statement has been doubted because the only real support for it is in the *Acta fratrum arvalium* of the 3rd century A.D. (cf. Latte, *op. cit.*, p. 207). Koch (*R.E.*, 8 A 2, 1777) defends Cicero's point of view and quotes in support certain passages from the literature which I find less convincing than Juvenal, 6, 386, which he does not quote. Whatever the case, Ovid is alone in his opinion concerning Vesta's prerogative.

his time to reach understanding of other people. That was how he made such happy choices in his associates and was able to attach them to himself. To quote only one example, he succeeded in entirely reconciling the Greeks to Roman domination and in teaching his subjects through Vergil's Aeneid that the principal ally of his ancestor the Trojan Aeneas was the Greek Evander. However it was this secondary function which must have prevented him from freely pouring out his heart on his personal attitudes in matters of religion. We even have a characteristic testimony about this. In his autobiography he himself spoke of the *Sidus Iulium*, the splendid comet which appeared at the time of the celebrations in honour of the dead Caesar, and he remarked that in the opinion of the public it was the soul of the Divus Iulius who had appeared in this comet. But Pliny, who tells the story (*N.H.* 2, 94), adds: 'In public he subscribed to this opinion. But at the bottom of his heart he indulged another interpretation. The comet had risen for him Augustus and in this comet he himself was rising to a new life.' We need not linger here to analyse this text.[18] But if we consider how marvellously everything succeeded to his touch from then on, how at Actium he routed Anthony and Cleopatra, ended the age of civil wars, and gave to the world the *pax Augusta*, we are prompted to ask what his most intimate thoughts may have been. Cicero, Vergil, and Horace recognized in him a divine being destined to give the world the *aurea aetas*. In the long run it was not only the provinces which loaded him with divine honours, but even in his own country people showed themselves more and more disposed to think him divine. Yet with it all he remained simple and modest in appearance—we have numerous testimonies for that.

Gardthausen (*Augustus* 1, 866) is a spokesman for many modern authors when he declares: 'Augustus, whose special concern it was to have re-established the Roman state on firm foundations believed that the only possible guarantee for the future must lie in a deep-felt revival of the Roman character and he saw religion as the most important means to this political end ... It can

[18] Cf. Wagenvoort, 'Vergils vierte Ekloge und das Sidus Iulium', *Mededel. Kon. Akad. v. Wetensch. afd. Lett.* 67 A No. 1 (1929), 17ff.; English translation in *Studies in Rom. Lit., Cult. and Rel.* (1956), 14ff.

hardly be supposed that he was really convinced at heart, for he had never in his political life allowed himself to be hindered or influenced by religious considerations.' Others on the contrary speak of a conversion after Actium, and Richard Heinze, whose book *Die Augusteische Kultur* (1930) is in my opinion one of the best yet written on Augustus, sees in it the influence of the Stoic teaching which in opposition to the opinion of Epicurus asserted the *providentia* of the divine nature (20, 2). For me this is not the principal factor. Undoubtedly the Stoic teachers of his youth, Arius of Alexandria and Athenodorus of Tarsus, exerted their influence upon him. But later on he showed much less interest in philosophy than in the ancient history of Rome and in poetry. Nepos, for instance, in his *Life of Atticus* relates that almost every day Augustus wrote a letter to his friend Atticus in which he sometimes put to him a question on antiquity, sometimes asked his opinion on a problem of poetry. This interest in poetry is of less concern to us here than the interest he took in antiquity, which may have been partly responsible for the preference he showed for the Vesta cult.

If I am not mistaken, Augustus developed a religious sentiment which had some connection with the Ciceronian conception of *pietas*, 'fidelity to the call of the gods' (see above p. 1ff.) which had also shaped the figure of the *pius Aeneas* of Vergil's *Aeneid* and which, if we go back far enough, did in fact originate in Stoic reflection. Augustus in his religious speculation included the gods, the Roman people, his family, and himself. He regarded himself as the descendant of Aeneas and Iulus, the continuer of the work of Romulus, but therewith knew himself, especially as he grew old, more and more dependent on the heavenly powers. So it was to them he addressed his prayers, particularly as with growing anxiety at the lack of a qualified successor he had to keep asking himself if he was not to see his whole life's work compromised.

How do we know that? From himself. He wrote to Tiberius (Suet. *Tib.* 21, 7), 'When I read and hear it said that this continual effort is exhausting you, may the gods destroy me if my whole body is not seized with shivering. I implore you to look after yourself, for if we were to hear that you were ill it would be like death for your mother and myself, and the whole empire of the

Roman people would be endangered. It matters little whether my health be good or bad if you are not well. I implore the gods to preserve you as we wish and to keep you in good health, today and always, if they do not hold the Roman people in detestation.' Tiberius knew Augustus through and through. His father-in-law had no need of pretence before him. Like the whole letter, the prayer throbs with real anxiety. For the *princeps* the prosperity of his house was at stake but so above all was that of the Roman people.

Secondly, I base myself on a letter to his grandson Gaius transmitted by Aulus Gellius (*Noct. Att.* 15, 7, 3). It is dated 13 September of A.D. 1, that is Augustus' 63rd birthday, and it is more or less filled with complaints about the absence of the young man, who was 20. The letter ends: 'I pray the gods that I may be granted for the time I still have to live to be in good health, to see the Republic in its happiest state, to see both of you conduct yourselves as brave men, and to be relieved by you from my post.' Do we not find here, with the flavour of a most genuine sincerity, the affection and pride of a grandfather, and the hope he places in his grandson's future, together with the wishes he has formed for his own house and his country?

Thirdly, when Drusus, whom he so loved, died and he pronounced his eulogy before the Assembly, he went so far as to pray the gods to make his dear Caesars men like Drusus and to reserve for himself later a death as glorious as his (Suet. *Claud.* 1). Here again we see him following the same thread.

It is true that the prayers I have quoted are addressed to the gods in general, not to Vesta in particular. But from the fact that on the birthdays of the imperial princes a *supplicatio Vestae* always took place in the temple of Augustus at Cumae (*C.I.L.* 10, 8375 = Dessau 108) we may infer that she herself was regarded as a deity who more than any other watched over the Imperial House. In the year 22 B.C., one year after the death of Marcellus, the Athenians decided to deify Livia and Julia and to sacrifice on the Acropolis to them at the same time as Hestia-Vesta [19] Would it be too bold to deduce the same sequence of ideas? Ovid who had already previously (*Ex Pont.* 1, 4, 56) in circumspect terms classed Livia

[19] *I.G.*, 3, 316; *Ath. Mitt.*, 14 (1889), 321.

herself among the gods beside Augustus and Tiberius later compare her in the same work (*Ex Pont*, 4, 13, 29) to Vesta, the chaste goddess, protectress of marriage. Between Augustus himself and Vesta there was according to Ovid a mystical bond. Vesta protected the pontiff (*Fast.* 3, 426: 'Vesta, protect your kinsman!') Augustus protects Vesta and the pledges of power (*pignora imperii*) which have been confided to her, the sacred fire in the Hall of State, the Penates, and the Palladium (*Fast.* 1, 528, 'Receive then, Vesta, the gods of Troy. The time will come when the same man will protect you, you and the world' and 3, 421, 'The eternal divinity of Augustus will watch over the eternal fire'). However, the protector himself is among those *pignora imperii* (*Fast.* 3, 422, in the words immediately preceding the passage quoted: 'behold the *pignora imperii* now united').

In prece totus eram—we set out from the astonishment caused us by such a fervent prayer addressed to Vesta, by a Roman in general and by Ovid in particular. And we asked ourselves if the poet in pronouncing these words could have had in mind the personality of Augustus, if he could have imagined so profound a surrender of himself in prayer to Vesta. It is my opinion that the reply we can now give to this question is affirmative.

XIII

CHARACTERISTIC TRAITS OF ANCIENT ROMAN RELIGION *

1. *Introduction*

To attempt any very brief account of the ancient religion of Rome must be a bold undertaking, even though we deliberately limit our terms of reference to indigenous cults and rites, excluding those deities which were gradually imported, together with their usual ceremonies of tendance, from elsewhere, that is from Etruria and Greece. For first we must ask whether the concept 'Roman religion' is bound up with the existence of the city of Rome and thus only begins with the foundation of Rome, or whether it is possible and justifiable to delve deeper into the past and perhaps by the research methods of comparative religion discover links with the original Indo-European homelands. Secondly, there is the question how far the religion of the Romans can be treated on its own, separately from that of the related tribes, the Oscans and Umbrians. Is it at all certain that the reputedly native deities of Rome all deserve this title and that none of them were taken over from neighbouring territories in prehistoric times? In the age of the Republic this often happened through the *evocatio*. When the Romans were besieging an enemy-city they used to pray that city's gods to hand it over to them, to give up their present abodes and settle in Rome, where they were promised a temple and cult. Thus we know, to take one instance, that at the end of the 4th century the guardian goddess of Veii was transferred to Rome after the destruction of her city and worshipped as Juno Regina. Who can say that similar things may not have happened in earlier times? Another difficulty is that we often cannot rely on the editing of texts in manuscripts and inscrip-

* The article is a revised version of an outline sketch which appeared in *Historia Mundi*, Vol. III (Bern 1954) pp. 485-500. 518, which at the editors' request has been much expanded and provided with additional footnotes.

tions.[1] And this is only one way in which external influence can operate. There have of course been many others. Finally, scholarship in recent years has given much attention to the problem whether the Etruscan and Greek influence—the latter too mostly mediated by the Etruscans—has not always been underestimated. Franz Altheim [2] has made important contributions to this topic, even though his findings need to be thoroughly overhauled.[3]

It would be nice to be able to go into all these questions in detail. But that is impossible here. Even with the restriction indicated, the subject matter is so wide-ranging and we have,

---

[1] As examples I quote two such passages, of which I offer emendations: first, the verse of Ennius (Fr. 16 V. = Persius, Sat., 6, 9) *Lunai portum, est operae, cognoscite, cives!* which I think should read *Lunai pratum* etc. (see H. Wagenvoort, 'Lunai pratum', *Mnemos. ser. IV* vol. XIX, 1966, pp. 344-348); secondly, the new inscription published by Margarita Guarducci, 'Legge sacra da un antico santuario di Lavinio', *Archaeol. classica* 3, 1951, pp. 99-103, *Lex sacra Lavinia*, which prescribes an offering to the goddess Ceres of *auliquoquibus*, 'entrails cooked in a pot', followed by the unintelligible words *vespernam poro*. The last word in my opinion must undoubtedly be *poplo* (see H. Wagenvoort, '*De lege sacra lavinia nuper reperta*', *Mnemos. ser. IV* vol. XIV, 1961, pp. 217-223). (Professor Schilling, *Aufstieg und Niedergang* I 2, p. 319, has evidently not seen my emendation). The text would then read: *Cerere auliquoquibus* (sc. *facito*), *vespernam poplo* (sc. *dato*), that is, the cooked entrails should be offered to Ceres, after the rest of the meat has been distributed to the people for supper according to the Greek rite.

[2] Franz Altheim, *Griechische Götter im alten Rom, Religionsgeschichtliche Versuche und Vorarbeiten* = *RVV*, Vol. XXII, Giessen 1930. Cf. his *Römische Religionsgeschichte, I. Die älteste Schicht.* (Sammlg. Göschen, No. 1035), Berlin 1931.

[3] I cannot go into details here. I only refer to H. J. Rose in his review (*Gnomon* 7, 1931, pp. 26ff.), who in general though not exclusively gives a very favourable opinion, while M. P. Nilsson (*Dtsche Lit. -Ztg.* 1931, Fascicle 47, pp. 224ff.) introduces a somewhat hesitant review with the words: 'The reviewer must confess that he has much more sympathy with the fundamental views of this author than with his detailed development. Against the sharp separation between the older completely indigenous religion of Rome and the later externally influenced religion, as first propounded by Mommsen and worked out in detail by Wissowa, Altheim has launched an attack based on the lively contacts between Italy and Greece from the seventh century B.C. onward, as shown by archaeological finds, and he asks whether it is justified to consider Rome even in ancient times so isolated as that separation assumes. I have long felt similar doubts. But whether the Etruscans were the intermediaries in all those cases so treated by the author seems to me questionable, despite the meaning and importance and wide distribution of the Etruscan culture.'

thanks to comparative religion, archaeology, and linguistics, so much new material that we can only hope to make a broad sketch from which the peculiar features of the ancient Roman religion may in some sense emerge. The question from which I shall above all else proceed is how to understand the relation between the gods proper (*dei*) and the impersonal powers (*numina*) which rule human life. Did the ancient Romans know personal gods at all, even in the sense that the human being could have any kind of personal relation with them, or practise a religion which could touch not only the intellect but also the heart? Many students answer this question with No, others are doubtful or at best recognize a certain development in the direction of divine personality or regard the personal gods (e.g. Jupiter, Mars) as rare exceptions. From the other side we are told that such a state of affairs is inconceivable with an Indo-European people. They cannot have completely renounced their links with the ancient Indians, Greeks, and Germans. Against that, recent studies have shown what an important part was played in Roman life by impersonal powers and what numerous magic rites they gave rise to. True, it is not possible in a primitive stage of development to draw a sharp distinction between magic and religion. The inconsistency is scarcely noticed. Only we do rightly wonder to observe that things did not fundamentally change even when the Romans had long left this stage behind them.[4] I shall now take a few of the more important points one by one.

2. *Religio*

There need be no objection to speaking of Roman religion at a time when Rome did not yet exist, let alone function as power centre of an empire. The expression in my opinion can legitimately be used for the *religio* of the ancestors of the Romans. If we could be sure that the Latin *religio* was derived from *re-ligare*, 'bind',

---

[4] Here I venture to insert some pages from my treatise on 'Roman Religion' from the Dutch compilation *Godsdiensten der Wereld*, 2nd Edn., ed. C. J. Bleeker, Amsterdam 1956, pp. 433ff. This will enable me to bring up those points which I should like to have seen discussed in Schilling's important contribution (see note 1). The pages in question are headed (in translation) 'On the threshold between Prehistory and the Historical Period. A. Dynamism.' I retain the original arrangement.

it would be some support for my view of the ancient Roman religion as a 'knowing oneself bound on all sides' in the sense that human life is continually beset by mysterious powers encompassing humanity and controlling its fate. But the correctness of this once freely asserted derivation is no longer so sure. It is well-known that today the generally preferred derivation of *religio* is that of A. Walde and J. B. Hoffmann (*Lateinisches Etymologisches Wörterbuch*,³ I, Heidelberg 1954, p. 352), from *religere* in the sense of 'misgiving', 'awe', particularly in religious matters, 'conscientiousness', 'fear of god', 'religious obligation', 'cult', 'religious usage', superstition', and so on. In support of it the favoured source is an important passage of Gellius (*Noctes Atticae* 4, 9, 1), where he quotes a fragment of an ancient tragic poet cited by Nigidius for the words *religentem esse oportet, religiosus ne fuas*.⁵ This certainly is important evidence, but it is not a proof. First, in dealing with such questions we must remember Eduard Norden's remarks. In his famous work *Die antike Kunstprosa* there are constant references to etymological word-play. It turns out that the ancient Latin tragedians also had a passion for such word-plays. We read (II, 889), 'Tragedy was highly rhetorical. Literary prose conceits were freely used'. Then Norden reminds us of the well-known fragment of Ennius preserved by Cicero (*Tusc.* 1, 35, 85.3, 19, 45): *haec omnia vidi inflammari, / Priamo vi vitam evitari, / Iovis aram sanguine turpari*. Here the word-play goes so far that the poet (cf. M. Pohlenz, pp. 2ff.) to achieve his jingle uses the verb *evitare* in the sense of 'to rob someone of life'. Such jokes, which were often popular, frequently developed into proverbs. So far as I can see we have no means of knowing how far the sentence *Deligere oportet quem velis diligere* (Rhetor ad Herenn. 4, 21, 29) became popular *proverbii vice*, even though A. Otto (*Sprichwörter* p. 106) included it among his proverbs. At any rate it is not clear whether the Rhetorician himself, who was only intending a joke, was aware of the etymological relationship between the two verbs. Even less clear is it in the case of Nigidius, who in the lines immediately following his tragedian's verse discusses the meaning of the adjective *religiosus* and comes

⁵ E. Norden, *Die antike Kunstprosa*, I ³, Leipzig-Berlin 1915. II ³, *ibid.* 1918; see its Index, under *Wortspiel*, II p. 968.

to the conclusion: *Quocirca religiosus is appellabatur, qui nimia et superstitiosa religione sese alligaverat, eoque res vitio assignabatur.*[6] For these reasons I do not think I am guilty of begging the question if I suppose that the average Roman at any rate regarded the word *religio* as constraint and derived from *religare*. Thus although I want to adopt the explanation *religio* = 'constraint', 'obligation', I should prefer to leave it at that for the moment. What is more important is to be clear that *religio* was the established term for the State religious service. For one point can be made in advance: the Roman religion, so far as it was the ancestral cult, was in historical times the state religion, that is to say, the magistrates were charged with supervising it and the priests too who were entrusted with the technical performance of the ritual were state-commissioners. This however refers exclusively to the *sacra publica*, that is, those acts performed in the name of the whole people or its sacral subdivisions by the responsible magistrates or priests. The *sacra privata* consisted first of all of divine service of the Genii, Lares, Penates, and Vesta in the home, at which the paterfamilias represented the whole family; and then also the communal cults of the clans (*gentes*). Although these private cults were not subject to any state rules, they were not wholly, in an absolute sense, free from state-supervision. The conservative Roman was firmly convinced that every prayer, every sacrifice was invalid if not performed with meticulous and precise adherence to customary rules and according to age-old forms and ceremonies which were often no longer understood. In case of need the priest was there to help him.

3. Numina

Often *deus*, 'god', and *numen* are hardly distinguished. It is true that the difference between the two words as the Romans understood them became blurred in course of time and that this was to be attributed especially to the influence of Greek philosophy. But originally the two words were not at all synonymous. *Numen* is in any case neuter, which gives pause for thought, and etymologically it means 'movement', which is an even better guide

---

[6] 'That is why a man was called *religiosus* if he had adopted' (better 'become enslaved to') 'a pietism so exaggerated and superstitious as to be accounted a fault'.

to a right understanding. With astonishment primitive man looks at every movement which he has not yet learnt to explain, the lashing sea, the howling wind, the clouds scudding across the sky, the flickering flame, the gushing spring, the sprouting bud. All these things must have behind or in themselves—more probably in themselves for nothing is seen behind—a moving force, a *numen*. The development of this word, so important for understanding the Roman popular religion, was thoroughly studied, almost at the same time, by two eminent scholars, Friedrich Pfister [7] and Herbert Rose.[8] Independently of one another they reached almost identical conclusions. Thus Pfister (*RE* XVII 17), col. 1290, 45) wrote: 'So this is an impersonal force which can work anywhere, the 'orenda' force, always present where we speak of the divine and holy; cf. *Handwörterbuch des deutschen Aberglaubens*, III, p. 1655ff. On the older view *numen* was attributed only to the gods, then also by transference (Cic.), to the Senate and *populus Romanus*, later to human beings. Thus *numen* belongs to the most ancient world of religious ideas and there can be no question of its being a recent term, as Birt [9] supposed. It is already attested in Accius,[10] and if it is not found in the Old Comedy, this is probably because of the sacral nature of the word, which ruled out its profane use in the mouth of a comedy hero. This 'orendistic' conception of god and holiness evolved in the case of *numen* as everywhere else (see above Vol. XV, pp. 2185ff.; Pfister, *Rel.d.Gr.u.R.*, pp. 122ff.), into the concept of personal gods, that is, *numen* acquired that meaning of 'god' which evolved out of the original meaning 'divine power' ...'

[7] F. Pfister, *Die Religion der Griechen und Römer*, Leipzig 1930, p. 122f., 185f.; article '*numen*' in Pauly-Wissowa, *RE* XVII (1937), col. 1273ff.

[8] H. J. Rose, *Primitive Culture in Italy*, London 1926, p. 7; *Idem*, 'Numen and Mana', *Harv. Theol. Rev*, 44, 1951, pp. 109ff. (cf. the same review 28, 1935, p. 237ff. and 42, 1949, p. 135ff. under the title '*Mana* in Greece and Rome').

[9] T. Birt, On Vergil, *Aeneid* I 8: *quo numine laeso*, *Berl. Philol. Wochenschr*. 38, 1918, p. 212.

[10] Lucius Accius, tragic poet, end of 2nd century B.C. Pfister is thinking of the passages *Acc*. 646 R (ed. Ribbeck): *Alia hic sanctitudo est, aliud nomen et numen Jovis* (Fragm. *apud* Nonius 173, 27.) 'Different is the nature of holiness, different the name and miraculous force of Jupiter' and *Acc*. E 92 R (Fragm. *apud* Varro, *De lingua latina* VII 85): *multis nomen vestrum numenque ciendo* (without context and hardly possible to translate).

Thus Pfister often speaks in this connection of 'orendistic ideas'. In comparative religious history the concept of this mysterious force is known to everyone,[11] especially in works of folklore, only there we have the difficulty that no modern language, nor Latin either, has a word for it. The upholders of the theory have been much criticized on this account. The criticism is not very profound. It has after all been universally observed that synthesis by abstraction is not exactly a characteristic of primitive intelligences. There are tribes which have special words for 'a white cow', 'a black cow', 'a dappled cow', but not a general word for 'a cow'. How much more understandable then is it that many peoples call by individual names the various dynamic forces which they think they recognize.[12] Thus the Roman, for instance, speaks of *numen* in the case of a deity or of a natural phenomenon which he attributes to divine action, but he calls it *imperium* when a human being has a great ascendancy over others, even too power over the growth of his crops.

Felicitas is their name for the innate talent of the general who wins a striking number of victories. We shall be discussing other words like *auctoritas* and *gravitas* later. All these words have one thing in common, that they signify remarkable powers which are hard to explain, but they are by no means synonymous. That is why modern scholarship has had recourse to the languages of peoples for whom the concept in question is still alive and crucial. This is the reason why words have been borrowed, *mana* from the Melanesians and more especially the New Zealand Maoris, *orenda* from the Iroquois, *tondi* from the Batak in Borneo, *elima* from the

[11] Cf. esp. W. Warde Fowler, *The Religious Experience of the Roman People*, London 1922, passim, see Index s.v. *mana*, and Nathan Söderblom, *Das Werden des Gottesglaubens*², Leipzig 1926, Chapter 1, 'The Primitives and ourselves', p. 1-9. Also K. Beth, *Religion und Magie bei den Kulturvölkern*², Leipzig-Berlin 1924; for the literature before 1930 F. Pfister, *Bursians Jahrbb. Suppl. Bd.* 229, 1930, pp. 108ff.: E. Arbmann, 'Seele und Mana; *Arch. Relig. wiss.* 19, 1931, p. 332; L. Deubner, *ARW* 33, 1936, p. 106; W. Eberhard, *ARW* 33, 1936, p. 318, G. van der Leeuw, *Phänomenologie der Religion*, Tübingen 1933, passim, see Index under '*Dynamismus*'; M. P. Nilsson, *A History of Greek Religion*², Oxford 1949, p. 81, 166, P. Boyancé, 'Le Mana dans la religion Romaine', *Journ. des Savants*, 1948, pp. 69ff.

[12] Cf. S. Kooyman, *Sahala tondi. De begrippen 'mana' en 'hau' bij enkele Sumatraanse volken*, Diss. Utrecht, 1942.

Bacwa in the Congo, *wakanda* from the Sioux, and so on. Meanwhile it need not surprise us that this proceeding on many sides gave rise to serious misgiving. Did it not bring the ancient Romans down to the level of these primitive peoples? That would be something like *lèse-majesté*. When we first make their acquaintance the Romans had been for centuries already out of the primitive phase. All the same, the culture of these conservative Romans, and their language too, are rich in 'survivals', relics of primitive times. Greece too shows traces of a similar world of ideas, but they are infinitely sparser. We must realize moreover that what we have here are no more than relics of prehistory, to which people had clung as to venerable fossils or which had acquired an entirely new sense. Nor are we moderns by any means free of such oddities. Not everyone who avoids walking under a ladder is conscious of sharing this reluctance with his distant forebears, strange though their reasons would be to him. Not everyone who has a noise in his ear and says, 'Somebody's talking about me', is conscious that the same deduction was drawn from this experience in classical antiquity and that the fear of magic was behind it, as we learn from the *Apology* of Apuleius and other sources. Only then it was the fear of magic, whereas today there is no danger of our being thought superstitious. Just so, it is no discredit to the ancient Romans to say that they inherited from their forebears a belief in a mysterious force, let us call it *mana*-like, even though we would gladly avoid the use of exotic words like *mana* and the misunderstanding to which they may give rise. For this reason the term 'dynamism' seems preferable. F. Pfister often pointed out that the Greek δύναμις could be synonymous with *mana*. He writes in one place (*Die Religion der Griechen und Römer*, 110), 'even the δύναμις of healing substances is a kind of *mana*, and so is that of magic spells; cf. Plato, *Charm.* 157 B; δύναμις ἐπῳδῆς', and later [13] he added (Orig. *c. Cels.* III 68) λόγοι ὡσπερεὶ ἐπῳδαὶ δυνάμεως πεπληρωμένοι, and earlier (I 30) παράδοξοι ἐξ ἐπῳδῶν δυνάμεις, also (Hippol. *ref.* IX 16, 1) ἐπαοιδαὶ δυνάμεων μεμεστωμέναι. Anyone trying to form a correct picture of the features of Roman religion must necessarily take account of dynamism with all the rest.

[13] F. Pfister, *RE*, Suppl. Bd. IV, (1924) p. 337, 6. Cf. S. Eitrem, 'Varia', *Symb. Osloenses II*, 1924, p. 71.

In conclusion I should like to illustrate the transition in meaning from *numen* to *deus* by a striking example.[14] On the frontier between Umbria and Etruria is a small lake, the *Lacus Vadimonis*, today called Laghetto di Bassano. Pliny *Epist*. 8, 20, 3ff. gives a detailed description of it. The lake is *sacer* and no boats are to be seen on it. What is even more remarkable is that it has floating islands. They are described at length by Pliny, and we get a clear picture of the profound impression made by the whole thing on the simple minds of the surrounding population. Undoubtedly Ovid's words (*Her*. 15, 158) about a *fons sacer* can be applied to the *Lacus Vadimonis; hunc multi numen habere putant*. There is already a reference in Nissen,[15] who says that the *Lacus Vadimonis* must have been named after an unknown god. In my opinion *Vādīmōn* is a *nomen agentis* from *vādere* and means 'the Wanderer'.[16] If I am right, the *numen* of the lake derived its name from the continual displacement of the islands and is thus an object lesson of a *numen* as moving force. Of course the *numen* is older than the name. It was there the moment people noticed the manifestation of an invisible unknown force. When the word *vādīmōn* was first uttered in reference to the *numen*, it was not yet a proper name, but must slowly have developed into one, and the *numen* became a god. That was the very thing for which a name was needed.[17] When Vergil (*Aen*. 8, 351ff.) tells how Evander conducts his guests in Rome, Aeneas and Iulus, around the district between Subura and the Forum, in the so-called Argiletum, he also shows them the wood there, the sacredness (*religio*) of which, the poet explains, had filled the peasants with awe and dread not only in prehistoric times but in his own lifetime still did so (note *jam tum*), for (*quis deus incertum est*) *habitat deus*. The word *numen* does not occur here but it is clear as daylight that it was hanging over Vergil's mind. There's a divinity here whose name we do not know but would

---

[14] Cf. H. Wagenvoort, *Roman Dynamism*, Oxford 1947, 77f.
[15] H. Nissen, *Italische Landeskunde*, II 1. *Die Städte*, Berlin 1902, p. 342.
[16] Hybrid formation of a *nomen agentis* with Greek suffix -μων (cf. γνώμων, ἡγεμών, see K. Brugmann-A. Thumb, *Griechische Grammatik*[4], Munich 1913, p. 222), and cf. Fest. 498 Linds.: *termonem Ennius* (ann. 479. 480 V.) *Graeca consuetudine dixit, quem nos nunc terminum* (see W. M. Lindsay, *The Latin Language*, Oxford 1894, p. 327).
[17] See the Accius passages above n. 10.

very much like to. Evander's fellow-countrymen, the Arcadians, had thought they saw Jupiter himself there when there was a tempest or thunderstorm. It can hardly be by chance that in both the passages from Accius (note 10) already quoted, our earliest sources for the occurrence of the word *numen*, it is combined with *nomen: nomen et numen Iovis* and *nomen vestrum numenque* (in this second case we unfortunately do not know what deities are addressed). Common names which were originally the names of *numina* could easily evolve into the names of deities. *Venus* originally was one of these, the 'eternal feminine' that 'attracts us', and so a mysterious force (Walde-Hofmann *s.v.* rightly refers to the adjective *venustus* and compares *onus: onustus;* to which I add *augus: augustus*, of which more below p. 245ff.). This force was personified and Venus became the name of the goddess of love.

4. *Prayer (preces)*

Characteristic of religious conditions in ancient Rome was the practice of prayer. Fowler [18] was right in part when he wrote: 'The whole public religion of the State, and to some extent also the private religion of the family became a mass of forms and formulae, and never succeeded in freeing itself from these fetters'. Only 'never' goes too far. It was particularly under Greek influence that the Romans learned to conceive of the relation between god and man more inwardly and with more dependence on an upright way of life. Even the comic playwright Plautus [19] can say: *facilius si qui pius est a dis supplicans | quam qui scelestust inveniet veniam sibi*.[20] Another comic playwright, Terence,[21] makes a boy beg his

---

[18] W. Warde Fowler, *The Religious Experience of the Roman People*, London 1922, p. 286.

[19] Plaut., *Rud.* 26f. According to F. Marx's commentary on the Plautus *Rudens*, Leipzig 1928, the playwright did not get this verse from his Greek source, the comedy of Diphilos. It was interpolated by another author in a second revision.

[20] 'Whoever is righteous when he prays to the gods will sooner get a favourable hearing than one who is wicked'.

[21] Ter., *Ad.* 704f. 'Better *you* pray to the gods than *me*, I'm sure they'll give you more of a hearing, you're a much better man than I am.' Here the playwright was certainly translating Menander. This must not be forgotten, as it was by P. Lejay, *Plaute*, Paris 1925, p. 183, who none the less correctly observed: *'Rien n'est plus étranger au formalisme précis du culte romain.'*

father: *tu potius deos comprecare, nam tibi eos certo scio, / quo vir melior multo es quam ego, obtemperaturos magis.*

Many years have passed since Pease [22] observed: 'Ancient prayers were usually uttered aloud rather than silently...Silent prayers were in the early period chiefly for magical purposes or for the attainment of wishes which the worshipper was ashamed or afraid to mention aloud, but later, especially in Christian usage, were far more generally employed (perhaps under the influence of such passages as Math. 6, 6).' Seneca judged differently—obviously not as a Stoic, but as a Roman. He wrote: [23] *Vota homines parcius facerent, si palam facienda essent; adeo etiam deos, quibus honestissime supplicamus, tacite malumus et intra nosmet ipsos precari.* Sudhaus [24] here rightly observes: 'The reason according to Seneca is a human sense of delicacy in not liking the posture of a suppliant even towards the gods. And yet the very expression he uses, *deos tacite malumus et intra nosmet ipsos precari*, seems to betray a different feeling very like the modern, when it resists the intrusion of a third person into personal communications with the deity.' To me it seems probable that Seneca was thinking of communications with the Lares and Penates.[25] We may well compare Cicero's words: *Ut enim deorum animi sine oculis, sine auribus, sine lingua sentiunt inter se quid quisque sentiat (ex quo fit ut homines, etiam cum tacite optent quid aut voveant, non dubitent quin di illud exaudiant) sic animi hominum . . . etc.*[26]

[22] A. S. Pease in his excellent commentary (Illinois 1929) on Cic. *Divin.*, 1, 129.

[23] Sen., *De benef.* 2, 1, 4. 'People would not be so free with their wishes if they had to be spoken aloud. To the gods especially, with whom we are at our most honest, we prefer to pray in silent self-communion'. How Seneca, as a Stoic, may have understood the meaning of prayer is not easy to determine. He writes (*Ep.* 41, 5), *Non sunt ad caelum elevandae manus nec exorandus aedituus ut nos ad aurem simulacri, quasi magis exaudiri possimus, admittat: prope est a te deus, tecum est, intus est.* 'We should not lift our hands up to heaven and importune the temple attendant to let us get closer to the ear of the divine image, as if we could so be better heard: god is near you, with you, inside you.' Cf. W. J. Richards, *Het Gebed by Seneca, die Stoisyn*, Diss. Utrecht 1964 (in Afrikaans).

[24] S. Sudhaus, 'Lautes und leises Beten', *ARW* 9, 1906, p. 200.

[25] Cf. Plaut., *Merc.* 834ff.; Ov., *Trist.* 1, 3, 43.

[26] Cic. *Div.* 1, 129: 'For just as the minds of the gods, without eyes, without ears, without a tongue, understand one another whatever they may want to say each to each (thus it is that men even when they wish or pray something in silence do not doubt that the gods hear it), so too...' etc.

In a way prayer is the yardstick of religion. Consequently it seems appropriate to dwell a little longer on it. Latin has two words for 'pray', *orare* and *precari* (see below). They are not synonymous. It is well-known that the primary meaning of *orare* is 'to be the spokesman'. It follows at once that it can originally have applied only to prayer spoken aloud [27] Sudhaus (p. 187) wrote: 'Silent or low-voiced prayer is not infrequently mentioned by the ancients, but it is always the exception. This applies particularly to public prayer, which is spoken aloud as a matter of course, but private prayer too ... was not silent without special reasons.[28]' Thus it was the priests and the magistrates—the latter under priestly supervision—who were responsible for the *oratio*. It was a popular use of words, first of all because it was ordinary people who had the feeling that a certain eloquence was required in addressing the gods, and this always commanded the respectful admiration of the people (we recall the words with which Homer (*Od.* 8, 170ff.) makes Odysseus describe people's astonished admiration of the orator: ἐρχόμενον δ'ἀνὰ ἄστυ θεὸν ὣς εἰσοράουσιν, 'and when he moves through the city, they stare at him as at a god'), and secondly because tradition demanded that fixed formulas (*certa verba*) should be used in public prayer and these were known only to the

[27] Cf. especially the words of A. S. Pease already quoted (n. 22). But we shall see that this statement is rather too one-sided.

[28] It goes almost without saying that silent prayer is the rule in matters of love. From Tibullus or his circle, for instance, we have a poem in which the girl Sulpicia for her lover's birthday prays to his *Genius* or *Deus Natalis* and ends with the words:

> *Optat idem iuvenis quod nos, sed tectius optat:*
> *nam pudet haec illum dicere verba palam.*
> *At tu, Natalis, quoniam deus omnia sentis,*
> *adnue; quid refert, clamne palamne roget?*

'The boy wants the same as me, but doesn't openly pour his heart out. He's too shy to say such things out loud. But you, his birth-god, a god from whom nothing is hidden, hear our prayer. What does it matter whether he says it to himself or openly?'

How dangerous it is, incidentally, to draw over-hasty conclusions in such matters can be gathered from a remark of Latte's (*Röm. Religionsgesch.* 41), 'The feeling of happiness or enthusiasm at the proximity of the deity is lacking among the Romans in contrast to the Greeks.' Can that be believed when in Ovid's prayer to Vesta quoted below (p. 236) we read, 'I was quite absorbed in my prayer. I became aware of a heavenly presence (*numen*) and the ground shone back joyously with purple light'?

priests. Wissowa [29] asserts, 'Prayer in the Roman conception is not so much a self-sufficient act of piety as the necessary oral accompaniment of every sacral procedure and performance which from the mortal side legalizes and perfects the sacral transaction and if uttered in the correct form at the same time compels the deity to take part in it.' In this connection it is significant that the priests and magistrates themselves, if all the indications are to be believed, avoided the words *orare* and *oratio*. They did not say *vos, deos, oro*, but used the verb *precari*, often with the addition of other verbs.[30] The use of *orare*, which gradually also invaded the private cult,[31] in the longer term became less usual, up to the time when the Christians took up the word again with a certain relish.[32]

Incidentally it would be a misunderstanding to suppose that heart and emotion were not involved in the religion of the Romans. Latte (p. 245) has correctly observed that the *supplicationes* ('days of prayer')—perhaps under Greek influence—became an occasion for the utterance of real emotions aloud. 'The participation of the whole people'—he writes—'in a religious act, the intensification of feeling provoked by it, had been until then unknown in Roman religion.'

I refer to one striking passage—a passage of the poet Ovid, be it noted, of whom Wilamowitz (*Der Glaube der Hellenen*, II, 338) had remarked that he had 'not a vestige of religion', a verdict with which Bömer in his Commentary [33] fully agrees. In the sixth

[29] G. Wissowa, *Religion und Kultus der Römer* ², Munich 1912, pp. 396f.

[30] Thus one does not say *vos, deos, oro* but e.g. *vos quaeso precorque* or *precor quaesoque* (this is how the *fratres Arvales* pray, see their '*acta*', ed. Henzen, pp. 122f.) Also *vos precor venerorque* or *vos precor veneror veniamque peto* (as when generals in the field perform various rites, such as *devotio* and *evocatio* (Liv., 8, 9, 6; Macr., *Sat*. 3, 9, 7; Tac., *Hist*. 4, 58).

[31] See Verg., *Aen*. 4, 203; 9, 24.

[32] E. Löfstedt, 'Peregrinatio Aetheriae, Philologischer Kommentar zur Peregrinatio Aetheriae, in: *Arbeten utgifna med understöd av Vilhelmo Ekmans Universitetsfond, Uppsala* 9, 1911, p. 41 (cf. id., *Syntactica*, Malmö 1956, 2, p. 463).

[33] F. Bömer, *Kommentar zu Ovid Fasti*, Heidelberg 1958, p. 14. Even such an enthusiastic admirer of Ovid as Emile Ripert did not venture to say more in his graceful book *Ovid, poet of love, gods, and exile* than 'The religion of beauty, that is all, on the whole, that Ovid practised.' '*La religion de la Beauté, voilà celle, somme toute, qu'Ovide pratiquait*'. Against that Carcopino pronounced an apt verdict (*Rencontres de l'histoire et de la littérature romaines*, Paris 1963): '*Deux hommes cohabitaient chez Ovide, le libertin et le philosophe, un sensuel et un mystique*'.

book of the *Fasti* (249-252) the poet prays to Vesta, goddess of the household hearth, and thus of family life, on the occasion of her feast, the *Vestalia*, on 9 June. It can hardly be a pretence of piety when he thus expresses his feelings:

Vesta, fave! Tibi nunc operata resolvimus ora,
  ad tua si nobis sacra venire licet.
In prece totus eram: caelestia numina sensi,
  laetaque purpurea luce refulsit humus.

That is, 'Vesta, be gracious! To you I open my lips in prayer now, if I am permitted to take part in your holy feast. I was entirely absorbed in prayer. Then I felt the divine presence, the joyful earth shone back with purple light'.

5. *Superstitio*

The original meaning of *superstitio* is uncertain. Usually it means 'superstition' but there is general agreement that it only acquired this unfavourable meaning by degrees. Recently the opinion has gained ground that it really means 'superiority' (literally 'to stand in combat over a prostrate opponent', from *super-stare*),[34] then 'superhuman power', 'soothsaying', even 'magic force', and finally that its meaning was degraded to 'superstition' by the guardians of *religio*. However that may be, the explanation does take very good account of Roman views in historical times. On the one hand the sober practical Roman found any suggestion of supernatural powers in individuals repugnant, and disliked magic, so far as he recognized it as such (which indeed he did not often do). On the other hand there is no lack of evidence that divination and magic had once been more highly esteemed. Is this internal contradiction perhaps connected with the fact that according to tradition the city of Rome grew out of the union of two very different tribes, the Latins and the Sabines, of whom the Latins were averse to everything supernatural in their cult while the Sabines

---

[34] Walde-Hofmann, *op. cit.* II, p. 632. How very obscure a word it was even to the ancients themselves is shown e.g. by Cicero, for whom *superstitio* was the behaviour of parents who continually implored the gods with sacrifices, *ut sui sibi liberi superstites essent*', 'that their children might survive them'! (*De nat. deor.*, 2). 72.

were entirely given over to it? In any case deep excavations of the Forum in Rome have proved that the tradition about a twin community of Latins and Sabines was historically founded in fact, and several duplicates, in the sphere of religion among others, are evidence of it, such as the existence of two gods of war side by side, Mars and Quirinus, and two parallel colleges of priests, *pontifices* and *augures*. The hypothesis is therefore tempting, all the more as it agrees very well with later clues, especially about the peculiarity of Sabine religious feeling.

For the rest, I can refer the reader to the full treatment of this theme by Professor Calderone (S. Calderone, 'Superstitio', *Aufstieg und Niedergang der röm. Welt* I 2, 377-396).

6. *The gods (dei)*

The Roman Pantheon contains innumerable gods, of whom only a few can be introduced here. Many of them being of foreign origin must in any case be eliminated from further consideration here by my self-imposed restriction of subject, though it would be an enthralling task to form an idea how the conflicts between the Greeks or Greek-influenced Etruscans and the Romans with their undoubted sense of inferiority in this respect must have developed in the early years of the Republic. The Romans made zealous efforts to assimilate their gods to the Greek gods, and where they could not find any similar figure, as in the case of the Apollo taken over from Cumae, they adopted the stranger complete with name and nature. It is obvious how much more difficult our task of singling out the old Roman elements in the religion thus becomes. There are other deities to which Altheim in particular assigns an Etruscan origin. He thinks that Vulcan was originally the tutelary god of the Etruscan Volca family, Saturn of the Satre family, Volturnus of the Velthur family—a theory difficult to prove but not to be lighly dismissed, though its author does undoubtedly go too far in his Etruscanization of Roman gods. Later, first because of the pressures of the Second Punic War and then little by little, in similar circumstances, when in the hour of crisis the help of its own gods failed it, Rome again took up foreign cults. The upper crust of Roman society tried wherever possible to resist this tendency, not so much for religious reasons or fear of foreign influence—after all, it was the state itself which had recognized the authority of the Sibylline books and at need sought the advice of the Etruscan entrail scanners (*haruspices*)— but from political motives. All novelty was dangerous because nobody could know in advance whether it might not impair the old Roman strength of character, the solidarity of the citizens and their power of endurance, in brief *virtus*. We thus see at once how energetically the Senate and Magistrates intervened the moment they felt the moral foundations of the state were endangered. We need consider all this no further for the moment. We have to concern ourselves first with the native *dei*—that is, what interests us now is the earliest phase of Roman religion, so far as it is accessible to us.

'Rich', 'wealthy' is rendered by the Latin *dives*. There is no doubt that this word is derived from *dīvus* (= *deus*), 'god'. It is to be translated 'standing under the protection of the gods', or perhaps more exactly 'having a (protecting) god' (cf. also Greek *eu-daimōn*).[35] Thus whereas in historical times we encounter almost exclusively group relations with the gods, this word proves that once upon a time certain gods were not only thought of as persons— the gods after all favoured one person more than another—but could also have personal relations with individuals. But this was not confined to early times. If we knew more about the *sacra privata*, on which we are much less well informed than on the *sacra publica*, though they had retained their original character in far greater purity, this could be more solidly demonstrated. One example must here suffice. In Vergil's first eclogue, and he as a country boy was well informed about domestic beliefs, the shepherd Tityrus meets the youthful Octavian, who has won his deepest gratitude by taking up the cause of the poor peasants threatened with the loss of their ploughland and pasture. He tells a mate about it in these words: 'I saw the young man—you know, the one in whose honour our altar smokes twelve days a year'

---

[35] See Walde-Hofmann, *op. cit.*, I, p. 338f. This etymology was already given by Varro, *De lingua latina*, 5, 9: *dives a divo, qui ut deus nihil indigere videtur*. Better probably Walde-Hofmann: '*divites* "the heavenly ones" = *caelites* in naive admiration of riches'. Cf. A. Ernout-A. Meillet, *Dictionnaire étymologique de la langue Latine*⁴, Paris 1959, s.v.: '*Les dieux européens étaient distributeurs de richesses* (Hom. δοτῆρες ἐάων)'.

(i.e. once a month). He thus indicates his tutelary deity, the *Lar familiaris*, who was worshipped in every farm-house. He had seen him face to face. What we have then is a divine epiphany. It has been said that such beliefs were brought from Greece to Rome. Of this we have no proof. Even if it were so, it would in no way affect the fact that the simple farmer had a very personal conception of his god.[36] This is after all proved by the fact that the words

---

[36] Divine epiphanies seem to have been fairly current among the ancient Romans. Their usual reaction was to be seized with fright—not at all like the Greeks (see H. Wagenvoort, '*Fas sit vidisse*', in: *Pro Regno, Pro Sanctuario, Festschrift für G. van der Leeuw*, Nykerk 1950, pp. 533-539). It is very striking that there is no trace of this in Vergil's first Eclogue. In other places Vergil shows himself very conscious of this reaction. In *Aen.* 4, 173ff. e.g. when Mercury appears to Aeneas at the orders of Zeus to remind him of his destiny Aeneas is quite overcome at his first appearance (279: *aspectu obmutuit amens*); his hair stands on end with fright, and the words stick in his throat (280: *arrectaeque horrore comae et vox faucibus haesit*) (cf. *Aen.* 3, 172ff. and generally R. Heinze, *Vergils epische Technik*, Leipzig-Berlin 1915, pp. 311f.). Of course it is no chance that an encounter with the *Lar familiaris* is an exception, and does not upset the countryman, being as he is a homely spirit closely concerned with the family's affairs (G. Wissowa, *Religion und Kultus der Römer*, ²1912, p. 169) and evidently an intimate and reliable friend of the farmer and even of his slaves. It almost looks as if the Romans in ancient times had learnt when young to utter an apotropaic prayer if a divinity appeared to them, in the words *fas sit vidisse*. This is of course improbable because there was never any catechism for the young. Nor were the priests ever concerned to write books of religious teaching. We must all the same be struck by the stereotyped appearance of this formula. After drawing the portrait of a wise Stoic (*Ep.* 115, 4) as that of a superman, Seneca asks: 'Who will not, on meeting such a man, stand amazed as if by a *numinis occursu* (meeting with a *Numen*) and pray silently *fas sit vidisse*' ('let it not be reckoned to me for a sin—*nefas*—to have seen him'). Thus the Einsiedel poet (*poet. lat. min.* 3 p. 61 Baehr. = *Anthol. lat.* 725 Riese, 26) and with unimportant variants Liv. 1, 16, 6f.; Ov. *Fast.* 6, 7. Her. 16, 63. He at any rate was considered a personal god. By contrast, the fact that names like Jupiter and Mamers (the god who became Mars) were originally vocatives is no doubt to be explained by the fact that the people in the earliest times only knew these gods from the prayers of the priests and took their names from them. They must have been fairly strange to them. How far it can be a question of personal gods is difficult to say. It depends what is understood by a personal deity. A. von Domaszewski ('Dei certi und dei incerti', *ARW*, 10, 1907, p. 7. The title refers to Varro's division of the gods into *dei certi*, that is deities whose nature and significance can be discovered for certain, and *incerti*, with whom that was no longer (i.e. 1st century B.C.) the case. This too the author did not correctly understand, see Wissowa, *op. cit.* 37, 3; Peter, *Roschers Lexicon*, 2, 1, pp. 129ff.), incidentally a not always reliable guide in religious studies, once wrote,

deus, dīvus, really mean 'shining' 'radiant,' and the 'radiant ones' can hardly have much to do with the impersonal *Numina*.

Matters are much more difficult, as I have said, when we turn our attention to the state gods. Let us begin with Jupiter, the sky god and father of gods and men. In his origins we know that he was a mighty personality, as has already been remarked and is particularly emphasized by Dumézil. To a certain extent his name confirms it, for the first syllable (Jupiter from *Dieu-pater*) means the radiant sky, so that he is the 'radiant sky-father'. But in fact he had long ceased to be that. As in Greece, Jupiter in Italy was the god of rain and wind, of tempest and thunderstorm. It is true that we possess a fragment of the ancient poet Ennius (about 200 B.C.): 'Look at this shining sky, which everyone calls Jupiter', but we do not know the context. He does however speak of the shining sky in another passage, 'whatever it may be'. In Cicero's work *On the Nature of the Gods* the former of these two passages is quoted four times (II 2, 4; II 25, 65; III 4, 10; III 16, 40). The discussion there should be read to get an idea how little the speakers were able to make of it. The metamorphosis into a rain god need not incidentally surprise us. It is obvious that once upon a time in their original home the sight of the cloudless sky was a cause of delight and gave rise to its identification with the supreme god. But after the Indo-European tribes had settled in the south, in Greece and Italy, rain was much more often prayed for than sunny weather and the transformation of Jupiter into a rain-giving god, though still confusing, was completed. The form of his name is noteworthy. It is a vocative. The nominative *Dies-piter* survived only as an archaistic form. How is this to be explained? In my opinion by the fact that there was a time when the name was

as long ago as the beginning of our century: 'The god thought of as personal came about no differently from the tree thought of as personal. Just as the living will in the tree expresses itself in effects, so too the sky was thought of as a person. Out of the steady circumscription of the *numen* and the lasting effects of the expressions of its will has grown the personal god, the *deus*.' Although it is creditable in him to have realized, and been perhaps the first to do so, the significance of the concept of *numen* for the understanding of the development of the Roman religion, his theory must be rejected, first, because in all these shades of meaning it too strongly emphasizes the 'Will' instead of the 'Movement', and secondly because he generalizes too much, as if all gods had developed out of *numina*.

hardly in current use any longer among the people but was yet preserved in mass consciousness through the prayer formulas anxiously guarded and faithfully transmitted by a conservative priesthood. There are other cases of this kind. We shall be discussing a second one later.

Thus not much can be made of the personal character of Jupiter in historical times. And his importance as a protector of morals, of which a good deal is made occasionally, rests almost exclusively on his function as a god of oaths. Here I can only point out that the usual giving of oaths in the open air is evidence of his original nature but in the course of time had become a fossil rite.

If Jupiter had been the husband of Juno from time immemorial, we should of course be compelled to revise our verdict. But there is not a trace to be found [37] of an Old Italic divine couple Jupiter-Juno. We do not even know whether the sky god in the mists of prehistory had a wife. It may be remarked in passing that there is no good reason for the frequent denial that an original Roman mythology ever existed. The Frankfurt school of religious historians (W. F. Otto and his pupils) have proved this clearly enough, even though they have sometimes tried to prove too much. We simply have no idea how much purely Roman substance was lost under the crushing superiority of Greek thought and storytelling.

Zeus was married indeed. Consequently a consort must be assigned to him, possibly a worthy substitute for majestic Hera. So recourse was had to Juno. Her name means 'youth', obviously sharpened to 'woman's sexual maturity' (her old epithet *Sororia* for example means 'who makes the breasts swell'). To all appearance, therefore, this goddess, long before the time we are now talking about, had evolved out of a *numen* and gradually taken under her protection the whole sexual life of woman—in this at least wholly comparable to the Greek Hera—marriage, menstruation, birth, the moon too and the month because of the influence of the moon periods on

---

[37] Cf. Latte, (*Röm. Religionsgesch.* p. 151f.) on the Jupiter-Juno-Minerva triad: 'It is characteristic of the Roman development that compared with Jupiter the two other deities beside Jupiter are pushed right into the background; their real cult in Rome is the result of later cult transferences and attaches to special sanctuaries.'

the physical life of woman. Every woman besides had her *iuno*, significantly enough for the original sense of the word (the parallelism between the female *iuno* and the male *genius* seems to have been an invention of imperial times).

A second highly respectable god was Mars (or *Mavors*, Oscan *Mamers*). In the last few decades there have been lively discussions about the nature of this god. It is unfortunate that the brevity of the present treatment prevents me from giving a summary of them. The name has not yet been elucidated despite many attempts. There seems to be no doubt that Mamers came about through doubling of the stem and was formed from a vocative (cf. the invocation '*Ares, Ares*' in Homer, and the vocative *Marmar* in the time-honoured cult song of the priesthood of the *fratres Arvales*). It is certain that Mars from very early times enjoyed great popularity among the Italic tribes. Many called a month after him. The Marsi were called after him themselves. The Romans called their sons after him Marcus, and the Oscans Mamercus. It is not too bold to infer from facts such as these, first, that Mars was a universally Italic god, and secondly that the human worshipper had a markedly personal relationship with him. It is true that among the Sabellian tribes, in the Oscan language domain, he seems at an early date to have lost a good deal of his influence. This may be deduced from the fact that the oldest divine triad, which was worshiped on the Roman Capitol (and later gave way to Jupiter, Juno, and Minerva) consisted of Jupiter, Mars, and Quirinus, the last of whom was a Sabine god in all essentials identical with his Roman colleague Mars. This of course does not mean, as has been supposed, that therefore the Sabines had not yet known Mars as a god of their own, but it does mean that he had been pushed out of his position among them by a competitor. A gratifying confirmation of this view is to be found in the very fact that they were the ones with whom the name Mars did not persist but was replaced by a vocative form, just as we have observed in the case of the name Jupiter. A further point is that Quirinus is really an adjective and probably means 'spear-wielding'. It may thus very probably be an old epithet of Mars the spear-bearer which, as so often happens, has caused the splitting off of a new deity.

In Republican times Mars was exclusively a god of war. For this he is no doubt indebted to the levelling tendencies of Graeco-Roman god identification, for Ares, with whom Mars was identified was concerned solely with the equipment of war. Not so with Mars. In the song already referred to above, of the 'brotherhood of the ploughland' (*fratres Arvales*), and in an old prayer handed down to us by Cato for the 'purification' (*lustratio*) of the fields he is invoked as god concerned with agriculture, even though an unusual representative of the genre. He not only confers blessings but is prone to anger. Therefore he is feared, because he sends harvest failures and cattle plagues. The manner in which attempts were made to appease Mars in time of distress is characteristic. A *ver sacrum* was vowed to him, that is to say the whole yield of one spring in the fruits of the field and orchards, in cattle and even new-born children. The latter, it is true, were not killed but, so soon as they were grown, cast out of the community. From historical records only one such example survives, from the Second Punic War. Then a *ver sacrum* was performed not to Mars but to Jupiter, but it can with certainty be inferred from the records that this was a modification of an ancient custom.

All the same Mars has a different face also. For when the young people who fell victim to the *ver sacrum* found themselves compelled to seek a new place of settlement, it was the animals sacred to Mars which appeared as their leaders and conducted them to a suitable spot. So the wolf (*hirpus*) was said to have led the Hirpini, the woodpecker (*picus*) the Picentes, and the bull (*bos*) the inhabitants of the Samnite capital Bovianum.[38] The bull in fact was considered by the Samnites especially as an animal of Mars. Samnite coins show on the obverse the god himself, on the reverse a bull throwing a she-wolf (the Roman one) to the ground. We are thus made aware here of a brighter side to his character.

Like most fertility gods Mars commanded life and death. His power extended to the underworld. The same applied to his counterpart Quirinus. His special priest, the *flamen Quirinalis*, still put in an appearance in historical times on the very occasion when

---

[38] Of course it is not impossible that popular etymology has played a part in this case. Even then, however, it is still important for the relations between god and people.

ceremonies were consecrated to the dead. The 'Mars field' (*campus Martius*), near Rome beside the Tiber, named after Mars, had been in ancient times a memorial cemetery where there was also an underground altar (*tarentum*, or better *terentum*) [39] which later at any rate was dedicated to Dispater and Proserpine, the god and goddess of the underworld, and according to tradition had been founded in the year 249 B.C. when the war with Carthage threatened to take a fatal turn, and then at intervals of about a century was opened up for a feast of sacrifice. Connected with it was the celebration of nocturnal 'games' (*ludi tarentini* or *terentini*, which later evolved into secular feasts, one of which was held by Augustus). Yet there is no doubt that the altar on the 'Mars field' originally belonged to Mars himself as a vegetation and death god, for three ancient authors testify that the Campus Martius was dedicated to Mars.

Such a god, who combined in himself life and death and—what is perhaps more significant—after whom the father named his son, must have counted more for the Roman uninfluenced by Greek teaching doctrines than any impersonal *numen*. He was for him an active god, strong of will and demanding respect.

A brief word may be added here about the ancient Roman ideas of the underworld. They were always very vague. The resort of the dead was thought of as an enormously large underground space narrowing upwards and coming out on earth in a small opening, rather like an *orca* or spherical jar with a long narrow neck. It was called Orcus for this reason.[40] The name was then transferred to the god of the underworld himself. Both in Greece and in Italy many such openings (*fauces*), usually chasms, were known, so deep as to seem like ways of approach to the dead. There are many indications that the one-time ancestors lived in a mountainous and volcanic region, where they threw their gifts to the dead, even human sacrifices, down such chasms to secure their favour.

---

[39] See H. Wagenvoort, *Studies in Roman Literature, Culture and Religion*, Leiden 1956, p. 122f. and *passim* (see Index).

[40] The view is defended by the author in *Studi e Materiali di Storia delle Religioni* 14, 1938, pp. 35ff. (= *Studies* etc. (n. 39 above) pp. 102ff.) W. Mackauer dissents, *RE* XVIII (1939) s.v. *Orcus*, Col. 928, 26ff.

7. Dynamism (Belief in impersonal forces)

In the study of religions today we often meet with the word 'dynamism'—it was introduced by Bertholet—to denote the belief in independently working forces which reside in the inorganic as well as in the organic, in things as well as in men. As soon as these forces are credited with a 'soul' or even a will, the word generally used is 'animism', though this has appeared with so many different meanings as to be hardly usable in serious work. The term 'pre-deism', which has been used occasionally in place of 'animism', is to be deplored because it assumes the dynamistic point of view to be chronologically prior to belief in god. This is in fact often the case and there are many individual instances of it especially on Roman territory, but it must be rejected as a universal rule and we have seen that even in Rome there are considerable objections to such a generalization.

I should like to add some further remarks to my observations above on the concept of *numen*, which can be regarded as an introduction to the present section. First, anyone interested in the Emperor Augustus must ask himself how it came about that the Senate resolved, on the proposal of Munatius Plancus, to confer the title *Augustus* on Octavian. So far as we know, this epithet had never before been applied to any man but was generally current for objects consecrated to temple use. What does *augus-to-s* then mean? Linguists agree that it must mean 'who has experienced increase' (*augus* from *augeo*, cf. *onustus, venustus*). The obsolete word *augus* (Vedic ojaš) was originally an s-stem, gen. *auguris* (cf. *augurium*), in Old Latin also *augĕris*.[41]

The poet Ovid also dealt with these questions and wrote (*Fast.* 1, 609)

> *sancta vocant augusta patres, augusta vocantur*
> *templa sacerdotum rite dicata manu.*
> *huius et augurium dependet origine verbi*
> *et quodcumque sua Jupiter auget ope.*[42]

---

[41] According to Priscian, *Gramm. Lat.*, ed. Keil, 2, 27, 17 the forms *auger*, gen. *augeris* were known in ancient times.

[42] 'Our fathers call sanctuaries "august", temples duly consecrated by the priest's hand are called "august". From the same root as this verb "*augurium*" too and whatever Jupiter "increases" (*auget*) in wealth are both derived'.

It is clear to him that *augustus* is derived from *augere* and related to *augurium*. Clear too that it is synonymous with *sanctus*—or let us rather say with *sacer*, 'consecrated', for *sancire* is 'to make *sacer*'. Finally he mentions consecration by the priest's laying on of hands—by the *sacer-dot-s*, that is, the 'holy-maker' or 'consecrator' (*sacer* and *dare*). We must now notice another word, not used just for any priest but originally for the one who as 'increaser', i.e. as bestower of *mana*, for instance consecrates a temple. For him the word that denoted the power of increase, *augus*, was personified. From this came *augur*. If it was a private person he was called *auctor*. That is how the different shades of meaning can be explained. A new word for capacity, the power of increase, now occurs: *auctoritas*. And the act of consecration is called *augurium* (see my *Roman Dynamism*, p. 12). The object of this increase is as I have said *sacer*. Consequently *augere*, when the act of a priest, is synonymous with *consecrare*, to make *sacer*, cf. Suet., *Aug.* 71: *loca quoque religiosa et in quibus augurato quid consecratur augusta dicuntur*, 'religious places too and those in which anything is consecrated by the augur's power are called "august"'. It is no coincidence that the epithets *sacer* and *augustus* are often linked.[43] When a temple was to be consecrated and dedicated to a deity the *consecratio* by the priest preceded the *dedicatio* by the magistrate. That is logical. A temple not yet consecrated could not be handed over to a deity. The consecration itself was done by laying on of hands, that is, the priest, the *pontifex*, *postem tenebat*, held the door-post, so that his mysterious force could flow over into the building like an electric current.[44]

We often read in ancient authors that a *numen* dwells in a tree, in a rock, in a spring. This originally meant a motive force not understood but felt as in confrontation with a human being.

In the section on *numina*, when I attempted also to throw some light on the nature of dynamism, which in many ways gave Roman religion a peculiar quality, it unfortunately became clear that an

[43] E.g. Cic., *Nat. Deor.* 2, 62. 79; Liv., *Praef.* 7, 45, 5, 3; Pomp. Mela 1, 13, 75: Man., 5.540; Stat., *Theb.* 10, 757; cf. Macr., *Sat.*, 1, 20, 7.
[44] G. Wissowa, *op. cit.* p. 385, wrongly observes: '*Geschieht diese Überantwortung (nämlich des Eigentumsrechtes am Tempel) an die Gottheit von Staatswegen, so ist die Dedication zugleich Consecration*'. He constantly confuses the two concepts also in his articles in the *RE*.

adequate treatment of the topic would be far outside the scope of this chapter. I thus cannot avoid referring the reader to my book *Roman Dynamism* already quoted.

To conclude, I must warn the reader in the interest of objectivity that eminent scholars have strongly, often irritably, objected to dynamistic theories. But irritation is seldom conducive to sound reasoning. The reason for this exasperation is often found to be a distaste for the use of words like '*Mana*'. Even the word 'primitive' in this context is much deplored by some. To prevent any misunderstanding, let me observe once and for all that the Romans of historical times had long since emerged from the primitive phase, but that in consequence of their conservatism and relative lack of imagination their language and mores for centuries again and again betrayed their spiritual origins.

Even H. J. Rose had to defend himself against Stefan Weinstock, an excellent scholar, who had reviewed his book *Ancient Roman Religion*. London 1949, in the *Journ. of Rom. Stud. 39*, 1949, pp. 166ff. and raised five objections: '1. the word *numen* is not found earlier than Accius; 2. it is not used in old prayers and in relevant antiquarian texts nor, for instance, in the *Arval Acts*; 3. it still denotes occasionally 'nodding, inclination' in Cicero and Lucretius; 4. religious usage begins to prevail at the same time, i.e. in the last century of the Republic, and so we often find *numen Jovis, deorum,* or the like, sometimes joined to other words, such as *vis*; 5. the predication that something or somebody is or has a *numen* does not occur until the Augustan period.' Rose answered in detail in his article '*Numen* and *Mana*' (*Harvard Theol. Rev. 44*, 1951, pp. 109-120) and quite rightly remarked (p. 110) that if his views were rejected 'a new explanation must be sought for a large group of fundamentally important phenomena.'

Later G. Dumézil (the scholar who made his reputation by comparing, through better knowledge of Sanskrit than most of his fellows, the ancient Indian and Roman religions and thus solving several individual problems) again took up arms against what he chose to call 'Manaism' [45] and launched a crusade against it.

---

[45] Discussion with Professor Dumézil is not always easy. Only once was public discussion prolonged. Because so-called *mana* is universally regarded as something concrete, material, which when it occurs in human beings can

Evidently he also called his students to arms, and it is touching how they rallied to his crusade and how faithfully they echoed 'their Master's voice'.[46]

so to speak be removed by an operation, and because it is also regarded as something remarkably heavy, in my book *Roman Dynamism* I had connected it hypothetically with the Roman concept of *gravitas*. This word has gradually acquired the sense of *auctoritas* and is frequently associated with it. Comparison with the Hebrew *Kâbôd* and Sanskrit *Guru* was in my opinion a strong argument in favour of this (pp. 168ff.). Previously (pp. 106f.) I had written: 'There is, in addition, the *gravitas* of magic words, e.g. *terroribus omnibus verba graviora* (referring to a magician's conjurations, Quint., *decl.* 10, p. 206, L.) Admiration and reverence for the magic power of speech, particularly of oratory, are often expressed in terms borrowed directly from worship. So in Tacitus, *dial.* 4, 4, the poet Maternus speaks of *sanctiorem illam et augustiorem eloquentiam;* another participant in the same dialogue, Aper, of *numen et caelestis vis* (*eloquentiae*) and Quintilian at the end of his *Institutio oratoria* (12, 11, 30) extols *ipsam. . .orandi maiestatem, qua nihil dii immortales melius homini dederunt.* Dumézil in an article ('Maiestas et gravitas', *Rev. de Philol.* 26, 1952, pp. 7ff.) raised objections and wrote: '*On se démande comment M. Wagenvoort a pu placer ce texte* (*le seul de ceux qu'il cite qui contienne maiestas. . .*)' (Here be it noted that in my book there was not yet any mention of *maiestas*, only of *gravitas*): it was my opponent himself who spoke of '*Maiestas and gravitas*' and thus anticipated *maiestas*, probably because he felt safer there than where I dealt with *gravitas* alone. For *maiestas*, the 'being-greater' does not contain any element of *mana*. Nor did I ever say it did. On the contrary I declared (*Rom. Dyn.* p. 120): 'Strictly speaking this *maiestas* (*mag-jes-tat-s*) or "being greater" does not belong to our present study, but it is difficult to leave it out of our consideration because it is important to observe how, in the long run, this notion either took the place of *gravitas* or for a long time a place beside it as having a synonymous meaning.'

Dumézil, regardless of all this, took refuge in mockery. After pointing out in my reply ('Gravitas et maiestas', *Mnemos. ser. IV* vol. V, 1952, p. 297) that it was only necessary to read my context without prejudice in order to discover that the passage quoted did not in any way deal with *maiestas* but only with *gravitas* and especially with *gravis* in combination with certain substantives, I mentioned that this adjective often serves to express the reverence which simple people are accustomed to bestow on the speaker who can captivate an audience in words which often have a religious colour. In my opinion Quintilian's *maiestas orandi* was an example of this though he did not use the word *gravis*. I likewise on p. 207, 2 compared the famous passage in Homer, *Od.* 8, 170ff. where the poet describes a speaker as clothed in gracious beauty by some god. What was my opponent's next retort? He wrote '(Maiestas et gravitas' II, *Rev. de Philol.* 28, 1954, p. 19): '*Quant aux objections qui sont faites à mes objections, beaucoup m'ont d'abord déconcerté, puis enchanté, car elles reviennent à dire que j'ai eu tort de croire que, si l'auteur de* "Roman Dynamism" *cite tel, tel, et tel texte, c'est pour appuyer la thèse dynamiste. Pas du tout: ils ne l'appuyent pas, en effet, mais ne voulaient pas l'appuyer. Par exemple* (*p.* 296) *l'orandi maiestas de la fin*

Some further remarks in conclusion. Here and there the old ideas lie almost untouched on the surface. Thus in Rome in the Regia, the old royal palace, the spears of Mars were kept. Presumably this dated from a time when the weapons of war were stored in a consecrated place in time of peace, probably in the king's house.

de l'Institution Oratoire, citée Roman Dynamism, *p. 107, à propos du* 'magic power of speech', *n'est qu'une façon de parler de Quintilien dont M. W. n'entendait tirer aucune conséquence quant à la valeur de maiestas.*' Now comes another example. After I had made it clear in my book that *maiestas*, as I said, was not properly speaking a '*mana* word' (that was my first conclusion) I found myself obliged by Latin usage to modify this opinion so far as to allow that in course of time the word did approach the meaning of *gravitas* in certain associations, for instance in *maiestas populi* (Val. Max. 8, 15, ext. 1; Liv., 23, 43, 10; Flor., 2, 13, 8; Plin., *N.H.* 22, 6; furthermore, with an appeal to F. R. Lehmann, *Mana. Eine begriffsgeschichtliche Untersuchung auf ethnologischer Grundlage*, Leipzig 1915, p. 119). That was the second, later conclusion, in no way contradictory of the first. In this sense I wrote, p. 125, '*Maiestas populi*, in the primitive sense, is the "*mana* of the ruling tribe".' Since Dumézil in connection with my quoted examples had disputed my explanation of *maiestas* in the latter sense, that is, with a religious colour, since it was '*inutile de supposer un rapport de cette maiestas bien concrète, bien physique, avec quelque forme de "sacredness"* ' (Dumézil p. 19, 7) I was able to demolish his argument, as I venture to claim, by reference to *Aen.* 6, 48ff. (about the Sibyl), *maiorque videri, / nec mortale sonans, adflata est numine quando iam propiore dei*, and more especially to Valerius Flaccus 4, 548ff., speaking of the *vates* Phineus, '*tam largus honos, tam mira senectae maiestas infusa; vigor novus auxerat artus.*' Is a *maiestas* thus infused into someone '*bien physique*'? How can we think so? The man has experienced *augus*, he has become *augustus*, even though the poet does not use this word (for *vigor* see *Rom. Dyn.* 128f., which does not unfortunately include this passage). For Dumézil this all counts for nothing. In his reply he insists (p. 19): '*M. W. n'a nullement voulu suggérer une interprétation dynamiste du texte de Virgile. Comment ne pas se réjouir d'apprendre cela? On sait maintenant comment lire "Roman Dynamism".*' No, he has given us a striking, luckily obvious example how not to read it.

I hope this detailed digression concerning a difference of opinion among scholars will not cause annoyance. On the one hand, I regard dynamism with absolute conviction as an important trait of Roman religion and would regret any aspersions cast on this view. On the other, Professor Dumézil justly enjoys such prestige among his French *confrères—sit venia verbo;* that too is a '*mana* word' (*Rom. Dyn.* p. 106)—that he might very easily be credited with the last word on the subject. Fortunately it does not yet look as bad as that. On many sides my observations have been applauded. One unexpected and unintended success, though here not entirely to the point, is that many representatives of non-Western peoples, especially of Indonesia, have found a new reflection of themselves in my theories and gained a new understanding of their own rites and customs. A young Chinese research worker, a student of Waszink in Leiden, found there the solution

This custom is still found today among primitive peoples. Weapons are thought of as full of force, especially when they have wounded a man and thus been bathed in enemy blood, for blood is strongly *mana*-bearing. But repeatedly we are told, especially by Livy, of the occurrence of terrible portents. The spears had moved of their own accord. Then the Senate had to take all kinds of precautions to avert the threatened evil. Probably the omen portended an approaching war, that is, the spears brought the war about. It is not essential in such a case that the movement should also be visible. On the other hand it is noteworthy that according to another tradition men are able for their own benefit to activate the force in the spear. We are told, for instance, that formerly a general on going into battle shook one of Mars's spears and called out 'Mars, awake!' This exclamation is proof enough that animistic and dynamistic ideas have combined. The act itself, however, is older than the exclamation and shows how a man could operate on the *mana* in a thing.

of a well-known problem (Tjan Tsoe-Som, 'On the Rendering of the Word Ti as Emperor', *Journ. Amer. Orient. Soc.* 71, 1951, pp. 119ff). But even on studies of Roman religion they have not been without influence. I am not of course including the writings of my own students. Only recently there appeared the excellent dissertation of H. S. Versnel, also a student of Waszink, under the title *Triumphus, an Inquiry into the Origins, Development and Meaning of the Roman Triumph*, Leiden 1970, in which my book is mentioned throughout with approval, though not without healthy criticism (I need only mention e.g. p. 5, after a mention of my name with others, 'In too many instances they over-emphasize the data that fit in with the theory concerned, whilst leaving out those that do not.' Thank you, Mr. Versnel, probably you are right).

[46] It would be superfluous to mention them all here. As only one example, by no means the worst, I refer to the otherwise valuable work of Huguette Fugier, *Recherches sur l'Expression du Sacré dans la langue latine*, Paris 1963. In my review, *Gnomon* 38, 1966, pp. 38off., I observed: 'Obviously she has heard the war-cry, *Agitedum ite mecum, in manaistas et primitivistas signa inferamus*, and she too has taken up arms. The use of the Austronesian word *mana* in reference to early Roman ideas is of course proscribed, it is taboo. Strangely enough *tabu* itself is not taboo, even though it is found rather embarrassing and put in inverted commas. Nor were the distant ancestors of the Romans ever "primitive", they were "*archaiques*". Since the idea itself can hardly be disputed, we speak instead of "*une force sacrée*", "*une force numineuse*" (sic!), "*une force immanente*", "*une force vitale*", "*une force végétative*", "*une force défensive*", altogether in nine separate places. To speak of "*mana*" would be a gross misdemeanour! I find that too much of a good thing.'

Against that, not all men were equally capable. In fact the field commander and the priest possessed a *mana* of their own and through it could gain ascendancy over a different *mana*. Thus the commander was thought able to influence the fertility of the soil, he fertilized it. Similar views are encountered far and wide in anthropological literature. Properly considered, the verb *imperare* ('command', 'rule') originally meant 'awaken to life', 'fertilize'. The field commander who gave his men orders (*imperabat*) to attack an enemy position, engendered in them by his magic words the force to carry out his orders.

Imperium is thus a form of the transmission of mysterious force. There are many such forms, and the most important is probably touching, physical contact. For *mana* works like an electric current.

It will be enough to give a few examples. The priesthood of the *Fetiales* had the task of managing relations between Rome and the neighbouring states. It was involved in declarations of war, making of treaties, and so on. Its leader bore the title *pater patratus*. Before he can carry out his mission—we are still in the time of the kings—he must be consecrated in it by the king. This consecration consists of being touched by a tuft of grass gathered on the *Arx* (the citadel), the centre and holiest place of Rome. The force of the soil has penetrated the grass and when the priest's head in its turn is touched by the grass a new, mysterious force is instilled in it. It is clearly shown that the force comes from the soil by the prescription that the tuft must be pulled up root, earth, and all— the grass alone would not be enough. The consecration rite for an improvised altar is another example belonging to this context. When an army on the march, for instance, wants to sacrifice to the gods, a stone altar may be put up for the purpose but can only be consecrated by laying turf on it, 'living' turf at that, with the original force of the soil still freshly adhering. The ancient meaning of this custom incidentally, like that of many others, was no longer understood by later Romans.

So far we have considered consecration by transference of *mana* from the soil. But frequently the human individual—primarily the magistrate or priest—was the source of the force which by touch or the laying on of hands was transferred to another human being or a thing. It often happened that a general in the field sacrificed his own life or that of some warrior to the gods of the underworld in order to obtain deliverance or victory for the community. This consecration, called *devotio*, was performed by laying on of hands. If it was himself that the magistrate was sacrificing, he touched his own chin, since the toga had been raised to cover his head which was therefore not free. This ritual was rooted in the conviction that no sacrifice was acceptable to the gods—note the co-existence of dynamistic magic with belief in gods—if it was not *sacrum*, consecrated or 'tabu'. The word for 'sacrifice', *sacrificare*, 'make *tabu*' in fact, originally signified an act which preceded the actual sacrifice of the victim. An example of the consecration of things by a magistrate can be found in Tacitus, when he records the laying of the foundation stone of the new temple on the Capitol by the Emperor Vespasian, after the old one had been destroyed by fire. The praetor, whose task it was, addressed a prayer to Jupiter, Juno, Minerva, and the other guardian deities of the empire, and touched the ceremonial bands in which the stone was wrapped.

Priests too were required to perform such ceremonies. During the time of the kings when the throne had become vacant and the inauguration of the new king was to take place, a priest, an augur, stood at the left hand of the chosen candidate, laid his right hand on his head and in this position addressed a prayer to Jupiter to implore his favour and to submit the election for his approval. Things too could be consecrated by priests in this fashion. For example, before cult ceremonies could take place in a newly built temple, it had to be consecrated by a magistrate. He for this purpose sought the expert help of a member of the college of *Pontifices*. The priest would speak the appropriate formula before him to ensure that he made no mistake such as would invalidate the whole ceremony, and had to hold the door-post of the temple as he did so. There can be no doubt that this holding of the door-post by the priest was the very thing which gave the temple its sacral character.

It seems an appropriate point to observe that certain divine beings owe their existence to dynamistic views of this kind. The fact that the part of the temple grasped by the Pontifex was the door-post was not a chance one. A door, or indeed any passage way, has been 'powerful' not only in the eyes of an ancient Roman but in those of primitive man of all times and places. The house door separates one's own from the stranger's, often the ill-disposed stranger's at that. It is the symbol of 'my house is my castle'. No, that is the wrong way of putting it. Abstractions such as symbols are not known to primitive man. A door keeps out the enemy, even the demons, that is where it shows its power. Other gates too have their share in this power. As you go out or in, you come into a different sphere, become a different person. It is the same as with the *terminus*, the boundary stone. This is not only a symbol of the separation of plots and of property but—nobody knows how—it makes property, it keeps and protects it, and does so at a time when there are no land registers. Just as the god Terminus has evolved from the boundary stone, so in course of time the passageway, the door, the gate is raised to divine self-sufficiency and becomes the god Janus (i.e. 'way', 'passage').

Thus the magic contact passes on mysterious force, but also extracts it from things. That is the explanation for instance of the touching of the altar so often mentioned, which has evolved from the sacred stone charged with *mana*. When praying or swearing an oath the necessary force is got from it by touching. When, later on, the suppliant embraced the altar or the divine image, that was probably derived from Greek notions and had in any case lost all connection with the original meaning of the gesture.

The polarity of these phenomena shows itself also in another way. The touching can just as well have a bad effect and there are many unwanted contacts which must be avoided. Infectious diseases, for instance, come about through contact, that is in primitive eyes through radiation of bad *mana*. Note that the contact does not have to be direct. Among the ancestors of the Romans it was probably just as with the New Zealand Maoris, whose *mana* concept was at first understood by investigators as something purely psychic. Then they gradually learnt to distinguish a system of thought totally different from our own and to understand *mana* often as something concrete, a substance however fine. We might say, it radiates atomically. It is no chance that atomism played an important part in ancient philosophy so early. Consequently it works also at a distance. We recall the influence of the 'evil eye'. It was much the same with the magic word, which was already referred to and was once thought of as having physical substance. Homer's 'winged words' remind us of a notion according to which words floated through the air on little wings. Among the Greeks, incidentally, such survivals are extremely rare. For them the dynamistic point of view in historical times had been completely lived down.

I have already indicated how a *numen* could be personified and attain the rank of a deity. Two characteristic instances are worth closer consideration.

In the oldest Roman festival calendar, one of our most important sources for the knowledge of the religion of Rome in its earliest centuries, the name of the goddess Venus does not occur, any more than in the oldest sacral documents. The outstanding scholar Varro (born 116 B.C.) was already convinced that her worship was fairly recent. He was undoubtedly right about that. The name Venus was originally neuter and is derived from a root which recurs for instance in the German *Wonne*. It meant 'power of attraction', but in a rather less abstract sense than in our usage. It was a fluid of remarkably strong effects. It was probably attributed by preference to women, though two derivatives already had a general sense. The adjective *venustus*, 'attractive' or 'charming' was not used exclusively of women. The verb *venerari*, 'to take to oneself', 'to worship' (of a deity), was used of men and women. How it had been used originally we can no longer determine.

There is another line of thought leading to the same conclusion. The Roman year originally began with the month of March. The names of the first four months were *Martius, Aprilis, Maius, Junius*. The first, third, and fourth are named after the deities Mars, Maia, and Juno. Until recently the name *Aprilis* was differently explained. Now there seems growing agreement, and rightly so, that the ancient interpretation connecting it with the Greek goddess Aphrodite is by no means so unfounded. Only it must then be derived from the shorter form of the name, Aphro, by which the goddess was also called in Greece, and which must have come by way of the Etruscans. How did this happen? The Etruscans, or Romans under their influence, wanted to call the first two months after the Greek divine couple Ares and Aphrodite.

But they looked for the names of native deities who could be equated with them. For the war god Ares they chose Mars, although as I have explained above the warlike function was only a secondary part of his nature. If there had been a cult of Venus, the second month would of course have been called after her, *'Venerius'* for example. They did not do so because they did not yet know of such a goddess. Thus the fact that in due course the *numen* Venus evolved into the goddess Venus is no doubt attributable to the pressure of Greek mythology and the ambition to set as many native deities as possible alongside the Greek.

A second case is rather different but also instructive. It concerns Ceres, the goddess of growth. Once or twice in very ancient times we encounter a god Cerus. There was a natural desire to see in him a husband of Ceres but that is pure speculation. It seems less speculative that the name Cerus gives a hint of the origin of both deities. It contains a root which means to '(make) grow'. In my opinion there are still surviving traces of an old substantive *cerus (gen. *cereris, like *venus*, gen. *veneris*), which meant 'growth' 'motive force', in other words the mysterious force in the soil, which in the first place caused the plant world to turn green and blossom but as we have seen could also be used for other purposes. *Cerēs* on the contrary (gen. again *cerĕris*) was an adjective to begin with, 'promoting growth', 'full of motive force'), and was particularly said of the earth, when it was deified—*Terra cerĕs, Tellus Cerĕs.* Ancient writers were still acquainted with these combinations. This character of the goddess Earth split off and acquired an independent existence. Consequently later generations had great difficulty in separating Tellus and Ceres. The two were always being confused. One strange misunderstanding was caused by the expression *Initia cerĕris*, the name of a feast of Ceres. The proceedings of the Romans themselves have accustomed us to translate it 'Mysteries of Ceres', although nobody has succeeded in explaining how on earth *initia* ('entry', 'beginning') could have acquired the meaning 'mysteries'. Elsewhere I have argued at length that what we have here is a very ancient spring-festival, which was called 'Beginning of Growth' and then no longer understood, the word *cerus* having gone out of use, so that the second word of the combination *initia cerĕris* became *Cerēris*, 'of the goddess Ceres'. Thus the word *initia* had at first nothing to do with mysteries. The idea only came in after Ceres had been identified with the Greek Demeter.

I am well aware that these few pages are far from having given a complete survey of the ancient Roman religion, let alone the foreign elements which I have deliberately excluded. I have merely tried to the best of my ability to sketch the two main lines which stretch side by side as far as our view can reach into the ancient past, the two directions which, however dissimilar and irreconcilable they may seem, can none the less be demonstrated also among other Indo-European peoples and which have again and again influenced one another. Religion and Magic in ancient Rome went hand in hand. It is difficult to say whether and how far magic in historical times had lost its original sense and become a mere survival. But it is advisable to bear in mind that Roman magic had nothing in common with the absurdities of abstruse superstition known elsewhere and later imported into Rome from the Hellenistic world. The Roman mind, not profound but always acute, shows even in its magical practice a certain transparent and well-considered logic. It is a thrilling spectacle to see how in religious matters too it wrestled with the steady advance of Greek theories.

INDEX OF AUTHORS CITED

Selected

Accius		64, 104	206
fr. 5f.	170	68, 108	187
fr. E92	228	Charisius	
fr. 646	228	1, 76, 3	32
Acta Fratrum Arvalium		Cicero	
p. 122f. Henzen	202	Balb. 35	43
Afranius		Brut. 33, 126	8
fr. 83R	171	Cat. M. 38	45
fr. 380f. R	188	Clu. 194	204
Anthol. Lat.		de or. 1, 2, 5	7
452 R	46, 170	2, 164	42
Alcaeus		2, 343ff.	80
fr. 15	157	div. 1, 79	184
fr. 22	157	1, 129	207, 233
Apuleius		2, 29	184
Apol. 48	46	dom. 16	71
61	208	ep. ad Att. 6, 6, 3	63
Met. IV, 28-VI, 24	84-92	ep. ad Corn. Nep. fr. 2, 5	61
Aristides		ep. ad fam. 9, 22, 2	153
Apol. 11, 3	87	fin. 3, 22, 73	9
Arnobius		4, 22	66ff.
2, 73	136	har. resp. 3	73
4, 7ff.	22	23	48
Augustinus		imp. Gn. Pomp. 10	69
C.D. 4, 18	61	28	60
4, 21	22, 61	47	68
4, 23f.	61	inv. 1, 94	63, 69, 80
4, 34	22	2, 22, 66	7
5, 24	61	2, 53, 161	7
6, 10	179	leg. 2, 36	135
19, 21, 2	14	Marc. 191	70
Conf. 1, 14	212	Mil. 6	69
Caesar		N. D. 1, 2, 3	9
B.C. 2, 38	74	1, 2, 4	11
B.G. 5, 24, 1	74	1, 41, 116	9
7, 29, 3	74f.	1, 59	177
7, 80, 2	74	2, 2, 4	240
Cato		2, 7, 9	68
Agr. 50	29	2, 23	178
83	30	2, 25, 65	240
132	29, 31	2, 67	218
134	171	3, 4, 10	240
Catullus		3, 16, 40	240

INDEX OF AUTHORS CITED

3, 86	68	422.31	135
off. 1, 2, 33-35	4	Fronto	
1, 118	64	Ep. 2, 2, 1	46
1, 130	173	Gaius	
2, 8, 27	6	4, 11	79
2, 17, 58	5	Gellius	
3, 6, 28	11	N. A. 4, 9, 1	226
part. or. 22, 78	8	11, 6, 5f.	123
Phil. 5, 40	67	13, 23, 1	205
14, 37	67	13, 23, 2	174
Pis. 70	173	15, 7, 3	221
Planc. 33, 80	8	Herodotus	
Prov. 35	71	1, 171	157
Rab. 2, 5	176	Hippolytus	
rep. 1, 2, 3	12	Ref. 9, 16, 1	230
1, 4, 8	4	Homerus	
1, 21, 34	12	Od. 8, 170ff.	197, 234
1, 29, 45	12	17, 541ff.	47
3, 6, 9	13	Horatius	
6, 16	8	Od. 3, 3, 57ff.	19
Rosc. 136	72	4, 7, 15ff.	19
Top. 90	9	4, 14, 3	216
Tusc. 1, 35, 85	226	Sat. 2, 6, 13	198
3, 19, 45	226	Livius	
4, 71	190	1, 22, 2	45
5, 37	122	1, 31, 7	176
Verr. 4, 6, 12	8	1, 38, 6	181
5, 187	131	1, 56, 2	181
Curtius		3, 7, 8	205
4, 3, 23	142	3, 54, 9	79
Digest.		5, 21, 3	202
47, 7, 2	78	6, 27, 1	70
Diod. Sic.		8, 9, 6	171, 202
3, 60	89	10, 24, 16	68
14, 77, 4	131	22, 56, 4f.	142, 144
Dion. Hal.		23, 43, 10	43, 45
Ant. Rom. 1, 33	131f.	29, 3, 15	45
4, 15	178	30, 30, 11	78
Ennius		30, 30, 23	77
Ann. fr. 20V²	198	38, 48	67-70
fr. 52V²	171	39, 51, 6	55
Epictetus		40, 52, 5	66, 71ff.
Diatr. 1, 29, 21	208	42, 12, 2	63
Festus (editio Lindsay)		45, 41, 6	74
144	143	Livius Andron.	
242	37	Od. fr. 19R	202
260	153	Lucianus	
270	36	Adv. indoctos 13, 3	208
322	178	Amor. 37	88
402	172	Dial Deor. 1, 4	88

INDEX OF AUTHORS CITED

2, 1	88	3, 417	215
de Salt. 7	88	3, 421f.	222
Lucilius (editio Marx)		3, 426	222
fr. 206	171	3, 604f.	218
fr. 667	75	3, 697	215
Lucretius		4, 949-954	217
6, 806f.	185	5, 571	215
6, 816f.	185	6, 249-252	208, 210-222, 236
Macrobius		6, 537ff.	50
Sat. 3, 6, 11	36	Heroid. 7, 129	34
3, 9, 7	171	15, 158	231
3, 11, 1	137	16, 25	187
3, 11, 9	137	Met. 4, 539ff.	49
3, 19, 4	65	7, 953	205
3, 20, 3	79	8, 682	205
Marcus Aurelius		9, 268ff.	49
2, 2	170	10, 647	95
Martialis		14, 113	97
2, 46, 8	27	15, 777	215
Monumentum Ancyranum, see		15, 868	216
Res Gestae Divi Augusti		Pont. 1, 2, 73	216
Nemesianus		1, 4, 44	216
Ecl. 2, 14	187	1, 4, 56	216, 221
Nepos		2, 9, 65	201
Att.	220	4, 13, 29	222
Lys. 1, 1	70	Trist. 1, 3, 43ff.	205
Reg. 2, 3	70	5, 2, 35	216
Timol. 2, 1	63	5, 10, 52	216
Nonius		5, 11, 20	216
p. 64 M (Varro)	178	Pacuvius	
p. 173, 27 M (Accius)	228	fr. 102 R	185
p. 480 M (Varro)	171	fr. 125 R	199
p. 529 M (Varro)	198	fr. 177 R	198
Obsequens,		fr. 296 R	171
Prodig. 8, 62	180	Paulus (editio Lindsay)	
Origenes,		35	172
c. Cels. 1, 30	230	50	148
3, 68	230	53.21	135
Ovidius		80	191
Amor. 1, 2, 29ff.	191	81	145
3, 5, 36	187	231	153
3, 9, 19	34	246	147
3, 10	123	287	32
3, 10, 1	143	Pausanias	
3, 10, 43	143	2, 11, 3	140
Ars am. 3, 82	45	Placidius	
Fasti 1, 90	213	Gloss. IV M 6	183
1, 528	222	in Stat. Theb. 4, 527	178
1, 530	216	Plato	
1, 609ff.	245	Charm. 157B	230

INDEX OF AUTHORS CITED

Plautus
  Asin. 662 — 199
      686 — 199
  Amphitr. 196 — 73
  Aul. 354 — 137
  Capt. 244 — 198
  Curc. 121 — 181
      432 — 199
      471 — 179
  Mil. 651 — 173
      657 — 173
  Most. 414 — 75
  Pers. 189 — 177
  Poen. 255f. — 173
      950f. — 169
      1113 — 173
      1176ff. — 173
  Rud. 26ff. — 203, 212, 232
      305 — 169
      320 — 173
  Truc. 714 — 173
Plinius
  Epist. 8, 20, 3ff. — 231
Plinius
  N. H. 2, 94 — 219
      2, 208 — 183
      3, 136 — 73
      7, 200 — 157
      15, 119 — 180, 186
      16, 108 — 79
      16, 249ff. — 96, 99
      26, 19 — 64
      28, 23 — 47, 169
      28, 24 — 46, 170
      28, 27 — 48
      31, 49 — 185
      34, 137 — 121
Plutarchus
  fort. Rom. 7,
  Q. R. 23 — 82
      97 — 178
  Cic. 45, 3 — 148
  Fab. Max. 18, 2 — 78
  Numa 12 — 142
  Sulla 6, 6 — 178
      35, 6 — 82
Porphyrio
  ad. Hor., Od. 3, 18 — 195
Propertius
  2, 25, 4 — 176
  3, 24, 17ff. — 191
Publilius Syrus
  36 — 77
Quintilianus
  Decl. 10, p. 206 L — 49
  Inst. or. 12, 11, 30 — 48
Res Gestae Divi Augusti
  10 — 214
Rhet. ad Her.
  4, 21, 29 — 226
  4, 27 — 69
  4, 28 — 69, 80
Sallustius
  Cat. 8, 3 — 74
      9-11 — 6
  or. Macr. ad pleb. 19 — 45
Schol. Aesch. Prom. 496f. — 154
Schol. Bern. Verg. Ecl. 3, 104 — 145
Schol. Stat. Theb. 1, 91 — 183
Seneca
  Ag. 35 — 27
      855 — 95
  Apoc. 11 — 32
  Ben. 2, 1, 4 — 207, 233
  Contr. 3 praef. 8 — 80
  Ep. 41, 5 — 207, 233
    115, 4 — 239
  fr. 123H — 204
  H. O. 1773 — 24
  Oct. 147 — 27
Servius
  ad Verg. Aen. 1, 519 — 176
      6, 48ff. — 51
      7, 84 — 182
      7, 456 — 190
      7, 563 — 183
      8, 60 — 170
      8, 183 — 36
      8, 363 — 36
      12, 779 — 28
  ad Ecl. 5, 65 — 77
  ad Georg. 1, 344 — 137
      2, 126f. — 65
Sextus Empiricus
  Adv. Phys. I, 124 — 10
Solinus
  2, 14 — 191
Statius
  Silvae 4, 8, 50 — 140
Strabo

INDEX OF AUTHORS CITED

14, 660	157	3, 1, 5	133f.
Suetonius		Vegetius	
Aug. 71	246	Mil. 2, 18	80
84, 2	218	Vergilius	3, 16
Claud. 1	221	Aen. 1, 330	79
Tib. 21, 7	220	1, 378	16
Tacitus		2, 245	79
Dial. 4, 4	48	2, 296	217
Terentius		3, 246	79
Ad. 447	27	4, 173ff.	239
704ff.	204, 232	4, 331ff.	17
And. 119f.	173	4, 448f.	191
Hec. 686	199	4, 597ff.	17
848	173	4, 625ff.	17
858	173	6, 48f.	50, 249
Phorm. 378	177	6, 137	93f.
1008	28	6, 143	94
Tertullianus		6, 205ff.	94
Apol. 14, 1	36	6, 229ff.	65
De anima 50, 4	64	6, 230	79
(Corpus) Tibullianum		6, 408ff.	94, 97
3, 11	206	6, 412ff.	56
4, 5	206	6, 636	93
Valerius Flaccus		7, 568ff.	183
2, 336	170	7, 750ff.	65
4, 548ff.	51, 249	8, 60	170
Valerius Maximus		8, 620	157
1, 1, 1	131	8, 351ff.	231
4, 1, 10	203	9, 771ff.	65
5, 10, 2	74ff.	12, 89	157
6, 21	177	12, 820ff.	43
Varro		Ecl. 1	238
L. L. 5, 68	144	5, 65	79
6, 47	178	Georg. 2, 126	65
6, 54	34	2, 518	75
7, 85	228	4, 534ff.	176
8, 71	32	Vitruvius	
R. R. 1, 1, 6	167	1, 4, 12	195
2, 4, 9f	117, 133f	Xenophon	
2, 10, 6	189	Anab. 3, 2, 9	47

INDEX OF SUBJECTS

Adonis 87f.
Aeneas 216, 220, 231
aestus 185, 187, 189
aeternitas 216
Ahtu Iuvip. 175
Ahtu Marti 175
Angerona 21-24
angitia 21
Antony (Mark) 15
Aphrodite 87ff., 91
Apollo 214, 217
Aprilis 254
Ara Maxima 34-36
arbor felix 78f.
Asvamedha 159
auctoritas 229, 246
augur(es) 237, 246
Augustus 16-20, 210-222, 245
aurea aetas 214, 219
auspicium 73

Balder 96
bone-marrow 154

Campus Martius 244
Carneades 13f.
Cautes 89, 148f., 164f.
Cautopates 89, 148f., 164f.
Ceres 114-146, 255
Cloaca Maxima 181, 186
Cloacina, Cluacina 179f., 185f.
consecratio 246
contact, see touching
contagio 33f.
'Cupid and Psyche' 84-92, 106-108

daps 31f.
dedicatio 246
deus 225, 227, 231, 237ff.
devotio 252
Dioscuri 126f.
divinity (of Augustus) 216, 219
—(of Livia) 216, 221
divus 238, 240
door 252f.

ductus 72f.
Dumézil (crusade against 'manaism') 39-58, 247ff.
δύναμις 230
dynamism 230f., 245ff.

edepol 124ff.
Eleusinia 124ff.
epiphany 239
Eros 88, 90, 92
Etruscan influence 223f., 237
etymological word play 226
Euander 219, 231
evocatio 223
extempore prayer 200, 202f., 205f.

fanum 26
fecunditas, fecundus 59, 75
felicitas, felix 59-81, 229
fertilis 59, 75
fetiales 251
Fisica 193ff.
Florifertum 145
fortuna 70, 77
fratres Arvales 242f.
Frutis 191ff.
funeral wedding 86, 90f.

genius 227, 242
golden bough 93-113
gravis, gravitas 39-58, 229, 248
Greek influence 223f., 237, 239

hands, laying on of— 246, 252
haruspices 238
Heres Martea 175
Heries Iunonis 175
Hesperus 89-92
horse sacrifice 159
humanitas 2-8
humanity 3-7, 13ff., 20

imperare 251
imperator(ius) 59, 62f., 68f., 73, 76ff.

INDEX OF SUBJECTS

imperium 72f., 76f., 229, 251
indigenous cults 223-256
Initia Cereris 114-146, 255f.
initia Eleusinia 123ff.
Ishtar 87, 90f., 103f.
Iulus 220, 231
iuno 242

Janus 218, 253
Juno 241f.
Juno Sororia 241
Jupiter 174, 232, 240ff.
Iupiter Arborator 145f.

Lacus Vadimonis 231
Lar(es) 204f., 207, 212, 227, 239
lex sacra Lavinia 224
Libitina 178f., 185f.
Lua Saturni 174
ludi saeculares 214
ludi tarentini (terentini) 244
lustratio 243

mactare 169, 211
magic 168ff., 201, 225, 252f.
maiestas 39-58, 248f.
mana 39-58, 228, 247
Mars 237, 242f.
—(spears of —) 249f.
mecastor 124, 128
Mefitis (Mephitis) 181ff., 194f.
Mefitis Fisica, see Fisica
Mens 190f.
Milky Way 160
mistletoe 94ff.
Mithras 89, 148-165
mundus Cereris 145

numen 183ff., 225, 227ff., 245ff.

oath 125
October Horse 147-159
orare 197-209, 234f.
orator 197f.
Orcus 137-141, 244
orenda 228f.

Palladium 222
Panaetius 3ff., 10-14, 20
pater patratus 251

pax 176f.
pax Augusta 219
Penates 204f., 207, 217, 222, 227
penis 153
pietas 1-20, 220
pignora imperii 222
pol 128f.
pollucere 35f.
Polybius 3
pontifex maximus 214f., 217
pontifices 237, 252
Posidonius 10ff., 15, 20
prayer 170, 197-209, 211ff., 232-236
praying aloud 197-209, 234f.
precari 171, 197-209, 234f.
preces 170f., 232ff.
private cult vs. public cult 200, 203f., 227, 238
profanare, profanus 25-38
Proserpina 137f., 144
provenire, proventus 74f.
proverb 226

Quirinus 237, 242ff.

rainbow 160
Regia 249
religio 7, 8, 16, 225ff., 231
religiosus 226f.
ringing in the ears, see tingling
Romulus 220

Sabines 236f.
sacer 246, 252
Salacia Neptuni 174
Scipio the Younger 3f.
senescere 45
Sibylline Books 190f.
Sidus Iulium 219
silent prayer 197-209, 234ff.
Silvanus 30f.
sneezing 47, 169
Stoa 207, 211, 220
Sulla felix 81f.
superstitio 236f.
superstition 16ff.
supplicatio 202f., 212, 235
supplicatio Vestae 221

tail 147-165

Tammuz 87f., 90f., 103f.
tarentum (terentum) 244
Tellus 255
terminus, Terminus 253
Thanatos 88f.
Thracian Rider 149-165
tingling of the ears 46, 170
tinnitus auris 46
touching 246, 251f.
trias Capitolina 242
triumph 66f.

Underworld 244

venenum 175f.
venerari 168ff.

venia 176ff.
Venus 166-196, 254f.
Venus Cloacina, see Cloacina
Venus Erycina 190
Venus Fisica, see Fisica
Venus Frutis, see Frutis
Venus Iovia 174ff.
Venus Libitina (Libentina, Lubentina), see Libitina
Venus Mefitis, see Mefitis
venustas 167, 173
venustus 167, 171ff.
ver sacrum 243
Vesta 210-222, 227, 236
virtus 62f., 67-70, 76, 80